Recipe Collection Showcases a Year of Fantastic Eating!

2003 was another fabulous year for *Taste of Home*—America's No. 1 cooking magazine—so don't be surprised if you have a hard time deciding which of the recipes in this cookbook to try first!

2004 Taste of Home Annual Recipes contains every single delicious recipe published during 2003, plus 24 bonus recipes…that's 500 in all! It's packed with family-favorite dishes shared by fellow cooks from across the country.

So whether you're fixing dinner for your own family, cooking for a holiday crowd or simply whipping up something for yourself, you'll have plenty of fitting recipes from which to choose. To get you started, take a sneak peek at the winners of our six national recipe contests.

• Bountiful Buffet. Holiday celebrations lend themselves to buffet-style dining. Party guests will eagerly stand in line for festive dishes like grand-prize winner Chocolate Velvet Dessert (p. 128) and Loaded Baked Potato Salad (p. 34), which landed second-place honors.

• Great Coffee Cakes. On a crisp morning, there's nothing quite like cozying up to a warm slice of homemade coffee cake. Raspberry Streusel Coffee Cake (p. 86) got the "top of the morning" rating from our judges, with Lemon Curd Coffee Cake (p. 88) coming in a close second.

• Cheery Cherries. Whether tart or sweet, cherries have a knack for brightening up baked goods, salads, condiments and entrees with a burst of juicy flavor. Cherry Chip Scones (p. 96) were chosen as the pick of the contest crop, while Sweet Cherry Pork Chops (p. 73) placed second.

• Picnics and Potlucks. Warm-weather get-togethers prompt a potpourri of take-along dishes, from tangy potato or pasta salads to baked beans and brownies. Contest winner Parmesan Chicken (p. 73) and second-place Watermelon Slice Cookies (p. 110) will make any family reunion, church picnic or summer party a flavor feast.

• Onions and Garlic. There's no doubt about it, when you want to give a recipe a little "oomph", you can count on onions and garlic. Onion Beef Au Jus (p. 44) made the most of those potent bulbs and won top honors…Southwestern Onion Rings (p. 29) took second place.

• Wings and Drums. Lip-smacking chicken wings and drumsticks can perk up a party…and make fun finger food for a casual meal, too. Once the taste-testing wingding was done, our judges drummed up Tempura Chicken Wings (p. 19) as the first-place winner with Grilled Wing Zingers (p. 7) second in the pecking order.

With 500 recipes in this colorful big cookbook, you won't run out of choices anytime soon. You're sure to find something special for everyone and every occasion.

CARRY-IN CONTEST WINNERS. Parmesan Chicken (p. 73) won the grand prize and Watermelon Slice Cookies (p. 110) took second place in our national picnics and potlucks contest.

2004 Taste of Home Annual Recipes

Editor: Jean Steiner
Art Director: Lori Arndt
Food Editor: Janaan Cunningham
Associate Editors: Julie Schnittka,
Heidi Reuter Lloyd
Graphic Art Associates: Ellen Lloyd,
Catherine Fletcher

Taste of Home®

Executive Editor: Kathy Pohl
Food Editor: Janaan Cunningham
Associate Food Editor: Diane Werner
Managing Editor: Ann Kaiser
Assistant Managing Editor: Barbara Schuetz
Art Director: Emma Acevedo
Copy Editor: Kristine Krueger
Senior Recipe Editor: Sue A. Jurack
Test Kitchen Director: Karen Johnson
Senior Home Economist: Patricia Schmeling
Test Kitchen Home Economists: Tamra Duncan,
Sue Draheim, Mark Morgan RD, Karen Wright
Test Kitchen Assistants: Kris Lehman,
Megan Taylor
Editorial Assistants: Barb Czysz,
Mary Ann Koebernik
Food Stylists: Joylyn Jans, Kristin Koepnick
Food Photographers: Rob Hagen, Dan Roberts
Senior Food Photography Artist:
Stephanie Marchese
Food Photography Artist: Julie Ferron
Photo Studio Manager: Anne Schimmel
Graphic Art Associates: Ellen Lloyd,
Catherine Fletcher
Chairman and Founder: Roy Reiman
President: Russell Denson

Taste of Home Books
©2003 Reiman Media Group, Inc.
5400 S. 60th St., Greendale WI 53129

International Standard Book Number:
0-89821-384-3
International Standard Serial Number:
1094-3463

PICTURED AT RIGHT. Clockwise from upper left: Pepperoni Pizza Quiche, Chicken Spinach Quiche, Double-Crust Onion Quiche and Potato-Crust Chicken Quiche (p. 74); Grilled Corn on the Cob, Three Potato Salad, Blueberry Pound Cake and Zesty Sloppy Joes (p. 161); Chocolate Berry Angel Torte (p. 119); Cheesy Ham 'n' Rice Soup (p. 45); Cranberry Fool, Creamy Mashed Potatoes and Artichoke Beef Steaks (p. 256).

Taste of Home 2004
Annual Recipes

PICTURED ON FRONT COVER. From top: Chocolate Velvet Dessert (p. 128), Beans 'n' Caramelized Onions (p. 262) and Sweet Cherry Pork Chops (p. 73).

PICTURED ON BACK COVER. From top: Blueberry Cheesecake Ice Cream (p. 141), Creamy Peach Pie (p. 122) and Cream Cheese Brownies (p. 110).

FOR ADDITIONAL COPIES of this book, write *Taste of Home* Books, P.O. Box 908, Greendale WI 53129.

To order by credit card, call toll-free 1-800/344-2560 or visit our Web site at www.reimanpub.com.

Snacks & Beverages

Get ready for compliments when you serve any of these super snacks and refreshing beverages at your next get-together.

— 🍴 🍴 🍴 —

PERFECT PARTY FOOD. Clockwise from upper left: Blackberry Lemonade (p. 20), Apple-Cinnamon Snack Mix (p. 14), Bite-Size Crab Quiches (p. 10), Glazed Meatballs (p. 25), Grilled Wing Zingers (p. 7) and Chive Egg Dip (p. 28).

with sauce. Broil 4-6 in. from the heat for 20-25 minutes, turning and basting every 5 minutes or until wings are well coated. **Yield:** 10-12 servings.

Editor's Note: 3 pounds of uncooked chicken wing sections (wingettes) may be substituted for the whole chicken wings. Omit cutting wings and discarding tips. When cutting or seeding hot peppers, use rubber or plastic gloves to protect your hands. Avoid touching your face.

— 🍷 🍷 🍷 —

Garlic Dip

I've been making this dip for years, and now my grown daughters fix it for their families. My mom makes it, too, and her motto is, "You can never have too much garlic." —*Jauneen Hosking, Wind Lake, Wisconsin*

☑ Uses less fat, sugar or salt. Includes Nutritional Analysis and Diabetic Exchanges.

    1 package (8 ounces) cream cheese, softened
  1/2 cup sour cream
    1 tablespoon milk
1-1/2 teaspoons Worcestershire sauce
    3 garlic cloves, minced
  1/4 teaspoon salt
  1/8 teaspoon pepper
Fresh vegetables *and/or* pretzels

In a small mixing bowl, beat the cream cheese, sour cream, milk, Worcestershire sauce, garlic, salt and pepper. Serve with vegetables and/or pretzels. **Yield:** 1-1/2 cups.

Nutritional Analysis: 1/4 cup of dip (prepared with fat-free cream cheese and reduced-fat sour cream) equals 68 calories, 2 g fat (2 g saturated fat), 10 mg cholesterol, 333 mg sodium, 4 g carbohydrate, trace fiber, 7 g protein. **Diabetic Exchange:** 1/2 fat-free milk.

— 🍷 🍷 🍷 —

Raspberry Barbecue Wings

(Pictured above)

I came up with this recipe when I got tired of the same old wings. These are baked with onion and garlic, then broiled and basted with a mixture of raspberry jam, barbecue sauce and jalapeno peppers. The sauce is also excellent on pork...and is great for dipping. —*Sandra Fisher, Missoula, Montana*

  2/3 cup barbecue sauce
  2/3 cup seedless raspberry jam
    3 tablespoons finely chopped onion
    1 to 2 jalapenos, seeded and finely chopped
    2 teaspoons minced garlic, *divided*
    2 teaspoons liquid smoke, optional, *divided*
  1/4 teaspoon salt
  15 whole chicken wings (about 3 pounds)
    1 small onion, sliced
    1 cup water

In a small bowl, combine the barbecue sauce, jam, chopped onion, jalapenos, 1 teaspoon garlic, 1 teaspoon liquid smoke if desired and salt; mix well. Cover and refrigerate for at least 2 hours.

Cut chicken wings into three sections; discard wing tip section. Place the chicken wings in a greased 15-in. x 10-in. x 1-in. baking pan. Top with sliced onion and remaining garlic. Combine the water and remaining liquid smoke if desired; pour over wings. Cover and bake at 350° for 30 minutes or until juices run clear.

Transfer wings to a greased broiler pan; brush

Cheesy Corn Spread

Canned Mexicorn lends a sweet twist to this cheesy crowd-pleaser. The zippy cracker spread gets its "heat" from jalapeno and red pepper. Refrigeration improves its flavor even more. —*Jan Henderson Smackover, Arkansas*

    1 can (11 ounces) Mexicorn, drained
  1/2 cup sour cream
  1/2 cup mayonnaise
    1 can (4 ounces) chopped green chilies, undrained
  1/4 cup chopped onion

1 jalapeno pepper, seeded and finely chopped*
1 tablespoon ground cumin
1 tablespoon picante sauce
3 cups (12 ounces) shredded cheddar cheese
1/2 cup chopped sweet red pepper
Assorted crackers

In a bowl, combine the first eight ingredients; stir in cheese. Sprinkle with red pepper. Cover and chill for 4 hours. Serve with crackers. **Yield:** 4 cups.

*Editor's Note: When cutting or seeding hot peppers, use rubber or plastic gloves to protect your hands. Avoid touching your face.

— 🏆 🏆 🏆 —

Grilled Wing Zingers

(Pictured on page 4)

My husband fine-tuned this recipe—and the results were spectacular! These spicy-hot grilled wings are true party pleasers.
—Angela Roster
Greenbackville, Virginia

40 whole chicken wings* (about 8 pounds)
2 cups packed brown sugar
2 cups hot sauce
1/2 cup butter *or* margarine, cubed
2 tablespoons cider vinegar
1/4 cup sugar
1/2 cup Italian seasoning
1/4 cup dried rosemary, crushed
1/4 cup paprika
1/4 cup chili powder
1/4 cup pepper
2 tablespoons cayenne pepper
1 cup blue cheese salad dressing
1/2 cup ranch salad dressing
Celery sticks

Cut chicken wings into three sections; discard wing tip section. In a large saucepan, bring the brown sugar, hot sauce, butter and vinegar to a boil. Reduce heat; simmer, uncovered, for 6-8 minutes or until butter is melted and sauce is heated through. Cool.

In a gallon-size resealable plastic bag, combine sugar, seasonings and 1 cup of sauce. Add chicken wings in batches. Seal bag; toss to coat. Grill wings, uncovered, over indirect medium heat for 12-15 minutes or until juices run clear, turning once and basting occasionally with remaining sauce.

In a small bowl, combine blue cheese and ranch salad dressings; serve with chicken wings and celery sticks. **Yield:** 25-30 servings.

*Editor's Note: 8 pounds of uncooked chicken wing sections (wingettes) may be substituted for the whole chicken wings. Omit the first step.

Salmon Mousse Cups

(Pictured below)

I make these tempting little tarts frequently for parties. They disappear at an astonishing speed, so I usually double or triple the recipe. The salmon-cream cheese filling and flaky crust will melt in your mouth.
—Fran Rowland, Phoenix, Arizona

1 package (3 ounces) cream cheese, softened
1/2 cup butter (no substitutes), softened
1 cup all-purpose flour
FILLING:
1 package (8 ounces) cream cheese, softened
1 cup fully cooked salmon chunks *or* 1 can (7-1/2 ounces) salmon, drained, bones and skin removed
2 tablespoons chicken broth
2 tablespoons sour cream
1 tablespoon finely chopped onion
1 teaspoon lemon juice
1/2 teaspoon salt
2 tablespoons minced fresh dill

In a small mixing bowl, beat the cream cheese and butter until smooth. Add flour; mix well. Shape into 24 balls; press onto the bottom and up the sides of greased miniature muffin cups. Bake at 350° for 10-15 minutes or until golden brown. Cool for 5 minutes before removing from pans to wire racks to cool completely.

For filling, in a mixing bowl, beat the cream cheese until smooth. Add the salmon, broth, sour cream, onion, lemon juice and salt; mix well. Spoon into the shells. Refrigerate for at least 2 hours. Sprinkle with dill. **Yield:** 2 dozen.

Warm Black Bean Dip

(Pictured below)

Cumin and chili powder pack plenty of zip into this chunky bean dip, which is served warm. It's a great make-ahead dish for any kind of party or get-together.
—Lynda Cavanaugh, De Forest, Wisconsin

✓ Uses less fat, sugar or salt. Includes Nutritional Analysis and Diabetic Exchanges.

  1 small onion, chopped
  2 garlic cloves, minced
  1 teaspoon canola *or* vegetable oil
  1 can (15 ounces) black beans, rinsed and drained
1/2 cup diced fresh tomato
1/3 cup picante sauce
1/2 teaspoon ground cumin
1/2 teaspoon chili powder
1/4 cup shredded reduced-fat Mexican cheese blend *or* cheddar cheese
1/4 cup minced fresh cilantro *or* parsley
  1 tablespoon lime juice
Baked tortilla chips

In a large nonstick skillet, saute onion and garlic in oil until tender. Add the beans; mash gently. Stir in the tomato, picante sauce, cumin and chili powder. Cook and stir just until heated through. Remove from the heat; stir in cheese, cilantro and lime juice. Serve warm with chips. **Yield:** 2 cups.

    Nutritional Analysis: One serving (1/4 cup dip) equals 73 calories, 2 g fat (1 g saturated fat), 3 mg cholesterol, 270 mg sodium, 10 g carbohydrate, 3 g fiber, 4 g protein. **Diabetic Exchanges:** 1/2 starch, 1/2 lean meat.

Garlic-Cheese Chicken Wings

I developed this recipe several years ago using chicken breasts, then decided to try it on wings as an appetizer—and it was a hit! If you like garlic, you're sure to enjoy these tender zesty bites. —Donna Pierce
Lady Lake, Florida

  2 large whole garlic bulbs
  1 tablespoon plus 1/2 cup olive *or* vegetable oil, *divided*
1/2 cup butter *or* margarine, melted
  1 teaspoon hot pepper sauce
1-1/2 cups seasoned bread crumbs
3/4 cup grated Parmesan cheese
3/4 cup grated Romano cheese
1/2 teaspoon pepper
 15 whole chicken wings* (about 3 pounds)

Remove papery outer skin from garlic (do not peel or separate cloves). Cut top off garlic bulbs. Brush with 1 tablespoon oil. Wrap each bulb in heavy-duty foil. Bake at 425° for 30-35 minutes or until softened. Cool for 10-15 minutes.

    Squeeze softened garlic into a blender or food processor. Add butter, hot pepper sauce and remaining oil; cover and process until smooth. Pour into a shallow bowl. In another shallow bowl, combine the bread crumbs, cheeses and pepper.

    Cut chicken wings into three sections; discard wing tip section. Dip chicken wings into the garlic mixture, then coat with crumb mixture. Place on a greased rack in a 15-in. x 10-in. x 1-in. baking pan; drizzle with any remaining garlic mixture. Bake, uncovered, at 350° for 50-55 minutes or until chicken juices run clear. **Yield:** 10-12 servings.

    *Editor's Note: 3 pounds of uncooked chicken wing sections (wingettes) may be substituted for the whole chicken wings. Omit cutting wings and discarding tips.

— 🏆 🏆 🏆 —

Ranch Ham Roll-Ups

(Pictured above right)

These pretty pinwheel appetizers are easy to make and fun to nibble. They have a yummy filling of cream cheese and ranch dressing that's layered with ham. I prepare them the night before and slice before serving.
—Charlie Clutts, New Tazewell, Tennessee

  2 packages (8 ounces *each*) cream cheese, softened
  1 envelope ranch salad dressing mix
  3 green onions, chopped
 11 flour tortillas (8 inches)
 22 thin slices deli ham

RING IN the new year with Ranch Ham Roll-Ups and Smoked Salmon Cheesecake (shown above, left to right).

In a small mixing bowl, beat the cream cheese and salad dressing mix until smooth. Add onions; mix well. Spread about 3 tablespoons over each tortilla; top each with two ham slices. Roll up tightly and wrap in plastic wrap. Refrigerate until firm. Unwrap and cut into 3/4-in. slices. **Yield:** about 7-1/2 dozen.

— ☕ ☕ ☕ —

Smoked Salmon Cheesecake

(Pictured above)

We live on Kodiak Island off the coast of Alaska, and salmon is one of our favorite foods. This elegant dish was the star attraction at an open house we hosted at my husband's business. —Becky Applebee
Chiniak, Alaska

> 3 **tablespoons dry bread crumbs**
> 5 **tablespoons grated Parmesan cheese,** *divided*
> 1/2 **cup chopped onion**
> 1/2 **cup chopped green pepper**
> 3 **tablespoons butter** *or* **margarine**
> 4 **packages (three 8 ounces, one 3 ounces) cream cheese, softened**
> 1/2 **cup heavy whipping cream**
> 1/4 **teaspoon pepper**
> 4 **eggs**
> 5 **ounces smoked salmon, diced**
> 1/2 **cup shredded Swiss cheese**
> **Assorted crackers**

Grease the bottom and sides of a 9-in. springform pan. Combine the bread crumbs and 2 tablespoons Parmesan cheese; sprinkle into pan, coating bottom and sides. Set aside.

In a skillet, saute onion and green pepper in butter until tender; set aside. In a mixing bowl, beat cream cheese until fluffy. Beat in the cream, pepper and remaining Parmesan cheese. Add eggs; beat on low speed just until combined. Fold in the onion mixture, salmon and Swiss cheese.

Wrap a double thickness of heavy-duty foil around bottom of prepared pan. Pour salmon mixture into pan. Place in a larger baking pan. Fill larger pan with hot water to a depth of 1-1/2 in. Bake at 325° for 35-40 minutes or until center is almost set. Cool on a wire rack for 1 hour. Refrigerate overnight.

Remove foil and sides of pan. Cut cheesecake into wedges; serve with crackers. **Yield:** 12-14 servings.

Autumn Tea

(Pictured above)

I've been serving beverages made with various flavors of green tea at gatherings, and people are always surprised by the results. This blend features flavors we associate with fall—apple, cranberry and pumpkin pie spice. Serve it either warm or cold.
—Sandra McKenzie, Braham, Minnesota

✓ Uses less fat, sugar or salt. Includes Nutritional Analysis and Diabetic Exchanges.

- 5 **individual tea bags**
- 5 **cups boiling water**
- 5 **cups unsweetened apple juice**
- 2 **cups cranberry juice**
- 1/2 **cup sugar**
- 1/3 **cup lemon juice**
- 1/4 **teaspoon pumpkin pie spice**

Place tea bags in a large heat-proof bowl; add boiling water. Cover and steep for 8 minutes. Discard tea bags. Add the remaining ingredients to tea; stir until sugar is dissolved. Serve warm or over ice. **Yield:** 3 quarts.

Nutritional Analysis: One 1-cup serving (prepared with reduced-calorie cranberry juice and sugar substitute) equals 66 calories, trace fat (trace saturated fat), 0 cholesterol, 4 mg sodium, 17 g carbohydrate, trace fiber, trace protein. **Diabetic Exchange:** 1 fruit.

Bite-Size Crab Quiches

(Pictured on page 4)

These mouth-watering morsels make an appealing appetizer when you invite a few friends to the house after a movie or ball game. —Virginia Ricks, Roy, Utah

✓ Uses less fat, sugar or salt. Includes Nutritional Analysis and Diabetic Exchanges.

- 1 **tube (10.2 ounces) large refrigerated buttermilk biscuits**
- 1 **can (6 ounces) crabmeat, drained, flaked and cartilage removed** *or* **1 cup chopped imitation crabmeat**
- 1/2 **cup shredded Swiss cheese**
- 1 **egg**
- 1/2 **cup milk**
- 1/2 **teaspoon dill weed**
- 1/4 **teaspoon salt**

Separate each biscuit into five equal pieces. Press onto the bottom and up the sides of 24 ungreased miniature muffin cups (discard remaining piece of dough). Fill each cup with 2 teaspoons crab and 1 teaspoon Swiss cheese. In a small bowl, combine the egg, milk, dill and salt; spoon about 1-1/2 teaspoons into each cup.

Bake at 375° for 15-20 minutes or until edges are golden brown. Let stand for 5 minutes before removing from pans. Serve warm. **Yield:** 2 dozen.

Nutritional Analysis: One serving (2 quiches, prepared with reduced-fat cheese and fat-free milk) equals 91 calories, 1 g fat (trace saturated fat), 30 mg cholesterol, 332 mg sodium, 12 g carbohydrate, trace fiber, 7 g protein. **Diabetic Exchanges:** 1 lean meat, 1/2 starch.

Rhubarb Cooler

I've shared this recipe with many people who tell me it's one of the best beverages they've ever had. It's an attractive and fizzy refresher. —Hazel McMullin, Amherst, Nova Scotia

✓ Uses less fat, sugar or salt. Includes Nutritional Analysis and Diabetic Exchanges.

- 3 **pounds fresh** *or* **frozen rhubarb, chopped (about 10 cups)**
- 2 **quarts water**
- 1 **tablespoon grated orange peel**
- 2 **cups sugar**
- 1/2 **cup lemon juice**
- 1/2 **cup orange juice**
- 1/8 **teaspoon salt**
- 6 **cups lemon-lime soda, chilled**

In a Dutch oven, bring rhubarb, water and orange peel to a boil. Reduce heat; simmer, uncovered, for 10-15 minutes or until rhubarb is very tender. Cool slightly. Strain through cheesecloth; discard pulp.

Return liquid to the pan. Stir in the sugar, lemon juice, orange juice and salt. Cook and stir over medium heat until sugar is dissolved. Cover and refrigerate until chilled.

To serve, pour 2/3 cup rhubarb mixture over ice; add 1/3 cup soda. **Yield:** 3 quarts.

Nutritional Analysis: One 1/2-cup serving (prepared with sugar-free soda) equals 81 calories, trace fat (trace saturated fat), 0 cholesterol, 21 mg sodium, 20 g carbohydrate, 1 g fiber, 1 g protein. **Diabetic Exchange:** 1-1/2 fruit.

— 🛒 🛒 🛒 —

Aussie Sausage Rolls

I was born and raised in Australia, but moved to the U.S. when I married my husband. When I long for a taste of home, I bake up a batch of these sausage rolls and share them with neighbors or co-workers. —Melissa Landon
Port Charlotte, Florida

1-1/4 **pounds bulk pork sausage**
   1 **medium onion, finely chopped**
   2 **teaspoons snipped chives**
   2 **teaspoons minced fresh basil *or* 1/2**
     teaspoon dried basil
   2 **garlic cloves, minced**
   1 **teaspoon paprika, *divided***
1/2 **teaspoon salt**
1/4 **teaspoon pepper**
   1 **package (17.3 ounces) frozen puff pastry, thawed**

In a bowl, combine the sausage, onion, chives, basil, garlic, 3/4 teaspoon paprika, salt and pepper. Unfold pastry onto a lightly floured surface. Roll each pastry sheet into an 11-in. x 10-1/2-in. rectangle. Cut widthwise into 3-1/2-in. strips.

Spread 1/2 cup of sausage mixture down the center of each strip. Fold pastry over and press edges together to seal. Cut each roll into six pieces. Place seam side down on a rack in a shallow baking pan. Sprinkle with remaining paprika. Bake at 350° for 20-25 minutes or until golden brown. **Yield:** 3 dozen.

— 🛒 🛒 🛒 —

Crescent-Wrapped Drumsticks

(Pictured at right)

Looking for a different way to do drumsticks? A friend shared this recipe with me. The drums are sauteed in barbecue sauce, then wrapped in crescent roll dough that's sprinkled with Parmesan cheese and Italian seasoning. My husband loves them! —Paula Plating
Colorado Springs, Colorado

   8 **chicken drumsticks**
1/4 **cup butter *or* margarine**
1/2 **cup barbecue sauce**
   1 **tube (8 ounces) refrigerated crescent rolls**
   1 **egg, lightly beaten**
   2 **teaspoons grated Parmesan cheese**
   2 **teaspoons Italian seasoning**
   2 **teaspoons sesame seeds, toasted**

Remove and discard skin from drumsticks. In a large skillet, melt butter over medium heat; stir in the barbecue sauce. Add chicken. Bring to a boil. Reduce heat; cover and simmer for 30 minutes or until a meat thermometer reads 170°, turning occasionally. Remove chicken from pan; cool slightly.

Separate crescent dough into eight triangles; place in a lightly greased 15-in. x 10-in. x 1-in. baking pan. Brush dough with some of the beaten egg; sprinkle with Parmesan cheese and Italian seasoning.

Place the meaty portion of each drumstick at the tip of each triangle, with the bony portion extended beyond one long side of triangle. Wrap drumstick in dough; place seam side down. Brush with remaining egg; sprinkle with sesame seeds. Bake at 375° for 13-15 minutes or until golden brown and a meat thermometer reads 180°. **Yield:** 8 servings.

Tropical Tea

Brew a batch of this fragrant, flavorful tea in a slow cooker for your next family gathering.
—Irene Helen Zundel, Carmichaels, Pennsylvania

✓ Uses less fat, sugar or salt. Includes Nutritional Analysis and Diabetic Exchanges.

6 cups boiling water
6 individual tea bags
1-1/2 cups orange juice
1-1/2 cups unsweetened pineapple juice
1/3 cup sugar
1 medium navel orange, sliced and halved
2 tablespoons honey

In a 5-qt. slow cooker, combine the boiling water and tea bags. Cover and let stand for 5 minutes. Discard the tea bags. Stir in the remaining ingredients. Cover and cook on low for 2-4 hours or until heated through. Serve warm. **Yield:** about 2-1/2 quarts.

Nutritional Analysis: One serving (1 cup) equals 82 calories, trace fat (0 saturated fat), 0 cholesterol, 1 mg sodium, 21 g carbohydrate, trace fiber, trace protein. **Diabetic Exchange:** 1-1/2 fruit.

—— 🍶 🍶 🍶 ——

Almond Snack Mix

Sliced almonds and almond extract set this crunchy Chex mix apart from other versions. We always keep the ingredients on hand so we can whip up this yummy snack at a moment's notice. But be warned—once you start eating it, you can't stop! —Lisa Hess
Bountiful, Utah

1 package (17.6 ounces) Rice Chex
2-3/4 cups sliced almonds
1 cup sugar
1 cup light corn syrup
3/4 cup butter (no substitutes)
1 teaspoon almond extract

Place cereal and almonds in a large bowl; set aside. In a heavy saucepan, combine the sugar, corn syrup and butter. Bring to a boil over medium heat, stirring occasionally, until a candy thermometer reads 250° (hard-ball stage).

Remove from the heat; stir in extract. Pour over cereal mixture and mix well. Spread onto waxed paper-lined baking sheets; cool. Toss to break apart. Store in an airtight container. **Yield:** 5 quarts.

Editor's Note: We recommend that you test your candy thermometer before each use by bringing water to a boil; the thermometer should read 212°. Adjust your recipe temperature up or down based on your test.

Pepperoni Pizza Spread

(Pictured at right)

When I serve this savory spread, I have copies of the recipe with me because so many people ask for one. The cheesy concoction is loaded with popular pizza ingredients, including pepperoni, olives, mushrooms and onion. It's wonderful on crackers of all kinds.
—Connie Milinovich, Cudahy, Wisconsin

2 cups (8 ounces) shredded mozzarella cheese
2 cups (8 ounces) shredded cheddar cheese
1 cup mayonnaise*
1 cup chopped pepperoni
1 can (4 ounces) mushroom stems and pieces, drained and chopped
1/2 cup chopped onion
1/2 cup chopped green pepper
1 can (6 ounces) ripe olives, drained and chopped
1 cup chopped stuffed olives
Crackers, breadsticks *and/or* French bread

In a large bowl, combine the first nine ingredients. Transfer to an 11-in. x 7-in. x 2-in. baking dish. Bake, uncovered, at 350° for 25-30 minutes or until edges are bubbly and lightly browned. Serve with crackers, breadsticks and/or French bread. **Yield:** 6 cups.

*Editor's Note: Reduced-fat or fat-free mayonnaise may not be substituted for regular mayonnaise in this recipe.

—— 🍶 🍶 🍶 ——

Chili Cheddar Pinwheels

(Pictured above right)

These baked Southwestern bites, made with convenient crescent roll dough, will steal the show at your next get-together. Picante sauce, green chilies and chili powder perk up the cream cheese filling. They'll disappear in no time. —Mary Dorchester
Midland, Texas

1 package (8 ounces) cream cheese, softened
1 cup (4 ounces) shredded cheddar cheese
1 can (4 ounces) chopped green chilies, drained
2 tablespoons picante sauce
1/2 teaspoon chili powder
1/4 teaspoon garlic salt
1/4 teaspoon onion powder
2 tubes (8 ounces *each*) refrigerated crescent rolls
Additional chili powder, optional

PERK UP holiday parties with Pepperoni Pizza Spread, Cold Chicken-Cheese Kabobs and Chili Cheddar Pinwheels (shown above, clockwise from top).

In a mixing bowl, beat cream cheese. Add the cheddar cheese, chilies, picante sauce, chili powder, garlic salt and onion powder. Separate each tube of crescent roll dough into four rectangles; press perforations to seal. Spread about 1/4 cup cheese mixture over each rectangle. Roll up jelly-roll style, starting with a short side. Wrap in plastic wrap and chill for at least 1 hour.

Cut each roll into eight slices; place on ungreased baking sheets. Sprinkle with additional chili powder if desired. Bake at 350° for 10-12 minutes or until golden brown. **Yield:** 64 appetizers.

— 🍶 🍶 🍶 —

Cold Chicken-Cheese Kabobs

(Pictured above)

These cute kabobs will add pizzazz to any party...and you don't even have to get out the grill! Spicy marinated chicken cubes are browned in a skillet, then skewered with cheese cubes and tiny tomatoes.
—Sherine Gilmour, Brooklyn, New York

☑ Uses less fat, sugar or salt. Includes Nutritional Analysis and Diabetic Exchanges.

1/2 teaspoon salt
1/2 teaspoon chili powder
1/8 teaspoon pepper
1/2 pound boneless skinless chicken breast, cubed
1/2 cup balsamic vinegar *or* red wine vinegar
2 teaspoons olive *or* canola oil
1 block (5 ounces) mozzarella cheese, cubed
18 cherry *or* grape tomatoes

Combine the salt, chili powder and pepper; rub into chicken cubes. Place in a bowl; add vinegar. Cover and refrigerate for 1-8 hours. In a skillet, cook chicken in oil until juices run clear. Cool slightly. Alternately thread chicken, cheese and tomatoes onto wooden skewers. Refrigerate until serving. Serve cold. **Yield:** 8 servings.
Nutritional Analysis: One serving (prepared with part-skim mozzarella) equals 93 calories, 4 g fat (2 g saturated fat), 26 mg cholesterol, 264 mg sodium, 3 g carbohydrate, trace fiber, 12 g protein.
Diabetic Exchanges: 1 meat, 1 vegetable.

Fried Onion Rings

(Pictured above)

For this satisfying snack, sweet Vidalia onion rings are deep-fried to a crispy golden brown, then served with a cool and zesty lime dipping sauce.
—Christine Wilson, Sellersville, Pennsylvania

   1 large Vidalia *or* sweet onion
 3/4 cup all-purpose flour
 1/4 cup cornmeal
 1/2 teaspoon baking powder
 1/2 teaspoon salt
 1/4 teaspoon baking soda
 1/4 teaspoon cayenne pepper
   1 egg
   1 cup buttermilk
Oil for deep-fat frying
LIME DIPPING SAUCE:
 2/3 cup mayonnaise
   3 tablespoons honey
   2 tablespoons lime juice
   2 tablespoons spicy brown *or* horseradish
      mustard
   1 teaspoon prepared horseradish

Cut onion into 1/2-in. slices; separate into rings. In a bowl, combine the flour, cornmeal, baking powder, salt, baking soda and cayenne. Combine the egg and buttermilk; stir into dry ingredients just until moistened.

In an electric skillet or deep-fat fryer, heat 1 in. of oil to 375°. Dip onion rings into batter. Fry a few at a time for 1 to 1-1/2 minutes on each side or until golden brown. Drain on paper towels (keep warm in a 300° oven). In a small bowl, combine sauce ingredients. Serve with onion rings. **Yield:** 4 servings.

Tangy Barbecue Wings

Spicy ketchup, vinegar, molasses and honey blend together in a tangy sauce that makes these chicken wings lip-smacking good. —Sherry Pitzer, Troy, Missouri

    25 whole chicken wings* (about 5 pounds)
 2-1/2 cups hot and spicy ketchup
   2/3 cup white vinegar
   1/2 cup plus 2 tablespoons honey
   1/2 cup molasses
     1 teaspoon salt
     1 teaspoon Worcestershire sauce
   1/2 teaspoon onion powder
   1/2 teaspoon chili powder
   1/2 to 1 teaspoon liquid smoke, optional

Cut chicken wings into three sections; discard wing tip section. Place chicken wings in two greased 15-in. x 10-in. x 1-in. baking pans. Bake, uncovered, at 375° for 30 minutes; drain. Turn wings; bake 20-25 minutes longer or until juices run clear. Meanwhile, in a large saucepan, combine the remaining ingredients. Bring to a boil. Reduce heat; simmer, uncovered, for 25-30 minutes.

Drain wings; place a third of them in a 5-qt. slow cooker. Top with about 1 cup sauce. Repeat layers twice. Cover and cook on low for 3-4 hours. Stir before serving. **Yield:** 15-20 servings.

***Editor's Note:** 5 pounds of uncooked chicken wing sections (wingettes) may be substituted for the whole chicken wings. Omit the first step.

—— 🥤 🥤 🥤 ——

Apple-Cinnamon Snack Mix

(Pictured on page 4)

This colorful and crunchy concoction with a sweet-spicy coating is great for parties or just snacking.
—Virginia Krites, Cridersville, Ohio

   3 cups Apple Jacks cereal
   2 cups pecan halves
   1 cup whole blanched almonds
   1 cup chow mein noodles
 1/2 cup sugar
   1 tablespoon ground cinnamon
 1/4 teaspoon salt
   1 egg white

In a large bowl, combine the cereal, nuts and chow mein noodles. In a small bowl, combine the sugar, cinnamon and salt; stir in egg white. Pour over the cereal mixture and toss to coat. Transfer to a greased 15-in. x 10-in. x 1-in. baking pan. Bake, uncovered, at 300° for 45 minutes, stirring every 15 minutes. **Yield:** 6 cups.

Mint Mocha Shakes

Cool off with this yummy ice cream drink that delightfully blends chocolate, coffee and mint flavors.
—Edna Hoffman, Hebron, Indiana

2 **cups milk**
1 **teaspoon vanilla extract**
1/8 **teaspoon mint extract**
1 **envelope (.77 ounce) instant cappuccino Irish cream mix**
2 **cups chocolate ice cream, softened**

In a blender, combine all ingredients; cover and process until blended. Stir if necessary. Pour into chilled glasses; serve immediately. **Yield:** 4 servings.

Mexican Chicken Wings

I make these spicy appetizers for parties and football games and never have any leftovers. The hot wings contrast nicely with the cool but zippy dip. When the wings run out, we use the extra cilantro dip on tortilla chips for a fast snack. —*Barbara McConaughey Houlton, Wisconsin*

12 **whole chicken wings (about 2-1/2 pounds)**
1/3 **cup all-purpose flour**
1/3 **cup cornmeal**
1 **tablespoon ground cumin**
1-1/2 **teaspoons salt**
1-1/2 **teaspoons pepper**
3/4 **teaspoon cayenne pepper**
JALAPENO CILANTRO DIP:
2-1/2 **cups (20 ounces) sour cream**
3 **cups loosely packed fresh cilantro *or* parsley leaves**
6 **green onions, cut into 3-inch pieces**
4 **jalapeno peppers, seeded**
3 **teaspoons salt**

Cut chicken wings into three sections; discard wing tip section. In a large resealable plastic bag, combine the flour, cornmeal, cumin, salt, pepper and cayenne. Add chicken wings, a few at a time, and shake to coat. Transfer to a greased 13-in. x 9-in. x 2-in. baking pan. Bake, uncovered, at 375° for 50-55 minutes or until juices run clear and coating is set, turning once.

Meanwhile, in a blender or food processor, combine the dip ingredients; cover and process until blended. Refrigerate until serving. Serve with wings. **Yield:** 8-10 servings (3-2/3 cups dip).

Editor's Note: 2-1/2 pounds of uncooked chicken wing sections (wingettes) may be substituted for the whole chicken wings. Omit the first step. When cutting or seeding hot peppers, use rubber or plastic gloves to protect your hands. Avoid touching your face.

Almond Fudge Pops

(Pictured below)

These rich-tasting frozen treats are oh-so-creamy, kids and grown-ups love 'em! It's hard to eat just one. They're simple to prepare and great to keep in the freezer. Sometimes I'll substitute pecans for the almonds. —*Debby Pion, Lakeland, Florida*

1 **envelope whipped topping mix**
1/2 **cup cold milk**
1/2 **teaspoon vanilla extract**
3/4 **cup hot fudge ice cream topping**
2 **tablespoons water**
1 **cup finely chopped almonds, toasted, *divided***
6 **disposable plastic cups (3 ounces)**
6 **Popsicle sticks**

In a mixing bowl, beat the topping mix, milk and vanilla on low speed until blended. Beat on high until soft peaks form, about 4 minutes. In a large bowl, combine the fudge topping and water; fold in the topping mixture and 1/2 cup of almonds.

Pour into plastic cups. Cover with heavy-duty foil; insert sticks through foil. Place in a 9-in. square pan. Freeze until firm. Remove foil and cups. Roll the frozen pops in remaining almonds. **Yield:** 6 servings.

Mushrooms Make For Fun Munching

CAPS OFF to the good cooks who recommended these marvelous mushroom recipes! Flavorful ingredients pack plenty of punch in these delicious dishes that are great appetizers or side dishes.

Why not try one or more of these reader-favorite recipes today? No doubt the compliments will mushroom at your dinner table.

— 🍴 🍴 🍴 —

Mushroom Turnovers

(Pictured below)

I love these tasty little turnovers hot or cold. They're great for parties or for serving at home. I'm recently "transplanted" from Pennsylvania—the nation's top mushroom producer. A friend gave me this recipe while I was living there. —Joanne Migliozzi-Beers
Mesquite, Nevada

> 1 package (8 ounces) cream cheese, softened
> 1/2 cup butter *or* margarine, softened
> 1-1/2 cups all-purpose flour
> **FILLING:**
> 1/2 pound fresh mushrooms, finely chopped
> 1 medium onion, finely chopped
> 2 tablespoons butter *or* margarine
> 1/4 cup sour cream
> 2 tablespoons all-purpose flour
> 1 teaspoon salt

SAVORY BITES. Mushroom Turnovers, Marinated Mushrooms and Sausage Mushroom Appetizers (shown below, top to bottom) are popular party fare or can add appeal to any meal.

1/2 teaspoon dried thyme
 1 egg
 2 teaspoons water

In a small mixing bowl, beat cream cheese and butter until smooth. Gradually beat in flour until well blended. Shape pastry into a ball. Cover and refrigerate for 1 hour. Meanwhile, in a large skillet, saute mushrooms and onion in butter until tender. Stir in the sour cream, flour, salt and thyme. Remove from the heat; set aside.

Roll dough into 1-in. balls; place on ungreased baking sheets. Flatten into 3-in. circles. In a small bowl, beat the egg and water; brush over pastry. Place about 1 teaspoon mushroom filling in the center of each circle. Fold pastry over and seal edges. Brush tops with remaining egg mixture. Bake at 450° for 10-12 minutes or until golden brown. **Yield:** 3-1/2 dozen.

— ☕ ☕ ☕ —

Marinated Mushrooms

(Pictured at left)

This is a nice way to serve mushrooms as an appetizer...and it also makes a great side dish for any type of meat. Sometimes I add these tangy mushrooms to salads for extra flavor, too. —Brenda Swan
Alexandria, Pennsylvania

 2 pounds fresh mushrooms
 1 envelope (.7 ounce) Italian salad dressing mix
 1 cup water
1/2 cup olive *or* vegetable oil
1/3 cup cider vinegar
 2 tablespoons lemon juice
 1 tablespoon sugar
 1 tablespoon minced fresh parsley
 1 tablespoon soy sauce
 2 teaspoons crushed red pepper flakes
 3 garlic cloves, minced
1/2 teaspoon salt
1/8 teaspoon pepper
Leaf lettuce, optional

Remove mushroom stems (discard or save for another use). Place caps in a large saucepan and cover with water. Bring to a boil. Reduce heat; cook for 3 minutes, stirring occasionally. Drain and cool.

In a jar with a tight-fitting lid, combine the salad dressing mix, water, oil, vinegar, lemon juice, sugar and seasonings; shake well. Place mushrooms in a bowl; add dressing and stir to coat. Cover and refrigerate for 8 hours or overnight. Serve in a lettuce-lined bowl if desired. **Yield:** 4 cups.

Sausage Mushroom Appetizers

(Pictured below left)

These hors d'oeuvres are oh-so-good! For fun variations, I sometimes substitute venison or crabmeat for the pork sausage in the stuffing. Either way, they're delicious. —Sheryl Siemonsma
Sioux Falls, South Dakota

48 large fresh mushrooms
 2 eggs, lightly beaten
 1 pound bulk pork sausage, cooked and crumbled
 1 cup (4 ounces) shredded Swiss cheese
1/4 cup mayonnaise*
 3 tablespoons butter *or* margarine, melted
 2 tablespoons finely chopped onion
 2 teaspoons spicy brown *or* horseradish mustard
 1 teaspoon garlic salt
 1 teaspoon Cajun seasoning
 1 teaspoon Worcestershire sauce

Remove mushroom stems (discard or save for another use); set caps aside. In a large bowl, combine the remaining ingredients. Stuff into the mushroom caps. Place in two greased 13-in. x 9-in. x 2-in. baking dishes. Bake, uncovered, at 350° for 16-20 minutes or until heated through. **Yield:** 4 dozen.

*Editor's Note: Reduced-fat or fat-free mayonnaise may not be substituted for regular mayonnaise in this recipe.

More About Mushrooms

WE'VE harvested a few helpful hints about white or "button" mushrooms:

● Since mushrooms need air circulation, store them on a shelf in the fridge rather than in the crisper drawer. Keep them in their original packaging, or spread the mushrooms in a single layer on a plate and cover with a slightly damp paper towel. Moisten the towel every day.
 —*Taste of Home Test Kitchen*

● Mushrooms bruise easily, so handle them as little as possible. Be careful not to stack anything on top of them. —*Christine Wilson*
Sellersville, Pennsylvania

● Wipe mushrooms gently with a damp cloth or paper towel to clean them. If it's necessary to wash mushrooms, quickly rinse them in a colander and pat dry immediately with paper towels.
 —*Patty Kile, Greentown, Pennsylvania*

Honey-Glazed Wings

My family loves these chicken wings that are mildly seasoned with honey, ginger, soy sauce and chili sauce. Tasty and tender, they're sure to be a hit at your next get-together. They're a crowd-pleaser!
—*Marlene Wahl, Baldwin, Wisconsin*

15 whole chicken wings* (about 3 pounds)
1/2 cup honey
1/3 cup soy sauce
 2 tablespoons vegetable oil
 2 tablespoons chili sauce
 2 teaspoons salt
 1 teaspoon garlic powder
 1 teaspoon Worcestershire sauce
1/2 teaspoon ground ginger

Cut chicken wings into three sections; discard wing tip section. Set aside chicken wings. In a saucepan, combine the honey, soy sauce, oil, chili sauce, salt, garlic powder, Worcestershire sauce and ginger. Cook and stir until blended and heated through. Cool to room temperature. Place the chicken wings in a large resealable plastic bag; add honey mixture. Seal bag and turn to coat. Refrigerate for at least 8 hours or overnight.

 Drain and discard marinade. Place wings in a well-greased 15-in. x 10-in. x 1-in. baking pan. Bake, uncovered, at 375° for 30 minutes. Drain; turn wings. Bake 20-25 minutes longer or until chicken juices run clear and glaze is set. **Yield:** 10-12 servings.

 *Editor's Note: 3 pounds of uncooked chicken wing sections (wingettes) may be substituted for the whole chicken wings. Omit the first step.

Cracker Snack Mix

Family and friends will munch this fun mix of crackers, nuts and ranch dressing by the handfuls! Everyone is sure to find something they like. If not, substitute other snack packages to vary the flavors.
—*Sharon Nichols, Brookings, South Dakota*

12 cups original flavor Bugles
 6 cups miniature pretzels
 1 package (11 ounces) miniature butter-flavored crackers
 1 package (10 ounces) Wheat Thins
 1 package (9-1/4 ounces) Cheese Nips
 1 package (7-1/2 ounces) nacho cheese Bugles
 1 package (6 ounces) miniature Parmesan fish-shaped crackers
 1 cup mixed nuts *or* peanuts
 1 bottle (10 *or* 12 ounces) butter-flavored popcorn oil
 2 envelopes ranch salad dressing mix

In a very large bowl, combine the first eight ingredients. In a small bowl, combine oil and salad dressing mix. Pour over cracker mixture; toss to coat evenly. Transfer to four ungreased 15-in. x 10-in. x 1-in. baking pans. Bake at 250° for 45 minutes, stirring every 15 minutes. Cool completely, stirring several times. **Yield:** about 8 quarts.

—— 🏳 🏳 🏳 ——

Lemon-Orange Iced Tea
(Pictured at left)

I finally hit on a recipe for iced tea that doesn't have the aftertaste of artificial sweetener. This tangy drink is perfect for folks who need to monitor their sugar intake. —*Dawn Lowenstein, Hatboro, Pennsylvania*

✓ Uses less fat, sugar or salt. Includes Nutritional Analysis and Diabetic Exchanges.

 2 quarts cold water, *divided*
 6 individual tea bags
 2 sprigs fresh mint
 1 tub sugar-free lemonade soft drink mix*
 2 cups orange juice

In a saucepan, bring 1 qt. of water to a boil. Remove from the heat. Add tea bags and mint; let stand for 10 minutes. Discard tea bags and mint. Pour tea into a large pitcher. Add lemonade drink mix, orange juice and remaining water; stir well. Refrigerate until chilled. Serve over ice. **Yield:** 10 servings.

 Nutritional Analysis: One serving (1 cup) equals 27 calories, 0 fat (0 saturated fat), 0 cholesterol, 1 mg sodium, 5 g carbohydrate, 0 fiber, trace protein. **Diabetic Exchange:** 1/2 fruit.

*Editor's Note: This recipe was tested with Crystal Light lemonade-flavored low-calorie soft drink mix. Four to six tubs come in one container.

— 🍷 🍷 🍷 —

Baked Onion Rings

These crispy, lightly browned rings are a healthy alternative to the deep-fried version. Thyme and paprika enhance the flavor of the tender onions.
—Della Stamp, Long Beach, California

✓ Uses less fat, sugar or salt. Includes Nutritional Analysis and Diabetic Exchanges.

- 1 **pound sweet onions**
- 3 **egg whites**
- 1 **cup dry bread crumbs**
- 2 **teaspoons dried thyme**
- 1 **teaspoon salt**
- 1 **teaspoon paprika**
- 1/4 **teaspoon pepper**

Cut onions into 1/2-in. slices; separate into rings and place in a bowl. Cover with ice water; soak for 30 minutes. Drain.

In a small mixing bowl, beat the egg whites until foamy. In another bowl, combine the bread crumbs, thyme, salt, paprika and pepper. Divide the crumb mixture among three large resealable plastic bags. Dip a third of the onions in the egg whites; add a few rings at a time to crumb mixture and shake to coat. Place on a baking sheet coated with nonstick cooking spray.

Repeat with remaining onions and crumb mixture. Bake at 400° for 20 minutes or until lightly browned and crisp. **Yield:** 4 servings.

Nutritional Analysis: One serving equals 169 calories, 2 g fat (trace saturated fat), 0 cholesterol, 865 mg sodium, 31 g carbohydrate, 3 g fiber, 8 g protein. **Diabetic Exchange:** 2 starch.

— 🍷 🍷 🍷 —

Tempura Chicken Wings

(Pictured above right)

When I moved to Kansas City from Texas, I brought many of my mom's best-loved recipes with me, including these saucy sweet-and-sour wings. This recipe turned a friend of mine, who's not a fan of chicken, into a real wing lover. —*Susan Wuckowitsch*
Lenexa, Kansas

- 15 **whole chicken wings* (about 3 pounds)**
- 1 **cup cornstarch**

- 3 **eggs, lightly beaten**
- **Oil for deep-fat frying**
- 1/2 **cup sugar**
- 1/2 **cup white vinegar**
- 1/2 **cup currant jelly**
- 1/4 **cup soy sauce**
- 3 **tablespoons ketchup**
- 2 **tablespoons lemon juice**

Cut chicken wings into three sections; discard wing tip section. Place cornstarch in a large resealable plastic bag; add chicken wings, a few at a time, and shake to coat evenly. Dip wings in egg. In an electric skillet or deep-fat fryer, heat oil to 375°. Fry wings for 8 minutes or until golden brown and juices run clear, turning occasionally. Drain on paper towels.

In a small saucepan, combine the sugar, vinegar, jelly, soy sauce, ketchup and lemon juice. Bring to a boil. Reduce heat; simmer, uncovered, for 10 minutes.

Place chicken wings in a greased 15-in. x 10-in. x 1-in. baking pan. Pour half of the sauce over wings. Bake, uncovered, at 350° for 15 minutes. Turn wings; top with remaining sauce. Bake 10-15 minutes longer or until chicken juices run clear and coating is set. **Yield:** 10-12 servings.

*Editor's Note: 3 pounds of uncooked chicken wing sections (wingettes) may be substituted for the whole chicken wings. Omit the first step.

Moisten wonton edges with egg mixture; fold opposite corners over filling and press to seal. Heat remaining vegetable oil in a large skillet. Cook wontons in batches for 1-2 minutes on each side or until golden brown, adding additional oil if needed. **Yield:** 5 dozen.

— ▼ ▼ ▼ —

Ginger-Orange Wings

The sweet-and-sour sauce in this recipe was originally for pork spare ribs, but my family has always enjoyed it this way. The longer the wings sit in the ketchup, ginger and orange marmalade sauce, the better they taste. They can be served warm or cold.
—Lora Fletcher, Lyons, Oregon

      25 whole chicken wings* (about 5 pounds)
       2 cups all-purpose flour
       3 teaspoons seasoned salt
       2 teaspoons garlic salt
     1/3 cup vegetable oil
       2 cups orange marmalade
       1 cup ketchup
     1/2 cup soy sauce
     3/4 teaspoon ground ginger

Cut chicken wings into three sections; discard wing tip section. In a large resealable plastic bag, combine the flour, seasoned salt and garlic salt. Add chicken wings, a few at a time, and shake to coat. In a large skillet, fry wings in oil, a few at a time, for 3-4 minutes on each side or until golden and crispy.

Drain pan drippings; return all chicken to the pan. Combine the marmalade, ketchup, soy sauce and ginger; pour over chicken and stir to coat. Cover and cook over medium-low heat for 10-15 minutes or until wings are well coated. **Yield:** 15-20 servings.

*Editor's Note: 5 pounds of uncooked chicken wing sections (wingettes) may be substituted for the whole chicken wings. Omit the first step.

— ▼ ▼ ▼ —

Korean Wontons

(Pictured above)

These fried dumplings, filled with vegetables and beef, are very easy to prepare, and the ingredients are inexpensive. I hope you try them!   *—Christy Lee*
Horsham, Pennsylvania

       2 cups shredded cabbage
       1 cup canned bean sprouts
     1/2 cup shredded carrots
   1-1/2 teaspoons plus 2 tablespoons vegetable
            oil, *divided*
     1/3 pound ground beef
     1/3 cup sliced green onions
   1-1/2 teaspoons sesame seeds, toasted
     1/2 teaspoon ground ginger
            or 1-1/2 teaspoons minced fresh
            gingerroot
       3 garlic cloves, minced
   1-1/2 teaspoons sesame oil
     1/2 teaspoon salt
     1/2 teaspoon pepper
       1 package (12 ounces) wonton wrappers
       1 egg, lightly beaten
       3 tablespoons water

In a wok or large skillet, stir-fry cabbage, bean sprouts and carrots in 1-1/2 teaspoons oil until tender; set aside. In a small skillet, cook beef over medium heat until no longer pink; drain. Add to the vegetable mixture. Stir in the onions, sesame seeds, ginger, garlic, sesame oil, salt and pepper.

Place about 1 tablespoon of filling in the center of each wonton wrapper. Combine egg and water.

— ▼ ▼ ▼ —

Blackberry Lemonade

(Pictured on page 4)

This is a great beverage for any summer gathering, whenever blackberries are in season—usually June and July. It has a tangy, refreshing flavor.
—Rich Murray, Nevada, Missouri

       4 cups water, *divided*
       1 cup sugar
       1 cup lemon juice
       1 tablespoon grated lemon peel
       1 cup blackberries
       1 to 2 drops blue food coloring, optional

In a large saucepan, bring 2 cups water and sugar to a boil. Boil for 2 minutes, stirring occasionally. Remove from the heat. Stir in the lemon juice, lemon peel and remaining water; cool slightly.

In a blender, combine 1 cup of lemon mixture and the blackberries; cover and process until blended. Strain and discard seeds. Pour blackberry mixture and remaining lemon mixture into a pitcher; stir well. Add food coloring if desired. Refrigerate until chilled. Serve over ice. **Yield:** about 1-1/2 quarts.

— 🏆 🏆 🏆 —

Deep-Fried Chicken Wings

A soy sauce marinade with sesame seeds and green onion adds flavor to these deep-fried wings. My mom got the recipe from a friend in Vancouver, British Columbia and passed it on to me. My husband loves chicken wings, and these are by far his favorite.
—Tami McLean, Brampton, Ontario

  15 **whole chicken wings* (about 3 pounds)**
1/2 **cup cornstarch**
1/4 **cup all-purpose flour**
1/4 **cup sugar**
  2 **teaspoons sesame seeds**
1-1/2 **teaspoons salt**
  2 **eggs**
1/4 **cup vegetable oil**
  5 **teaspoons soy sauce**
  2 **green onions, finely chopped**
Oil for deep-fat frying

Cut chicken wings into three sections; discard wing tip section. In a large bowl, combine the cornstarch, flour, sugar, sesame seeds and salt. Combine the eggs, oil and soy sauce; gradually whisk into dry ingredients until blended. Stir in onions. Add chicken wings and stir to coat. Cover and refrigerate for at least 3 hours.

Remove wings and discard the batter. In an electric skillet or deep-fat fryer, heat 1-1/2 in. of oil to 375°. Fry wings, 8-10 at a time, for 5-6 minutes on each side or until chicken juices run clear. Drain on paper towels. **Yield:** 10-12 servings.

*Editor's Note: 3 pounds of uncooked chicken wing sections (wingettes) may be substituted for the whole chicken wings. Omit the first step.

— 🏆 🏆 🏆 —

Five-Fruit Salsa

(Pictured at right)

Scoop this chunky fresh-tasting salsa onto a cinnamon tortilla chip and you'll have to go back for more.
—Catherine Dawe, Kent, Ohio

☑ Uses less fat, sugar or salt. Includes Nutritional Analysis and Diabetic Exchanges.

  2 **cups chopped fresh cantaloupe**
  6 **green onions, chopped**
  3 **kiwifruit, peeled and finely chopped**
  1 **medium navel orange, peeled and finely chopped**
  1 **medium sweet yellow pepper, chopped**
  1 **medium sweet red pepper, chopped**
  1 **can (8 ounces) crushed unsweetened pineapple, drained**
  2 **jalapeno peppers, seeded and chopped***
  1 **cup finely chopped fresh strawberries**
CINNAMON TORTILLA CHIPS:
  10 **flour tortillas (8 inches)**
1/4 **cup butter *or* stick margarine, melted**
1/3 **cup sugar**
  2 **teaspoons ground cinnamon**

In a bowl, combine the first eight ingredients. Cover and refrigerate for 8 hours or overnight. Drain if desired. Just before serving, stir in strawberries.

For chips, brush tortillas with butter; cut each into eight wedges. Combine sugar and cinnamon; sprinkle over the tortillas. Place on ungreased baking sheets. Bake at 350° for 10-14 minutes or just until crisp. Serve with fruit salsa. **Yield:** 8 cups salsa and 80 chips.

Nutritional Analysis: One serving (1/2 cup salsa with 5 chips) equals 170 calories, 5 g fat (2 g saturated fat), 8 mg cholesterol, 189 mg sodium, 29 g carbohydrate, 2 g fiber, 4 g protein. **Diabetic Exchanges:** 2 fruit, 1 fat.

*Editor's Note: When cutting or seeding hot peppers, use rubber or plastic gloves to protect your hands. Avoid touching your face.

Heavenly Deviled Eggs

BE AN ANGEL and do something delicious with hard-cooked eggs left over from Easter!

Each of these deviled egg recipes takes a little different approach to perking up the flavor in those classic egg delights. Enjoy all three versions suggested by *Taste of Home* readers.

— 🥄 🥄 🥄 —

Cute Egg Chicks

(Pictured below)

These big-eyed chicks will steal the show at your Easter table or on a buffet!
—Tami Escher
Dumont, Minnesota

12 hard-cooked eggs
1/2 cup mayonnaise
1/2 cup shredded Parmesan cheese
2 teaspoons finely chopped onion
1/2 teaspoon curry powder
1/2 teaspoon prepared mustard
1/8 teaspoon pepper
3 stuffed olives
1 small sweet red pepper

Cut a thin slice from the bottom of each egg so it sits flat. Cut a zigzag pattern a third down from the top of each egg. Carefully remove yolks and place in a small bowl; mash with a fork. Add the mayonnaise, Parmesan cheese, onion, curry, mustard and

pepper; stir until well blended. Spoon yolk mixture into the egg white bottoms; replace tops.

Cut olives into slices for eyes. Cut 12 small triangles from red pepper for beaks. Gently press the eyes and beaks into egg yolk filling. Refrigerate until serving. **Yield:** 1 dozen.

— 🍴 🍴 🍴 —

Zippy Deviled Eggs

(Pictured at right)

I take these eggs to our monthly retirement potluck...and if I don't bring them, I get told about it. A few splashes of hot sauce liven up these eggs, which are so easy to make. —Marbeth Balensiefer
Sun City, California

  12 **hard-cooked eggs**
1/4 **cup mayonnaise**
  3 **tablespoons chili sauce**
  1 **teaspoon prepared mustard**
1/4 **teaspoon hot pepper sauce**
Paprika

Slice eggs in half lengthwise; remove yolks and set whites aside. In a small bowl, mash yolks. Stir in the mayonnaise, chili sauce, mustard and hot pepper sauce. Pipe or stuff into egg whites. Sprinkle with paprika. Refrigerate until serving. **Yield:** 1 dozen.

— 🍴 🍴 🍴 —

Bacon-Cheddar Deviled Eggs

(Pictured at right)

I created this recipe a few years ago when I was craving something different to do with hard-cooked eggs. I combined three of my favorite foods—bacon, eggs and cheese—in these deviled eggs. I've received many compliments on their special taste. —Laura LeMay
Deerfield Beach, Florida

  12 **hard-cooked eggs**
1/2 **cup mayonnaise**
  4 **bacon strips, cooked and crumbled**
  2 **tablespoons finely shredded cheddar cheese**
  1 **tablespoon honey mustard***
1/4 **teaspoon pepper**

Slice eggs in half lengthwise; remove yolks and set whites aside. In a small bowl, mash yolks. Stir in the mayonnaise, bacon, cheese, mustard and pepper. Stuff into egg whites. Refrigerate until serving. **Yield:** 1 dozen.

*Editor's Note: As a substitute for honey mustard, combine 1-1/2 teaspoons Dijon mustard and 1-1/2 teaspoons honey.

BACON-CHEDDAR Deviled Eggs and Zippy Deviled Eggs (shown above, from top) make eggscellent appetizers any time of year.

Deviled Egg Tips

DID you know that the cooking term "deviled" means to highly season a food with a spice such as pepper or mustard? Keep these tips in mind next time you're making deviled eggs:

● To avoid having my deviled eggs slide together and get messy on the way to a party, I use a muffin tin to transport them. I put one egg in each cup. At the gathering, you can either transfer them to a plate or serve them as is.
—*Michelle Armistead, Marlboro, New Jersey*

● Put the filling for deviled eggs into a resealable plastic bag, then snip off a corner to pipe the filling into your hard-cooked egg whites.
—*Taste of Home Test Kitchen*

Almond Curry Spread

Curry and chutney combine nicely in this out-of-the-ordinary spread. For dippers, use thick apple slices, carrot sticks, crackers, cocktail bread or a combination of these. —Barbara Beard, Lexington, Kentucky

> 2 packages (8 ounces *each*) cream cheese, softened
> 1/2 cup chopped green onions
> 1/3 cup chopped sweet red pepper
> 1 tablespoon curry powder
> 2 teaspoons Worcestershire sauce
> 2 teaspoons Dijon mustard
> 1 teaspoon ground nutmeg
> 1 jar (9 ounces) chutney
> 1/2 cup slivered almonds, toasted
> Assorted fruit, vegetables *or* crackers

In a mixing bowl, beat cream cheese until smooth. Add onions, red pepper, curry powder, Worcestershire sauce, mustard and nutmeg; mix well. Spread onto a platter. Top with chutney; sprinkle with almonds. Serve with fruit, vegetables or crackers. **Yield:** 8-10 servings.

Sesame Chicken Bites

(Pictured above)

So tender and tasty, these chicken appetizers are enhanced by a honey-mustard dipping sauce. I used to spend several days creating hors d'oeuvres for our holiday open house, and these bites were among the favorites. —Kathy Green, Layton, New Jersey

> 1/2 cup dry bread crumbs
> 1/4 cup sesame seeds
> 2 teaspoons minced fresh parsley
> 1/2 cup mayonnaise
> 1 teaspoon onion powder
> 1 teaspoon ground mustard
> 1/4 teaspoon pepper
> 1 pound boneless skinless chicken breasts, cut into 1-inch cubes
> 2 to 4 tablespoons vegetable oil
> HONEY-MUSTARD SAUCE:
> 3/4 cup mayonnaise
> 4-1/2 teaspoons honey
> 1-1/2 teaspoons Dijon mustard

In a large resealable plastic bag, combine the bread crumbs, sesame seeds and parsley; set aside. In a small bowl, combine the mayonnaise, onion powder, mustard and pepper. Coat chicken in mayonnaise mixture, then add to crumb mixture, a few pieces at a time, and shake to coat.

In a large skillet, saute chicken in oil in batches until juices run clear, adding additional oil as needed. In a small bowl, combine sauce ingredients. Serve with the chicken. **Yield:** 8-10 servings.

Warm Bacon Cheese Spread

My friends threaten not to come by unless this dip is on the menu! The rich spread bakes right in the bread bowl and goes well with almost any dipper. Plus, cleanup is a breeze.
—Nicole Marcotte
Smithers, British Columbia

> 1 round loaf (1 pound) sourdough bread
> 1 package (8 ounces) cream cheese, softened
> 1-1/2 cups (12 ounces) sour cream
> 2 cups (8 ounces) shredded cheddar cheese
> 1-1/2 teaspoons Worcestershire sauce
> 3/4 pound sliced bacon, cooked and crumbled
> 1/2 cup chopped green onions
> Assorted crackers

Cut the top fourth off the loaf of bread; carefully hollow out the bottom, leaving a 1-in. shell. Cut the removed bread and top of loaf into cubes; set aside.

In a mixing bowl, beat the cream cheese. Add the sour cream, cheddar cheese and Worcestershire sauce until combined; stir in bacon and onions. Spoon into bread shell. Wrap in a piece of heavy-duty foil (about 24 in. x 17 in.). Bake at 325° for 1 hour or until heated through. Serve with crackers and reserved bread cubes. **Yield:** 4 cups.

Cappuccino Punch

When I tried this punch at a friend's wedding shower, I had to have the recipe. Guests will eagerly gather around the punch bowl when you ladle out this frothy mocha ice cream drink. —Rose Reich, Nampa, Idaho

1/2 cup sugar
1/4 cup instant coffee granules
1 cup boiling water
2 quarts milk
1 quart vanilla ice cream, softened
1 quart chocolate ice cream, softened

In a small bowl, combine the sugar and coffee; stir in boiling water until dissolved. Cover and refrigerate until chilled. Just before serving, pour coffee mixture into a 1-gal. punch bowl. Stir in milk. Add scoops of ice cream; stir until melted. **Yield:** about 1 gallon.

— 🍴 🍴 🍴 —

Glazed Meatballs

(Pictured on page 4)

Allspice adds a bit of a twist to traditional barbecue meatballs in this recipe. —Nancy Horsburgh, Everett, Ontario

2 eggs
2/3 cup milk
1-1/4 cups soft bread crumbs
1 tablespoon prepared horseradish
1-1/2 pounds ground beef
1 cup water
1/2 cup chili sauce
1/2 cup ketchup
1/4 cup maple syrup
1/4 cup soy sauce
1-1/2 teaspoons ground allspice
1/2 teaspoon ground mustard

In a bowl, beat eggs and milk. Stir in bread crumbs and horseradish. Crumble beef over mixture and mix well. Shape into 1-1/2-in. balls. Place in a lightly greased 15-in. x 10-in. x 1-in. baking pan. Bake at 375° for 15-20 minutes or until meat is no longer pink.

In a large saucepan, combine the remaining ingredients. Bring to a boil; add the meatballs. Reduce heat; cover and simmer 15 minutes or until heated through, stirring occasionally. **Yield:** about 3-1/2 dozen.

— 🍴 🍴 🍴 —

Crispy Onion Wings

(Pictured at right)

My wife, daughters and I often enjoy these buttery wings while watching TV on Saturday nights. The crisp coating of french-fried onions, cornmeal and potato chips is also great on the chicken tenders I make from cut-up boneless chicken breast. —Jonathan Hershey, Akron, Ohio

12 whole chicken wings* (about 2-1/2 pounds)
2-1/2 cups crushed potato chips
1 can (2.8 ounces) french-fried onions, crushed
1/2 cup cornmeal
2 teaspoons dried oregano
1 teaspoon onion salt
1 teaspoon garlic powder
1 teaspoon paprika
2 eggs, beaten
1/4 cup butter *or* margarine, melted

Line a 15-in. x 10-in. x 1-in. baking pan with foil and grease the foil; set aside. Cut chicken wings into three sections; discard wing tip section. In a large resealable plastic bag, combine the potato chips, onions, cornmeal and seasonings; mix well. Dip chicken wings in eggs. Place in the bag, a few at a time; shake to coat and press crumb mixture into chicken.

Place wings in prepared pan; drizzle with butter. Bake, uncovered, at 375° for 30-35 minutes or until chicken juices run clear and coating is crisp. **Yield:** 8-10 servings.

*Editor's Note: 2-1/2 pounds of uncooked chicken wing sections (wingettes) may be substituted for the whole chicken wings. Omit cutting wings and discarding tips.

Southern Spiced Pecans

(Pictured below)

Pop these tasty pecans in your mouth...and you'll immediately want more. A mix of salty and sweet, the nuts are seasoned with cumin, cayenne, sugar and salt. They make a great hostess gift, too. —Carol Feaver
Marion, Ohio

      1/4 cup butter *or* margarine
  1-1/2 teaspoons ground cumin
      1/4 teaspoon cayenne pepper
        3 cups pecan halves
        2 tablespoons sugar
        1 teaspoon salt

In a large skillet, melt butter. Add the cumin and cayenne; cook and stir for 1 minute. Remove from the heat; stir in the pecans, sugar and salt until well coated. Spread in a single layer in a greased 15-in. x 10-in. x 1-in. baking pan.
    Bake at 300° for 25-30 minutes or until lightly browned, stirring occasionally. Cool. Store in an airtight container. **Yield:** 3 cups.

Creamy Chicken Spread

Every time I take this eye-catching log to a party, it's gone in no time. This mild spread smooths easily onto crackers. —Charlene Barrows, Reedley, California

✓ Uses less fat, sugar or salt. Includes Nutritional Analysis and Diabetic Exchanges.

        1 package (8 ounces) cream cheese, softened
      1/4 cup mayonnaise
        2 tablespoons lemon juice
      1/2 teaspoon salt
      1/4 teaspoon ground ginger
      1/8 teaspoon pepper
      1/8 teaspoon hot pepper sauce
        2 cups finely chopped cooked chicken breast
        2 hard-cooked eggs, finely chopped
      1/4 cup sliced green onions
Diced pimientos and additional sliced green onions
Assorted crackers and snack bread

In a small mixing bowl, combine the first seven ingredients; mix well. Stir in chicken, eggs and green onions. Shape into an 8-in. x 2-in. log. Garnish with pimientos and onions. Cover and chill. Remove from the refrigerator 15 minutes before serving. Serve with crackers and snack bread. **Yield:** 3 cups.
    Nutritional Analysis: 1/4 cup of spread (prepared with reduced-fat cream cheese and fat-free mayonnaise) equals 100 calories, 5 g fat (3 g saturated fat), 67 mg cholesterol, 223 mg sodium, 3 g carbohydrate, trace fiber, 10 g protein. **Diabetic Exchanges:** 1 lean meat, 1 fat.

Deep-Fried Potato Skins

The combination of potatoes, cheese, bacon and garlic dip in this recipe is fantastic. The skins can be served as an appetizer or as a side dish with any entree you choose. We like them with prime rib.
—Leslie Cunnian, Peterborough, Ontario

        4 large baking potatoes
        2 cups (16 ounces) sour cream
        1 envelope onion soup mix
        1 tablespoon finely chopped onion
        5 garlic cloves, minced
Dash hot pepper sauce
Oil for deep-fat frying
      1/2 cup shredded cheddar cheese
      1/2 cup shredded Swiss cheese
   6 to 8 bacon strips, cooked and crumbled
        4 teaspoons minced chives *or* green onion

Bake potatoes at 400° for 1 hour or until tender. Meanwhile, for dip, combine the sour cream, soup mix, onion, garlic and hot pepper sauce in a bowl. Cover and refrigerate until serving.

When potatoes are cool enough to handle, cut in half lengthwise. Scoop out pulp, leaving a 1/4-in. shell (save pulp for another use). With a scissors, cut each potato half into three lengthwise strips. In an electric skillet or deep-fat fryer, heat oil to 375°. Fry skins in oil for 2-3 minutes or until golden brown and crisp.

Place potato skins in a 15-in. x 10-in. x 1-in. baking pan. Combine the cheeses and bacon; sprinkle over potatoes. Broil 4 in. from the heat for 1-2 minutes or until cheese is melted. Sprinkle with chives. Serve with the dip. **Yield:** 2 dozen.

Asparagus Sesame Rolls

(Pictured at right)

These appealing appetizers are nice-looking on a buffet and always disappear fast. The cheeses and asparagus blend for a delicious flavor. They're quick to fix, too. —_Donna Folk, Berwick, Pennsylvania_

- **12 fresh asparagus spears**
- **12 bread slices,* crusts removed**
- **1 package (8 ounces) cream cheese, softened**
- **1/2 cup crumbled blue cheese**
- **6 tablespoons butter _or_ margarine, melted**
- **1 tablespoon sesame seeds, toasted**

Trim asparagus spears to 6 in. Flatten bread with a rolling pin. In a small mixing bowl, beat the cream cheese and blue cheese until combined. Spread over bread; top with an asparagus spear and roll up tightly. Roll in butter; place seam side down on a greased baking sheet. Sprinkle with sesame seeds. Bake at 375° for 14-16 minutes or until bottom is lightly browned. **Yield:** 1 dozen.

*Editor's Note: This recipe was tested with original Pepperidge Farm bread.

Bread Bowl Fondue

Veggies and toasted bread cubes make the perfect dippers for this thick, rich ham and cheese dip. Served in a bread bowl, it looks so pretty on a buffet table. —_June Mullins, Livonia, Missouri_

- **1 unsliced round bread (1 pound)**
- **8 ounces process cheese (Velveeta), cubed**
- **2 cups (16 ounces) sour cream**
- **1 package (8 ounces) cream cheese, softened**
- **1 cup diced fully cooked ham**
- **1/2 cup chopped green onions**
- **1 can (4 ounces) chopped green chilies**
- **1 teaspoon Worcestershire sauce**
- **2 tablespoons vegetable oil**
- **1 tablespoon butter _or_ margarine, melted**
- **Assorted fresh vegetables**

Cut the top fourth off the loaf of bread; set top aside. Carefully hollow out bottom, leaving a 1/2-in. shell. Cube removed bread; set aside.

In a bowl, combine the process cheese, sour cream and cream cheese. Stir in the ham, green onions, chilies and Worcestershire sauce. Spoon into bread shell; replace top. Wrap tightly in heavy-duty foil and place on a baking sheet. Bake at 350° for 60-70 minutes or until the filling is heated through.

Meanwhile, toss reserved bread cubes with oil and butter. Place in a 15-in. x 10-in. x 1-in. baking pan. Bake for 10-15 minutes or until golden brown, stirring occasionally. Unwrap loaf and remove bread top; stir filling. Serve with vegetables and toasted bread cubes. **Yield:** 5 cups.

in the center. Using a serrated knife, cut into 1/2-in. slices. Place on parchment paper-lined baking sheets; flatten to 1/4-in. thickness. Refrigerate for 15 minutes.

In a small bowl, beat egg and water; brush over slices. Bake at 375° for 12-14 minutes or until puffed and golden brown. Serve warm. **Yield:** 1-1/2 dozen.

— 🍵 🍵 🍵 —

Cheesy Chive Crisps

These snack bites are great to keep on hand for guests. Since the recipe makes a lot, you might want to freeze some of the cheese logs for future use. Be sure to thaw them in the refrigerator for 2 to 3 hours before slicing and baking.
—Eve McNew
St. Louis, Missouri

   1 cup butter (no substitutes), softened
   3 cups (12 ounces) shredded sharp cheddar cheese
   2 cups all-purpose flour
1/4 cup minced chives
1/2 teaspoon salt
1/2 teaspoon hot pepper sauce
Dash garlic salt
   2 cups crisp rice cereal

In a large mixing bowl, cream the butter and cheese until blended. Beat in the flour, chives, salt, hot pepper sauce and garlic salt. Stir in the cereal. Shape mixture into four 6-1/2-in. x 1-1/2-in. logs. Wrap in plastic wrap. Refrigerate for 1 hour or until firm.

Unwrap logs and cut into 1/4-in. slices. Place slices on ungreased baking sheets. Bake at 325° for 20-25 minutes or until edges are crisp and lightly browned. Remove to wire racks to cool. Store in the refrigerator. **Yield:** about 9 dozen.

— 🍵 🍵 🍵 —

Onion Brie Appetizers
(Pictured above)

Guests will think you spent hours preparing these cute appetizers, but they're really easy to assemble using purchased puff pastry. And the tasty combination of Brie, caramelized onions and caraway is terrific.
—Carole Resnick, Cleveland, Ohio

   2 medium onions, thinly sliced
   3 tablespoons butter *or* margarine
   2 tablespoons brown sugar
1/2 teaspoon white wine vinegar *or* cider vinegar
   1 sheet frozen puff pastry, thawed
   4 ounces Brie *or* Camembert, rind removed, softened
   1 to 2 teaspoons caraway seeds
   1 egg
   2 teaspoons water

In a large skillet, cook the onions, butter, brown sugar and vinegar over medium-low heat until onions are golden brown, stirring frequently. Remove onions with a slotted spoon and cool to room temperature.

On a lightly floured surface, roll puff pastry into an 11-in. x 8-in. rectangle. Spread Brie over pastry. Cover with the onions; sprinkle with caraway seeds. Roll up one long side to the middle of the dough; roll up the other side so the two rolls meet

Chive Egg Dip
(Pictured on page 4)

I just love the combination of cream cheese and chives...and it goes so well with the other savory ingredients in this dip.
—Ruth Peterson
Jenison, Michigan

   2 packages (3 ounces *each*) cream cheese, softened
1/4 cup milk
   2 tablespoons mayonnaise
   1 teaspoon prepared mustard
   1 teaspoon Worcestershire sauce

1/4 teaspoon salt
Dash pepper
   2 hard-cooked eggs, chopped
1/4 cup minced chives
Sweet pepper pieces *or* assorted crackers

In a small mixing bowl, beat the cream cheese until smooth. Gradually beat in milk and mayonnaise until blended. Add the mustard, Worcestershire sauce, salt and pepper. Stir in eggs and chives; mix well. Serve with peppers or crackers. Refrigerate leftovers. **Yield:** 1-1/2 cups.

Southwestern Onion Rings

These light crispy onion rings are sliced thin and spiced just right with garlic powder, cayenne pepper, chili powder and cumin. My family likes them alongside grilled burgers. They're even good as leftovers.
—Tamra Kriedeman, Enderlin, North Dakota

   2 large sweet onions
2-1/2 cups buttermilk
   2 eggs
   3 tablespoons water
1-3/4 cups all-purpose flour
   2 teaspoons salt
   2 teaspoons chili powder
   1 to 2 teaspoons cayenne pepper
   1 teaspoon sugar
   1 teaspoon garlic powder
   1 teaspoon ground cumin
Oil for deep-fat frying

Cut onions into 1/4-in. slices; separate into rings. Place in a bowl; cover with buttermilk and soak for 30 minutes, stirring twice. In another bowl, beat eggs and water. In a shallow dish, combine the flour, salt, chili powder, cayenne, sugar, garlic powder and cumin. Drain onion rings; dip in egg mixture, then coat with flour mixture.

In an electric skillet or deep-fat fryer, heat 1 in. of oil to 375°. Fry onion rings, a few at a time, for 1 to 1-1/2 minutes on each side or until golden brown and crisp. Drain on paper towels. **Yield:** 8 servings.

Hot Spiced Cider

Next time you're entertaining, stir up a batch of this nicely spiced cider. The wonderful aroma will make your guests feel welcome on a chilly day.
—Kim Wallace, Dover, Ohio

   1 gallon apple cider *or* apple juice
   1 cup orange juice
1/4 cup maple syrup
1/2 teaspoon orange extract
1/2 teaspoon lemon extract
   4 cinnamon sticks
   2 teaspoons whole cloves
   1 teaspoon whole allspice

In a Dutch oven, combine the first five ingredients. Place the cinnamon sticks, cloves and allspice on a double thickness of cheesecloth; bring up corners of cloth and tie with string to form a bag. Add to the pan.

Cook, uncovered, over medium heat for 10-15 minutes or until flavors are blended (do not boil). Discard spice bag. **Yield:** 4-1/2 quarts.

Garlic Treats Are Doggone Good

PET LOVERS will want to bake a batch of these tasty snacks for their canine friends.

"Dogs love garlic and cheese," says Judy Hede of Bemidji, Minnesota, who shared the puppy-pleasing recipe. "So my dog thinks these are the cat's meow!"

Garlic-Cheese Dog Biscuits

1-1/4 cups shredded cheddar cheese
1/4 cup stick margarine, softened
1-1/2 cups whole wheat flour
   1 to 4 garlic cloves, minced
Dash salt
   6 to 8 tablespoons milk

In a mixing bowl, beat the cheese and margarine. Add the flour, garlic and salt; mix well. Add enough milk to form a stiff dough. Cover and refrigerate for 30 minutes.

Roll out dough to 1/4-in. thickness. Cut with  a bone-shaped cookie cutter. Place on an ungreased baking sheet. Bake at 375° for 15-20 minutes or until edges are golden brown. Remove to wire racks. Biscuits will harden as they cool. **Yield:** 1-1/2 to 2 dozen (depending on cookie cutter size).

Sweet-Sour Sausage Bites

(Pictured below)

As a pastor's wife, I frequently entertain church groups in my home, so I'm always looking for new recipes. These quick and easy appetizers are not only delicious, they're colorful, too. I've made them many times.
—Maretta Bullock, McNeil, Arkansas

- 1/2 pound fully cooked smoked sausage, cut into 1/2-inch slices
- 1 can (20 ounces) pineapple chunks
- 4 teaspoons cornstarch
- 1/2 teaspoon salt
- 1/2 cup maple syrup
- 1/3 cup water
- 1/3 cup white vinegar
- 1 large green pepper, cut into 3/4-inch pieces
- 1/2 cup maraschino cherries

In a large skillet, saute the sausage for 3-5 minutes or until lightly browned. Drain on paper towels; set aside. Drain pineapple, reserving juice; set the pineapple aside.

In a large skillet, combine the cornstarch, salt and reserved pineapple juice until smooth. Stir in the syrup, water and vinegar. Bring to a boil; cook and stir for 2-3 minutes or until thickened. Add the sausage, green pepper, cherries and pineapple. Simmer, uncovered, for 5 minutes or until peppers are crisp-tender. Transfer to a shallow serving dish. Serve with toothpicks. **Yield:** 4 cups.

Crunchy Cheese Toasts

(Pictured below)

Cayenne pepper lends a little zip to these crisp and cheesy treats. They look and taste like they're a lot of trouble to make, but they're not. That's my favorite kind of recipe! —Camille Langford, Branson, Missouri

- 1 loaf (1 pound) French bread
- 1/2 cup olive *or* vegetable oil
- 1 teaspoon dried thyme
- 1/4 to 1/2 teaspoon cayenne pepper
- 2 cups (8 ounces) shredded Mexican cheese blend *or* cheddar cheese

Cut French bread into 54 slices, about 1/4 in. thick. Place on ungreased baking sheets. In a small bowl, whisk the oil, thyme and cayenne until blended. Brush over bread slices. Sprinkle with cheese. Bake at 300° for 12-15 minutes or until bread is golden brown and cheese is bubbly. Serve warm. **Yield:** 4-1/2 dozen.

———— 🍶 🍶 🍶 ————

Pizza Rolls

This is my husband's version of store-bought pizza rolls, and our family loves them. Although they take some time to make, they freeze well. So when we're through, we get to enjoy the fruits of our labor for a long time! —Julie Gaines, Normal, Illinois

- 4 cups (16 ounces) shredded pizza cheese blend *or* mozzarella cheese

YOU'LL HAVE TIME to enjoy the party when you serve simple snacks like Sweet-Sour Sausage Bites and Crunchy Cheese Toasts (shown below, left to right).

1 pound bulk Italian sausage, cooked and
  drained
2 packages (3 ounces *each*) sliced
  pepperoni, chopped
1 medium green pepper, finely chopped
1 medium sweet red pepper, finely chopped
1 medium onion, finely chopped
2 jars (14 ounces *each*) pizza sauce
32 egg roll wrappers
Vegetable oil for frying
**Additional pizza sauce for dipping, warmed,
  optional**

In a large bowl, combine the cheese, sausage,
pepperoni, peppers and onion. Stir in pizza sauce
until combined. Place about 1/4 cup filling in the
center of each egg roll wrapper. Fold bottom corner
over filling; fold sides toward center over filling.
Moisten remaining corner with water and roll up
tightly to seal.

   In an electric skillet, heat 1 in. of oil to 375°. Fry
pizza rolls for 1-2 minutes on each side or until
golden brown. Drain on paper towels. Serve with
additional pizza sauce if desired. **Yield:** 32 rolls.

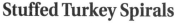

Stuffed Turkey Spirals

(Pictured above right)

*To create these impressive appetizers, I roll up turkey
breast halves with ham and cheese, bake and slice
them, then serve them with a creamy basil sauce.
They're great for a buffet because you can prepare
them ahead and bake them right before serving.*
   —*Renee Aupperle, Litiz, Pennsylvania*

2 boneless skinless turkey breast halves
  (1 pound *each*)
1/4 cup olive *or* vegetable oil, *divided*
4 teaspoons dried basil, *divided*
1 pound thinly sliced deli ham
1 pound thinly sliced Swiss cheese
1 teaspoon salt
1 teaspoon pepper
BASIL SAUCE:
2 cups mayonnaise
1/2 cup milk
1 to 2 tablespoons dried basil
1 teaspoon sugar

Cut each turkey breast horizontally from the long
side to within 1/2 in. of opposite side. Open flat;
cover with plastic wrap. Flatten into 12-in. x 10-in.
x 1/2-in. rectangles. Remove plastic; top each with
1 teaspoon oil and 1 teaspoon basil. Layer with ham
and cheese to within 1 in. of edges. Roll up jelly-
roll style, starting with a long side; tie with kitchen

string. Place on a rack in a roasting pan.
   In a small bowl, combine salt, pepper and remaining oil and basil; spoon some over turkey.
Bake at 325° for 75-90 minutes or until a meat thermometer reads 170°, basting occasionally with
remaining oil mixture.
   In a blender or food processor, combine the
sauce ingredients; cover and process until blended. Cool turkey for 5 minutes before slicing; serve
with basil sauce. **Yield:** about 30 servings.

Party Punch

*Filled with delicious citrus flavors, this lively beverage
will brighten any setting. I usually make two to three
batches for family gatherings, and there's never any
left over.*   —*Verna Doerksen, MacGregor, Manitoba*

2 cups sugar
2-1/2 cups boiling water
1 bottle (48 ounces) grapefruit juice
1 can (46 ounces) orange juice
1 can (46 ounces) pineapple juice
1 cup lemon juice
2 liters lemon-lime soda, chilled

In a large bowl, dissolve sugar in water. Add juices.
Refrigerate for 2 hours or until chilled. Just before
serving, stir in soda. **Yield:** 7-1/2 quarts.

Salads & Dressings

Feast your eyes on these refreshing salads featuring fresh fruits, vegetables, pasta, beans and more—you won't know which to toss together first!

IT'S A TOSS-UP. Clockwise from upper left: Flank Steak Spinach Salad (p. 34), Parsnip Carrot Salad (p. 36), Picnic Pasta Salad (p. 37), Sticks 'n' Stones Salad (p. 34) and Cranberry Cherry Salad (p. 35).

Loaded Baked Potato Salad

(Pictured above)

I revamped my mother's potato salad recipe to taste more like baked potatoes with all the fixin's, which I love. It's now the most requested dish at family gatherings…even my mother asked for the recipe!
—*Jackie Deckard, Solsberry, Indiana*

    5 pounds small unpeeled red potatoes,
       cubed
    1 teaspoon salt
  1/2 teaspoon pepper
    8 hard-cooked eggs, chopped
    1 pound sliced bacon, cooked and
       crumbled
    2 cups (8 ounces) shredded cheddar cheese
    1 medium Vidalia *or* sweet onion, chopped
    3 dill pickles, chopped
1-1/2 cups (12 ounces) sour cream
    1 cup mayonnaise
    2 to 3 teaspoons prepared mustard

Place the potatoes in a greased 15-in. x 10-in. x 1-in. baking pan; sprinkle with salt and pepper. Bake, uncovered, at 425° for 40-45 minutes or until tender. Cool in pan on a wire rack.

In a large bowl, combine the potatoes, eggs, bacon, cheese, onion and pickles. In a small bowl, combine the sour cream, mayonnaise and mustard; pour over the potato mixture and toss to coat. Serve immediately. **Yield:** 20 servings.

Flank Steak Spinach Salad

(Pictured on page 32)

Moist marinated steak, wild rice, almonds and veggies blend together nicely in this colorful main-dish salad. Years ago, a friend gave me the idea for this recipe, and with some tweaking, it's become a favorite of ours.
—*Freddie Johnson, San Antonio, Texas*

    4 beef flank steaks (about 1 pound *each*)
    1 bottle (16 ounces) Italian salad dressing,
       divided
1-1/4 cups uncooked wild rice
    2 packages (6 ounces *each*) fresh baby
       spinach
  1/2 pound fresh mushrooms, sliced
    1 large red onion, thinly sliced
    1 pint grape tomatoes, halved
    1 package (2-1/2 ounces) slivered almonds,
       toasted

Place steaks in a gallon-size resealable plastic bag; add 3/4 cup salad dressing. Seal bag and turn to coat. Refrigerate overnight. Prepare the rice according to package directions. In a bowl, combine rice with 1/2 cup salad dressing. Cover and refrigerate overnight.

Drain and discard marinade from steaks. Grill steaks, uncovered, over medium heat for 6-8 minutes on each side or until meat reaches desired doneness (for rare, a meat thermometer should read 140°; medium, 160°; well-done, 170°). Let stand for 10 minutes. Thinly slice against the grain; cool to room temperature.

To serve, arrange spinach on a large platter. Top with the rice, mushrooms, onion, tomatoes and steak. Sprinkle with almonds; drizzle with remaining salad dressing. **Yield:** 16 servings.

— 🛒 🛒 🛒 —

Sticks 'n' Stones Salad

(Pictured on page 32)

"Sticks" of celery and carrots tossed with water chestnuts ("stones") are nicely coated in a dill and Dijon mustard dressing. This salad is a big hit with our children—it's a great way to get them to eat their vegetables. Not only do they love the taste, but they also love the name of the recipe! —*Nancy Zicker
Port Orange, Florida*

✓ Uses less fat, sugar or salt. Includes Nutritional Analysis and Diabetic Exchanges.

    5 celery ribs, julienned
    2 large carrots, julienned
    1 can (8 ounces) sliced water chestnuts,
       drained

2 tablespoons olive *or* canola oil
2 tablespoons cider vinegar
1 teaspoon sugar
1 teaspoon Dijon mustard
1/2 teaspoon salt
1/4 teaspoon dill weed

Place celery and carrots in a saucepan; cover with water. Bring to a boil. Cook, uncovered, for 3-4 minutes; drain and rinse with cold water. Drain thoroughly. Transfer to a large bowl; add the water chestnuts. In a small bowl, whisk the oil, vinegar, sugar, mustard, salt and dill. Pour over vegetables and toss to coat. **Yield:** 4 servings.

Nutritional Analysis: One serving (3/4 cup) equals 121 calories, 7 g fat (1 g saturated fat), 0 cholesterol, 396 mg sodium, 14 g carbohydrate, 5 g fiber, 1 g protein. **Diabetic Exchanges:** 3 vegetable, 1 fat.

Green Bean Chicken Salad

(Pictured below right)

I dress green beans, tomatoes and chicken in a pleasant basil vinaigrette to make this refreshing salad. The flavors really blend well in the refrigerator, so this salad tastes even better the second day.
—*Kylene Konosky, Jermyn, Pennsylvania*

✓ Uses less fat, sugar or salt. Includes Nutritional Analysis and Diabetic Exchanges.

1/3 cup red wine vinegar *or* cider vinegar
1/4 cup minced fresh basil *or* 4 teaspoons dried basil
1 tablespoon plus 2 teaspoons olive *or* canola oil, *divided*
2 teaspoons sugar
1/8 teaspoon salt
1 pound boneless skinless chicken breasts, cubed
1 pound fresh green beans, trimmed
2 plum tomatoes, chopped

In a large bowl, whisk the vinegar, basil, 1 tablespoon of oil, sugar and salt; set aside. In a nonstick skillet, saute chicken in remaining oil over medium heat until juices run clear. Add to vinaigrette and toss to coat.

Place green beans in a steamer basket in a saucepan over 1 in. of water. Bring to a boil; cover and steam for 5-10 minutes or until crisp-tender. Add to chicken mixture. Add tomatoes and toss to coat. Cover and refrigerate for at least 1 hour. Toss before serving. **Yield:** 4 servings.

Nutritional Analysis: One serving (1-1/4 cups) equals 225 calories, 7 g fat (1 g saturated fat), 66

mg cholester-ol, 152 mg sodium, 11 g carbohydrate,5 g fiber, 28 g protein. **Diabetic Exchanges:** 3 very lean meat, 2 vegetable, 1 fat.

Cranberry Cherry Salad

(Pictured on page 32)

I like to make this refreshing salad for summer get-togethers. It's also a great side dish during the Thanksgiving and Christmas seasons. Everybody just loves it!
—*Betsy Bianco, Wheaton, Missouri*

1 can (14-1/2 ounces) pitted tart red cherries
1 package (3 ounces) cherry gelatin
1 can (8 ounces) jellied cranberry sauce
1 package (3 ounces) lemon gelatin
1 cup boiling water
1 package (3 ounces) cream cheese, softened
1/3 cup mayonnaise
1 can (8 ounces) crushed pineapple, undrained
1/2 cup heavy whipping cream, whipped
1 cup miniature marshmallows

Drain cherries, reserving juice; set cherries aside. Add water to juice to measure 1 cup; transfer to a saucepan. Bring to a boil. Add cherry gelatin; stir until dissolved. Whisk in cranberry sauce until smooth. Add cherries; pour into an 11-in. x 7-in. x 2-in. dish. Refrigerate until firm.

In a bowl, dissolve lemon gelatin in boiling water. In a small mixing bowl, beat the cream cheese and mayonnaise. Gradually beat in lemon gelatin until smooth. Stir in pineapple. Refrigerate until almost set. Fold in whipped cream and marshmallows. Spoon over cherry layer. Refrigerate until firm. **Yield:** 8-10 servings.

Berry Slaw

(Pictured below)

As a family, we're trying to cut down on the fat in our diets without giving up good taste. This crisp cabbage salad, featuring strawberries and cranberries, is a great warm-weather pick-me-up.
—Harriet Stichter, Milford, Indiana

☑ Uses less fat, sugar or salt. Includes Nutritional Analysis and Diabetic Exchanges.

 1/4 cup cider vinegar
 1/4 cup unsweetened apple *or* cranberry juice
 1 teaspoon sugar
 1/2 teaspoon salt
 1/4 teaspoon white pepper
 6 cups shredded cabbage
 1-1/2 cups sliced fresh strawberries
 1/2 cup dried cranberries

In a large bowl, combine the vinegar, apple juice, sugar, salt and pepper; add cabbage. Toss gently to coat. Cover and refrigerate for at least 8 hours or overnight, stirring occasionally. Just before serving, stir in strawberries and cranberries. **Yield:** 6 servings.

Nutritional Analysis: One serving (3/4 cup) equals 74 calories, trace fat (trace saturated fat), 0 cholesterol, 212 mg sodium, 17 g carbohydrate, 4 g fiber, 2 g protein. **Diabetic Exchange:** 1 fruit.

Cherry Waldorf Salad

I combine apples with cherries and cranberries to give a new twist to the classic Waldorf salad.
—Marie Hattrup, The Dalles, Oregon

 2 large apples (about 1 pound), chopped
 1 tablespoon lemon juice
 2 celery ribs, chopped
 1 cup fresh *or* frozen pitted tart cherries, halved
 1/2 cup dried cranberries
 1/2 cup slivered almonds, toasted
 1/4 cup mayonnaise
 1/4 cup sour cream
 2 tablespoons honey
 1/8 teaspoon salt

In a large salad bowl, toss apples with lemon juice. Add the celery, cherries, cranberries and almonds. In a small bowl, whisk the mayonnaise, sour cream, honey and salt until well blended. Pour over salad and toss to coat. Cover and refrigerate for 1 hour before serving. **Yield:** 6-8 servings.

— 🃏 🃏 🃏 —

Parsnip Carrot Salad

(Pictured on page 33)

Because my husband's garden produced an overabundance of parsnips, I experimented and came up with this combination. *—Marge Campbell Waymart, Pennsylvania*

☑ Uses less fat, sugar or salt. Includes Nutritional Analysis and Diabetic Exchanges.

 3 cups sliced peeled parsnips
 3/4 cup sliced peeled carrots
 3 tablespoons orange juice
 1 tablespoon olive *or* canola oil
 1-1/2 teaspoons lemon juice
 3/4 teaspoon Dijon mustard
 3 tablespoons minced chives
 3/4 teaspoon celery seed

Place the parsnips and carrots in a large saucepan; cover with water. Bring to a boil. Reduce heat; cover and simmer for 8-10 minutes or until crisp-tender. Meanwhile, in a small bowl, whisk the orange juice, oil, lemon juice and mustard until blended.

Drain the vegetables; add orange juice mixture and toss to coat. Sprinkle with the chives and celery seed. Serve warm. **Yield:** 4 servings.

Nutritional Analysis: One serving (1/2 cup) equals 124 calories, 4 g fat (1 g saturated fat), 0 cholesterol, 42 mg sodium, 22 g carbohydrate, 6 g fiber, 2 g protein. **Diabetic Exchanges:** 1 starch, 1 vegetable, 1/2 fat.

Tarragon Salad Dressing

I whisk together tarragon, chives, parsley and Dijon mustard in this delightful vinaigrette. The fast-to-fix dressing will add a fresh tang to any bowl of mixed greens. —Marie Hoyer, Lewistown, Montana

    1/2 cup olive _or_ vegetable oil
    1/3 cup red wine vinegar _or_ cider vinegar
      2 tablespoons minced fresh tarragon _or_ 2
        teaspoons dried tarragon
      1 teaspoon Dijon mustard
      1 garlic clove, minced
    1/2 teaspoon salt
    1/2 teaspoon pepper
    1/2 teaspoon minced chives
    1/2 teaspoon minced fresh parsley
Salad greens

In a jar with a tight-fitting lid, combine the first nine ingredients; shake well. Serve over salad greens. **Yield:** 3/4 cup.

Picnic Pasta Salad

(Pictured on page 33)

My family's not big on traditional pasta salads made with mayonnaise, so when I served this colorful version that uses Italian dressing, it was a big hit. —Felicia Fiocchi, Vineland, New Jersey

      1 package (12 ounces) tricolor spiral pasta
      1 package (10 ounces) refrigerated tricolor
        tortellini
      1 jar (7 ounces) marinated artichoke hearts,
        undrained
    1/2 pound fresh broccoli florets (about 1-3/4
        cups)
     12 ounces provolone cheese, cubed
     12 ounces hard salami, cubed
      1 medium sweet red pepper, chopped
      1 medium green pepper, chopped
      1 can (15 ounces) garbanzo beans _or_
        chickpeas, rinsed and drained
      2 cans (2-1/4 ounces _each_) sliced ripe
        olives, drained
      1 medium red onion, chopped
      4 garlic cloves, minced
      2 envelopes Italian salad dressing mix

Cook spiral pasta and tortellini according to package directions. Drain and rinse in cold water. Place in a large bowl; add the artichokes, broccoli, provolone cheese, salami, peppers, beans, olives, onion and garlic.

Prepare salad dressing according to package directions; pour over salad and toss to coat. Serve immediately or refrigerate. **Yield:** 14-16 servings.

Cashew Turkey Pasta Salad

(Pictured above)

Cashews add a nice crunch to this grilled turkey and spiral pasta combo. I first tasted this salad at a baby shower and asked the hostess for her recipe. Since then, I've served it for many occasions. —Karen Wyffels, Lino Lakes, Minnesota

      2 bone-in turkey breast halves, skin
        removed
      3 cups uncooked tricolor spiral pasta
      2 celery ribs, diced
      6 green onions, chopped
    1/2 cup diced green pepper
  1-1/2 cups mayonnaise
    3/4 cup packed brown sugar
      1 tablespoon cider vinegar
  1-1/2 teaspoons salt
  1-1/2 teaspoons lemon juice
      2 cups salted cashew halves

Grill turkey, covered, over medium heat for 25-30 minutes on each side or until juices run clear. Cool slightly. Cover and refrigerate until cool. Meanwhile, cook pasta according to package directions; drain and rinse in cold water.

Chop turkey; place in a large bowl. Add the pasta, celery, onions and green pepper. In a small bowl, combine the mayonnaise, brown sugar, vinegar, salt and lemon juice; pour over pasta mixture and toss to coat. Cover and refrigerate for at least 2 hours. Just before serving, stir in cashews. **Yield:** 12 servings.

Cherry Brie Tossed Salad
(Pictured above)

Draped in a light vinaigrette and sprinkled with cherries and almonds, this pretty salad is a variation of a recipe that's been passed around at school and church functions and even birthday parties. Everyone wants a copy of the recipe.
—Toni Borden
Wellington, Florida

DRESSING:
1 cup cider vinegar
1/2 cup sugar
1/4 cup olive *or* vegetable oil
1 teaspoon ground mustard
1-1/2 teaspoons poppy seeds
SALAD:
1/3 cup sugar
3/4 cup sliced almonds
8 cups torn romaine
8 ounces Brie *or* Camembert,* rind removed, cubed
1 package (6 ounces) dried cherries

In a jar with a tight-fitting lid, combine the dressing ingredients; shake until the sugar is dissolved.

For salad, in a heavy saucepan, heat sugar over medium-low heat until melted, about 10 minutes (do not stir). When sugar is melted, stir in almonds until coated and lightly toasted. Spread on foil to cool; break apart.

In a large salad bowl, combine the romaine, cheese and cherries. Shake dressing; drizzle over salad. Sprinkle with sugared almonds and toss to coat. **Yield:** 8-10 servings.

*Editor's Note:** Swiss cheese can be substituted for Brie or Camembert.

— 🍴 🍴 🍴 —

Three-Bean Garden Salad

This comes from a recipe I originally found in a bean cookbook. It took quite a few failures to come up with this winning combination. I hope you enjoy it as much as we do!
—Mary Kaye Rackowitz
Marysville, Washington

1 package (10 ounces) frozen lima beans
1 can (16 ounces) kidney beans, rinsed and drained
1 package (9 ounces) frozen cut green beans, thawed
8 ounces fresh mushrooms, sliced
1 pint cherry tomatoes, halved
1/4 cup thinly sliced green onions
DRESSING:
2/3 cup lemon juice
1/3 cup sugar
1/3 cup olive *or* vegetable oil
1-1/4 teaspoons salt
3/4 teaspoon Italian seasoning
1/2 teaspoon dried basil
1/2 teaspoon pepper

Cook lima beans according to package directions. Rinse in cold water; drain and place in a medium bowl. Add kidney and green beans, mushrooms, tomatoes and onions. Combine dressing ingredients. Pour over salad; mix gently to coat. Cover and chill for at least 5 hours, stirring occasionally. **Yield:** 10-12 servings.

— 🍴 🍴 🍴 —

Tuna-Stuffed Tomatoes

Each summer, I look forward to making this main-dish salad when I have a bumper crop of fresh tomatoes in my vegetable garden.
—Patricia Collins
Imbler, Oregon

1 can (12 ounces) tuna, drained and flaked
4 ounces cheddar cheese, cut into 1/4-inch cubes
1/2 to 3/4 cup mayonnaise
1/2 cup chopped celery
1/4 cup chopped onion
2 tablespoons chopped dill pickle
1 tablespoon dill pickle juice
1/4 teaspoon salt
1/8 teaspoon *each* celery seed and pepper

5 **medium tomatoes, cored**
Bacon bits, optional

In a bowl, combine tuna, cheese, mayonnaise, celery, onion, pickle, pickle juice, salt, celery seed and pepper. Chill. Cut tomatoes, not quite through, into quarters; place on individual plates and spread apart. Spoon 1/2 cup salad into each. Garnish with bacon bits if desired. **Yield:** 5 servings.

— ☕ ☕ ☕ —

Submarine Sandwich Salad

If your family's like mine, they won't be able to resist this salad loaded with meat, produce…even bread! The recipe can be easily doubled, so I often prepare it for potlucks.   —Julie Vogl, Cumberland, Iowa

  5 to 6 cups torn lettuce
  1 to 2 hard rolls, cubed
  1 medium tomato, chopped
1/2 cup thinly sliced red onion
1/2 cup shredded Swiss cheese
  2 ounces *each* ham, turkey and salami,
    julienned
1/2 cup sliced pepperoni
DRESSING:
1/3 cup vegetable oil
  2 tablespoons tarragon *or* white wine
    vinegar
1/4 to 1/2 teaspoon dried oregano
1/4 teaspoon salt
1/8 teaspoon garlic powder
Dash pepper

Combine lettuce, rolls, tomato, onion, cheese, ham, turkey, salami and pepperoni in a large bowl. In a small bowl, combine dressing ingredients; mix well. Pour over salad; toss to coat. Serve immediately. **Yield:** 6 servings.

— ☕ ☕ ☕ —

Summer Fruit Salad

(Pictured at right)

A tangy cream cheese dressing makes this refreshing salad special. I've found it's a big hit at potlucks, whether served as a salad or dessert. It makes a luscious finale on those sultry summer days when baking is out of the question.   —James Korzenowski
Dearborn, Michigan

PINEAPPLE CREAM CHEESE DRESSING:
1/3 cup sugar
  4 teaspoons cornstarch
1/4 teaspoon salt

  1 cup pineapple juice
1/4 cup orange juice
  2 tablespoons lemon juice
  2 eggs, lightly beaten
  2 packages (3 ounces *each*) cream cheese,
    softened
SALAD:
  2 cups sliced fresh strawberries
  2 cups pineapple tidbits
1-1/2 cups seedless green *or* red grapes, halved
1-1/2 cups diced peaches *or* nectarines
  1 cup fresh blueberries *or* raspberries
1/4 cup sugar
Leaf lettuce

In a small saucepan, combine the sugar, cornstarch and salt. Stir in the juices until smooth. Bring to a boil; cook and stir for 2 minutes or until thickened. Remove from the heat.

Stir a small amount into the eggs; return all to the pan, stirring constantly. Cook and stir until mixture reaches 160° and is thickened. Remove from the heat; cool slightly. In a small mixing bowl, beat cream cheese until smooth. Add juice mixture; mix well. Cover and refrigerate overnight.

In a large bowl, combine the fruit. Sprinkle with sugar; toss to coat. Cover and refrigerate overnight. Serve in a lettuce-lined bowl with the dressing. **Yield:** 8 servings.

Soups & Sandwiches

Nothing beats the classic combination of a steaming bowl of soup and a piled-high sandwich for a comforting lunch or light supper.

SO HAPPY TOGETHER. Clockwise from upper left: Slow Cooker Barbecue Beef (p. 45), Onion Beef Au Jus (p. 44), Cheesy Ham Braid (p. 42) and Zucchini Tomato Soup (p. 42).

Turkey Barbecue

(Pictured above)

Cayenne and lemon pepper add zip to this tantalizing shredded turkey that will have guests lining up for seconds. The well-seasoned meat takes some time to prepare, but it's well worth the effort. —Tammy Schill Omaha, Nebraska

      1 turkey (about 12 pounds)
  1/2 cup butter *or* margarine, melted
      2 tablespoons Worcestershire sauce
      2 tablespoons steak sauce
      1 tablespoon garlic powder
      1 tablespoon onion powder
      1 tablespoon lemon-pepper seasoning
      1 tablespoon pepper
      2 to 3 teaspoons cayenne pepper
  1/4 teaspoon salt
      1 cup chicken broth
    12 sandwich rolls, split
Lettuce leaves and tomato slices, optional

Place turkey, breast side up, on a rack in a roasting pan. Combine the butter, Worcestershire sauce, steak sauce and seasonings; rub 3 tablespoons over turkey. Cover and refrigerate remaining butter mixture. Bake turkey, uncovered, at 325° for 3 to 3-1/2 hours or until a meat thermometer reads 180°, basting occasionally with pan drippings.

Remove turkey; pour drippings into a saucepan. When turkey is cool enough to handle, remove meat from the bones. Shred turkey and return to the roasting pan. Add broth and remaining butter mixture to the drippings; bring to a rolling boil. Pour over shredded turkey.

Cover and bake at 325° for 25-30 minutes or until heated through. Serve on rolls with lettuce and tomato if desired. **Yield:** 12 servings.

Cheesy Ham Braid

(Pictured on page 41)

Our congregation is full of wonderful cooks, so we enjoy many potluck meals throughout the year. I like to share this chewy and cheesy braid I got from a family friend. —Becky Houston, Grand Junction, Tennessee

      1 package (16 ounces) hot roll mix
      1 cup warm water (120° to 130°)
      1 egg, lightly beaten
      2 tablespoons butter *or* margarine,
        softened, *divided*
  1/2 cup chopped onion
  1/2 cup chopped green pepper
      2 cups chopped fully cooked ham
1-1/2 cups (6 ounces) shredded cheddar cheese
      1 cup (8 ounces) ricotta cheese
      1 tablespoon minced fresh parsley
      1 egg white
      1 tablespoon cold water

In a large bowl, combine the hot roll mix and contents of yeast packet. Stir in the warm water, egg and 1 tablespoon butter. Turn onto a lightly floured surface; knead for 5 minutes. Cover and let rest for 5 minutes. In a skillet, saute onion and green pepper in remaining butter until tender. Remove from the heat; stir in ham, cheeses and parsley.

On a greased baking sheet, roll dough into a 15-in. x 10-in. rectangle. Spoon ham mixture lengthwise down the center of dough. On each long side, cut 1-in.-wide strips about 2 in. into the center. Starting at one end, fold alternating strips at an angle across filling. Pinch ends to seal. Cover and let rise in a warm place for 15 minutes or until almost doubled.

In a small bowl, beat egg white and cold water; brush over dough. Bake at 375° for 25-30 minutes or until golden brown. Let stand for 10 minutes before slicing. Serve warm. Refrigerate leftovers. **Yield:** 6-8 servings.

Zucchini Tomato Soup

(Pictured on page 40)

There's garden-fresh flavor in every spoonful of this easy-to-make soup. I like it for a low-calorie lunch, along with a roll and fruit for dessert. It serves just two, so you don't end up with leftovers. —Nancy Johnson Laverne, Oklahoma

✓ Uses less fat, sugar or salt. Includes Nutritional Analysis and Diabetic Exchanges.

2 small zucchini, coarsely chopped
1/4 cup chopped red onion
1-1/2 teaspoons olive *or* canola oil
1/8 teaspoon salt
1 cup spicy hot V8 juice
1 small tomato, cut into thin wedges
Dash *each* pepper and dried basil
2 tablespoons shredded cheddar cheese, optional
1 to 2 tablespoons cooked crumbled bacon, optional

In a skillet, saute the zucchini and onion in oil until crisp-tender. Sprinkle with salt. Add the V8 juice, tomato, pepper and basil; cook until heated through. Garnish with cheese and bacon if desired. **Yield:** 2 servings.

Nutritional Analysis: One serving (calculated without cheese and bacon) equals 89 calories, 4 g fat (1 g saturated fat), 0 cholesterol, 545 mg sodium, 12 g carbohydrate, 3 g fiber, 3 g protein. **Diabetic Exchanges:** 2 vegetable, 1/2 fat.

— 🍴 🍴 🍴 —

Shredded Barbecued Beef

I work for the Delaware Department of Transportation and prepare this simple dish during storm emergencies or for lunch get-togethers. —Jan Walls
Camden, Delaware

1 teaspoon celery salt
1 teaspoon garlic powder
1 teaspoon onion powder
1 fresh beef brisket* (3 to 5 pounds), halved
3 tablespoons liquid smoke, optional
1 tablespoon hot pepper sauce
1 bottle (18 ounces) barbecue sauce
12 sandwich rolls, split

Combine the celery salt, garlic powder and onion powder; rub over brisket. Place in a 5-qt. slow cooker. Combine liquid smoke if desired and hot pepper sauce; pour over brisket. Cover and cook on low for 6-8 hours or until the meat is tender.

Remove roast and cool slightly. Strain cooking juices, reserving 1/2 cup. Shred meat with two forks; place in a large saucepan. Add the barbecue sauce and reserved cooking juices; heat through. Serve about 1/3 cup meat mixture on each roll. **Yield:** 12 servings.

***Editor's Note:** This is a fresh beef brisket, not corned beef.

Chicken Noodle Soup

(Pictured below)

I cook most of the weekend meals and share weekday cooking duties with my wife. I also like to take food to neighbors, co-workers and our parents. And I try to send things like this hearty soup to people I know are sick. —Terry Kuehn, Waunakee, Wisconsin

1 stewing chicken (about 4 pounds), cut up
3 quarts water
2 cans (14-1/2 ounces *each*) chicken broth
5 celery ribs, coarsely chopped, *divided*
4 medium carrots, coarsely chopped, *divided*
2 medium onions, quartered, *divided*
2/3 cup coarsely chopped green pepper, *divided*
1-1/4 teaspoons pepper, *divided*
1 bay leaf
2 teaspoons salt
8 ounces uncooked medium egg noodles

In a large kettle, combine the chicken, water, broth, half of the celery, carrots, onions and green pepper, 1/2 teaspoon pepper and the bay leaf. Bring to a boil. Reduce heat; cover and simmer for 2-1/2 hours or until the chicken is tender. Chop the remaining onion; set aside.

Remove chicken from broth. When cool enough to handle, remove meat from bones and cut into bite-size pieces. Discard bones and skin; set chicken aside. Strain broth and skim fat; return broth to kettle. Add salt, chopped onion and remaining celery, carrots, green pepper and pepper. Bring to a boil. Reduce heat; cover and simmer for 10-12 minutes or until vegetables are crisp-tender. Add noodles and chicken. Cover and simmer for 12-15 minutes or until noodles are tender. **Yield:** 16 servings.

Italian Turkey Burgers

(Pictured below)

Seasoned with oregano and Parmesan cheese, these burgers are a delicious change-of-pace entree. I serve them on crusty Italian bread with warmed spaghetti sauce. —Mary Tallman, Arbor Vitae, Wisconsin

✓ Uses less fat, sugar or salt. Includes Nutritional Analysis and Diabetic Exchanges.

- 1/4 cup canned crushed tomatoes
- 2 tablespoons grated Parmesan cheese
- 1/2 teaspoon garlic powder
- 1/2 teaspoon dried oregano
- 1/4 teaspoon salt
- 1/4 teaspoon pepper
- 1 pound ground turkey *or* veal
- 8 slices Italian bread, toasted
- 1/2 cup meatless spaghetti sauce, warmed

In a bowl, combine the first six ingredients. Crumble turkey over mixture and mix well. Shape into four 3/4-in.-thick oval-shaped patties. Coat grill rack with nonstick cooking spray before starting the grill. Grill patties, uncovered, over medium heat for 6-8 minutes on each side or until meat is no longer pink. Place each patty on a slice of bread; top with spaghetti sauce and another slice of bread. **Yield:** 4 servings.

Nutritional Analysis: One serving (prepared with lean ground turkey) equals 306 calories, 12 g fat (3 g saturated fat), 92 mg cholesterol, 680 mg sodium, 24 g carbohydrate, 2 g fiber, 25 g protein. **Diabetic Exchanges:** 3 lean meat, 1-1/2 starch, 1 fat.

— 🍵 🍵 🍵 —

Onion Beef Au Jus

(Pictured on page 41)

Garlic, onions, soy sauce and onion soup mix flavor the tender beef in these savory hot sandwiches served with a tasty rich broth for dipping. The seasoned beef makes delicious cold sandwiches, too. —Marilyn Brown West Union, Iowa

- 1 boneless beef rump roast (4 pounds)
- 2 tablespoons vegetable oil
- 2 large sweet onions, cut into 1/4-inch slices
- 6 tablespoons butter *or* margarine, softened, *divided*
- 5 cups water
- 1/2 cup soy sauce
- 1 envelope onion soup mix
- 1 garlic clove, minced
- 1 teaspoon browning sauce, optional
- 1 loaf (1 pound) French bread
- 1 cup (4 ounces) shredded Swiss cheese

In a Dutch oven over medium-high heat, brown roast on all sides in oil; drain. In a large skillet, saute onions in 2 tablespoons of butter until tender. Add the water, soy sauce, soup mix, garlic and browning sauce if desired. Pour over roast. Cover and bake at 325° for 2-1/2 hours or until meat is tender.

Let stand for 10 minutes before slicing. Return meat to pan juices. Slice bread in half lengthwise; cut into 3-in. sections. Spread remaining butter over bread. Place on a baking sheet. Broil 4-6 in. from the heat for 2-3 minutes or until golden brown. Top with beef and onions; sprinkle with cheese. Broil 4-6 in. from the heat for 1-2 minutes or until cheese is melted. Serve with pan juices. **Yield:** 12 servings.

— 🍵 🍵 🍵 —

Shrimp Chowder

This zippy chowder is chock-full of shrimp and vegetables, so it satisfies hearty appetites, but the skim milk and reduced-sodium broth help keep fat and calories to a minimum. —Michelle Conley Evanston, Wyoming

✓ Uses less fat, sugar or salt. Includes Nutritional Analysis and Diabetic Exchanges.

- 1 pound red potatoes, peeled and cubed
- 2-1/2 cups reduced-sodium chicken broth
- 3 celery ribs, chopped
- 8 green onions, chopped
- 1/2 cup chopped sweet red pepper
- 1-1/2 cups skim milk
- 1/4 cup all-purpose flour
- 1/2 cup evaporated skim milk
- 1-1/2 pounds uncooked medium shrimp, peeled and deveined
- 2 tablespoons minced fresh parsley
- 1/2 teaspoon paprika
- 1/2 teaspoon Worcestershire sauce

1/8 teaspoon cayenne pepper
1/8 teaspoon pepper

In a large saucepan, bring the potatoes, broth, celery, onions and red pepper to a boil. Reduce heat; cover and simmer for 13-15 minutes or until vegetables are tender. Stir in skim milk. Gently mash vegetables with a potato masher, leaving some chunks of potatoes.

Combine flour and evaporated milk until smooth; gradually stir into potato mixture. Bring to a boil; cook and stir for 2 minutes or until thickened. Stir in the remaining ingredients. Return to a boil. Cook and stir for 2-3 minutes or until shrimp turn pink. **Yield:** 8 servings.

Nutritional Analysis: One serving (1 cup) equals 192 calories, 2 g fat (trace saturated fat), 130 mg cholesterol, 334 mg sodium, 21 g carbohydrate, 2 g fiber, 23 g protein. **Diabetic Exchanges:** 2-1/2 lean meat, 1 starch, 1 vegetable.

Slow Cooker Barbecue Beef

(Pictured on page 40)

This juicy shredded beef is so popular at summer gatherings. The tender meat is slow-cooked in a savory sauce. It makes a big batch...enough for seconds.
—*Colleen Nelson, Mandan, North Dakota*

 1 boneless beef sirloin tip roast (about 3 pounds), cut into large chunks
 3 celery ribs, chopped
 1 large onion, chopped
 1 medium green pepper, chopped
 1 cup ketchup
 1 can (6 ounces) tomato paste
1/2 cup packed brown sugar
1/4 cup cider vinegar
 3 tablespoons chili powder
 2 tablespoons lemon juice
 2 tablespoons molasses
 2 teaspoons salt
 2 teaspoons Worcestershire sauce
 1 teaspoon ground mustard
 8 to 10 sandwich rolls, split

Place beef in a 5-qt. slow cooker. Add the celery, onion and green pepper. In a bowl, combine the ketchup, tomato paste, brown sugar, vinegar, chili powder, lemon juice, molasses, salt, Worcestershire sauce and mustard. Pour over beef mixture. Cover and cook on low for 8-9 hours or until meat is tender.

Skim fat from cooking juices if necessary. Shred beef. Toast rolls if desired. Use a slotted spoon to serve beef on rolls. **Yield:** 8-10 servings.

Cheesy Ham 'n' Rice Soup

(Pictured above)

Here's a real gem! After tasting a similar soup at a popular restaurant in the Twin Cities, I came up with my own version. Everyone who tastes it says it's wonderful. Adding the almonds at the end gives the soup a fun crunch. —*Nicole Weir, Hager City, Wisconsin*

 4 celery ribs, chopped
 1 large onion, chopped
1/4 cup butter *or* margarine
 4 medium carrots, shredded
1/3 cup all-purpose flour
 1 teaspoon salt
1/2 teaspoon pepper
 2 cups half-and-half cream
 8 ounces process cheese (Velveeta), cubed
 4 cups cooked wild rice
 3 cups cubed fully cooked ham
2-2/3 cups cooked brown rice
 3 tablespoons chicken bouillon granules
 8 cups water
Slivered almonds, optional

In a saucepan, saute celery and onion in butter until tender. Add carrots; cook and stir for 1-2 minutes. In a large kettle or Dutch oven, combine the flour, salt and pepper. Gradually stir in cream. Bring to a boil; cook and stir for 2 minutes or until thickened.

Remove from the heat; stir in cheese until melted. Stir in the wild rice, ham, brown rice, bouillon, celery mixture and water. Return to a boil. Sprinkle with almonds if desired. **Yield:** 12 servings.

Onion Cream Soup

(Pictured above)

My whole family loves this hearty soup, especially on cool autumn evenings. It's rich and creamy with a mild onion-cheese flavor. When I need an easy dinner, I stir up this soup and serve it with warm crusty bread and a crisp salad.
—Janice Hemond
Lincoln, Rhode Island

> 2 cups thinly sliced sweet onions
> 6 tablespoons butter *or* margarine, ***divided***
> 1 can (14-1/2 ounces) chicken broth
> 2 teaspoons chicken bouillon granules
> 1/4 teaspoon pepper
> 3 tablespoons all-purpose flour
> 1-1/2 cups milk
> 1/4 cup diced process cheese (Velveeta)
> Shredded cheddar cheese and minced fresh parsley

In a large skillet, cook onions in 3 tablespoons butter over medium-low heat until tender. Add the broth, bouillon and pepper; bring to a boil. Remove from the heat.

In a large saucepan, melt the remaining butter. Stir in flour until smooth; gradually add milk. Bring to a boil; cook and stir for 1-2 minutes or until thickened. Reduce heat; add process cheese and onion mixture. Cook and stir until heated through and cheese is melted. Garnish with cheddar cheese and parsley. **Yield:** 4 servings.

— 🥤 🥤 🥤 —

Ground Venison Burgers

Even folks who aren't fans of venison will enjoy these zippy burgers, deliciously topped with pepper cheese and a cool lime-mustard mayonnaise. My son, who's an avid hunter, gave me this super recipe.
—Jerry Honeyager, North Prairie, Wisconsin

> 1/3 cup mayonnaise
> 1 teaspoon lime juice
> 1 teaspoon Dijon mustard
> 1/2 teaspoon grated lime peel
> 1/3 cup chopped green onions
> 3 tablespoons plain yogurt
> 2 tablespoons finely chopped jalapeno pepper*
> 1/2 teaspoon salt
> 1/2 teaspoon pepper
> 2 pounds ground venison
> 8 hamburger buns, split
> 8 slices pepper Jack cheese

In a small bowl, combine mayonnaise, lime juice, mustard and peel. Cover; refrigerate until serving.

In a bowl, combine the onions, yogurt, jalapeno, salt and pepper. Crumble meat over mixture and mix well. Shape into eight patties. Pan-fry, grill or broil until meat is no longer pink. Serve on buns; top with cheese and mayonnaise mixture. **Yield:** 8 servings.

Editor's Note: When cutting or seeding hot peppers, use rubber or plastic gloves to protect your hands. Avoid touching your face.

— 🥤 🥤 🥤 —

Pinto Bean Chili

Cumin and chili powder season this traditional chili. Quesadillas on the side make this Southwestern soup a meal. —Sandy Dilatush, Denver, Colorado

> 1 pound dried pinto beans
> 2 pounds ground beef
> 1 medium onion, chopped
> 3 celery ribs, chopped
> 3 tablespoons all-purpose flour
> 4 cups water
> 2 tablespoons chili powder
> 2 tablespoons ground cumin
> 1/2 teaspoon sugar
> 1 can (28 ounces) crushed tomatoes
> 2 teaspoons cider vinegar
> 1-1/2 teaspoons salt
> **CHILI CHEESE QUESADILLAS:**
> 2 cans (4 ounces *each*) chopped green chilies
> 12 flour tortillas (6 inches)
> 3 cups (12 ounces) shredded cheddar cheese
> 3 teaspoons vegetable oil

Place beans in a Dutch oven or soup kettle; add water to cover by 2 in. Bring to a boil; boil for 2 minutes. Remove from the heat; cover and let stand for 1 hour. Drain and rinse beans, discarding liquid.

In a Dutch oven, cook the beef, onion and celery over medium heat until meat is no longer pink; drain. Stir in flour until blended. Gradually stir in water. Add beans, chili powder, cumin and sugar. Bring to a boil.

Reduce heat; cover and simmer for 1-1/2 hours or until beans are tender. Stir in tomatoes, vinegar and salt; heat through, stirring occasionally.

Meanwhile, for quesadillas, spread about 1 tablespoon of chilies on half of each tortilla. Sprinkle with 1/4 cup of cheese; fold in half. In a large skillet, cook tortillas in 1 teaspoon of oil over medium heat until lightly browned on each side, adding more oil as needed. Serve with chili. **Yield:** 6-8 servings.

— 🥣 🥣 🥣 —

Super Bowl Bread Bowls

You'll score points when you spoon the halftime meal into these hearty bowls. The bread's spongy texture makes it the perfect container for the full-flavored chowder. —Darlene Alexander, Nekoosa, Wisconsin

  1/2 cup water (70° to 80°)
    1 cup warm milk (70° to 80°)
    2 tablespoons butter *or* margarine, softened
    2 tablespoons sugar
1-1/2 teaspoons salt
    4 cups all-purpose flour
    2 packages (1/4 ounce *each*) active dry
       yeast
    1 egg white, beaten
VEGETABLE CHOWDER:
    1 large onion, chopped
    3 celery ribs, chopped
    6 tablespoons butter *or* margarine
3-1/2 cups frozen mixed vegetables, thawed
    6 tablespoons all-purpose flour
4-1/2 cups milk
    4 bacon strips, cooked and crumbled
    2 teaspoons chicken bouillon granules
  3/4 teaspoon seasoned salt
  1/2 teaspoon pepper

In bread machine pan, place the first seven ingredients in order suggested by manufacturer. Select dough setting (check dough after 5 minutes of mixing; add 1 to 2 tablespoons of water or flour if needed).

When the cycle is completed, turn dough onto a lightly floured surface. Divide into six portions; shape into balls. Place on greased baking sheets. Cover and let rise in a warm place until doubled, about 30 minutes. Brush with egg white. Bake at 375° for 20-25 minutes or until golden brown. Cool on wire racks. To make bowls, cut the top fourth off of bread; carefully hollow out bottom of each, leaving a 1/4-in. shell.

For chowder, in a large saucepan, saute onion and celery in butter until tender. Add mixed vegetables. Stir in flour until blended. Gradually stir in milk until combined. Bring to a boil; cook and stir for 2 minutes or until thickened. Stir in bacon, bouillon, seasoned salt and pepper until bouillon is dissolved. Serve in bread bowls. **Yield:** 6 servings.

— 🥣 🥣 🥣 —

Black Bean Rice Burgers
(Pictured below)

A salsa and sour cream sauce helps dress up these hearty vegetarian burgers. My fiance, who's a confirmed meat-and-potatoes man, loves them.
—Laura Wimbrow, Ocean City, Maryland

✓ Uses less fat, sugar or salt. Includes Nutritional Analysis and Diabetic Exchanges.

    1 can (15 ounces) black beans, rinsed and
       drained
    1 cup cooked brown rice
    1 small onion, finely chopped
    1 egg, lightly beaten
    2 tablespoons plus 1/4 cup salsa, *divided*
  1/4 cup reduced-fat sour cream
    4 lettuce leaves
    4 slices reduced-fat cheddar cheese (1
       ounce *each*)
    4 hamburger buns, split

In a large bowl, mash beans with a fork. Add the rice, onion, egg and 2 tablespoons salsa; mix well. Drop by 1/2 cupfuls into a large nonstick skillet coated with nonstick cooking spray. Flatten to 1/2-in. thickness. Cook over medium heat for 4-5 minutes on each side or until firm and browned.

In a small bowl, combine sour cream and remaining salsa. Place a lettuce leaf, burger, sour cream mixture and slice of cheese on each bun. **Yield:** 4 servings.

Nutritional Analysis: One sandwich equals 368 calories, 9 g fat (5 g saturated fat), 20 mg cholesterol, 875 mg sodium, 52 g carbohydrate, 8 g fiber, 20 g protein. **Diabetic Exchanges:** 3 starch, 1 vegetable, 1 lean meat, 1 fat.

Side Dishes & Condiments

Tired of serving the same-old thing alongside main courses? These complementary side dishes and condiments are a tasty new twist on traditional favorites.

TASTE SENSATIONS. Clockwise from upper left: Cardamom Carrots (p. 53), Three-Fruit Relish (p. 54), Triple-Onion Baked Potatoes (p. 56), Rosemary Au Gratin Potatoes (p. 50) and Cranberry Pearl Onions (p. 52).

Acorn Squash Feta Casserole

(Pictured above)

I get loads of compliments on this out-of-the-ordinary casserole whenever I serve it. The recipe marries squash and feta cheese with onion, garlic, bell peppers and a sprinkling of sunflower kernels. Leftovers are delicious hot or cold! —Maisy Vliet
Holland, Michigan

   2 large acorn squash (about 1-1/2 pounds *each***)**
   1 medium onion, chopped
   2 garlic cloves, minced
   3 tablespoons butter *or* **margarine**
 1/2 cup chopped green pepper
 1/2 cup chopped sweet red pepper
   2 eggs
   1 cup (8 ounces) plain yogurt
   1 cup crumbled feta cheese
1-1/4 teaspoons salt
 1/2 teaspoon pepper
Dash cayenne pepper, optional
 1/4 cup sunflower kernels

Cut squash in half; discard seeds. Place squash cut side down in a greased 15-in. x 10-in. x 1-in. baking pan. Bake at 375° for 35-40 minutes or until tender; cool slightly. Carefully scoop out squash; place in a bowl and mash.

In a skillet, saute onion and garlic in butter until tender. Add peppers; saute until crisp-tender. In a large bowl, whisk eggs and yogurt until blended. Stir in squash, onion mixture, feta cheese, salt, pepper and cayenne if desired. Transfer to a greased 11-in. x 7-in. x 2-in. baking dish.

Sprinkle with sunflower kernels.

Cover and bake at 375° for 25 minutes. Uncover; bake 25-30 minutes longer or until a knife inserted near the center comes out clean. **Yield:** 6-8 servings.

—— ▼ ▼ ▼ ——

Rosemary Au Gratin Potatoes

(Pictured on page 48)

Rosemary, garlic and Parmesan cheese season the tender potato slices in this delectable side dish. It's sure to satisfy family and guests alike. —Jean Minner
New Castle, Pennsylvania

 1/4 cup butter *or* **margarine**
 1/4 cup all-purpose flour
   2 cups half-and-half cream
   1 tablespoon minced fresh rosemary *or* **1 teaspoon dried rosemary, crushed**
   1 garlic clove, minced
   1 teaspoon salt
 1/4 teaspoon pepper
   3 pounds potatoes, peeled and cut into 1/8-inch slices
 2/3 cup grated Parmesan cheese

In a large saucepan, melt butter over medium heat. Stir in flour until smooth. Gradually add the cream. Bring to a boil; cook and stir for 2 minutes or until thickened. Remove from the heat. Stir in the rosemary, garlic, salt, pepper and potatoes.

Transfer to a greased 13-in. x 9-in. x 2-in. baking dish. Sprinkle with Parmesan cheese. Cover and bake at 350° for 45 minutes. Uncover; bake 10-15 minutes longer or until potatoes are tender. **Yield:** 8-10 servings.

—— ▼ ▼ ▼ ——

Sage Mashed Potatoes

My daughters and I get together on Friday nights to try out new recipes, and we like to use a lot of herbs. I don't care for mashed potatoes, but sage and onion make these irresistible. —Harriet Stichter
Milford, Indiana

✓ Uses less fat, sugar or salt. Includes Nutritional Analysis and Diabetic Exchanges.

   4 medium potatoes, peeled and cut into 1/8-inch slices
   1 medium onion, chopped
 1/4 cup water
   2 tablespoons olive *or* **canola oil**
   1 tablespoon minced fresh sage *or* **1 teaspoon rubbed sage**

1/2 teaspoon salt
1/8 teaspoon pepper
1/2 cup reduced-fat plain yogurt

In a greased 11-in. x 7-in. x 2-in. baking dish, layer the potatoes and onion. Combine the water, oil, sage, salt and pepper; pour over potato mixture. Cover and bake at 450° for 45-50 minutes or until potatoes are tender, stirring twice. Transfer to a mixing bowl; add yogurt and mash. **Yield:** 6 servings.
Nutritional Analysis: One serving (2/3 cup) equals 130 calories, 5 g fat (1 g saturated fat), 1 mg cholesterol, 211 mg sodium, 21 g carbohydrate, 3 g fiber, 4 g protein. **Diabetic Exchange:** 1-1/2 starch.

Apple 'n' Pepper Saute

This colorful side dish blends apple slices, red onion rings and sweet pepper strips in a soy sauce and herb glaze. —Emily Guidry, Breaux Bridge, Louisiana

✓ Uses less fat, sugar or salt. Includes Nutritional Analysis and Diabetic Exchanges.

3 medium sweet peppers, julienned
1 small red onion, sliced and separated into rings
1 medium apple, sliced
2 tablespoons olive *or* canola oil
1 tablespoon reduced-sodium soy sauce
2 garlic cloves, minced
1/4 teaspoon dried rosemary, crushed
1/4 teaspoon dried basil

In a large nonstick skillet, saute the peppers, onion and apple in oil until crisp-tender. Stir in the soy sauce, garlic, rosemary and basil. Cook and stir until heated through. **Yield:** 6 servings.
Nutritional Analysis: One serving (2/3 cup) equals 83 calories, 5 g fat (1 g saturated fat), 0 cholesterol, 103 mg sodium, 10 g carbohydrate, 2 g fiber, 1 g protein. **Diabetic Exchanges:** 2 vegetable, 1 fat.

Asparagus in Corn Crepes
(Pictured at right)

It's impressive on a buffet, but this dish is not as complicated as it looks. Thin sweet corn pancakes are wrapped around fresh asparagus and topped with an easy cream cheese sauce and pistachios. The flavors blend so well! —Lillian Julow, Gainesville, Florida

2 cups fresh *or* frozen corn, thawed
1 cup all-purpose flour
1 cup half-and-half cream

4 eggs
1/4 cup butter *or* margarine, melted
1 teaspoon salt
1/2 teaspoon pepper
CREAM SAUCE:
1 cup milk
1 package (8 ounces) cream cheese, cubed
1/4 teaspoon salt
1/8 teaspoon pepper
1/8 teaspoon ground nutmeg
60 thin asparagus spears (about 2 pounds), trimmed
1 cup chopped pistachios

In a food processor or blender, cover and process corn until pureed. Add the flour, cream, eggs, butter, salt and pepper; pulse until blended. Cover and refrigerate for 1 hour.
Heat a lightly greased 8-in. nonstick skillet; pour 1/4 cup batter into the center of skillet. Lift and tilt pan to evenly coat bottom. Cook until top appears dry; turn and cook 15-20 seconds longer. Remove to a wire rack. Repeat with remaining batter, greasing skillet as needed. When cool, stack the crepes with waxed paper or paper towels in between.
In a small saucepan, heat milk and cream cheese over low until melted; stir until blended. Stir in the salt, pepper and nutmeg; keep warm. Steam the asparagus for 3-4 minutes or until crisp-tender.
Place stack of crepes on a microwave-safe plate. Microwave on high for 10-15 seconds or until warmed. To assemble, fold each crepe around four asparagus spears. Place seam side down on a serving dish; drizzle with cream sauce. Garnish with pistachios. Serve immediately. **Yield:** 15 servings.

Cheesy Zucchini Medley

(Pictured below)

I constantly crave the wholesome goodness of fresh garden vegetables, so I fix this quick and delicious dish as often as possible. It's wonderful to make on camping trips. —Ruth Ann Stelfox, Raymond, Alberta

✓ Uses less fat, sugar or salt. Includes Nutritional Analysis and Diabetic Exchanges.

    4 medium zucchini, cut into 1/4-inch slices
    1 large sweet onion, thinly sliced and
      separated into rings
    1 medium sweet yellow pepper, julienned
    1 medium green pepper, julienned
    2 garlic cloves, minced
    2 tablespoons canola *or* vegetable oil
1/4 teaspoon salt
1/4 teaspoon pepper
    1 cup (4 ounces) shredded cheddar cheese
1/2 cup shredded mozzarella cheese

In a large skillet, saute the zucchini, onion, peppers and garlic in oil until crisp-tender. Sprinkle with salt and pepper; mix well. Sprinkle with cheeses. Remove from the heat. Let stand for 2-3 minutes or until cheese begins to melt. **Yield:** 8 servings.
    Nutritional Analysis: One serving (3/4 cup) equals 135 calories, 10 g fat (4 g saturated fat), 19 mg cholesterol, 198 mg sodium, 7 g carbohydrate, 2 g fiber, 7 g protein. **Diabetic Exchanges:** 1 vegetable, 1 lean meat, 1 fat.

Cranberry Pearl Onions

(Pictured on page 48)

This unusual combination of pearl onions and cranberries is surprisingly delicious. There's plenty of thick, dark red sauce, and the onions have a sweet-tangy taste. They'll melt in your mouth!
    —Lesley Tragesser, Charleston, Missouri

    8 cups water
    3 packages (10 ounces *each*) fresh pearl
      onions
    1 tablespoon butter *or* margarine
    1 tablespoon vegetable oil
1-1/2 cups cranberry juice
1/2 teaspoon salt
    1 can (16 ounces) jellied cranberry sauce
1/2 teaspoon lemon juice

In a large saucepan, bring water to a boil. Add onions; boil for 3 minutes. Drain and rinse in cold water; peel.
    In a large skillet, cook onions in butter and oil over medium heat until lightly browned, about 5 minutes. Add cranberry juice and salt. Bring to a boil. Reduce heat to medium-low; cover and cook just until onions are tender. Add cranberry sauce and lemon juice; cook and stir until mixture is thick and syrupy. **Yield:** 6 servings.

— 🍃 🍃 🍃 —

Basil Jelly

We grow lots of basil for our local farmers market, and this is a unique way to use it. The jelly is really good with cream cheese as an appetizer. I also like to combine a jar with 1 cup of barbecue sauce and simmer mini meatballs or cocktail wieners in the mixture.
    —Sue Gronholz, Beaver Dam, Wisconsin

    1 quart water
    2 cups firmly packed fresh basil leaves,
      finely chopped
    1 package (1-3/4 ounces) powdered fruit
      pectin
    3 drops green food coloring, optional
    5 cups sugar

In a large saucepan, bring water and basil to a boil. Remove from the heat; cover and let stand for 10 minutes. Strain and discard basil. Return 3-2/3 cups liquid to the pan. Stir in pectin and food coloring if desired. Return to a rolling boil over high heat. Stir in sugar. Boil for 1 minute, stirring constantly. Remove from the heat; skim off foam.
    Pour hot liquid into hot sterilized jars, leaving 1/4-in. headspace. Adjust caps. Process for 15 minutes in a boiling-water bath. **Yield:** 6 half-pints.

Cardamom Carrots

(Pictured on page 48)

These slightly sweet carrots with a hint of cardamom go over big whenever I serve them. They're particularly nice at holidays. I especially like this dish because it's so easy to prepare. —Joan Hallford
North Richland Hills, Texas

    2 pounds carrots, cut into 2-inch julienned strips
    1 teaspoon salt
    1/4 cup butter *or* margarine
    1/4 cup packed brown sugar
    1 teaspoon ground cardamom
    1 teaspoon grated orange peel

Place 1 in. of water in a saucepan; add carrots and salt. Bring to a boil; reduce heat. Cover and simmer for 7-9 minutes or until crisp-tender; drain. In a large skillet, combine the butter, brown sugar, cardamom and orange peel. Cook and stir over medium heat for 1-2 minutes or until sauce is thickened. Add carrots; toss to coat. **Yield:** 8 servings.

Hearty Baked Beans

This saucy dish is flavorful and filling, chock-full of ground beef, bacon and four varieties of beans. I've had the recipe for over 10 years and make it often for big appetites at home and potlucks at work and church. —Cathy Swancutt, Junction City, Oregon

    1 pound ground beef
    2 large onions, chopped
    3/4 pound sliced bacon, cooked and crumbled
    4 cans (15 ounces *each*) pork and beans
    1 bottle (18 ounces) honey barbecue sauce
    1 can (16 ounces) kidney beans, rinsed and drained
    1 can (15-1/4 ounces) lima beans, rinsed and drained
    1 can (15 ounces) black beans, rinsed and drained
    1/2 cup packed brown sugar
    3 tablespoons cider vinegar
    1 tablespoon liquid smoke, optional
    1 teaspoon salt
    1/2 teaspoon pepper

In a large skillet, cook beef and onions over medium heat until meat is no longer pink; drain. Transfer to a 5-qt. Dutch oven. Stir in the remaining ingredients. Cover and bake at 350° for 1 hour or until heated through. **Yield:** 18 servings.

Tangy Cherry Relish

(Pictured above)

This flavorful blend of cherries, onion, green pepper and carrot perks up chicken or turkey nicely. When my mom served it at a holiday meal, I just had to have this quick-and-easy recipe. —Sue Bellamy
Roblin, Manitoba

    1 cup cherry preserves
    1 cup dried cherries
    2 tablespoons cider vinegar
    1/2 cup chopped onion
    1/4 cup chopped green pepper
    1/4 cup shredded carrot
    1/2 teaspoon salt
    1/2 teaspoon dried basil

Cut cherries in preserves into small pieces; place preserves in a saucepan. Add the dried cherries and vinegar. Bring to a boil. Reduce heat; simmer, uncovered, for 5 minutes. Remove from the heat; cool. Stir in the remaining ingredients. Cover and refrigerate overnight. Serve with turkey or chicken. **Yield:** 2 cups.

Chunky Peach Spread

(Pictured above)

This fruity spread captures the taste of summer! Low in sugar, it's not overly sweet…and the fresh peach flavor really comes through. You'll want to try it on everything from bagels to waffles. —Rebecca Baird
Salt Lake City, Utah

✓ Uses less fat, sugar or salt. Includes Nutritional Analysis and Diabetic Exchanges.

> **7 medium peaches (2 to 2-1/2 pounds)**
> **1/3 cup sugar**
> **1 tablespoon lemon juice**
> **1 envelope unflavored gelatin**
> **1/4 cup cold water**

Drop peaches in boiling water for 1 minute or until peel has softened. Immediately dip fruit in ice water. Peel and chop peaches. In a large saucepan, combine the peaches, sugar and lemon juice. Bring to a boil. Mash peaches. Reduce heat; simmer, uncovered, for 5 minutes.

Meanwhile, in a small bowl, sprinkle gelatin over cold water; let stand for 2 minutes. Remove peach mixture from the heat; stir in gelatin mixture until dissolved. Cool for 10 minutes. Pour into jars. Refrigerate for up to 3 weeks. **Yield:** about 3-1/2 cups.

Nutritional Analysis: One serving (2 tablespoons) equals 21 calories, trace fat (0 saturated fat), 0 cholesterol, 1 mg sodium, 5 g carbohydrate, trace fiber, trace protein. **Diabetic Exchange:** Free food.

— ▼ ▼ ▼ —

Onion Tart

Onion lovers are sure to be asking for second helpings of this appetizing tart—it uses two kinds of onions! Parmesan and feta cheese, nutmeg and hot pepper sauce enhance the flavor nicely. With its quiche-like filling, the dish is ideal for a brunch or buffet.
—Christine Andreas, Huntingdon, Pennsylvania

> **1 unbaked pastry shell (9 inches)**
> **2 medium sweet onions, thinly sliced**
> **2 tablespoons olive *or* vegetable oil**
> **3 eggs**
> **1/2 cup crumbled feta cheese**
> **1/2 teaspoon salt**
> **1/4 teaspoon coarsely ground pepper**
> **1/8 teaspoon ground nutmeg**
> **1/8 teaspoon hot pepper sauce**
> **3/4 cup half-and-half cream**
> **1/2 cup milk**
> **1 tablespoon Dijon mustard**
> **6 green onions, thinly sliced**
> **2 tablespoons minced chives**
> **1/3 cup grated Parmesan cheese**

Line unpricked pastry shell with a double thickness of heavy-duty foil. Bake at 450° for 8 minutes. Remove foil; bake 5 minutes longer. Cool on a wire rack. In a small skillet, saute onions in oil until tender; cool.

In a food processor, combine the eggs, feta cheese, salt, pepper, nutmeg and hot pepper sauce; cover and process until smooth. Gradually add cream and milk; process until blended.

Brush the inside of crust with mustard. Sprinkle the green onions, chives and sauteed onions over crust. Carefully pour egg mixture over onions. Top with Parmesan cheese. Bake at 375° for 30-40 minutes or until a knife inserted near the center comes out clean. **Yield:** 6 servings.

— ▼ ▼ ▼ —

Three-Fruit Relish

(Pictured on page 49)

A deep red color and nice tangy flavor make this relish a hit whenever I serve it. It's great at Thanksgiving and Christmas—or anytime. I keep frozen cranberries on hand so we can enjoy it year-round.
—Maureen Alexander, San Jose, California

1 cup sugar
1/2 cup orange marmalade
1 teaspoon lemon juice
1 package (12 ounces) fresh *or* frozen
  cranberries, finely chopped
2 cups fresh raspberries
2 medium tart apples, diced

In a large bowl, combine the sugar, marmalade and lemon juice; mix well. Stir in the cranberries, raspberries and apples. Cover and refrigerate until serving. Stir before serving. **Yield:** 5 cups.

— 🎺 🎺 🎺 —

Potato Squash Casserole

Butternut squash teams up with sliced potatoes and fla-vorful pork sausage in this hearty autumn casserole. The rich, creamy cheese sauce adds to the down-home taste. —Peggy Burdick, Burlington, Michigan

4 small potatoes, peeled and thinly sliced
1 small butternut squash, peeled, seeded
  and thinly sliced
1 tablespoon water
1/4 teaspoon salt
1/8 teaspoon pepper
1/2 pound uncooked bulk pork sausage
1 small onion, chopped
2 tablespoons all-purpose flour
1-1/2 cups heavy whipping cream, *divided*
1 cup (4 ounces) shredded cheddar cheese

In a microwave-safe bowl, combine the potatoes, squash and water. Cover and cook on high for 5 minutes or until crisp-tender. Place half of the mixture in a greased 2-qt. baking dish. Sprinkle with salt and pepper. Crumble sausage over potato mixture. Top with onion and remaining potato mixture.

In a small bowl, combine flour and 1/4 cup cream until smooth; stir in remaining cream. Pour over potato mixture. Cover and bake at 350° for 30 minutes. Uncover; bake for 20-30 minutes or until potatoes are tender. Sprinkle with cheese; bake 5 minutes longer or until cheese is melted. **Yield:** 4-6 servings.

Editor's Note: This recipe was tested in an 850-watt microwave.

— 🎺 🎺 🎺 —

Cheese Sauce for Veggies

This tasty cheese sauce, flavored with ground mustard, curry and marjoram, is especially good over broccoli and cauliflower. I like to add a sprinkling of crumbled bacon on top. —Ruth Bogdanski, Grants Pass, Oregon

2 cups (8 ounces) shredded cheddar cheese
3/4 cup plus 2 tablespoons evaporated milk

3/4 teaspoon ground mustard
1/2 teaspoon dried marjoram
Dash to 1/8 teaspoon curry powder

In a small saucepan, combine all ingredients. Cook and stir over medium-low heat until the cheese is melted. Serve warm over broccoli or other cooked vegetables. **Yield:** 1-1/2 cups.

— 🎺 🎺 🎺 —

Creamy Sweet Onions

(Pictured below)

Well coated with a tangy sour cream and celery seed dressing, these sweet-sour onions can sure dress up a juicy burger. My sister likes to serve them as a side sal-ad when our family gets together in summer up at the lake.   —Ethel Lowey, Fort Frances, Ontario

5 large white onions, thinly sliced
2-1/4 cups sugar
1-1/2 cups cider vinegar
1-1/2 cups water
4 teaspoons salt
1 cup (8 ounces) sour cream
3 tablespoons mayonnaise *or* salad dressing
1/4 teaspoon celery seed
Salt and pepper to taste

Place the onions in a large bowl. In a saucepan, combine the sugar, vinegar, water and salt. Bring to a boil; pour over onions. Cover and refrigerate overnight.

Drain onions, discarding liquid. In a bowl, combine the sour cream, mayonnaise, celery seed, salt and pepper; mix well. Add onions and toss to coat. **Yield:** 4 cups.

Harvard Beets

(Pictured below)

These saucy sweet-tart beets with their deep cherry color will have folks talking at your next dinner party! Serve them warm as a side dish or chilled in a salad with cottage cheese. —Nancy Griffin
Simpsonville, South Carolina

      3 cans (15 ounces *each*) whole beets
      2 tablespoons whole cloves
      1 cup sugar
      1 cup white vinegar
      3 tablespoons vegetable oil
      3 tablespoons ketchup
  1/8 teaspoon salt
      3 tablespoons cornstarch
      1 teaspoon vanilla extract

Drain beets, reserving 1-1/2 cups juice. Cut beets into wedges; set juice and beets aside. Place the cloves on a double thickness of cheesecloth; bring up corners of cloth and tie with string to form a bag.

In a large saucepan, combine the sugar, vinegar, oil, ketchup and salt. Add spice bag; bring to a boil. Reduce heat; cover and simmer for 15 minutes. Discard spice bag.

In a small bowl, combine cornstarch and reserved beet juice until smooth. Stir into sugar mixture. Bring to a boil; cook and stir for 2 minutes or until thickened. Add beets and vanilla; heat through. **Yield:** 6-8 servings.

— 🏺 🏺 🏺 —

Apple Syrup

This delicious alternative to maple syrup makes a great change-of-pace topper for French toast and other morning meals. My husband doesn't feel deprived when I serve this syrup with his waffles and pancakes. —Barbara Hill, Oil Springs, Ontario

☑ Uses less fat, sugar or salt. Includes Nutritional Analysis and Diabetic Exchanges.

      1 tablespoon cornstarch
  1/4 teaspoon ground cinnamon
  1/4 teaspoon ground nutmeg
1-1/4 cups unsweetened apple juice
Sugar substitute equivalent to 4 teaspoons sugar

In a small saucepan, combine the cornstarch, cinnamon, nutmeg and apple juice until smooth. Bring to a boil; cook and stir for 2 minutes or until thickened. Remove from the heat; stir in sugar substitute. **Yield:** 1-1/4 cups.
  Nutritional Analysis: One serving (2 tablespoons) equals 20 calories, trace fat (trace saturated fat), 0 cholesterol, 1 mg sodium, 5 g carbohydrate, trace fiber, trace protein. **Diabetic Exchange:** Free food.

— 🏺 🏺 🏺 —

Triple-Onion Baked Potatoes

(Pictured on page 49)

I've been making twice-baked potatoes since I got married 19 years ago, and I'm constantly changing my recipe. This version features a rich filling of onions, bacon, sour cream and cheese. I like to serve these potatoes with baked ham. —Char Shanahan
Schererville, Indiana

      4 large baking potatoes
      1 pound sliced bacon, diced
  1/2 cup finely chopped red onion
  1/2 cup finely chopped yellow onion
  1/2 cup sour cream
      2 tablespoons milk
      1 cup diced American cheese
  1/2 cup shredded cheddar cheese
      4 green onions, finely sliced

Bake potatoes at 400° for 1 hour or until tender. Meanwhile, in a large skillet, cook the bacon over medium heat until crisp; remove to paper towels. Drain, reserving 1 tablespoon drippings. In the

drippings, saute red and yellow onions until tender; set aside.

When potatoes are cool enough to handle, cut in half lengthwise. Scoop out pulp, leaving an 1/8-in. shell. In a mixing bowl, beat the pulp, sour cream and milk until creamy. Stir in sauteed onions, American cheese and 1 cup of bacon. Spoon into potato shells.

Place potatoes on a baking sheet. Bake at 400° for 25 minutes. Sprinkle with cheddar cheese, green onions and remaining bacon. Bake 5-10 minutes longer or until the cheese is melted. **Yield:** 8 servings.

Corn Cobbler

While thinking of a shortcut for what we Pennsylvania Dutch call "Corn Pie", I thought of using biscuit mix instead of the usual pie dough. I tried my version on some friends who were visiting, and they scraped the dish clean!
—Vivian Hippert
Richland, Pennsylvania

   2 cups diced peeled potatoes
   1/2 cup chopped onion
 1-1/2 teaspoons salt
   1/2 teaspoon pepper
     2 cups water
     4 cups fresh corn
 2-3/4 cups milk, *divided*
   1/4 cup sliced green onions
     2 tablespoons minced fresh parsley
     6 hard-cooked eggs, sliced
     3 cups biscuit/baking mix

Place potatoes, onion, salt, pepper and water in a large saucepan. Bring to a boil and boil, uncovered, for 5 minutes. Add corn; return to boiling and boil for 2 minutes. Drain. Add 1-3/4 cups milk, green onions and parsley.

Pour into a greased 13-in. x 9-in. x 2-in. baking dish. Top with eggs. Mix biscuit mix and remaining milk until smooth; drop by teaspoonfuls onto corn mixture. Bake at 450° for 13-15 minutes or until golden brown. **Yield:** 6-8 servings.

Cooking Fresh Corn

Plunge husked ears of corn into a large kettle of boiling water. Don't salt during cooking, since salt can harden kernels. Boil until tender, about 8 to 10 minutes; less for just-picked corn.

Herbed Apricots 'n' Carrots
(Pictured above)

There's plenty of flavor in this bright side dish that's quick and easy to prepare but special enough for company. I season sliced carrots and dried apricots with a pleasant blend of dill, fennel, brown sugar and dry mustard. —Jodi Rice, Appleton, Wisconsin

☑ Uses less fat, sugar or salt. Includes Nutritional Analysis and Diabetic Exchanges.

   8 medium carrots, sliced
   9 dried apricots, sliced
   1 tablespoon butter *or* stick margarine
   1 tablespoon brown sugar
   1 tablespoon snipped fresh dill *or* 1 teaspoon dill weed
 1/2 teaspoon fennel seed, crushed
 1/8 teaspoon ground mustard

Place carrots and apricots in a saucepan; cover with water. Bring to a boil. Cover and cook for 8 minutes or until carrots are crisp-tender; drain. Add the remaining ingredients; stir until butter is melted. **Yield:** 6 servings.

Nutritional Analysis: One serving (1/2 cup) equals 114 calories, 3 g fat (2 g saturated fat), 8 mg cholesterol, 58 mg sodium, 21 g carbohydrate, 2 g fiber, 2 g protein. **Diabetic Exchanges:** 1 starch, 1 vegetable.

Main Dishes

Your family will eagerly gather around the dinner table when any of these mouth-watering main dishes is on the menu.

MAKE MOUTHS WATER. Clockwise from upper left: Breaded Sirloin (p. 83), Chicken with Chive Sauce (p. 77), Marinated Rib Eyes (p. 70), Spinach Feta Pizza (p. 61) and Chicken Veggie Alfredo (p. 62).

Swiss Cheese Lasagna

(Pictured above)

An old favorite from my mother-in-law's collection, this recipe is now a staple for our family. We like to serve it with garlic bread, Caesar salad and coleslaw.
—Susan Rourke, Dartmouth, Nova Scotia

> 1 pound ground beef
> 1 large onion, chopped
> 1 garlic clove, minced
> 3 cups water
> 1 can (12 ounces) tomato paste
> 2 teaspoons salt
> 1/2 to 1 teaspoon dried rosemary, crushed
> 1/4 teaspoon pepper
> 1 package (8 ounces) lasagna noodles
> 8 ounces sliced Swiss cheese
> 1 carton (12 ounces) small-curd cottage cheese
> 1/2 cup shredded mozzarella cheese

In a large skillet, cook the beef, onion and garlic over medium heat until meat is no longer pink; drain. Stir in the water, tomato paste, salt, rosemary and pepper. Bring to a boil. Reduce heat; simmer, uncovered, for 30 minutes.

Meanwhile, cook lasagna noodles according to package directions; drain. In a greased 13-in. x 9-in. x 2-in. baking dish, layer a third of the meat sauce, noodles and Swiss cheese. Repeat layers. Top with cottage cheese and the remaining Swiss cheese, noodles and sauce. Sprinkle with mozzarella cheese.

Cover and bake at 350° for 30 minutes. Uncover; bake 10-15 minutes longer or until bubbly. Let stand for 10 minutes before serving. **Yield:** 12 servings.

Jim's Honey-Glazed Ham

The aroma of this ham cooking in the oven is absolutely wonderful. It comes out moist, juicy and lightly browned.   *—Jim Whelan, Sebastian, Florida*

> 1 boneless fully cooked ham (3 to 5 pounds)
> 1/2 cup water
> 1 cup honey
> 1/2 cup packed brown sugar
> 1 teaspoon ground cloves
> 1/2 teaspoon ground mustard

Score the ham, making diamond shapes 1/2 in. deep. Place on a rack in a well-greased foil-lined roasting pan. Add water to pan. In a small bowl, combine the honey, brown sugar, cloves and mustard; pour over ham.

Bake, uncovered, at 350° for 1-1/2 to 2 hours or until a meat thermometer reads 140°, basting with pan juices often. Add additional water to the pan if necessary. **Yield:** 15-18 servings.

Garlic-Lime Pork Chops

Cilantro, lime and hot pepper sauce lend south-of-the-border pizzazz to boneless pork chops in this recipe. Pretty enough for company, these chops are tender, juicy and delicious.   *—Paula Marchesi*
Lenhartsville, Pennsylvania

✓ Uses less fat, sugar or salt. Includes Nutritional Analysis and Diabetic Exchanges.

> 1/3 cup fat-free Italian salad dressing
> 1/3 cup salsa
> 4-1/2 teaspoons lime juice
> 4-1/2 teaspoons minced fresh cilantro *or* parsley
> 4 garlic cloves, minced
> 1-1/4 teaspoons grated lime peel
> 1/4 teaspoon hot pepper sauce
> 6 boneless lean pork loin chops (5 ounces *each*)

In a bowl, combine the first seven ingredients. Pour 1/2 cup into a large resealable plastic bag; add the pork chops. Seal bag and turn to coat; refrigerate for 8 hours or overnight. Cover and refrigerate remaining marinade.

Drain and discard marinade from chops. Place on a broiler pan rack. Broil 4 in. from the heat for 7 minutes on each side or until juices run clear, basting with reserved marinade. **Yield:** 6 servings.

Nutritional Analysis: One serving equals 189 calories, 6 g fat (2 g saturated fat), 90 mg cholesterol, 194 mg sodium, 2 g carbohydrate, trace fiber, 30 g protein. **Diabetic Exchange:** 4 lean meat.

—— 🥄 🥄 🥄 ——

Spinach Feta Pizza

(Pictured on page 58)

You won't miss the tomato sauce and pepperoni when you bite into this pizza. Garlic, onion and basil season the spinach and cheese topping. —Wilma Lombardo
Santa Fe, New Mexico

✓ Uses less fat, sugar or salt. Includes Nutritional Analysis and Diabetic Exchanges.

     3/4 cup water (70° to 80°)
       2 tablespoons olive *or* canola oil
     1/2 teaspoon sugar
     1/2 teaspoon salt
       2 cups bread flour
       2 teaspoons active dry yeast
TOPPING:
       1 garlic clove, minced
     1/8 teaspoon garlic salt
       2 cups chopped fresh spinach
       1 small red onion, sliced and separated into
          rings
       1 cup sliced fresh mushrooms
       1 cup (4 ounces) shredded mozzarella cheese
     1/4 cup crumbled feta cheese
     1/2 teaspoon dried basil

In bread machine pan, place the first six ingredients in order suggested by manufacturer. Select dough setting (check dough after 5 minutes of mixing; add 1 to 2 tablespoons of water or flour if needed).

When cycle is completed, turn dough onto a lightly floured surface. Knead for 1 minute. Cover and let rest for 15 minutes. Roll into a 12-in. circle. Transfer to a greased 12-in. pizza pan. Cover and let rise in a warm place until puffed, about 20 minutes.

Sprinkle with garlic and garlic salt. Top with the spinach, onion, mushrooms, cheeses and basil. Bake at 400° for 35-40 minutes or until crust is golden and cheese is melted. Let stand for 5 minutes before slicing. **Yield:** 6 slices.

Nutritional Analysis: One slice equals 287 calories, 10 g fat (4 g saturated fat), 16 mg cholesterol, 401 mg sodium, 37 g carbohydrate, 2 g fiber, 12 g protein. **Diabetic Exchanges:** 2 starch, 2 fat, 1 vegetable.

Pheasant with Cranberry Sauce

(Pictured below)

My Uncle Stanley, an avid hunter and fisherman, encouraged me to try game cooking, and this recipe is one of my successes. The tangy orange-cranberry sauce that complements the tender meat makes it ideal for the holidays. —Sharon Shamosh
Rockville Center, New York

       1 pheasant (2 to 3 pounds)
     1/4 teaspoon salt, *divided*
     1/4 teaspoon pepper, *divided*
       2 tablespoons butter *or* margarine, melted
       1 package (12 ounces) fresh *or* frozen
          cranberries, thawed
       1 cup sugar
       1 cup orange juice
     1/2 teaspoon ground cinnamon
       2 tablespoons grated orange peel

Sprinkle cavity of pheasant with 1/8 teaspoon salt and 1/8 teaspoon pepper. Place pheasant on a rack in a shallow roasting pan. Brush with butter; sprinkle with remaining salt and pepper. Cover and bake at 350° for 45 minutes. Uncover; bake 30-45 minutes longer or until a meat thermometer reads 160°, basting with pan juices frequently.

Meanwhile, in a large saucepan, combine the cranberries, sugar, orange juice and cinnamon. Cook over medium heat for 10-12 minutes or until the berries begin to pop, stirring frequently. Stir in the orange peel. Simmer 5 minutes longer. Serve with the pheasant. **Yield:** 3-4 servings.

Venison Cordon Bleu

(Pictured below)

For this recipe, I roll up venison steaks with slices of ham and Swiss cheese before baking. I serve them with crusty French bread for dipping in the pan juices.
—Janette Yingling, Clear, Alaska

    4 venison tenderloin steaks (5 ounces *each*)
1/2 teaspoon salt
1/4 teaspoon pepper
    4 thin slices Swiss cheese
    4 thin slices fully cooked ham
    2 tablespoons butter *or* margarine
    1 cup beef broth

Flatten steaks to 1/4-in. thickness; sprinkle with salt and pepper. Top each with a slice of cheese and ham; roll up tightly. Secure with toothpicks.

In a large skillet, brown roll-ups in butter on all sides. Transfer to an ungreased 11-in. x 7-in. x 2-in. baking dish. Pour broth over top. Bake, uncovered, at 350° for 25-30 minutes or until a meat thermometer reads 160° and the meat juices run clear. **Yield:** 4 servings.

— ☕ ☕ ☕ —

Pork and Pinto Beans

I first tasted this dish at an office potluck, and now I serve it often when company comes. I set out an array of toppings and let everyone fix their own taco salad.
—Darlene Markel, Salem, Oregon

    1 pound dried pinto beans
    1 boneless pork loin roast (3 to 4 pounds), halved
    1 can (14-1/2 ounces) stewed tomatoes

    5 medium carrots, chopped
    4 celery ribs, chopped
1-1/2 cups water
    2 cans (4 ounces *each*) chopped green chilies
    2 tablespoons chili powder
    4 garlic cloves, minced
    2 teaspoons ground cumin
    1 teaspoon dried oregano
Dash pepper
    2 packages (10-1/2 ounces *each*) corn tortilla chips *or* 30 flour tortillas (9 inches)
Chopped green onions, sliced ripe olives, chopped tomatoes, shredded cheddar cheese, sour cream *and/or* shredded lettuce

Place beans in a saucepan; add water to cover by 2 in. Bring to a boil; boil for 2 minutes. Remove from the heat; cover and let stand for 1 hour.

Drain and rinse beans; discard liquid. Place roast in a 5-qt. slow cooker. In a bowl, combine beans, tomatoes, carrots, celery, water, chilies, chili powder, garlic, cumin, oregano and pepper. Pour over roast. Cover; cook on high for 3 hours. Reduce heat to low; cook 5 hours or until beans are tender.

Remove meat; shred with two forks and return to slow cooker. With a slotted spoon, serve meat mixture over corn chips or in tortillas; serve with toppings of your choice. **Yield:** 10 servings.

— ☕ ☕ ☕ —

Chicken Veggie Alfredo

(Pictured on page 58)

My family loves this dinner—it's easy to make and a great way to save time after a busy day.
—Jennifer Jordan, Hubbard, Ohio

    4 boneless skinless chicken breast halves
    1 tablespoon vegetable oil
    1 jar (16 ounces) Alfredo sauce
    1 can (15-1/4 ounces) whole kernel corn, drained
    1 cup frozen peas, thawed
    1 jar (4-1/2 ounces) sliced mushrooms, drained
1/2 cup chopped onion
1/2 cup water
1/2 teaspoon garlic salt
1/4 teaspoon pepper
Hot cooked linguine

In a large skillet, brown chicken in oil. Transfer to a slow cooker. In a bowl, combine Alfredo sauce, corn, peas, mushrooms, onion, water, garlic salt and pepper. Pour over chicken. Cover and cook on low for 6-8 hours. Serve over linguine. **Yield:** 4 servings.

Reuben Casserole

This is a great dish to serve for St. Patrick's Day—or anytime. It features corned beef, sauerkraut and other ingredients that make Reuben sandwiches so popular. It's always well received at a potluck.
—_Margery Bryan, Royal City, Washington_

- 1 jar (16 ounces) sauerkraut, rinsed and well drained
- 1-1/4 cups chopped cooked corned beef (about 1 pound)
- 1 cup (8 ounces) sour cream
- 1 small onion, chopped
- 1 garlic clove, minced
- 1 cup (4 ounces) shredded Swiss cheese
- 2 slices rye bread, cubed
- 2 tablespoons butter _or_ margarine, melted

In a bowl, combine first five ingredients. Transfer to a greased 11-in. x 7-in. x 2-in. baking dish. Sprinkle with cheese and bread; drizzle with butter. Bake, uncovered, at 350° for 25-30 minutes or until heated through. **Yield:** 4 servings.

Santa Fe Cornmeal Pizza

(Pictured above right)

You'll love the cornmeal crust of this "knife-and-fork" pizza that has been a hit with our family for years. —_Mirien Church, Aurora, Colorado_

- 1 cup cornmeal
- 1-1/3 cups water, _divided_
- 6 tablespoons grated Parmesan cheese, _divided_
- 1 medium onion, chopped
- 1 small green pepper, julienned
- 1 garlic clove, minced
- 2 tablespoons olive _or_ vegetable oil
- 1 can (8 ounces) tomato sauce
- 8 fresh mushrooms, sliced
- 3/4 teaspoon _each_ dried basil and oregano
- 1/4 teaspoon pepper
- 1 can (15 ounces) black beans, rinsed and drained
- 1-1/2 cups (6 ounces) shredded mozzarella cheese, _divided_
- 1/2 cup sliced ripe olives

In a small bowl, combine the cornmeal and 2/3 cup water. In a saucepan, bring the remaining water to a boil. Gradually whisk in the cornmeal mixture; cook and stir until thickened. Stir in 2 tablespoons Parmesan cheese. When cool enough to handle, pat into a greased 12-in. pizza pan. Bake at 375° for 15 minutes or until lightly browned. Cool slightly.

Meanwhile, in a skillet, saute onion, green pepper and garlic in oil until tender. Add tomato sauce, mushrooms, basil, oregano and pepper. Cover; cook for 5 minutes. Add beans. Sprinkle 1/2 cup mozzarella and 2 tablespoons Parmesan over crust. Top with bean mixture and remaining cheeses. Sprinkle with olives. Bake at 375° for 15-20 minutes or until cheese is melted. **Yield:** 4-6 servings.

Partridge with Wild Rice

This flavorful game bird recipe features tender partridge on a bed of well-seasoned wild rice. You can use whatever type of bird you have in your area.
—_Gary Miller, Riggins, Idaho_

- 1 package (6.7 ounces) brown and wild rice mix with mushrooms
- 1/4 cup all-purpose flour
- 2 partridge game birds (14 ounces _each_), split lengthwise
- 2 tablespoons vegetable oil
- 1 cup milk
- 1/4 teaspoon pepper

Prepare rice according to package directions. Place flour in a large resealable plastic bag; add game birds and shake to coat. In a large skillet, cook birds in oil until browned; remove. Add milk and pepper to skillet; cook and stir until heated through.

Place the rice in a greased 9-in. square baking dish. Top with game birds and milk mixture. Bake, uncovered, at 350° for 40-50 minutes or until a meat thermometer reads 180° and meat is tender. **Yield:** 2 servings.

Best Baby-Back Ribs

(Pictured above)

My dad encouraged me when I was young to pursue my interest in cooking. As I got older, I experimented more, and there were many successes, including these ribs. —*Rick Consoli, Orion, Michigan*

    4 pounds pork baby-back ribs
    1 teaspoon garlic powder
    1 teaspoon seasoned salt
    1 teaspoon pepper
    1 medium onion, sliced
    1 cup ketchup
    1 cup chili sauce
1/4 cup packed brown sugar
    1 tablespoon dried minced onion
    1 tablespoon liquid smoke
    1 tablespoon molasses

Place ribs bone side down in a large roasting pan. Combine garlic powder, seasoned salt and pepper; sprinkle over ribs. Top with sliced onion. Cover tightly and bake at 350° for 2-1/2 hours.

In a bowl, combine the remaining ingredients. Drain fat from pan; discard sliced onion. Brush ribs with half of barbecue sauce. Cover and bake 30 minutes longer or until ribs are tender. Serve with remaining sauce. **Yield:** 4 servings.

Tomato Meat Loaf

My husband is on a low-fat diet, so I try to make dishes that are lower in fat, sugar and salt but still have flavor. This meat loaf, topped with slices of tomato, is tasty. —*Linda Begley, Stoutsville, Missouri*

☑ Uses less fat, sugar or salt. Includes Nutritional Analysis and Diabetic Exchanges.

    1 egg, lightly beaten
1/2 cup fat-free milk
1/4 cup ketchup
    1 cup quick-cooking oats
    1 slice white bread, crumbled
    4 saltines, crushed
1/2 teaspoon salt
1/4 teaspoon pepper
    2 pounds lean ground beef
    1 medium tomato, sliced

In a large bowl, combine the first eight ingredients. Crumble beef over mixture and mix well. Shape into a loaf in a greased 13-in. x 9-in. x 2-in. baking dish. Bake, uncovered, at 350° for 1 hour.

Arrange tomato slices over loaf. Bake 30 minutes longer or until meat is no longer pink and a meat thermometer reads 160°. **Yield:** 8 servings.

Nutritional Analysis: One serving equals 299 calories, 13 g fat (5 g saturated fat), 69 mg cholesterol, 442 mg sodium, 17 g carbohydrate, 1 g fiber, 27 g protein. **Diabetic Exchanges:** 3 lean meat, 1 starch, 1 fat.

———— 🍴 🍴 🍴 ————

Venison Dumpling Stew

Dill-seasoned dumplings top this homey stew featuring tender venison, carrots and potatoes. —*Elizabeth Smith, Middlebury, Vermont*

1/4 cup all-purpose flour
    1 pound venison stew meat, cut into 1-inch cubes
    3 tablespoons butter *or* margarine
    4 to 5 cups water
  10 bay leaves
    2 teaspoons beef bouillon granules
    3 tablespoons Worcestershire sauce
    1 teaspoon salt
1/2 to 3/4 teaspoon pepper
    5 medium potatoes, peeled and cubed
    5 medium carrots, peeled and cut into 3/4-inch slices
    1 medium onion, chopped
DILLED DUMPLINGS:
    1 cup all-purpose flour
    1 teaspoon baking powder
1/2 teaspoon salt

1/2 teaspoon dill weed
1 egg
1/2 cup milk

In a large resealable plastic bag, combine flour and venison; shake to coat. In a Dutch oven, brown meat in butter. Add water; stir to scrape browned bits from pan. Add bay leaves, bouillon, Worcestershire sauce, salt and pepper. Bring to a boil. Reduce heat; cover and simmer for 1 hour or until meat is tender. Discard bay leaves. Add potatoes, carrots and onion. Cover and simmer for 25 minutes.

For dumplings, in a bowl, combine the flour, baking powder, salt and dill. Stir in the egg and milk just until moistened. Drop by tablespoonfuls onto simmering stew. Cover and simmer for 15 minutes (do not lift cover) or until dumplings test done. Serve immediately. **Yield:** 4 servings.

— 🚩 🚩 🚩 —

Kung Pao Wings

Served over hot cooked rice, these delicious drummettes have plenty of personality—with sweet red pepper for color, red pepper flakes for zip and peanuts for crunch. —*Kathleen Evans, Lacey, Washington*

8 whole chicken wings* (about 1-1/2 pounds)
2 tablespoons sugar
2 teaspoons cornstarch
1/4 cup water
1/4 cup soy sauce
2 tablespoons lemon juice
1/4 teaspoon crushed red pepper flakes
1 tablespoon vegetable oil
1 small sweet red pepper, diced
1/2 cup diced onion
1 to 2 garlic cloves, minced
1/3 cup peanuts
Hot cooked rice

Cut chicken wings into three sections; discard wing tip section. Set aside chicken wings. In a small bowl, combine sugar, cornstarch, water, soy sauce, lemon juice and pepper flakes until blended; set aside. In a large skillet, heat oil over medium-high heat. Cook chicken wings, uncovered, for 10-15 minutes or until juices run clear, turning occasionally.

Add the red pepper, onion and garlic; cook for 3-5 minutes or until vegetables are crisp-tender. Stir cornstarch mixture; add to skillet. Bring to a boil; cook and stir for 2 minutes or until sauce is thickened and vegetables are tender. Sprinkle with peanuts. Serve with rice. **Yield:** 4 servings.

*Editor's Note: 1-1/2 pounds of uncooked chicken wing sections (wingettes) may be substituted for the whole chicken wings. Omit the first step.

Shrimp Vegetable Stir-Fry

(Pictured below)

My family loves seafood, and this colorful, fresh-tasting stir-fry doesn't take long to prepare. —*Cathy Dawe Kent, Ohio*

✓ Uses less fat, sugar or salt. Includes Nutritional Analysis and Diabetic Exchanges.

1/3 cup reduced-fat Italian salad dressing
1 tablespoon reduced-sodium soy sauce
1/2 teaspoon ground ginger
1 medium carrot, julienned
3/4 cup fresh snow peas
1 small zucchini, julienned
1 small red onion, halved and thinly sliced
1/2 cup sliced fresh mushrooms
1/2 medium sweet yellow pepper, julienned
1/2 medium sweet red pepper, julienned
1 pound uncooked medium shrimp, peeled and deveined
3 cups hot cooked rice

In a small bowl, combine the salad dressing, soy sauce and ginger; set aside 2 tablespoons. In a large skillet or wok, cook and stir carrot in remaining dressing mixture over medium heat for 5 minutes. Stir in the remaining vegetables. Cook and stir for 5-7 minutes or until crisp-tender. Remove vegetables with a slotted spoon and keep warm.

Add shrimp and reserved dressing mixture to the pan. Cook and stir over medium heat until shrimp turn pink. Return vegetables to pan; heat through. Serve over rice. **Yield:** 4 servings.

Nutritional Analysis: One serving (1-1/4 cups stir-fry mixture with 3/4 cup rice) equals 299 calories, 4 g fat (1 g saturated fat), 174 mg cholesterol, 487 mg sodium, 36 g carbohydrate, 3 g fiber, 27 g protein. **Diabetic Exchanges:** 2 starch, 2 lean meat, 1 vegetable.

Deep-Dish Hunter's Pie

(Pictured below)

My husband, an avid hunter, loves the garlic mashed potato topping on this dish. —Christina Rulien
Marysville, Washington

1-1/2 pounds potatoes, peeled and cubed
   3 garlic cloves, minced
 1/4 cup milk
   1 tablespoon butter *or* margarine
 1/4 teaspoon dried rosemary, crushed
 1/2 teaspoon salt
 1/8 teaspoon pepper
FILLING:
   1 cup sliced fresh mushrooms
   1 cup sliced carrots
 1/2 cup chopped onion
 1/4 cup chopped green pepper
   1 tablespoon butter *or* margarine
   2 cups cubed cooked venison
1-1/2 cups beef broth
 1/4 teaspoon dried thyme
 1/8 teaspoon ground nutmeg
   3 tablespoons all-purpose flour
   3 tablespoons cold water
 1/3 cup shredded cheddar cheese
   2 tablespoons minced parsley

Cook potatoes in boiling water until tender; drain and mash. Add next six ingredients; set aside. In a skillet, saute mushrooms, carrots, onion and green pepper in butter until tender. Add venison, broth, thyme and nutmeg. Bring to a boil. Reduce heat; cover and simmer for 25-30 minutes or until meat and vegetables are tender.

Combine the flour and water until smooth; stir into skillet. Bring to a boil; cook and stir for 2 minutes or until thickened. Transfer to a greased 2-qt. baking dish. Spread mashed potatoes over the top. Bake, uncovered, at 350° for 30-40 minutes or until bubbly. Sprinkle with cheese. Bake 5 minutes longer or until cheese is melted. Sprinkle with parsley. **Yield:** 6 servings.

— ☕ ☕ ☕ —

Chicken with Cherry Sauce

This tender moist chicken bakes in a savory sauce that combines cherries with soy sauce, orange juice and ginger. —Linda Grubb, Poland, Indiana

   1 pound fresh *or* frozen pitted sweet
     cherries
 1/2 cup orange juice
 1/2 cup soy sauce
 1/4 cup packed brown sugar
 1/4 cup honey
   2 tablespoons lemon juice
   1 garlic clove, minced
 1/2 teaspoon ground ginger *or* 2 teaspoons
     minced fresh gingerroot
   1 broiler/fryer chicken (3 to 4 pounds),
     cut up
   3 tablespoons butter *or* margarine

Set aside 3/4 cup cherries. In a blender, combine orange juice and remaining cherries; cover and process until smooth. Add soy sauce, brown sugar, honey, lemon juice, garlic and ginger; set aside.

In a large skillet over medium heat, brown chicken on all sides in butter. Place chicken skin side down in an ungreased 13-in. x 9-in. x 2-in. baking dish. Top with cherry sauce. Bake, uncovered, at 350° for 20 minutes; turn chicken. Top with reserved cherries. Bake, uncovered, 25-30 minutes longer until chicken juices run clear. **Yield:** 4-6 servings.

— ☕ ☕ ☕ —

Slow-Cooked Spaghetti Sauce

After searching for a tomato sauce that didn't taste like it was only for spaghetti, I set out to make my own. The result was this versatile sauce that's great on pizza, too. —David Shields, Barberton, Ohio

   1 pound ground beef
   4 cans (14-1/2 ounces *each*) diced
     tomatoes, undrained
   6 cans (6 ounces *each*) tomato paste
   1 cup beef broth
 1/4 cup packed brown sugar
   3 tablespoons minced fresh marjoram *or* 1
     tablespoon dried marjoram

2 tablespoons garlic powder
2 tablespoons minced fresh basil _or_ 2
  teaspoons dried basil
2 tablespoons minced fresh oregano _or_ 2
  teaspoons dried oregano
2 tablespoons minced fresh parsley
1 teaspoon salt
1 bay leaf
Hot cooked spaghetti

In a large skillet, cook beef over medium heat until no longer pink; drain. Transfer to a 5-qt. slow cooker. Stir in tomatoes, tomato paste, broth, brown sugar and seasonings; mix well. Cover; cook on low for 6-8 hours or until bubbly. Discard bay leaf. Serve over spaghetti. **Yield:** 12-14 servings.

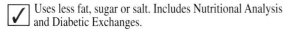

Seafood Soft Tacos

A delicate fish flavor enhances these taste-tempting tacos. I've even tried this recipe with octopus and squid.   _—Jack Hunter, Harlingen, Texas_

✓ Uses less fat, sugar or salt. Includes Nutritional Analysis and Diabetic Exchanges.

1 pound fresh _or_ frozen flounder*
1/3 cup chopped green pepper
1/4 cup chopped onion
1 to 2 tablespoons olive _or_ canola oil
1 medium plum tomato, chopped
1/4 teaspoon salt
1/8 teaspoon garlic powder
1/8 teaspoon ground cumin
1/8 teaspoon pepper
4 flour tortillas (8 inches), warmed
1 tablespoon minced fresh cilantro _or_
  parsley
1 medium lime, cut into wedges

Place fish in a greased 11-in. x 7-in. x 2-in. baking dish. Bake, uncovered, at 350° for 20-25 minutes or until fish flakes with a fork; cut into 1-in. pieces.

In a large skillet, saute green pepper and onion in oil until crisp-tender. Stir in the tomato, salt, garlic powder, cumin and pepper; cook and stir for 1 minute. Add fish; cook and stir until heated through. Spoon filling on one side of tortillas. Sprinkle with cilantro; fold in half. Serve with lime wedges. **Yield:** 4 servings.

*Editor's Note: Cod, red snapper, haddock, ocean perch or any lean fish may be substituted.

Nutritional Analysis: One taco (prepared with 1 tablespoon oil) equals 295 calories, 8 g fat (1 g saturated fat), 54 mg cholesterol, 490 mg sodium, 29 g carbohydrate, 1 g fiber, 26 g protein. **Diabetic Exchanges:** 3 very lean meat, 2 starch, 1 fat.

Cumin Chicken with Apples

(Pictured above)

A mixture of onions, apples and mushrooms seasoned with cumin and Worcestershire sauce enhances this tender chicken dish.   _—Raymonde Bourgeois_
Swastika, Ontario

4 chicken legs with thighs
2 tablespoons butter _or_ margarine
2 medium apples, chopped
2 small onions, halved and sliced
1 can (4-1/2 ounces) mushroom stems and
  pieces, drained
1 tablespoon all-purpose flour
1 can (10-3/4 ounces) condensed cream of
  mushroom soup, undiluted
1/2 cup water
1 tablespoon ground cumin
1 teaspoon Worcestershire sauce
3/4 teaspoon salt
1/4 teaspoon pepper
1/4 teaspoon chili powder
Hot cooked rice

In a large skillet, brown chicken in butter. Transfer to a greased 13-in. x 9-in. x 2-in. baking dish. In the drippings, saute apples, onions and mushrooms until apples are crisp-tender. Add flour, soup, water, cumin, Worcestershire sauce, salt and pepper; mix well. Pour over chicken.

Cover and bake at 350° for 1 hour or until the chicken juices run clear. Sprinkle with chili powder. Serve over rice. **Yield:** 4 servings.

Rack of Lamb

(Pictured above)

I first started cooking in college and have continued to do so ever since. Grilling is what I like best, but I bake this rack of lamb in the oven for the best results.
—Bob Paffenroth, Brookfield, Wisconsin

    4 racks of lamb (1 to 1-1/2 pounds *each*),
        trimmed
    2 tablespoons Dijon mustard
    1 cup soft bread crumbs
  1/4 cup minced fresh parsley
  1/4 teaspoon *each* salt and pepper
  1/4 cup butter *or* margarine, melted
    1 garlic clove, minced

Place lamb on a rack in a greased large roasting pan; brush with mustard. In a small bowl, combine the bread crumbs, parsley, salt and pepper. Press onto the meat. Combine butter and garlic; drizzle over the meat. Bake, uncovered, at 350° for 35-40 minutes or until meat reaches desired doneness (160° for medium-well, 170° for well-done). **Yield:** 8 servings.

— 🍽 🍽 🍽 —

Mashed Potato Meat Loaf

I created this recipe when my children were young and "meat loaf shy". They loved the potato surprise inside and the sauce that has a mild zip. —Dava Beck Amarillo, Texas

1-1/3 cups water
  1/3 cup milk
    2 tablespoons butter *or* margarine
1-1/2 teaspoons salt, *divided*

1-1/3 cups mashed potato flakes
    1 egg, beaten
  1/2 cup quick-cooking oats
  1/2 cup chopped green pepper
  1/3 cup chopped onion
  3/4 teaspoon pepper
    1 pound lean ground beef
    1 can (11-1/2 ounces) picante V8 juice
  1/4 cup ketchup

In a saucepan, bring water, milk, butter and 1/2 teaspoon salt to a boil. Remove from the heat; stir in potato flakes. Let stand for 30 seconds. Fluff with a fork; set aside.

In a bowl, combine the egg, oats, green pepper, onion, pepper and remaining salt. Crumble beef over mixture and mix well. On a piece of waxed paper, pat beef mixture into a 12-in. x 8-in. rectangle. Spoon mashed potatoes lengthwise down the center third to within 1 in. of edges. Bring long sides over potatoes to meet in center; seal seam and edges.

Place seam side up in a greased 13-in. x 9-in. x 2-in. baking dish. Bake, uncovered, at 350° for 30 minutes; drain. Pour V-8 juice over loaf. Top with ketchup. Bake 18-22 minutes longer or until meat is no longer pink and a meat thermometer reads 160°. Let stand for 5 minutes before slicing. **Yield:** 4-6 servings.

— 🍽 🍽 🍽 —

Apricot Pineapple Ham

Tired of mixing up messy glazes to put on ham, I tried this simple recipe a few years ago. Young and old alike complimented me on the lovely, sweet and juicy ham— and I've prepared it this way ever since.
—Cathy Neve, Yakima, Washington

1/2 fully cooked bone-in ham (5 to 7 pounds)
    1 can (6 ounces) pineapple juice
    1 jar (10 ounces) pineapple preserves
    1 jar (10 ounces) apricot preserves
    2 cans (8 ounces *each*) sliced pineapple,
        drained
    1 jar (6 ounces) maraschino cherries with
        stems

Place ham on a rack in a roasting pan. Score the surface, making diamond shapes 1/2 in. deep. Pour pineapple juice over ham. Cover and bake at 325° for 1-1/4 hours.

Uncover; brush ham with preserves. Arrange pineapple slices and cherries on ham, securing with wooden toothpicks. Bake, uncovered, 25-30 minutes longer or until a meat thermometer reads 140° and the ham is heated through. Discard toothpicks. **Yield:** 10-14 servings.

Elk Wellington

My husband's an avid hunter and fisherman, so we often try new recipes with elk, deer, rabbit, turkey or fish. Our family loves this special dish. The elk fillets are dressed up in puff pastry and drizzled with a savory onion-mushroom sauce. —*Sandy Green*
Ignacio, Colorado

   8 elk fillets (about 4 ounces *each*)
   2 tablespoons olive *or* vegetable oil
1/2 pound fresh mushrooms, chopped
   2 tablespoons minced fresh parsley
   2 tablespoons snipped chives
   1 package (17-1/4 ounces) frozen puff
     pastry, thawed
   1 egg
   1 tablespoon cold water
MUSHROOM SAUCE:
1-1/3 cups finely chopped mushrooms
   1 medium onion, finely chopped
   2 tablespoons butter *or* margarine
   3 tablespoons all-purpose flour
   1 can (14-1/2 ounces) beef broth
   1 teaspoon browning sauce, optional
1/2 teaspoon tomato paste
1/4 teaspoon pepper

In a large skillet, brown elk fillets in oil on both sides; set aside. In a bowl, combine the mushrooms, parsley and chives; set aside.

On a lightly floured surface, roll out each sheet of pastry into a 16-in. square. Cut each into four 8-in. squares. Top each square with mushroom mixture and one fillet. Fold pastry over fillet; seal seams. Place seam side down on a rack in a 15-in. x 10-in. x 1-in. baking pan. Beat egg and cold water; brush over pastry. Bake at 350° for 30-35 minutes or until a meat thermometer reads 160°.

Meanwhile, for sauce, saute mushrooms and onion in butter in a saucepan until tender. Sprinkle with flour; stir until blended. Gradually stir in the broth, browning sauce if desired, tomato paste and pepper. Bring to a boil; cook and stir for 2 minutes or until thickened. Spoon over pastry. **Yield:** 8 servings.

— 🥤 🥤 🥤 —

Venison Meatballs

(Pictured at right)

These meatballs are a savory blend of ground venison and pork sausage, with water chestnuts for crunch. This is my husband's favorite venison recipe. Even my co-workers, who normally don't like game meat, enjoy it. —*Geraldine Mennear, Mastic, New York*

   1 egg, lightly beaten
   1 cup soft bread crumbs
   1 can (8 ounces) water chestnuts, drained
     and finely chopped
1/4 cup soy sauce
   2 teaspoons ground ginger
   1 garlic clove, minced
   1 pound ground venison
   1 pound bulk pork sausage
   3 to 4 teaspoons vegetable oil, *divided*
1/2 pound fresh mushrooms, sliced
   1 can (14-1/2 ounces) chicken broth
1-1/4 cups cold water, *divided*
   3 tablespoons cornstarch
Hot cooked noodles

In a bowl, combine the egg, bread crumbs, water chestnuts, soy sauce, ginger and garlic. Crumble the venison and sausage over the mixture and mix well. Shape into 1-in. balls. In a skillet over medium heat, brown meatballs in batches in 2 teaspoons oil, adding 1 teaspoon oil if needed. Transfer meatballs to a slow cooker.

In the same skillet, saute mushrooms in 1 teaspoon oil until tender. Stir in the broth and 1 cup cold water. Pour over the meatballs. Cover and cook on low for 4-5 hours or until a meat thermometer reads 160°.

Remove meatballs and mushrooms with a slotted spoon; keep warm. Strain cooking juices into a saucepan. Combine cornstarch and remaining water until smooth; add to saucepan. Bring to a boil; cook and stir for 2 minutes or until thickened. Serve over the meatballs, mushrooms and noodles. **Yield:** 8-10 servings.

Traditional Calzone

(Pictured below)

Serving this calzone at Easter has been a custom in my Italian family for over four generations. The filling is a delectable blend of Italian sausage and three types of cheese. —Joanne DiGirolamo, Des Plaines, Illinois

5-1/2 to 6 cups all-purpose flour
4-1/2 teaspoons sugar
1 tablespoon dried parsley flakes
1 package (1/4 ounce) quick-rise yeast
1-1/2 teaspoons salt
1-1/2 teaspoons dried basil
1-1/2 teaspoons dried rosemary, crushed
1/2 teaspoon garlic powder
1/2 teaspoon onion powder
1/4 teaspoon pepper
1-1/4 cups water
10 tablespoons butter *or* margarine
2 eggs
FILLING:
3 pounds bulk Italian sausage
3 cartons (15 ounces *each*) ricotta cheese
2 cups (8 ounces) shredded mozzarella cheese
1/2 cup grated Romano cheese
3 eggs, lightly beaten
1/4 cup dried parsley flakes
EGG WASH:
1 egg
2 tablespoons water

In a large mixing bowl, combine 4 cups flour, sugar, parsley, yeast, salt, basil, rosemary, garlic powder, onion powder and pepper. In a saucepan, heat water and butter to 120°-130°. Add to dry ingredients; beat just until moistened. Add eggs; beat until smooth. Stir in enough remaining flour to form a soft dough. Turn onto a floured surface; knead until smooth and elastic, 4-6 minutes. Place in a greased bowl, turning once to grease top. Cover and let rise in a warm place until doubled, 30 minutes.

Meanwhile, in a skillet, cook sausage until no longer pink; drain. Stir in cheeses, eggs and parsley; set aside. Punch dough down. On a lightly floured surface, roll out two-thirds of dough into an 18-in. x 15-in. rectangle. Transfer to a greased 13-in. x 9-in. x 2-in. baking dish (edges will hang over sides). Press onto bottom and up sides of dish.

Spread filling over crust. Roll out remaining pastry to fit top of dish; place over filling. Trim edges; pinch to seal. Cut slits in top. Beat egg and water; brush over top. Bake at 350° for 60-65 minutes or until a meat thermometer inserted into filling reads 160°. Let stand for 10 minutes; cut into squares. **Yield:** 15-20 servings.

— 🛒 🛒 🛒 —

Tangy Venison Stroganoff

For this recipe, I coat tender chunks of venison and chopped onion with a silky sour cream sauce.
—Ellen Spes, Caro, Michigan

1-1/2 pounds boneless venison steak, cubed
1 medium onion, sliced
1 can (10-1/2 ounces) condensed beef broth, undiluted
1 tablespoon Worcestershire sauce
1 tablespoon ketchup
1 teaspoon curry powder
1/2 teaspoon ground ginger
1/2 teaspoon salt
1/4 teaspoon pepper
4-1/2 teaspoons cornstarch
1/2 cup sour cream
2 tablespoons prepared horseradish
Hot cooked noodles

Place venison and onion in a slow cooker. Combine the next seven ingredients; pour over venison. Cover and cook on high for 3 to 3-1/2 hours or until meat is tender. In a small bowl, combine the cornstarch, sour cream and horseradish; mix well. Gradually stir into venison mixture. Cover and cook 15 minutes longer or until sauce is thickened. Serve over noodles. **Yield:** 4 servings.

— 🍴 🍴 🍴 —

Marinated Rib Eyes

(Pictured on page 58)

When spring comes to our house, out comes the grill! My husband does a great job cooking these steaks to perfection. —Sonja Kane, Wendell, North Carolina

1/2 cup butter *or* margarine, melted
1/4 cup lemon juice
1/4 cup ketchup
   2 tablespoons Worcestershire sauce
   2 tablespoons cider vinegar
   2 tablespoons olive *or* vegetable oil
   4 garlic cloves, minced
   1 teaspoon salt
   1 teaspoon sugar
1/2 teaspoon hot pepper sauce
Dash cayenne pepper
   6 beef rib eye steaks (12 ounces *each*)

In a large resealable bag, combine first 11 ingredients. Add steaks. Seal bag; turn to coat. Refrigerate 6 hours or overnight. Drain and discard marinade. Grill steaks, uncovered, over medium-hot heat for 8-10 minutes or until meat reaches desired doneness (for rare, a meat thermometer should read 140°; medium, 160°; well-done, 170°). **Yield:** 6 servings.

———— 🥄 🥄 🥄 ————

Crawfish Pizzas

These spicy pizzas were winners when I entered them in the International Crawfish Festival in Jackson.
—*Jackie Powell, Jayess, Mississippi*

1/2 cup *each* chopped green pepper, onion
      and green onions
   3 garlic cloves, minced
1/3 cup butter *or* margarine
   1 pound process cheese (Velveeta), cubed
   4 ounces cream cheese, cubed
1/4 cup mayonnaise
   1 tablespoon Worcestershire sauce
   1 teaspoon dried parsley flakes
1/2 to 1 teaspoon hot pepper sauce
1/2 teaspoon *each* cayenne pepper, pepper
      and Cajun seasoning
   2 pounds crawfish tails, cooked and peeled
Vegetable oil for frying
   10 flour tortillas (8 inches)
   2 cups (8 ounces) shredded Mexican blend
      cheese *or* cheddar cheese

In a large skillet, saute the green pepper, onions and garlic in butter until tender. Reduce heat to low. Add the process cheese, cream cheese and mayonnaise; cook and stir until melted. Stir in the Worcestershire sauce, parsley, hot pepper sauce and seasonings. Cook until slightly thickened. Add crawfish. Bring to a boil. Reduce heat; simmer, uncovered, for 10-15 minutes until heated through.
   Meanwhile, heat oil in a skillet. Fry each tortilla for 1-2 minutes on each side or until browned. Drain on paper towels. Spread 1/2 cup crawfish mixture on each tortilla. Sprinkle with cheese. Place on ungreased baking sheets. Bake at 350° for 4-5 minutes until cheese is melted. **Yield:** 10 servings.
   Editor's Note: Reduced-fat or fat-free mayonnaise may not be substituted for regular. Two pounds frozen salad shrimp can be substituted for crawfish.

———— 🥄 🥄 🥄 ————

Beef Rouladen

(Pictured above)

This is one of our most cherished dishes. My wife's aunt made it for us over 40 years ago. —*William Foster Haverhill, New Hampshire*

   2 pounds boneless beef top round steak
   6 bacon strips, halved
   12 small garlic dill pickles
   4 tablespoons vegetable oil, *divided*
   6 tablespoons all-purpose flour
   3 cups beef broth
   1 teaspoon dried savory
Salt and pepper to taste

Cut steak into twelve 4-in. x 3-in. pieces; flatten to 1/4-in. thickness. Place a bacon piece and pickle along a short side of each; roll up and secure with toothpicks. In a skillet, heat 2 tablespoons oil over medium-high heat. Brown roll-ups on all sides. Remove and keep warm.
   In same skillet, heat remaining oil. Stir in flour until smooth. Cook and stir over medium until golden brown, 5 minutes. Gradually blend in broth and savory, stirring constantly. Return roll-ups to pan. Cover; cook over low for 1-1/2 hours until tender. Season with salt and pepper. **Yield:** 6 servings.

Steak and Shrimp Kabobs

(Pictured above)

You'll make any get-together special with these attractive kabobs. For picnics, I assemble them at home and carry them in a large container.
—Karen Mergener, St. Croix, Minnesota

- 1 cup teriyaki sauce
- 1 can (6 ounces) pineapple juice
- 1/2 cup packed brown sugar
- 6 garlic cloves, minced
- 1/4 teaspoon Worcestershire sauce
- 1/8 teaspoon pepper
- 1 pound boneless beef sirloin steak, cut into 1-inch cubes
- 1 pound large uncooked shrimp, peeled and deveined
- 1 pound whole fresh mushrooms
- 2 large green peppers, cut into 1-inch pieces
- 2 medium onions, halved and quartered
- 1 pint cherry tomatoes
- 1-1/2 teaspoons cornstarch

In a large bowl, combine first six ingredients; mix well. Pour half of marinade into a large resealable plastic bag; add beef. Seal bag and turn to coat; refrigerate for 8 hours or overnight, turning occasionally. Cover and refrigerate remaining marinade.

Drain and discard marinade from beef. On metal or soaked wooden skewers, alternately thread beef, shrimp, mushrooms, green peppers, onions and tomatoes; set aside. In a small saucepan, combine cornstarch and reserved marinade until smooth. Bring to a boil; cook and stir for 1-2 minutes or until sauce is thickened.

Grill kabobs, covered, over indirect medium heat for 6 minutes, turning once. Baste with sauce.

Continue turning and basting for 8-10 minutes or until shrimp turn pink and beef reaches desired doneness. **Yield:** 6-8 servings.

— ▼ ▼ ▼ —

Cheesy Ham Macaroni

I'm often asked to bring this comforting casserole to potluck dinners, and it's a favorite of my family's, too. —Molly Seidel, Edgewood, New Mexico

- 1 package (8 ounces) elbow macaroni
- 6 tablespoons butter *or* margarine, *divided*
- 1/4 cup all-purpose flour
- 1/2 teaspoon salt
- Dash pepper
- 2 cups milk
- 2 cups (8 ounces) shredded sharp cheddar cheese
- 2 cups cubed fully cooked ham
- 1 can (4 ounces) mushroom stems and pieces, drained
- 1 jar (2 ounces) diced pimientos, drained
- 1/2 cup crushed butter-flavored crackers

Cook the macaroni according to package directions. Meanwhile, in a large saucepan, melt 4 tablespoons butter. Stir in the flour, salt and pepper until smooth; gradually whisk in milk. Bring to a boil; cook and stir for 1 minute or until thickened. Reduce heat. Add the cheese; cook and stir until melted. Stir in the ham, mushrooms and pimientos. Drain macaroni; stir into ham mixture.

Transfer to a greased shallow 2-1/2-qt. baking dish. Sprinkle with cracker crumbs; dot with remaining butter. Bake, uncovered, at 350° for 25-30 minutes until heated through. **Yield:** 8 servings.

— ▼ ▼ ▼ —

Three-Cheese Pesto Pizza

We love the flavor of this pizza because it's different from the traditional. The pesto, cheese and olive topping makes it delicious. —Pat Stevens, Granbury, Texas

- 1/2 cup chopped red onion
- 1/2 cup chopped sweet red pepper
- 1 tablespoon olive *or* vegetable oil
- 1 prebaked Italian bread shell crust (14 ounces)
- 1/2 cup prepared pesto sauce
- 1/2 cup chopped ripe olives
- 1 cup crumbled feta cheese
- 1 cup (4 ounces) shredded mozzarella cheese
- 1 cup shredded Parmesan cheese
- 2 plum tomatoes, thinly sliced

In a skillet, saute onion and red pepper in oil until tender. Place crust on an ungreased 12-in. pizza pan; spread with pesto. Top with onion mixture, olives, cheeses and tomatoes. Bake at 400° for 15-20 minutes or until cheese is melted. **Yield:** 4 servings.

— 🝰 🝰 🝰 —

Grilled Salmon with Creamy Tarragon Sauce

I accent succulent salmon with a zippy sauce featuring tarragon, green onions, lime juice and hot pepper sauce. —Joyce Turley, Slaughter, Kentucky

✓ Uses less fat, sugar or salt. Includes Nutritional Analysis and Diabetic Exchanges.

      1 salmon fillet (1 pound)
      1 tablespoon olive *or* canola oil
      1 cup (8 ounces) plain yogurt
  1/4 cup chopped green onions
      1 tablespoon minced fresh tarragon
         or 1 teaspoon dried tarragon
      1 tablespoon mayonnaise
      2 teaspoons lime juice
  1/2 to 1 teaspoon hot pepper sauce

Brush salmon on both sides with oil. Coat grill rack with nonstick cooking spray before starting the grill. Place salmon, skin side down, on grill rack. Grill, covered, over medium heat for 20-25 minutes or until fish flakes easily with a fork. Combine remaining ingredients. Serve with salmon. **Yield:** 4 servings.
   Nutritional Analysis: One serving (4 ounces of salmon with 2 tablespoons of sauce, prepared with fat-free yogurt and mayonnaise) equals 265 calories, 15 g fat (3 g saturated fat), 76 mg cholesterol, 130 mg sodium, 6 g carbohydrate, trace fiber, 25 g protein. **Diabetic Exchanges:** 4 lean meat, 1 fat.

— 🝰 🝰 🝰 —

Sweet Cherry Pork Chops

(Pictured on front cover)

I make pork chops often, so I like to experiment with different ideas. I dreamed up this recipe using ingredients that I had on hand. The cherry-orange sauce makes these chops special enough for guests.
—Shannon Mink, Columbus, Ohio

      4 boneless pork chops (1 inch thick)
      1 tablespoon vegetable oil
      1 cup orange juice
  3/4 cup pitted sweet cherries, halved
      2 green onions, sliced
  1/4 cup cherry preserves
      4 teaspoons cornstarch

      3 tablespoons cold water
Hot cooked rice

In a large skillet, brown pork chops in oil on both sides; drain. Add the orange juice, cherries and onions to skillet; bring to a boil. Reduce heat; simmer, uncovered, for 15 minutes or until a meat thermometer reads 160°, turning the chops twice.
   Remove chops; keep warm. Stir preserves into pan juices. In a bowl, combine cornstarch and cold water until smooth; stir into pan juices. Bring to a boil; cook and stir for 1-2 minutes until thickened. Serve over pork and rice. **Yield:** 4 servings.

— 🝰 🝰 🝰 —

Parmesan Chicken

(Pictured below)

This oven-fried chicken is perfect to prepare in advance and take on a picnic because it tastes good cold or warm. —Sharon Crider, St. Robert, Missouri

      1 cup all-purpose flour
      2 teaspoons salt
      2 teaspoons paprika
  1/4 teaspoon pepper
      2 eggs
      3 tablespoons milk
  2/3 cup grated Parmesan cheese
  1/3 cup dry bread crumbs
      1 broiler/fryer chicken (3 to 4 pounds), cut up

In a shallow bowl, combine flour, salt, paprika and pepper. In another shallow bowl, beat eggs and milk. In a third bowl, combine Parmesan cheese and bread crumbs. Coat chicken with flour mixture, dip in egg mixture, then roll in crumb mixture.
   Place in a well-greased 15-in. x 10-in. x 1-in. baking pan. Bake at 400° for 50-55 minutes or until chicken juices run clear. **Yield:** 4 servings.

Slice Into Quiche!

WHETHER it's for breakfast or brunch, a slice of quiche is sure to please! Quiche can take on delightfully different personalities, as these recipes demonstrate.

Use time-saving purchased frozen crusts...or make your own from scratch. You'll even find an easy hash brown crust here.

— ♟ ♟ ♟ —

Pepperoni Pizza Quiche

(Pictured below)

I put ever-popular ingredients into a pastry crust for this appealing "pizza pie". —Debbie White
Williamson, West Virginia

1 unbaked pastry shell (9 inches)
1 cup (4 ounces) shredded Swiss cheese, *divided*
4 eggs
1-1/2 cups half-and-half cream
1/2 teaspoon salt
1/2 teaspoon dried oregano
1/8 teaspoon cayenne pepper
1/8 teaspoon pepper
1 large onion, chopped
2 tablespoons vegetable oil
1 can (14-1/2 ounces) diced tomatoes, undrained
1/2 teaspoon dried thyme
1/4 teaspoon sugar

TRY SAVORY Pepperoni Pizza Quiche, Chicken Spinach Quiche, Double-Crust Onion Quiche or Potato-Crust Chicken Quiche (shown above, clockwise from top left) soon...or bake them all for a brunch!

1/8 teaspoon dried basil
12 slices pepperoni, chopped
1 cup (4 ounces) shredded mozzarella
   cheese
1/4 cup sliced ripe olives

Bake unpricked pastry shell at 375° for 11 minutes. Sprinkle with 2/3 cup Swiss cheese. In a bowl, whisk the eggs, cream, salt, oregano, cayenne and pepper; pour over cheese. Bake for 25-30 minutes or until a knife inserted near the center comes out clean.

Meanwhile, in a skillet, saute onion in oil until tender. Stir in the tomatoes, thyme, sugar and basil. Bring to a boil. Reduce heat; simmer, uncovered, for 15 minutes or until liquid has evaporated.

Sprinkle the remaining Swiss cheese over the quiche. Top with the tomato mixture. Sprinkle with the pepperoni, mozzarella cheese and olives. Bake 5 minutes longer or until the cheese is melted. Let stand for 15 minutes before cutting. **Yield:** 6-8 servings.

Chicken Spinach Quiche

(Pictured at left)

This delicious quiche features chicken, spinach and cheddar cheese, but you can use Swiss cheese instead if you'd like. The quiche is easy to prepare and cuts beautifully. —Barbara McCalley
Allison Park, Pennsylvania

1 cup (4 ounces) shredded cheddar cheese, *divided*
1 unbaked pastry shell (9 inches)
1 cup diced cooked chicken
1 package (10 ounces) frozen chopped spinach, thawed and squeezed dry
1/4 cup finely chopped onion
2 eggs
3/4 cup milk
3/4 cup mayonnaise*
1/4 teaspoon salt
1/8 teaspoon pepper

Sprinkle 1/4 cup cheese into the pastry shell. In a bowl, combine the chicken, 1/2 cup spinach, onion and remaining cheese (save remaining spinach for another use). Spoon into pastry shell. In a bowl, whisk the eggs, milk, mayonnaise, salt and pepper; pour over the chicken mixture.

Bake at 350° for 40-45 minutes or until a knife inserted near the center comes out clean. Let stand for 15 minutes before cutting. **Yield:** 6-8 servings.

***Editor's Note:** Reduced-fat or fat-free mayonnaise may not be substituted for regular mayonnaise in this recipe.*

Potato-Crust Chicken Quiche

(Pictured below left)

Shredded hash browns form the golden crust in this comforting quiche. Sometimes I'll substitute diced cooked ham, flaked tuna or sliced mushrooms for the chicken in this favorite recipe of mine.
—Halina D'Arienzo, Murrells Inlet, South Carolina

4 cups frozen shredded hash brown potatoes, thawed
3 tablespoons butter *or* margarine, melted
1 cup (4 ounces) shredded pepper Jack cheese
1 cup diced cooked chicken
4 eggs
1 cup half-and-half cream *or* milk
1/2 teaspoon salt

Pat hash browns with paper towels to remove excess moisture. Press into a well-greased 9-in. pie plate; brush with butter. Bake at 425° for 20-25 minutes or until lightly browned. Reduce heat to 350°.

Sprinkle cheese and chicken into the crust. In a mixing bowl, beat the eggs, cream and salt; pour over chicken. Bake for 20-25 minutes or until a knife inserted near the center comes out clean. Let stand for 5 minutes before cutting. **Yield:** 6-8 servings.

Double-Crust Onion Quiche

(Pictured at left)

In summer, our electric farm fencing business keeps us hopping, and I tend to fix quick meals like this hearty pie for husband Doug and me. I keep pie pastry on hand in the refrigerator or freezer just for this dish.
—Ruth Lee, Troy, Ontario

4 eggs
2 cups (8 ounces) shredded sharp cheddar cheese
1 large onion, quartered and sliced (about 1-1/2 cups)
4 bacon strips, cooked and crumbled
Salt and pepper to taste
Pastry for double-crust pie (9 inches)

In a mixing bowl, beat eggs. Add cheese, onion, bacon, salt and pepper; mix well. Line a 9-in. pie plate with bottom crust. Add egg mixture. Roll out remaining pastry to fit top of pie; place over filling. Trim, seal and flute edges; cut slits in top.

Cover edges loosely with foil. Bake at 375° for 10 minutes. Remove foil; bake 20-25 minutes longer or until the crust is golden brown. Refrigerate leftovers. **Yield:** 6-8 servings.

Pork Chops in Mustard Cream Sauce

(Pictured above)

I like to prepare foods I can eat for more than one meal or freeze and eat later so I don't have to cook a lot during the week. This recipe is one of my favorite creations.
—Bryan Cornett, Duluth, Georgia

1/4 cup plus 2 teaspoons all-purpose flour, *divided*
1/2 teaspoon salt
1/4 teaspoon pepper
   4 bone-in pork loin chops (1 inch thick), trimmed
   2 tablespoons vegetable oil
1/2 pound fresh mushrooms, sliced
   2 garlic cloves, minced
   1 cup beef broth
1/2 teaspoon dried rosemary, crushed
1/4 cup half-and-half cream
1/4 cup sour cream
   1 tablespoon Dijon mustard

In a large resealable plastic bag, combine 1/4 cup flour, salt and pepper. Add pork chops, one at a time, and shake to coat. In a large skillet, brown chops in oil over medium-high heat for 3-4 minutes on each side. Remove and set aside.

In the same skillet, saute mushrooms and garlic for 3 minutes. Add broth and rosemary; bring to a boil. Reduce heat to low; return pork to pan. Cover and simmer for 1 hour or until meat is very tender. Remove pork and keep warm.

In a small bowl, combine the half-and-half, sour cream, mustard and remaining flour until smooth.

Pour into skillet. Bring to a boil; cook and stir for 2 minutes or until thickened. Serve over pork chops. **Yield:** 4 servings.

Chicken Tarragon

This easy-to-fix entree combines moist chicken breasts with zucchini, carrots and mushrooms. I love tarragon, so I make this dish often.
—Ruth Peterson
Jenison, Michigan

   4 boneless skinless chicken breast halves
1/2 teaspoon paprika
1/3 cup butter *or* margarine, *divided*
   2 medium zucchini, julienned
   4 small carrots, julienned
   4 large mushrooms, sliced
   2 tablespoons minced fresh tarragon
   or 2 teaspoons dried tarragon
   1 tablespoon lemon juice
1/2 teaspoon salt
1/8 teaspoon pepper

Sprinkle chicken with paprika. In a large skillet, brown chicken in 2 teaspoons butter. Place the vegetables in a greased 13-in. x 9-in. x 2-in. baking dish. Top with chicken.

Melt the remaining butter; stir in the tarragon, lemon juice, salt and pepper. Pour over chicken and vegetables. Cover and bake at 350° for 30-35 minutes or until chicken juices run clear and vegetables are tender. **Yield:** 4 servings.

Apple-Topped Pork Loin

This succulent pork roast has a crisp topping of spiced apples.
—Susan Seymour, Valatie, New York

   2 tablespoons all-purpose flour
   1 teaspoon caraway seeds
   1 teaspoon ground mustard
3/4 teaspoon salt
1/2 teaspoon sugar
1/4 teaspoon rubbed sage
1/4 teaspoon pepper
   1 boneless pork loin roast (4 to 5 pounds)
   2 tablespoons olive *or* vegetable oil
APPLE TOPPING:
1-1/2 cups finely chopped peeled tart apples
1/2 cup packed brown sugar
1/4 teaspoon salt
1/4 teaspoon ground cinnamon
1/8 to 1/4 teaspoon ground mace

In a small bowl, combine the first seven ingredients; rub over roast. In a large skillet, heat oil; brown roast on all sides. Place on a rack in a shallow baking pan. Bake, uncovered, at 325° for 1-1/2 hours.

Combine the topping ingredients; spread over top of roast. Bake 1 to 1-1/2 hours longer or until a meat thermometer reads 160°. Let stand for 10 minutes before slicing. **Yield:** 12-15 servings.

— 🥤 🥤 🥤 —

Chicken with Chive Sauce

(Pictured on page 58)

Browned chicken gets a pleasant flavor boost from a creamy white sauce featuring chives and mushrooms and makes a lovely presentation when served over white or wild rice. —_Becky Baird, Salt Lake City, Utah_

    6 boneless skinless chicken breast halves
    4 tablespoons olive _or_ vegetable oil, _divided_
    1 cup sliced fresh mushrooms
  3/4 cup minced chives
    2 tablespoons all-purpose flour
  1/4 cup chicken broth
    2 cups half-and-half cream
Pinch ground nutmeg
Salt and pepper to taste
Hot cooked rice

In a large skillet, brown chicken in 2 tablespoons oil for 3-4 minutes on each side. Remove and keep warm. Saute mushrooms and chives in remaining oil for 2 minutes. Stir in the flour. Gradually whisk in the broth until blended. Stir in the cream, nutmeg, salt and pepper. Bring to a boil; cook and stir for 2-3 minutes or until thickened.

Return chicken to the pan; turn to coat. Cover and simmer for 7-9 minutes or until chicken juices run clear. Serve over rice. **Yield:** 6 servings.

— 🥤 🥤 🥤 —

Garlic-Onion Tomato Pizza

(Pictured at right)

You won't miss the traditional tomato sauce when you bite into a slice of this pizza—it is absolutely delicious! We like it hot or at room temperature. It makes a wonderful appetizer cut into small pieces...or you can use the same topping for bruschetta. —_Tammy Thomas, Sheboygan, Wisconsin_

    2 teaspoons cornmeal
    2 packages (1/4 ounce _each_) active dry yeast
    2 cups warm water (110° to 115°)
    5 to 6 cups all-purpose flour
    4 teaspoons plus 1 tablespoon olive _or_ vegetable oil, _divided_
    1 teaspoon salt
    2 medium sweet onions, thinly sliced
    8 large garlic cloves, halved
    6 to 8 plum tomatoes, cut lengthwise into eighths and seeded
    2 tablespoons dried oregano
    2 tablespoons dried parsley flakes
Pepper to taste
1-1/2 cups (6 ounces) shredded mozzarella cheese
  1/4 cup grated Romano cheese

Sprinkle cornmeal evenly over two greased 14-in. pizza pans; set aside. In a bowl, dissolve yeast in water; add 4-1/2 cups flour, 4 teaspoons oil and salt; beat until smooth. Add enough remaining flour to form a soft dough. Turn onto a floured surface; knead until smooth and elastic, about 6-8 minutes. Place in a greased bowl, turning once to grease top. Cover and let rise in a warm place until doubled, about 1 hour.

Punch dough down; divide in half. Press each portion into prepared pans. Prick dough with a fork. Bake at 450° for 4-5 minutes. Broil onions and garlic in batches 3-4 in. from the heat until softened and lightly browned. Broil tomato slices for 2 minutes on each side. Finely chop garlic.

Arrange onions, garlic and tomatoes over crusts. Sprinkle with oregano, parsley, pepper and cheeses; drizzle with remaining oil. Bake at 450° for 8-9 minutes or until cheese is melted. **Yield:** 2 pizzas (8 slices each).

Manicotti with Eggplant Sauce
(Pictured below)

This Italian-style dish has a hearty spinach and cheese filling and a well-seasoned tomato-eggplant sauce.
— *Barbara Nowakowski, North Tonawanda, New York*

✓ Uses less fat, sugar or salt. Includes Nutritional Analysis and Diabetic Exchanges.

- 1 small eggplant, peeled and chopped
- 1/2 cup chopped onion
- 2 garlic cloves, minced
- 1/2 teaspoon dried tarragon
- 1/4 teaspoon dried thyme
- 1 can (14-1/2 ounces) no-salt-added diced tomatoes, undrained
- 1 can (8 ounces) no-salt-added tomato sauce
- 1 package (10 ounces) frozen chopped spinach, thawed and well drained
- 1 cup reduced-fat ricotta cheese
- 1 cup (4 ounces) shredded part-skim mozzarella cheese, *divided*
- 1/2 cup egg substitute
- 1/4 cup grated Parmesan cheese
- 2 tablespoons minced fresh parsley
- 6 manicotti shells, cooked, rinsed and drained

In a large skillet coated with nonstick cooking spray, cook and stir the eggplant, onion, garlic, tarragon and thyme until vegetables are tender. Add tomatoes and tomato sauce; bring to a boil. Reduce heat; simmer, uncovered, for 3-4 minutes. Set aside.

In a large bowl, combine the spinach, ricotta, 1/2 cup mozzarella, egg substitute, Parmesan and parsley; mix well. Stuff into manicotti shells. Place in an 11-in. x 7-in. x 2-in. baking dish coated with nonstick cooking spray. Spoon eggplant sauce over manicotti; sprinkle with remaining moz-

zarella. Cover and bake at 350° for 25-30 minutes or until heated through. **Yield:** 6 servings.
Nutritional Analysis: One serving equals 252 calories, 8 g fat (5 g saturated fat), 26 mg cholesterol, 314 mg sodium, 29 g carbohydrate, 6 g fiber, 18 g protein. **Diabetic Exchanges:** 2 starch, 1 lean meat, 1 fat.

Italian-Style Duck

Tender duck breasts are smothered in a thick tomato sauce and melted mozzarella and cheddar cheeses in this delicious dish. — *Edna Watts, Arley, Alabama*

- 1 small onion, chopped
- 1 cup sliced fresh mushrooms
- 6 tablespoons butter *or* margarine, *divided*
- 1 can (29 ounces) tomato sauce
- 1/2 cup grated Parmesan cheese
- 1/2 cup minced fresh parsley, *divided*
- 1 envelope spaghetti sauce mix
- 1/2 cup all-purpose flour
- 1-1/2 teaspoons *each* onion salt and garlic salt
- 8 boneless skinless duck breast halves
- 1/2 cup shredded mozzarella cheese
- 1/2 cup shredded cheddar cheese
Hot cooked pasta

In a saucepan, saute onion and mushrooms in 2 tablespoons butter until tender. Stir in the tomato sauce, Parmesan cheese, 1/4 cup parsley and spaghetti sauce mix. Bring to a boil. Reduce heat; cover and simmer for 15 minutes, stirring occasionally.

In a shallow dish, combine the flour, onion salt and garlic salt; coat duck pieces. In a large skillet, brown duck on both sides in remaining butter. Place in an ungreased 13-in. x 9-in. x 2-in. baking dish. Top with tomato mixture; sprinkle with cheeses. Bake, uncovered, at 375° for 28-32 minutes or until a meat thermometer reads 180°. Sprinkle with remaining parsley. Serve with pasta. **Yield:** 8 servings.

Mexican Egg Casserole

Tomatoes and green chilies give color and zip to this cheesy egg bake. It makes a hearty breakfast or brunch entree. — *Mary Steiner, West Bend, Wisconsin*

- 1/2 cup all-purpose flour
- 1 teaspoon baking powder
- 12 eggs, lightly beaten
- 4 cups (16 ounces) shredded Monterey Jack cheese, *divided*
- 2 cups small-curd cottage cheese
- 2 plum tomatoes, seeded and diced

1 can (4 ounces) chopped green chilies, drained
4 green onions, sliced
1/2 teaspoon hot pepper sauce
1 teaspoon dried oregano
2 tablespoons minced fresh cilantro *or* parsley
1/2 teaspoon *each* salt and pepper
Salsa, optional

In a large bowl, combine flour and baking powder. Add eggs, 3-1/2 cups Monterey Jack cheese, cottage cheese, tomatoes, chilies, onions, hot pepper sauce, oregano, cilantro, salt and pepper. Pour into a greased 13-in. x 9-in. x 2-in. baking dish. Sprinkle with remaining Monterey Jack cheese.

Bake, uncovered, at 400° for 15 minutes. Reduce heat to 350°; bake 30 minutes longer or until a knife inserted near the center comes out clean. Let stand for 5 minutes before cutting. Serve with salsa if desired. **Yield:** 8 servings.

Turkey Tetrazzini

I make this recipe with leftover turkey, and it's a whole new meal! We look forward to having it after Christmas and Thanksgiving. —Susan Payne
Corner Brook, Newfoundland

1 package (7 ounces) thin spaghetti, broken in half
2 cups cubed cooked turkey
1 cup sliced fresh mushrooms
1 small onion, chopped
3 tablespoons butter *or* margarine
1 can (10-3/4 ounces) condensed cream of mushroom soup, undiluted
1 cup milk
1/2 teaspoon poultry seasoning
1/8 teaspoon ground mustard
1 cup (4 ounces) shredded cheddar cheese
1 cup (4 ounces) shredded mozzarella cheese
1 tablespoon shredded Parmesan cheese
Minced fresh parsley

Cook spaghetti according to package directions. Drain and place in a greased 11-in. x 7-in. x 2-in. baking dish. Top with turkey; set aside.

In a skillet, saute the mushrooms and onion in butter until tender. Whisk in the soup, milk, poultry seasoning and mustard until blended. Stir in the cheddar cheese; cook and stir over medium heat until cheese is melted. Pour over turkey.

Sprinkle with mozzarella and Parmesan cheeses (dish will be full). Bake, uncovered, at 350° for 25-30 minutes or until heated through and cheese is melted. Sprinkle with parsley. **Yield:** 4-6 servings.

Roasted Garlic Pork Supper

(Pictured above)

I grow sweet onions and garlic, so they're always on hand when I want to make this roast. —Joseph Obbie
Webster, New York

2 whole garlic bulbs
2 teaspoons olive *or* vegetable oil
1/2 teaspoon dried basil
1/2 teaspoon dried oregano
2 tablespoons lemon juice
1 boneless pork loin roast (4 to 5 pounds)
6 medium red potatoes, quartered
3 cups baby carrots
1 large sweet onion, thinly sliced
1-1/2 cups water
1 teaspoon salt
1/2 teaspoon pepper

Remove papery outer skin from garlic (do not peel or separate cloves). Cut top off garlic heads, leaving root end intact. Brush with oil; sprinkle with basil and oregano. Wrap each bulb in heavy-duty foil. Bake at 425° for 30-35 minutes or until softened. Cool for 10-15 minutes. Squeeze softened garlic into a small bowl. Add lemon juice; mix well. Rub over the roast.

Place roast in a shallow roasting pan. Arrange potatoes, carrots and onion around roast. Pour water into the pan. Sprinkle meat and vegetables with salt and pepper. Cover and bake at 350° for 1-1/2 hours. Uncover; bake 1-1/2 hours longer or until a meat thermometer reads 160°, basting often. Cover and let stand for 10 minutes before slicing. **Yield:** 10-12 servings.

onion and garlic in oil until crisp-tender. Stir in the tomato paste, broth, brown sugar and seasonings. Bring to a boil. Reduce heat; simmer, uncovered, for 30 minutes, stirring occasionally.

In a bowl, combine egg and ricotta cheese. Spread 1 cup vegetable mixture in a greased 8-in. square baking dish. Layer with two noodles (trimming to fit), half of ricotta mixture, 1-1/2 cups vegetable mixture and two more noodles. Top with remaining ricotta mixture, noodles and vegetable mixture.

Sprinkle with cheeses and Italian seasoning. Bake, uncovered, at 350° for 30-35 minutes or until bubbly and the cheese is melted. Let stand for 5 minutes before cutting. **Yield:** 4-6 servings.

Mushroom Cheese Chicken

There's a cheesy surprise tucked inside these rolled chicken breasts. The flavorful mushroom-mozzarella filling is perked up with chives and pimientos.
—*Anna Free, Plymouth, Ohio*

✓ Uses less fat, sugar or salt. Includes Nutritional Analysis and Diabetic Exchanges.

  4 boneless skinless chicken breast halves
    (5 ounces *each*)
1/2 teaspoon salt
Dash pepper
  2 tablespoons all-purpose flour
1/2 cup reduced-fat plain yogurt
1/2 cup shredded part-skim mozzarella cheese
1/2 cup canned mushroom stems and pieces
  1 tablespoon diced pimientos
  1 tablespoon minced fresh parsley
  1 tablespoon minced chives
TOPPING:
  1 tablespoon reduced-fat plain yogurt
  1 tablespoon dry bread crumbs
1/8 teaspoon paprika

Flatten chicken to 1/8-in. thickness; sprinkle with salt and pepper. In a small bowl, combine flour and yogurt until smooth. Stir in cheese, mushrooms, pimientos, parsley and chives. Spread down center of each piece of chicken. Roll up and tuck in ends; secure with toothpicks. Place seam side down in an 11-in. x 7-in. x 2-in. baking dish coated with nonstick cooking spray.

Brush yogurt over chicken. Combine bread crumbs and paprika; sprinkle over top. Bake, uncovered, at 350° for 20-25 minutes until chicken juices run clear. Discard toothpicks. **Yield:** 4 servings.

Nutritional Analysis: One serving equals 222 calories, 5 g fat (2 g saturated fat), 92 mg cholesterol, 544 mg sodium, 4 g carbohydrate, trace fiber, 39 g protein. **Diabetic Exchange:** 4 lean meat.

Vegetable Lasagna

(Pictured above)

I cooked up this fresh-tasting lasagna for vegetarian customers at a local grocery store, where I work part-time. —*Sam Hunsaker, Lawrence, Kansas*

  5 plum tomatoes, chopped
1-1/2 cups sliced fresh mushrooms
  1 medium sweet red pepper, julienned
  1 small yellow summer squash, cut into
    1/4-inch slices
  1 small zucchini, cut into 1/4-inch slices
  1 medium carrot, shredded
  1 small onion, chopped
  3 garlic cloves, minced
1/4 cup olive *or* vegetable oil
  1 can (12 ounces) tomato paste
  1 cup vegetable broth
  2 tablespoons brown sugar
  2 teaspoons dried oregano
  2 teaspoons dried basil
  1 teaspoon salt
1/2 teaspoon dried thyme
1/4 teaspoon pepper
  1 egg
  1 cup (8 ounces) ricotta cheese
  6 lasagna noodles, cooked and drained
  1 cup (4 ounces) shredded mozzarella
    cheese
1/4 cup shredded Parmesan cheese
  2 tablespoons grated Romano cheese
  2 teaspoons Italian seasoning

In a large saucepan, saute the tomatoes, mushrooms, red pepper, yellow squash, zucchini, carrot,

Pineapple Chicken Stir Fry

The brown sugar called for in this recipe gives the chicken a superior taste. —*Mel Miller, Perkins, Oklahoma*

  1 can (20 ounces) unsweetened pineapple
    tidbits
  2 tablespoons cornstarch
1/4 cup cider vinegar
1/4 cup ketchup
  2 tablespoons brown sugar
  2 tablespoons soy sauce
1/4 teaspoon ground ginger
1-1/2 pounds boneless skinless chicken breasts,
    cubed
  3 tablespoons vegetable *or* canola oil, *divided*
1/2 teaspoon garlic salt
  2 medium carrots, sliced
  1 medium green pepper, julienned
  1 medium tomato, cut into wedges
Hot cooked rice

Drain pineapple, reserving the juice; set pineapple aside. In a small bowl, combine cornstarch and reserved juice until smooth. Stir in the vinegar, ketchup, brown sugar, soy sauce and ginger; set aside.

In a wok or large skillet, stir-fry the chicken in 2 tablespoons oil for 5-6 minutes or until juices run clear; sprinkle with garlic salt. Remove and keep warm. Stir-fry the carrots in remaining oil for 4 minutes. Add green pepper; cook and stir until vegetables are crisp-tender. Add the chicken and pineapple.

Stir pineapple juice mixture; pour into pan. Bring to a boil; cook and stir for 1-2 minutes or until thickened. Add the tomato wedges. Serve over rice. **Yield:** 6 servings.

— 🝜 🝜 🝜 —

Cuban Ground Beef Hash

(Pictured below right)

Called "picadillo" in Spanish, this hash is wonderful served over white rice or even in a breakfast omelet.
—*Adrianna Still Cruz, Weston, Florida*

✓ Uses less fat, sugar or salt. Includes Nutritional Analysis and Diabetic Exchanges.

1-1/2 pounds ground beef
  1 medium green pepper, chopped
  1 medium onion, chopped
  1 can (14-1/2 ounces) diced tomatoes,
    undrained
  3 tablespoons tomato paste
1/3 cup raisins
1/3 cup sliced stuffed olives
  1 tablespoon cider vinegar
  3 garlic cloves, minced
  2 teaspoons ground cumin

1/2 teaspoon *each* salt and pepper
1/2 cup frozen peas
Hot cooked rice

In a large skillet, cook the beef, green pepper and onion over medium heat until meat is no longer pink; drain. Stir in tomatoes, tomato paste, raisins, olives, vinegar, garlic, cumin, salt and pepper. Bring to a boil. Reduce heat; cover and simmer for 5 minutes. Add peas; cover and cook 5 minutes longer or until heated through. Serve over rice. **Yield:** 6 servings.

Nutritional Analysis: One 3/4-cup serving (prepared with lean ground beef; calculated without rice) equals 262 calories, 10 g fat (4 g saturated fat), 56 mg cholesterol, 621 mg sodium, 18 g carbohydrate, 4 g fiber, 24 g protein. **Diabetic Exchanges:** 3 lean meat, 1 starch, 1/2 fat.

— 🝜 🝜 🝜 —

Crispy Onion Chicken

This golden brown chicken with its crunchy french-fried onion coating is great with baked potatoes.
—*Charlotte Smith, McDonald, Pennsylvania*

1/2 cup butter *or* margarine, melted
  1 tablespoon Worcestershire sauce
  1 teaspoon ground mustard
1/2 teaspoon garlic salt
1/4 teaspoon pepper
  4 boneless skinless chicken breast halves
  1 can (6 ounces) cheddar *or* original
    french-fried onions, crushed

In a shallow bowl, combine the butter, Worcestershire sauce, mustard, garlic salt and pepper. Dip chicken in the butter mixture, then coat with onions. Place in a greased 9-in. square baking pan. Top with any remaining onions; drizzle with any remaining butter mixture. Bake, uncovered, at 350° for 30-35 minutes or until chicken juices run clear. **Yield:** 4 servings.

Mustard-Glazed Pork Chops

(Pictured below)

My family loves these tender pork chops...but the spicy sauce is equally good on pork ribs and chicken.
—*Jeri-Lynn Sandusky, Hatch, Utah*

✓ Uses less fat, sugar or salt. Includes Nutritional Analysis and Diabetic Exchanges.

    1/2 cup packed brown sugar
    1/3 cup Dijon mustard
      5 tablespoons cider vinegar
      2 tablespoons molasses
      1 tablespoon ground mustard
      6 bone-in pork loin chops (6 ounces *each*)

In a small saucepan, whisk the brown sugar, Dijon mustard, vinegar, molasses and ground mustard until blended. Bring to a boil over medium heat, stirring frequently. Reduce heat; cover and simmer for 2-3 minutes or until thickened.

Place pork chops in a 13-in. x 9-in. x 2-in. baking dish coated with nonstick cooking spray. Top with sauce; turn to coat. Bake, uncovered, at 350° for 18-22 minutes or until juices run clear, basting occasionally. **Yield:** 6 servings.

Nutritional Analysis: One serving equals 258 calories, 9 g fat (3 g saturated fat), 58 mg cholesterol, 397 mg sodium, 25 g carbohydrate, trace fiber, 21 g protein. **Diabetic Exchanges:** 3 lean meat, 1-1/2 fruit.

— 🍶 🍶 🍶 —

Omelet Quesadilla

I came up with these crispy quesadillas because my family found breakfast burritos too messy. They're fast to fix, fun to eat, filling and healthy. —*Terri Capps*
Wichita, Kansas

✓ Uses less fat, sugar or salt. Includes Nutritional Analysis and Diabetic Exchanges.

      1 cup sliced fresh mushrooms
      2 tablespoons chopped onion
    1/2 cup egg substitute
      2 tablespoons chopped fresh tomato
      2 flour tortillas (10 inches)
      4 thin slices lean ham (1/2 ounce *each*)
    1/4 cup shredded part-skim mozzarella cheese
    1/4 cup shredded reduced-fat cheddar cheese
      3 tablespoons salsa

In a small nonstick skillet coated with cooking spray, saute mushrooms and onion until tender. Add egg substitute and tomato; cook and gently stir over medium heat until egg mixture is completely set.

Place one tortilla in a large ungreased nonstick skillet; top with ham, egg mixture, cheeses and remaining tortilla. Cook over medium heat, carefully turning once, until lightly browned on both sides and cheese begins to melt. Cut into four wedges. Serve with salsa. **Yield:** 2 servings.

Nutritional Analysis: One serving equals 423 calories, 11 g fat (5 g saturated fat), 27 mg cholesterol, 1,244 mg sodium, 42 g carbohydrate, 7 g fiber, 33 g protein. **Diabetic Exchanges:** 3 starch, 2 lean meat, 2 fat.

— 🍶 🍶 🍶 —

Crab Lasagna Roll-Ups

With their creamy filling and delicate crab flavor, these roll-ups are simply satisfying. —*Fran Rodgers*
Lake Geneva, Wisconsin

✓ Uses less fat, sugar or salt. Includes Nutritional Analysis and Diabetic Exchanges.

      1 carton (16 ounces) 1% cottage cheese
    1/2 cup egg substitute
    1/4 cup grated Parmesan cheese
      2 tablespoons Italian seasoning
      2 tablespoons minced fresh parsley
      1 teaspoon dried oregano
    1/2 teaspoon *each* dried basil and thyme
    1/4 teaspoon garlic powder
      1 package (8 ounces) imitation crabmeat, flaked
     12 lasagna noodles, cooked and drained
      2 cans (8 ounces *each*) no-salt-added tomato sauce

In a bowl, combine first nine ingredients. Add crab; mix well. Place 1/3 cup on each noodle; roll up. Place seam side down in a 13-in. x 9-in. x 2-in. baking dish coated with cooking spray. Top with tomato sauce. Cover; bake at 350° for 30-40 minutes until heated through. **Yield:** 6 servings.

Nutritional Analysis: One serving (2 roll-ups) equals 198 calories, 3 g fat (1 g saturated fat), 13 mg cholesterol, 755 mg sodium, 23 g carbohydrate, 1 g fiber, 19 g protein. **Diabetic Exchanges:** 2 very lean meat, 1-1/2 starch.

Cherry-Stuffed Pork Loin

(Pictured at right)

One of my best recipes is this pork loin, with its moist and tasty stuffing. —*Jim Korzenowski*
Dearborn, Michigan

    1 cup dried cherries
  1/2 cup water
  1/2 cup minced fresh parsley
    1 medium onion, chopped
    1 celery rib, diced
  1/4 cup shredded carrot
    1 tablespoon rubbed sage
    1 garlic clove, minced
    1 teaspoon minced fresh rosemary
    3 tablespoons butter *or* margarine
2-1/2 cups salad croutons
    1 cup chicken broth
  1/4 teaspoon ground nutmeg
  1/2 teaspoon pepper, *divided*
  1/4 teaspoon almond extract
    1 boneless whole pork loin roast (3 pounds)
GRAVY:
1-3/4 cups chicken broth
  1/2 cup water
  1/2 cup heavy whipping cream
  1/2 teaspoon minced fresh rosemary

In a small saucepan, bring cherries and water to a boil. Remove from heat; set aside (do not drain). In a skillet, saute parsley, vegetables and seasonings in butter until tender. Remove from heat. Stir in croutons, broth, nutmeg, 1/4 teaspoon pepper, extract and cherries. Let stand until liquid is absorbed.

Cut a lengthwise slit down the center of the roast to within 1/2 in. of bottom. Open roast so it lies flat; cover with plastic wrap. Flatten to 3/4-in. thickness. Remove plastic; spread stuffing over meat to within 1 in. of edges. Close roast; tie at 1-in. intervals with kitchen string. Place on a rack in a shallow roasting pan. Sprinkle with remaining pepper.

Bake, uncovered, at 350° for 1-1/2 to 2 hours or until a meat thermometer reads 160°. Let stand 10-15 minutes before slicing. Add broth and water to roasting pan; stir to loosen browned bits. Pour into a saucepan. Bring to a boil over medium-high heat; cook until reduced by half. Stir in cream and rosemary. Simmer, uncovered, until thickened. Serve with roast. **Yield:** 10-12 servings.

Breaded Sirloin

(Pictured on page 58)

This recipe calls for beef steaks to be dipped in an egg mixture, then coated in a combination of seasoned bread crumbs, grated cheese, parsley and garlic.
—*Sandra Lee Pippin, Aurora, Colorado*

    2 eggs
  1/2 cup milk
    1 cup seasoned bread crumbs
    3 tablespoons grated Parmesan cheese
    2 tablespoons minced fresh parsley
    2 garlic cloves, minced
  1/4 teaspoon salt
  1/8 teaspoon pepper
    2 pounds boneless beef sirloin steak (1-1/2 inches thick), cut into 1/4-inch slices
Oil for frying
    4 medium ripe tomatoes, sliced
    8 ounces sliced mozzarella cheese

In a shallow bowl, whisk eggs and milk. In another shallow bowl, combine bread crumbs, Parmesan cheese, parsley, garlic, salt and pepper. Dip steak in egg mixture, then coat with crumb mixture.

In a large skillet, heat 1-1/2 in. of oil. Brown steak over medium-high heat for 2-3 minutes on each side or until meat reaches desired doneness. Drain on paper towels. Transfer to a baking sheet. Top beef with tomato and cheese slices. Broil 4 in. from the heat for 1-2 minutes or until cheese is melted. **Yield:** 8 servings.

Breads, Rolls & Muffins

A basketful of breads is a welcome accompaniment to any meal.

—— 🍽 🍽 🍽 ——

DOUGH-LICIOUS! Clockwise from upper left: Apple Cheddar Scones (p. 98), Blueberry Almond Coffee Cake (p. 95), Maple Butter Twists (p. 90), Crispy French Toast (p. 96) and Raspberry Streusel Coffee Cake (p. 86).

In a mixing bowl, combine 1 cup flour, sugar, yeast, lemon peel and salt. In a saucepan, heat milk, water and butter to 120°-130°. Add to dry ingredients; beat until smooth. Add egg, egg yolk and 1/2 cup flour; beat for 2 minutes. Stir in enough remaining flour to form a soft dough. Turn onto a floured surface. Knead until smooth and elastic, about 5 minutes. Cover and let rest for 20-30 minutes. Punch dough down. Divide into three pieces; roll each into a 24-in. x 4-in. rectangle.

In a mixing bowl, beat filling ingredients. Spread over dough to within 1 in. of edges. Roll up, starting with a long side; pinch seams to seal. Place ropes on a floured surface; gently braid. Place in a well-greased 10-in. tube pan. Pinch ends to seal. Cover and let rise until doubled, about 30 minutes. Beat egg with water; brush over braid. Bake at 350° for 35-40 minutes. Carefully remove from pan to a wire rack. Combine the first five glaze ingredients; drizzle over warm braid. Top with almonds. **Yield:** 1 coffee cake.

Braided Almond Ring

(Pictured above)

An almond and lemon filling highlights this attractive yeast coffee cake that's perfect for breakfast, brunch or when guests drop by. It's worth the effort and has won me more than one Best of Show ribbon.
—Nancy Means, Moline, Illinois

3-1/2 to 4 cups all-purpose flour
  1/3 cup sugar
2-1/4 teaspoons quick-rise yeast
    1 tablespoon grated lemon peel
  1/2 teaspoon salt
  1/2 cup milk
  1/4 cup water
  1/4 cup butter *or* margarine, cubed
    1 egg
    1 egg yolk
ALMOND FILLING:
  1/3 cup almond paste
  1/3 cup finely chopped almonds
    1 egg white
    1 tablespoon grated lemon peel
EGG WASH:
    1 egg
    1 tablespoon water
GLAZE:
    2 tablespoons butter *or* margarine, softened
    2 cups confectioners' sugar
  1/2 teaspoon almond extract
  1/2 teaspoon vanilla extract
    2 to 3 tablespoons milk
  1/4 cup slivered almonds, toasted

Raspberry Streusel Coffee Cake

(Pictured on page 84)

One of my mother's friends used to bring this over at the holidays, and it never lasted long. With the tangy raspberry filling, tender cake and crunchy topping, it has become a favorite at our house. —Amy Mitchell
Sabetha, Kansas

3-1/2 cups unsweetened raspberries
    1 cup water
    2 tablespoons lemon juice
1-1/4 cups sugar
  1/3 cup cornstarch
BATTER:
    3 cups all-purpose flour
    1 cup sugar
    1 teaspoon baking powder
    1 teaspoon baking soda
    1 cup cold butter *or* margarine
    2 eggs, lightly beaten
    1 cup (8 ounces) sour cream
    1 teaspoon vanilla extract
TOPPING:
  1/2 cup all-purpose flour
  1/2 cup sugar
  1/4 cup butter *or* margarine, softened
  1/2 cup chopped pecans
GLAZE:
  1/2 cup confectioners' sugar
    2 teaspoons milk
  1/2 teaspoon vanilla extract

In a large saucepan, cook raspberries and water over medium heat for 5 minutes. Add lemon juice. Combine sugar and cornstarch; stir into fruit mixture. Bring to a boil; cook and stir for 2 minutes or until thickened. Cool.

In a large bowl, combine the flour, sugar, baking powder and baking soda. Cut in butter until mixture resembles coarse crumbs. Stir in eggs, sour cream and vanilla (batter will be stiff). Spread half into a greased 13-in. x 9-in. x 2-in. baking dish. Spread raspberry filling over batter; spoon remaining batter over filling. Combine topping ingredients; sprinkle over top. Bake at 350° for 40-45 minutes or until golden brown. Combine the glaze ingredients; drizzle over warm cake. **Yield:** 12-16 servings.

— ▆ ▆ ▆ —

Spiced Pumpkin Bread

This pretty quick bread is the only thing my kids will eat when they don't feel good. It's very comforting.
—Tammy Neubauer, Ida Grove, Iowa

3-1/2 **cups all-purpose flour**
　　3 **cups sugar**
　　2 **teaspoons baking soda**
　　2 **teaspoons salt**
　　2 **teaspoons ground allspice**
　　1 **teaspoon baking powder**
　　1 **teaspoon ground nutmeg**
　　1 **teaspoon ground cinnamon**
　1/2 **teaspoon ground cloves**
　　4 **eggs**
　　1 **can (15 ounces) solid-pack pumpkin**
　3/4 **cup vegetable oil**
　2/3 **cup water**

In a large bowl, combine the dry ingredients. In another bowl, combine the eggs, pumpkin, oil and water; mix well. Stir into dry ingredients just until moistened. Pour into three greased 8-in. x 4-in. x 2-in. loaf pans.

Bake at 350° for 50-60 minutes or until a toothpick inserted near the center comes out clean. Cool for 10 minutes before removing from pans to wire racks to cool completely. **Yield:** 3 loaves.

— ▆ ▆ ▆ —

Christmas Doughnuts

(Pictured at right)

Making these doughnuts has long been a custom in my French Canadian family. I remember helping with these tender treats as a child and eating the "holes" with my sister and brother. I loved their hint of lemon flavor! Carrying on the tradition, my husband, children
and I have made these yummy doughnuts every Christmas for many years. —Michelle Vander Byl
Portland, Ontario

　　6 **eggs**
　　2 **cups sugar**
　1/4 **cup vegetable oil**
　　1 **teaspoon lemon extract**
7-1/2 **cups all-purpose flour**
　　6 **teaspoons baking powder**
　　2 **teaspoons salt**
　　1 **teaspoon ground nutmeg**
　　1 **cup milk**
Oil for deep-fat frying
Confectioners' sugar, optional

In a mixing bowl, beat the eggs, sugar and oil. Add lemon extract; mix well. Combine the flour, baking powder, salt and nutmeg; stir into egg mixture alternately with milk. Cover and refrigerate overnight.

Divide dough in half. Roll out one portion to 1/4-in. thickness. Cut with a floured 1-1/2-in. round cookie cutter. Repeat with remaining dough. In an electric skillet or deep-fryer, heat oil to 375°. Fry doughnuts for about 4 minutes or until golden brown, turning once with a slotted spoon. Drain on paper towels. Dust with confectioners' sugar if desired. **Yield:** about 8 dozen.

Lemon Curd Coffee Cake

(Pictured below)

I tried this coffee cake recipe for my son's birthday a couple years ago and fell in love with the tart lemon filling. The powdered sugar glaze and coconut in the topping make it a pretty addition to a brunch or afternoon get-together. —Anne Wickman Endicott, New York

  1/2 **cup all-purpose flour**
  1/3 **cup sugar**
    3 **tablespoons cold butter** *or* **margarine**
  1/2 **cup flaked coconut**
BATTER:
2-1/4 **cups all-purpose flour**
  1/2 **teaspoon salt**
  1/2 **teaspoon baking powder**
  1/2 **teaspoon baking soda**
  3/4 **cup cold butter** *or* **margarine**
  2/3 **cup vanilla yogurt**
    1 **tablespoon lemon juice**
    2 **teaspoons grated lemon peel**
    1 **egg**
    1 **egg yolk**
  1/2 **cup lemon curd**

GLAZE:
  1/2 **cup confectioners' sugar**
    1 **teaspoon water**
    1 **teaspoon lemon juice**

In a bowl, combine flour and sugar. Cut in butter until mixture resembles coarse crumbs. Stir in coconut; set aside.

For batter, combine flour, salt, baking powder and baking soda in a bowl. Cut in butter until mixture resembles coarse crumbs. Combine yogurt, lemon juice, peel, egg and yolk; stir into crumb mixture just until moistened (batter will be stiff).

Spread 2 cups batter in a greased 9-in. springform pan; sprinkle with 3/4 cup of coconut mixture. Drop 1/2 teaspoonfuls of lemon curd over the top to within 1/2 in. of edge. Carefully spoon remaining batter over lemon curd; sprinkle with remaining coconut mixture.

Place pan on a baking sheet. Bake at 350° for 55-60 minutes or until a toothpick comes out clean. Cool for 10 minutes; remove sides of pan. Combine the glaze ingredients; drizzle over warm cake. **Yield:** 10-12 servings.

Coconut Chip Coffee Cake

I combined coconut, chocolate chips and walnuts to make the yummy filling in this coffee cake. My husband and two of my sons don't like coconut, but they still enjoy this recipe. —Char Fricke, St. Charles, Illinois

  1/2 **cup butter** *or* **margarine, softened**
    1 **cup sugar**
    2 **eggs**
    1 **teaspoon vanilla extract**
    2 **cups all-purpose flour**
    1 **teaspoon baking powder**
    1 **teaspoon baking soda**
  1/4 **teaspoon salt**
    1 **cup (8 ounces) sour cream**
FILLING/TOPPING:
  1/2 **cup sugar**
  1/2 **cup flaked coconut**
  1/2 **cup semisweet chocolate chips**
  1/2 **cup chopped walnuts**

In a mixing bowl, cream butter and sugar. Add the eggs, one at a time, beating well after each addition. Beat in vanilla. Combine the flour, baking powder, baking soda and salt; add to the creamed mixture alternately with sour cream.

Spoon half of the batter into a greased 10-in. tube pan. Combine the filling ingredients; sprinkle half over the batter. Repeat layers. Bake at 350° for 45-50 minutes or until a toothpick inserted near the center comes out clean. Cool for 10 minutes

before removing from pan to a wire rack. **Yield:** 12-16 servings.

— 🍴 🍴 🍴 —

Hazelnut Chip Scones

When I made a friend's scone recipe, I didn't have enough milk, so I substituted hazelnut-flavored nondairy creamer and added chocolate chips. Everyone loved them! —Elisa Lochridge, Aloha, Oregon

    4 cups all-purpose flour
    3 tablespoons sugar
    4 teaspoons baking powder
1/2 teaspoon salt
1/2 teaspoon cream of tartar
3/4 cup cold butter (no substitutes)
    1 egg, *separated*
1-1/2 cups refrigerated hazelnut nondairy
        creamer *or* half-and-half cream
1-1/2 cups semisweet chocolate chips
Additional sugar
SPICED BUTTER:
1/2 cup butter, softened
    3 tablespoons brown sugar
1/4 teaspoon ground cinnamon
1/4 teaspoon ground allspice
1/8 teaspoon ground nutmeg

In a bowl, combine the first five ingredients; cut in butter until crumbly. In a bowl, whisk egg yolk and creamer; add to dry ingredients just until moistened. Stir in the chocolate chips. Turn onto a floured surface; knead 10 times. Divide dough in half. Pat each portion into a 7-in. circle; cut into eight wedges. Separate wedges and place on greased baking sheets.

Beat egg white; brush over dough. Sprinkle with additional sugar. Bake at 425° for 15-18 minutes or until golden brown. Meanwhile, in a small mixing bowl, combine the spiced butter ingredients; beat until smooth. Serve with warm scones. **Yield:** 16 scones.

— 🍴 🍴 🍴 —

Caraway Rye Rolls

(Pictured above right)

The caraway and rye flavors really come through in these tender yeast rolls. A crispy golden crust and muffin shape make them an attractive addition to any meal. —Dot Christiansen, Bettendorf, Iowa

    2 packages (1/4 ounce *each*) active dry yeast
1/2 cup warm water (110° to 115°)
    2 cups warm small-curd cottage cheese
        (110° to 115°)

1/2 cup sugar
    2 eggs, beaten
    2 tablespoons caraway seeds
    2 teaspoons salt
1/2 teaspoon baking soda
    1 cup rye flour
    3 to 4 cups all-purpose flour

In a large mixing bowl, dissolve yeast in warm water. Add the cottage cheese, sugar, eggs, caraway seeds, salt, baking soda, rye flour and 1 cup all-purpose flour; mix well. Gradually stir in enough remaining all-purpose flour to form a sticky batter (do not knead). Cover and let rise in a warm place until doubled, about 1 hour.

Stir dough down. Turn onto a lightly floured surface; divide into 24 pieces. Place in well-greased muffin cups. Cover and let rise until doubled, about 35 minutes. Bake at 350° for 18-20 minutes or until golden brown. Cool for 1 minute before removing from pans to wire racks. **Yield:** 2 dozen.

🥄 *Flour Power*

All-purpose flour and bread flour have more gluten than whole wheat or rye flour. That's why most whole wheat or rye bread recipes contain a portion of all-purpose or bread flour—so they do not become too heavy and dense.

Cherry Cheese Loaves

(Pictured above)

This has become my "trademark" dessert. I'm asked to take it everywhere I go! Diagonal cuts in the dough give this coffee cake a pretty look without the extra work of braiding it.
—Carolyn Gregory
Hendersonville, Tennessee

   2 packages (1/4 ounce *each*) active dry
       yeast
1/2 cup warm water (110° to 115°)
   1 cup (8 ounces) sour cream
1/2 cup butter *or* margarine, cubed
1/2 cup sugar
   2 eggs
   4 cups all-purpose flour
FILLING:
   2 packages (one 8 ounces, one 3 ounces)
       cream cheese, softened
1/2 cup sugar
   1 egg
   1 teaspoon almond extract
   1 can (21 ounces) cherry pie filling
GLAZE:
   2 cups confectioners' sugar
1/4 cup milk
   1 teaspoon almond extract

In a large mixing bowl, dissolve yeast in warm water. In a saucepan, heat sour cream and butter to 110°-115°. Add to yeast mixture. Add sugar and eggs; mix well. Gradually add flour; mix well. Do not knead. Cover and refrigerate overnight.

In a small mixing bowl, beat cream cheese, sugar, egg and extract until smooth; set aside. Turn dough onto a lightly floured surface; divide into four portions. Roll each into a 12-in. x 8-in. rectangle. Spread a fourth of the cream cheese mixture down the center of each rectangle. Spoon a fourth of the pie filling over cream cheese. Fold lengthwise into thirds; pinch side seam and ends to seal. Place seam side down on greased baking sheets.

With a sharp scissors, make several 1-in. diagonal cuts near the center of loaves. Cover and let rise in a warm place until doubled, about 1 hour. Bake at 375° for 20-25 minutes or until lightly browned. Combine glaze ingredients; drizzle over warm loaves. Cool on wire racks. Refrigerate leftovers. **Yield:** 4 loaves.

Maple Butter Twists

(Pictured on page 85)

My stepmother passed on the recipe for this delicious yeast coffee cake that's shaped into pretty rings. When I make it for friends, they always ask for seconds.
—June Gilliland, Hope, Indiana

3-1/4 to 3-1/2 cups all-purpose flour
       3 tablespoons sugar
1-1/2 teaspoons salt
       1 package (1/4 ounce) active dry yeast
   3/4 cup milk
   1/4 cup butter *or* margarine
       2 eggs
FILLING:
   1/3 cup packed brown sugar
   1/4 cup sugar
       3 tablespoons butter *or* margarine, softened
       3 tablespoons maple syrup
4-1/2 teaspoons all-purpose flour
   3/4 teaspoon ground cinnamon
   3/4 teaspoon maple flavoring
   1/3 cup chopped walnuts
GLAZE:
   1/2 cup confectioners' sugar
   1/4 teaspoon maple flavoring
       2 to 3 teaspoons milk

In a mixing bowl, combine 1-1/2 cups flour, sugar, salt and yeast. In a saucepan, heat milk and butter to 120°-130°. Add to dry ingredients; beat just until moistened. Add eggs; beat on medium for 2 minutes. Stir in enough remaining flour to form a firm dough. Turn onto a floured surface; knead until smooth and elastic, about 5-7 minutes. Place in a greased bowl, turning once to grease top. Cover and let rise in a warm place until doubled, about 70 minutes.

In a small mixing bowl, combine the first seven filling ingredients; beat for 2 minutes. Punch dough down; turn onto a lightly floured surface. Divide in half; roll each into a 16-in. x 8-in. rectangle. Spread filling to within 1/2 in. of edges. Sprinkle with nuts. Roll up jelly-roll style, starting with a long side.

With a sharp knife, cut each roll in half lengthwise. Open halves so cut side is up; gently twist ropes together. Transfer to two greased 9-in. round baking pans. Coil into a circle. Tuck ends under; pinch to seal. Cover and let rise in a warm place until doubled, about 45 minutes. Bake at 350° for 25-30 minutes or until golden brown. Cool for 10 minutes; remove from pans to wire racks. Combine glaze ingredients; drizzle over warm cakes. **Yield:** 2 coffee cakes.

— 🥄 🥄 🥄 —

Apple Pear Coffee Cake

A friend gave me this recipe to make for a breakfast I was hosting. The pan was empty before the breakfast was over! It's one of my most-requested recipes, probably because it's a bit different.
—*Joanne Hoschette, Paxton, Massachusetts*

  1/2 **cup butter** *or* **margarine, softened**
    1 **cup sugar**
    2 **eggs**
    1 **teaspoon vanilla extract**
    2 **cups all-purpose flour**
    3 **teaspoons baking powder**
    1 **teaspoon baking soda**
  1/2 **teaspoon salt**
    1 **cup (8 ounces) sour cream**
1-1/4 **cups chopped peeled apples**
  1/2 **cup chopped peeled pear**
TOPPING:
    1 **cup packed brown sugar**
    1 **teaspoon ground cinnamon**
    2 **tablespoons cold butter** *or* **margarine**
  1/2 **cup chopped pecans**

In a large mixing bowl, cream butter and sugar. Add eggs and vanilla; beat well. Combine the flour, baking powder, baking soda and salt; add to creamed mixture alternately with sour cream. Fold in apples and pear. Pour into a greased 13-in. x 9-in. x 2-in. baking dish.

In a small bowl, combine brown sugar and cinnamon. Cut in butter until the mixture resembles coarse crumbs. Stir in pecans. Sprinkle over batter. Bake at 350° for 35-40 minutes or until a toothpick inserted near the center comes out clean. Cool on a wire rack. **Yield:** 12-15 servings.

Pumpkin Cheese Coffee Cake

(Pictured below)

This is one of my favorite recipes, especially in autumn. It is much easier to make than a traditional pumpkin roll—and it's always a crowd-pleaser!
—*Carlene Jessop, Hildale, Utah*

    2 **cups sugar**
    2 **eggs**
1-1/4 **cups canned pumpkin**
  1/4 **cup vegetable oil**
  1/2 **teaspoon vanilla extract**
2-1/4 **cups all-purpose flour**
    2 **teaspoons ground cinnamon**
    1 **teaspoon baking soda**
  1/2 **teaspoon salt**
FILLING:
    1 **package (8 ounces) cream cheese, softened**
    1 **egg**
    1 **tablespoon sugar**
TOPPING:
  3/4 **cup flaked coconut**
  1/2 **cup chopped pecans**
  1/4 **cup packed brown sugar**
  1/4 **teaspoon ground cinnamon**

In a large mixing bowl, beat sugar, eggs, pumpkin, oil and vanilla. Combine the flour, cinnamon, baking soda and salt; add to egg mixture and mix well. Pour into a greased 13-in. x 9-in. x 2-in. baking dish.

In a small mixing bowl, beat cream cheese, egg and sugar until smooth. Drop tablespoonfuls over batter; cut through batter with a knife to swirl. Combine topping ingredients; sprinkle over top. Bake at 350° for 35-40 minutes or until a toothpick comes out clean. Cool on a wire rack. **Yield:** 12-15 servings.

Walnut Orange Coffee Cake

(Pictured below)

My sister gave me this recipe about 40 years ago, and I still make it often. Whenever I take it to a gathering, there's rarely a crumb left—everyone loves the delightful orange flavor. —Janice Satanek
Hermitage, Pennsylvania

      1 cup quick-cooking oats
1-1/2 cups orange juice
  1/2 cup butter *or* margarine
1-1/2 cups sugar
  1/2 cup packed brown sugar
      2 eggs
      1 teaspoon vanilla extract
1-3/4 cups all-purpose flour
      1 teaspoon baking powder
      1 teaspoon baking soda
  1/2 teaspoon salt
  1/4 teaspoon ground cinnamon
  1/2 cup chopped walnuts
      1 tablespoon grated orange peel
TOPPING:
1-1/2 cups packed brown sugar
  3/4 cup butter *or* margarine, cubed
      3 tablespoons grated orange peel
      3 tablespoons orange juice
      3 cups flaked coconut
1-1/2 cups chopped walnuts

In a small bowl, stir oats and orange juice until softened; set aside. In a mixing bowl, cream butter and sugars; beat in eggs and vanilla until well combined. Combine the flour, baking powder, baking soda, salt and cinnamon; add to the creamed mixture alternately with oat mixture. Stir in walnuts and orange peel. Pour into a greased 13-in. x 9-in. x 2-in. baking dish. Bake at 350° for 25-30 minutes or until a toothpick inserted near the center comes out clean.

In a small saucepan, combine brown sugar, butter, orange peel and juice. Bring to a boil; reduce heat. Cook for 1 minute. Remove from the heat; stir in coconut and walnuts. Gently spread over warm cake. Broil 4 in. from the heat for 2 minutes or until the topping is bubbly. **Yield:** 12-15 servings.

— 🍵 🍵 🍵 —

Four-Herb Bread

Marjoram, thyme, basil and chives season this moist loaf. A friend gave me this recipe. The aroma while it's baking will make you think of a stuffed turkey roasting in the oven. —Sue Murphy
Greenwood, Michigan

✓ Uses less fat, sugar or salt. Includes Nutritional Analysis and Diabetic Exchanges.

1-1/4 cups water (70° to 80°)
      2 tablespoons butter *or* stick margarine, softened
      3 cups bread flour
      2 tablespoons nonfat dry milk powder
      2 tablespoons sugar
      1 tablespoon minced chives
      1 tablespoon minced fresh marjoram *or* 1 teaspoon dried marjoram
      1 tablespoon minced fresh thyme *or* 1 teaspoon dried thyme
      2 teaspoons minced fresh basil *or* 1/2 teaspoon dried basil
      1 teaspoon salt
      3 teaspoons active dry yeast

In bread machine pan, place all ingredients in order suggested by manufacturer. Select basic bread setting. Choose crust color and loaf size if available. Bake according to bread machine directions (check dough after 5 minutes of mixing; add 1 to 2 tablespoons of water or flour if needed). **Yield:** 1 loaf (1-1/2 pounds, 16 slices).

Nutritional Analysis: One slice equals 98 calories, 1 g fat (1 g saturated fat), 4 mg cholesterol, 165 mg sodium, 19 g carbohydrate, 1 g fiber, 4 g protein. **Diabetic Exchange:** 1 starch.

— 🍵 🍵 🍵 —

Apricot Coconut Coffee Cake

One of the senior members of our church brought this fruity treat to a Saturday morning wedding shower, and it was a big hit. I've made it several times since then and often get requests for the recipe. —Rita Hatfield
Cisco, Illinois

1 package (8 ounces) cream cheese,
  softened
1/2 cup butter *or* margarine, softened
1-1/4 cups sugar
  2 eggs
1/4 cup milk
  1 teaspoon vanilla extract
  2 cups all-purpose flour
  1 teaspoon baking powder
1/2 teaspoon baking soda
1/4 teaspoon salt
  1 can (12 ounces) apricot filling
TOPPING:
1/3 cup butter *or* margarine, softened
2/3 cup packed brown sugar
  1 teaspoon ground cinnamon
  2 cups flaked coconut

In a large mixing bowl, beat the cream cheese, butter and sugar until fluffy. Add eggs, one at a time, beating well after each addition. Add milk and vanilla; mix well. Combine the flour, baking powder, baking soda and salt; add to creamed mixture. Beat just until moistened.

Spread half of the batter into a greased 13-in. x 9-in. x 2-in. baking dish. Carefully spread apricot filling over batter; spread remaining batter over the top. Bake at 350° for 35-40 minutes or until golden brown.

In a mixing bowl, cream butter, brown sugar and cinnamon. Stir in coconut. Spoon over the cake. Broil 4 in. from the heat for 1-2 minutes or until golden brown. Cool on a wire rack. **Yield:** 12-15 servings.

— 🍴 🍴 🍴 —

Cinnamon-Swirl Coffee Ring

(Pictured above right)

I first sampled this coffee cake at an inn that serves a marvelous breakfast for its guests. It has a pretty cinnamon swirl and a hint of cardamom flavor. I like to make it for my Thursday morning quilt group.
—Stell Pierce, Franklin, Virginia

  3 cups all-purpose flour
  2 cups sugar
  1 teaspoon baking powder
  1 teaspoon baking soda
1/2 teaspoon salt
1/2 teaspoon ground cardamom
  1 package (8 ounces) cream cheese,
    softened
  3 eggs
  1 cup milk
1/2 cup butter *or* margarine, melted
  1 teaspoon vanilla extract
FILLING:
1/2 cup small-curd cottage cheese
2/3 cup sugar
  2 teaspoons ground cinnamon
Confectioners' sugar

In a large mixing bowl, combine the first six ingredients. In another mixing bowl, beat cream cheese until smooth. Beat in the eggs, milk, butter and vanilla. Gradually add to dry ingredients, beating until combined. For filling, combine cottage cheese, sugar and cinnamon in a small mixing bowl. Beat on medium speed for 2 minutes.

Spoon half of the batter into a greased 10-in. fluted tube pan; top with filling and remaining batter. Bake at 350° for 55-65 minutes or until a toothpick inserted near the center comes out clean. Cool for 10 minutes before removing from pan to a wire rack. Dust with confectioners' sugar if desired. **Yield:** 12-14 servings.

🥄 *Coffee Cake Clue*

Do you have a problem with fruit sinking to the bottom of your coffee cake? Try tossing the fruit with a small amount of flour called for in the recipe, then mixing it into the batter.

1 teaspoon vanilla extract

TOPPING:
3/4 cup all-purpose flour
1/2 cup sugar
1/2 cup cold butter *or* margarine

In a large bowl, combine the first four ingredients. Combine the egg, orange juice, butter and vanilla; stir into dry ingredients until well combined. Fold in the cranberries and orange peel. Pour into a greased 9-in. springform pan.

In a small mixing bowl, beat cream cheese and sugar until smooth. Add egg and vanilla; mix well. Spread over batter. Combine the flour and sugar; cut in butter until the mixture resembles coarse crumbs. Sprinkle over top.

Place pan on a baking sheet. Bake at 350° for 70-75 minutes or until golden brown. Cool on a wire rack for 15 minutes before removing sides of pan. **Yield:** 12 servings.

—————— 🥄 🥄 🥄 ——————

Macadamia Carrot Muffins

These muffins make a great snack for kids because they have so many healthy ingredients. I also turn to this recipe when I have to furnish muffins for church gatherings. —Shirley James
Buffalo Center, Iowa

1-1/2 cups All-Bran cereal
1 cup boiling water
3/4 cup packed brown sugar
1/4 cup molasses
1/2 cup vegetable oil
3 eggs
2 cups buttermilk
2-1/4 cups all-purpose flour
3-1/2 teaspoons baking soda
1 teaspoon salt
1-1/2 cups bran flakes cereal
1-1/3 cups shredded carrots
1 package (8 ounces) chopped dates
1 cup chopped macadamia nuts

In a bowl, combine All-Bran and boiling water; let stand for 10 minutes. In a mixing bowl, beat the brown sugar, molasses and oil. Add eggs, one at a time, beating well after each addition. Add buttermilk and soaked All-Bran; mix well. Combine the flour, baking soda and salt; add to creamed mixture just until combined. Stir in the bran flakes, carrots, dates and nuts.

Fill greased muffin cups two-thirds full. Bake at 400° for 15-18 minutes or until a toothpick comes out clean. Cool for 5 minutes before removing from pans to wire racks to cool completely. **Yield:** about 3 dozen.

Creamy Cranberry Coffee Cake

(Pictured above)

Chopped cranberries and orange peel give this coffee cake bursts of tart flavor, but a cream cheese layer on top sweetens it nicely. It's so lovely, you'll want to serve it when company comes. —Nancy Roper
Etobicoke, Ontario

2 cups all-purpose flour
1 cup sugar
1-1/2 teaspoons baking powder
1/2 teaspoon baking soda
1 egg
3/4 cup orange juice
1/4 cup butter *or* margarine, melted
1 teaspoon vanilla extract
2 cups coarsely chopped fresh *or* frozen cranberries
1 tablespoon grated orange peel

CREAM CHEESE LAYER:
1 package (8 ounces) cream cheese, softened
1/3 cup sugar
1 egg

Blueberry Almond Coffee Cake

(Pictured on page 85)

I've received many rave reviews for this tender coffee cake that's chock-full of blueberries and sliced almonds. Since it's not overly sweet, it's just the thing for breakfast or a light dessert. —Brenda Carr
Houston, Texas

  1 cup all-purpose flour
1/2 cup sugar
3/4 teaspoon baking powder
1/2 teaspoon salt
1/4 teaspoon baking soda
  1 egg
2/3 cup buttermilk
  2 tablespoons butter *or* margarine, melted
  1 teaspoon vanilla extract
1/4 teaspoon almond extract
  1 cup fresh *or* frozen blueberries,* *divided*
1/2 cup sliced almonds
  1 tablespoon brown sugar
1/4 teaspoon ground cinnamon

In a large bowl, combine the flour, sugar, baking powder, salt and baking soda. In another bowl, whisk the egg, buttermilk, butter and extracts until blended; stir into dry ingredients just until moistened. Stir in 2/3 cup blueberries. Pour into a greased 8-in. square baking dish. Top with remaining blueberries.

Combine the almonds, brown sugar and cinnamon; sprinkle over the top. Bake at 350° for 25-30 minutes or until a toothpick inserted near the center comes out clean. Cool on a wire rack. **Yield:** 9 servings.

*Editor's Note: If using frozen blueberries, do not thaw before adding to batter.

— 🛒 🛒 🛒 —

Easter Egg Bread

(Pictured at right)

I've made this Easter treat for 20 years! Colored hard-cooked eggs baked in the dough give this sweet bread such a festive look. Leave them out and it can be enjoyed anytime of year. My husband especially enjoys this bread with baked ham. —Heather Durante
Wellsburg, West Virginia

    6 to 6-1/2 cups all-purpose flour
1/2 cup sugar
    2 packages (1/4 ounce *each*) active dry yeast
    1 to 2 teaspoons ground cardamom
    1 teaspoon salt
1-1/2 cups milk
    6 tablespoons butter *or* margarine
    4 eggs
    3 to 6 hard-cooked eggs
Vegetable oil
    2 tablespoons cold water

In a large mixing bowl, combine 2 cups flour, sugar, yeast, cardamom and salt. In a saucepan, heat milk and butter to 120°-130°. Add to dry ingredients; beat just until moistened. Add 3 eggs; beat until smooth. Stir in enough remaining flour to form a soft dough. Turn onto a floured surface; knead until smooth and elastic, about 6-8 minutes. Place in a greased bowl, turning once to grease top. Cover and let rise in a warm place until doubled, about 45 minutes.

Dye hard-cooked eggs; lightly rub with oil. Punch dough down. Turn onto a lightly floured surface; divide dough into thirds. Shape each portion into a 24-in. rope. Place ropes on a greased baking sheet and braid; bring ends together to form a ring. Pinch ends to seal. Gently separate braided ropes and tuck dyed eggs into openings. Cover and let rise until doubled, about 20 minutes.

Beat water and remaining egg; gently brush over dough. Bake at 375° for 28-32 minutes or until golden brown. Remove from pan to a wire rack to cool. Refrigerate leftovers. **Yield:** 1 loaf.

Cherry Chip Scones

(Pictured below)

These buttery scones, dotted with dried cherries and vanilla chips, are so sweet and flaky that I even serve them for dessert. —Pamela Brooks
South Berwick, Maine

    3 cups all-purpose flour
    1/2 cup sugar
2-1/2 teaspoons baking powder
    1/2 teaspoon baking soda
    6 tablespoons cold butter (no substitutes)
    1 cup (8 ounces) vanilla yogurt
    1/4 cup plus 2 tablespoons milk, *divided*
1-1/3 cups dried cherries
    2/3 cup vanilla *or* white chips

In a large bowl, combine the flour, sugar, baking powder and baking soda. Cut in butter until the mixture resembles coarse crumbs. Combine yogurt and 1/4 cup milk; stir into crumb mixture just until moistened. Knead in the cherries and chips.

On a greased baking sheet, pat the dough into a 9-in. circle. Cut into eight wedges; separate wedges. Brush with the remaining milk. Bake at 400° for 20-25 minutes or until golden brown. Serve warm. **Yield:** 8 servings.

Honey Banana Muffins

Ground nutmeg enhances these delicious banana muffins. They're moist and filling. The best thing is they're healthy but don't taste it. —Gitel Alter
Brooklyn, New York

✓ Uses less fat, sugar or salt. Includes Nutritional Analysis and Diabetic Exchanges.

    1 cup whole wheat flour
    1/2 cup all-purpose flour
    1 teaspoon baking soda
    1/2 to 1 teaspoon ground nutmeg
    1/4 teaspoon salt
    2 eggs, lightly beaten
    1 cup mashed ripe banana (1 to 2 medium)
    1/2 cup unsweetened applesauce
    6 tablespoons honey
    1/2 cup golden raisins

In a large bowl, combine the first five ingredients. Combine the eggs, banana, applesauce and honey; stir into dry ingredients just until moistened. Fold in the raisins.

Coat muffin cups with nonstick cooking spray; fill two-thirds full with batter. Bake at 375° for 15-18 minutes or until a toothpick comes out clean. Cool for 5 minutes before removing from pans to wire racks. **Yield:** 14 muffins.

Nutritional Analysis: One muffin equals 119 calories, 1 g fat (trace saturated fat), 30 mg cholesterol, 142 mg sodium, 27 g carbohydrate, 2 g fiber, 3 g protein. **Diabetic Exchanges:** 1 starch, 1/2 fruit.

— 🥤 🥤 🥤 —

Crispy French Toast

(Pictured on page 84)

I lighten up my golden French toast with egg substitute and skim milk, then flavor it with orange juice, vanilla and a dash of nutmeg. The cornflake coating adds a fun crunch. —Flo Burtnett, Gage, Oklahoma

✓ Uses less fat, sugar or salt. Includes Nutritional Analysis and Diabetic Exchanges.

    1/2 cup egg substitute
    1/2 cup fat-free milk
    1/4 cup orange juice
    1 teaspoon vanilla extract
Dash ground nutmeg
    12 slices day-old French bread (3/4 inch thick)
1-1/2 cups crushed cornflakes

In a shallow dish, combine the egg substitute, milk, orange juice, vanilla and nutmeg. Add bread;

soak for 5 minutes, turning once. Coat both sides of each slice with cornflake crumbs. Place in a 15-in. x 10-in. x 1-in. baking pan coated with nonstick cooking spray. Bake at 425° for 10 minutes; turn. Bake 5-8 minutes longer or until golden brown. **Yield:** 12 slices.

Nutritional Analysis: One slice equals 147 calories, 1 g fat (trace saturated fat), trace cholesterol, 359 mg sodium, 28 g carbohydrate, 1 g fiber, 5 g protein. **Diabetic Exchange:** 2 starch.

— 📖 📖 📖 —

Blueberry Banana Bread

I combine blueberries and bananas in these tender, golden loaves. Whether you enjoy a slice as a snack or for breakfast, this bread is so flavorful, you won't need butter. —Sandy Flick, Toledo, Ohio

    2 cups all-purpose flour
    1 teaspoon baking soda
  1/2 teaspoon salt
  1/2 cup shortening
    1 cup sugar
    2 eggs
    2 teaspoons vanilla extract
    2 medium ripe bananas, mashed
    1 cup fresh blueberries

In a bowl, combine the flour, baking soda and salt. In a large mixing bowl, cream the shortening and sugar. Add eggs and vanilla; mix well. Beat in bananas. Gradually add the dry ingredients, beating just until combined. Fold in blueberries.

Pour into three greased 5-3/4-in. x 3-in. x 2-in. loaf pans. Bake at 350° for 30-35 minutes or until a toothpick inserted near the center comes out clean. Cool for 10 minutes before removing from pans to wire racks. **Yield:** 3 mini loaves.

— 📖 📖 📖 —

Whole Wheat Honey Rolls

(Pictured above right)

My husband loves whole wheat bread, so I have adapted most of my recipes to accommodate his taste buds. The creamy honey butter adds a little sweetness to these airy golden brown yeast rolls. —Linda Gunn Reynolds, Georgia

    2 packages (1/4 ounce *each*) active dry
      yeast
    2 cups warm buttermilk (110° to 115°)*
  1/2 cup butter (no substitutes), melted

  1/3 cup honey
    3 cups whole wheat flour
    1 teaspoon salt
    1 teaspoon baking soda
1-1/2 to 2-1/2 cups all-purpose flour
Additional melted butter
HONEY BUTTER:
    1 cup butter, softened
  1/2 cup honey

In a mixing bowl, dissolve yeast in warm buttermilk. Add the butter, honey, whole wheat flour, salt and baking soda. Beat until smooth. Stir in enough all-purpose flour to form a soft dough. Turn onto a floured surface; knead until smooth and elastic, about 6-8 minutes. Place in a greased bowl, turning once to grease top. Cover and let rise in a warm place until doubled, about 1 hour.

Punch dough down. Turn onto a lightly floured surface; divide into seven portions. Divide each portion into six pieces; shape each into a ball. Place 2 in. apart on greased baking sheets. Cover and let rise in a warm place until doubled, about 30 minutes.

Brush with melted butter. Bake at 400° for 12-16 minutes or until golden brown. Remove to wire racks to cool. In a small mixing bowl, beat butter and honey until smooth; serve with rolls. **Yield:** 3-1/2 dozen.

*Editor's Note: Warmed buttermilk will appear curdled.

Melt the remaining butter. In a bowl, whisk the eggs, milk, sour cream and melted butter. Make a well in dry ingredients; stir in egg mixture just until moistened. Spread into a greased 10-in. springform pan. Spoon onion mixture over the dough. Place pan on a baking sheet. Bake at 350° for 35-40 minutes or until a toothpick inserted near the center comes out clean. Serve warm. **Yield:** 10-12 servings.

Apple Cheddar Scones

(Pictured on page 84)

I often serve these golden scones for breakfast or brunch. Add a scoop of ice cream and they make a great dessert. —Jeanne Alexander
Qualicum Beach, British Columbia

1-3/4 cups all-purpose flour
    2 tablespoons sugar
1-1/2 teaspoons baking powder
    1/2 teaspoon salt
    1/4 teaspoon baking soda
    1/3 cup cold butter *or* margarine
    1 cup buttermilk
    1 cup (4 ounces) shredded cheddar cheese
    1 cup diced peeled apples

In a bowl, combine the first five ingredients. Cut in butter until mixture resembles coarse crumbs. Stir in buttermilk just until moistened. Gently fold in the cheese and apples. Turn onto a floured surface; knead 10 times.

Pat into a 9-in. circle. Cut into eight wedges. Separate wedges and place on a greased baking sheet. Bake at 450° for 12-15 minutes or until golden brown. **Yield:** 8 scones.

Amish Onion Cake

(Pictured above)

This rich, moist bread with an onion-poppy seed topping is a wonderful break from your everyday bread routine. You can serve it with any meat, and it's a nice accompaniment to soup or salad. I've made it many times and have often been asked to share the recipe.
—Mitzi Sentiff, Alexandria, Virginia

    3 to 4 medium onions, chopped
    2 cups cold butter *or* margarine, *divided*
    1 tablespoon poppy seeds
1-1/2 teaspoons salt
1-1/2 teaspoons paprika
    1 teaspoon coarsely ground pepper
    4 cups all-purpose flour
    1/2 cup cornstarch
    1 tablespoon baking powder
    1 tablespoon sugar
    1 tablespoon brown sugar
    5 eggs
    3/4 cup milk
    3/4 cup sour cream

In a large skillet, cook onions in 1/2 cup butter over low heat for 10 minutes. Stir in the poppy seeds, salt, paprika and pepper; cook until golden brown, stirring occasionally. Remove from the heat; set aside. In a bowl, combine the flour, cornstarch, baking powder and sugars. Cut in 1-1/4 cups butter until mixture resembles coarse crumbs.

Cardamom Cinnamon Knots

Crushed cardamom seeds and cinnamon season these yummy yeast rolls. My sister and I translated all the pinches and dashes in my mother's instructions for these rolls. After a couple of tries, we had a successful recipe. —Vivian Donner, Jackson, Michigan

    2 packages (1/4 ounce *each*) active dry yeast
    1 cup warm water (110° to 115°)
    1/2 teaspoon plus 2/3 cup sugar, *divided*
1-1/3 cups warm milk (110° to 115°)
    2/3 cup butter *or* margarine, cubed
    1/3 cup shortening

2 eggs, beaten
3/4 teaspoon salt
2 teaspoons cardamom seeds, crushed
8 to 8-1/2 cups all-purpose flour
1/4 cup ground cinnamon
ICING:
2 cups confectioners' sugar
5 tablespoons milk
1 tablespoon butter *or* margarine, melted
1/4 teaspoon vanilla extract

In a large mixing bowl, dissolve yeast in warm water. Add 1/2 teaspoon sugar; let stand for 5 minutes. Add the warm milk, butter, shortening, eggs, salt, cardamom, remaining sugar and 5 cups flour. Beat until smooth. Stir in enough remaining flour to form a soft dough. Turn onto a floured surface; knead until smooth and elastic, about 6-8 minutes. Place in a greased bowl, turning once to grease top. Cover and let rise in a warm place until doubled, about 1 hour.

Punch dough down. Turn onto a lightly floured surface; divide in half. Shape each portion into 18 balls. Roll each into an 8-in. rope; coat with cinnamon. Tie in a knot and tuck ends under. Place 2 in. apart on greased baking sheets. Cover and let rise in a warm place until doubled, about 30 minutes.

Bake at 375° for 15-20 minutes or until golden brown. Remove from pans to wire racks. Combine icing ingredients; drizzle over rolls. **Yield:** 3 dozen.

— 🥄 🥄 🥄 —

Pumpkin Date Bread

(Pictured at right)

Fall and Halloween are a time of harvest, and what better opportunity to combine two of the season's bounties—apples and pumpkin—to make this delightful quick bread? The brown sugar and nut topping gives it the finishing touch.
—Helen Phillips
Horseheads, New York

1 cup applesauce
1 cup canned pumpkin
2/3 cup vegetable oil
3 eggs
1/2 cup milk
1/3 cup molasses
1 teaspoon vanilla extract
3-2/3 cups all-purpose flour
2 cups sugar
2 teaspoons baking soda
2 teaspoons ground cinnamon
1 teaspoon ground nutmeg
1/2 teaspoon baking powder
1 cup chopped dates
1 cup chopped pecans
TOPPING:
1/4 cup packed brown sugar
1/4 cup chopped pecans
1/2 teaspoon ground cinnamon

In a large mixing bowl, combine the first seven ingredients; mix well. Combine the flour, sugar, baking soda, cinnamon, nutmeg and baking powder; gradually add to pumpkin mixture and mix well. Stir in dates and pecans. Pour into two greased 9-in. x 5-in. x 3-in. loaf pans.

Combine topping ingredients; sprinkle over batter. Bake at 350° for 55-65 minutes or until a toothpick comes out clean. Cool for 15 minutes before removing from pans to wire racks. **Yield:** 2 loaves.

✒ *Better Quick Breads*

Quick breads such as banana, zucchini and pumpkin taste and slice best when served a day after baking. Wrap the cooled bread in foil or plastic wrap; leave at room temperature overnight.

Pancakes Stack Up as Early-Morning Treats

YOU'LL FLIP over these four outstanding pancake recipes. While it's true that plain ol' griddle cakes are always good, these may set a new standard at your table. Each recipe has one or more special ingredients that makes the batter better!

Chocolate Chip Pancakes

(Pictured above)

This is a great breakfast for special days, but it mixes up so fast that it's perfect for busy mornings as well.
—LeeAnn Hansen, Kaysville, Utah

         2 cups all-purpose flour
     1/4 cup sugar
         2 tablespoons baking powder
         1 teaspoon salt
         2 eggs
 1-1/2 cups milk
     1/4 cup vegetable oil
     1/2 cup miniature chocolate chips
CINNAMON HONEY SYRUP:
         1 cup honey

     1/2 cup butter *or* margarine, cubed
     1 to 2 teaspoons ground cinnamon

In a bowl, combine the flour, sugar, baking powder and salt. Combine eggs, milk and oil; add to dry ingredients and mix well. Stir in chocolate chips. Pour the batter by 1/4 cupfuls onto a lightly greased hot griddle. Turn when bubbles form on top; cook until second side is golden brown. Keep warm.

Combine the syrup ingredients in a 2-cup microwave-safe bowl. Microwave, uncovered, on high until butter is melted and syrup is hot, stirring occasionally. Serve with pancakes. **Yield:** 6 servings.

— ▼ ▼ ▼ —

Ginger Pancakes

(Pictured at far right)

A sunny sauce nicely complements the ginger flavor in these pancakes. We often put a cube of cream cheese on top of the pancakes before pouring on the lemon sauce.
—Jenece Howard, Elko, Nevada

         2 cups biscuit/baking mix
 1-1/2 teaspoons ground ginger
         1 teaspoon ground cinnamon
     1/2 teaspoon ground cloves
         1 egg
 1-1/2 cups milk
     1/4 cup molasses
LEMON SYRUP:
     1/2 cup butter *or* margarine
         1 cup sugar
     1/4 cup water
         1 egg yolk, beaten
         3 tablespoons lemon juice

In a bowl, combine biscuit mix, ginger, cinnamon and cloves. In a small bowl, whisk egg, milk and molasses until blended; stir into dry ingredients just until moistened. Pour batter by 1/4 cupfuls onto a lightly greased hot griddle. Turn when bubbles form on top; cook until second side is golden brown. Keep warm.

For syrup, melt the butter in a small saucepan. Stir in the sugar, water, egg yolk and lemon juice. Bring to a boil over medium heat, stirring constantly. Remove from the heat. Serve warm with pancakes. **Yield:** 6 servings.

Banana Pancakes with Berries

(Pictured below right)

With strawberries, banana and a good buttermilk batter, this is my all-time favorite pancake recipe. I even serve these for dinner occasionally with some bacon or a slice of country ham. —*Katie Sloan*
Charlotte, North Carolina

2 cups sliced fresh strawberries
1/2 cup sugar
3 teaspoons vanilla extract
PANCAKES:
1 cup all-purpose flour
1 tablespoon sugar
1 teaspoon baking powder
1/2 teaspoon baking soda
1/2 teaspoon salt
1 egg
1 cup buttermilk
2 tablespoons vegetable oil
1 teaspoon vanilla extract
2 medium ripe bananas, cut into 1/4-inch slices
Whipped cream, optional

In a bowl, combine the strawberries, sugar and vanilla. Cover and refrigerate for 8 hours or overnight.

For pancakes, combine the flour, sugar, baking powder, baking soda and salt in a bowl. Combine the egg, buttermilk, oil and vanilla; stir into dry ingredients just until moistened.

Pour the batter by 1/4 cupfuls onto a lightly greased hot griddle; place 5-6 banana slices on each pancake. Turn when bubbles form on top; cook until second side is golden brown. Serve with strawberries and whipped cream if desired. **Yield:** 4 servings.

Zucchini Pancakes

(Pictured at right)

Flecks of zucchini give these savory, moist pancakes a pretty appearance. For a suppertime side dish, top them with spaghetti sauce and Parmesan cheese. —*Leann Meeds*
Klamath Falls, Oregon

1/2 cup all-purpose flour
1/2 cup grated Parmesan cheese
1/2 teaspoon dried oregano
Salt and pepper to taste
1-1/2 cups shredded zucchini
1 egg, beaten
2 tablespoons chopped onion
2 tablespoons mayonnaise
2 tablespoons butter *or* margarine
Sour cream, optional

In a bowl, combine the flour, Parmesan cheese, oregano, salt and pepper. Combine the zucchini, egg, onion and mayonnaise; stir into dry ingredients until well blended.

In a large skillet, melt butter. Drop zucchini mixture by cupfuls into skillet; press lightly to flatten. Fry until golden brown, about 2 minutes on each side. Drain on paper towels. Serve with sour cream if desired. **Yield:** 3 servings.

HOT OFF THE GRIDDLE. You'll enjoy the delightful difference in Zucchini Pancakes, Banana Pancakes with Berries and Ginger Pancakes (shown below, top to bottom).

Cookies & Bars

Take a peek inside this chapter—you'll find an appealing assortment of tasty morsels to tempt your family throughout the year!

— 🥄 🥄 🥄 —

TREATS ARE TOPS. Clockwise from upper left: Cranberry Crumb Bars (p. 104), Stained Glass Cutouts (p. 104), Butter Cookie Snowmen (p. 108), Giant Cherry Oatmeal Cookies (p. 105) and Apricot Pecan Bars (p. 109).

Chocolate Pecan Thumbprints
(Pictured below)

Every Christmas for over 30 years, I have rolled, cut, shaped and baked batches of cookies for family and friends. These melt-in-your-mouth morsels with a dollop of chocolate in the center are among my favorites.
—Jim Ries, Milwaukee, Wisconsin

> 1/2 **cup plus 1 tablespoon butter (no substitutes), softened, *divided***
> 1/4 **cup packed brown sugar**
> 1 **egg yolk**
> 1 **teaspoon vanilla extract**
> 1 **cup all-purpose flour**
> 1 **egg white, lightly beaten**
> 3/4 **cup finely chopped pecans**
> 3/4 **cup semisweet chocolate chips**

In a mixing bowl, cream 1/2 cup butter and brown sugar. Beat in egg yolk and vanilla. Gradually add flour; mix well. Cover and refrigerate for 2 hours or until easy to handle.

Roll dough into 1-in. balls. Dip in egg white, then coat with pecans. Place 2 in. apart on greased baking sheets. Using the end of a wooden spoon handle, make a 1/2-in. indentation in the center of each ball. Bake at 325° for 10 minutes. Press again into indentations with the spoon handle. Bake 10-15 minutes longer or until pecans are golden brown. Remove to wire racks to cool.

In a microwave-safe bowl, heat the chocolate chips and remaining butter until melted; stir until blended and smooth. Spoon into cooled cookies. **Yield:** about 1-1/2 dozen.

— 🍴 🍴 🍴 —

Cranberry Crumb Bars
(Pictured on page 102)

This family favorite features cream cheese and cranberry fillings, a tender crust and a nutty crunch.
—Charlene Baert, Winnipeg, Manitoba

> 1-1/2 **cups all-purpose flour**
> 1/3 **cup confectioners' sugar**
> 3/4 **cup cold butter *or* margarine**
> **FILLING:**
> 1 **package (8 ounces) cream cheese, softened**
> 1 **can (14 ounces) sweetened condensed milk**
> 1/4 **cup lemon juice**
> 2 **tablespoons cornstarch**
> 1 **tablespoon brown sugar**
> 1 **can (16 ounces) whole-berry cranberry sauce**
> **TOPPING:**
> 1/3 **cup all-purpose flour**
> 2 **tablespoons brown sugar**
> 1/4 **cup cold butter *or* margarine**
> 3/4 **cup finely chopped walnuts**

In a small bowl, combine flour and confectioners' sugar; cut in the butter until crumbly. Press into a greased 13-in. x 9-in. x 2-in. baking dish. Bake at 350° for 15-20 minutes or until edges are lightly browned. Reduce heat to 325°.

In a mixing bowl, beat cream cheese until smooth. Add milk and lemon juice; mix well. Pour over crust. In a bowl, combine the cornstarch and brown sugar. Stir in the cranberry sauce until combined. Spoon over cream cheese layer. For topping, combine the flour and brown sugar in a bowl; cut in butter. Fold in walnuts. Sprinkle over filling.

Bake at 325° for 40-45 minutes or until topping is golden brown. Cool on a wire rack. Cover and chill for 3 hours before cutting. **Yield:** 12-15 servings.

— 🍴 🍴 🍴 —

Stained Glass Cutouts
(Pictured on page 102)

These are delicious and festive-looking cookies with a "stained glass" heart in the center. —Dixie Terry
Goreville, Illinois

> 1/2 **cup butter (no substitutes), softened**
> 3/4 **cup sugar**

2 eggs
1 teaspoon vanilla extract
2-1/3 cups all-purpose flour
1 teaspoon baking powder
1/3 cup crushed clear red hard candy
1 cup vanilla frosting, optional
4 drops red food coloring, optional

In a mixing bowl, cream butter and sugar. Add eggs, one at a time, beating well after each addition. Beat in vanilla. Combine flour and baking powder; gradually add to creamed mixture. Cover and refrigerate for 3 hours or until easy to handle.

On a lightly floured surface, roll out dough to 1/8-in. thickness. Cut with a 4-in. heart-shaped cookie cutter dipped in flour. Cut out centers with a 1-1/4-in. heart-shaped cookie cutter; set aside to reroll. Place cookies 1 in. apart on lightly greased foil-lined baking sheets. Fill centers with crushed candy.

Bake at 375° for 7-9 minutes or until candy is melted and cookie edges begin to brown. Cool completely on baking sheets. Carefully peel cookies off foil. If desired, combine frosting and food coloring; pipe around edges. **Yield:** about 1-1/2 dozen.

Giant Cherry Oatmeal Cookies

(Pictured on page 103)

These colossal cookies taste best when golden around the edges and chewy in the center. With a glass of milk, they're polished off in no time by my grandchildren.
—*Irene McDade, Cumberland, Rhode Island*

1/2 cup shortening
1/2 cup butter *or* margarine, softened
3/4 cup packed brown sugar
1/2 cup sugar
2 eggs
1 teaspoon vanilla extract
2-1/2 cups old-fashioned oats
1-1/3 cups all-purpose flour
2 teaspoons apple pie spice
1/2 teaspoon baking powder
1/4 teaspoon baking soda
1/4 teaspoon salt
1-1/2 cups dried cherries, chopped
1/2 to 1 teaspoon grated orange peel

In a large mixing bowl, cream shortening, butter and sugars. Beat in the eggs and vanilla. Combine the oats, flour, apple pie spice, baking powder, baking soda and salt; gradually add to the creamed mixture. Stir in cherries and orange peel.

Drop by 1/3 cupfuls onto an ungreased baking sheet. Press to form a 4-in. circle. Bake at 375° for

9-12 minutes or until golden brown. Let stand for 1 minute before removing to wire racks to cool. **Yield:** 1 dozen.

Raspberry Walnut Shortbread

(Pictured above)

A sweet raspberry filling is sandwiched between a crispy crust and a crunchy brown sugar topping in these satisfying snack bars.
—*Pat Habiger*
Spearville, Kansas

1-1/4 cups plus 2 tablespoons all-purpose flour, *divided*
1/2 cup sugar
1/2 cup cold butter *or* margarine
1/2 cup raspberry jam
2 eggs
1/2 cup packed brown sugar
1 teaspoon vanilla extract
1/8 teaspoon baking soda
1 cup finely chopped walnuts

In a bowl, combine 1-1/4 cups flour and sugar; cut in butter until crumbly. Press into a greased 9-in. square baking pan. Bake at 350° for 20-25 minutes or until edges are lightly browned. Place on a wire rack. Spread jam over hot crust.

In a mixing bowl, beat eggs, brown sugar and vanilla. Combine baking soda and remaining flour; stir into the egg mixture just until combined. Fold in walnuts. Spoon over jam; spread evenly. Bake for 17-20 minutes or until golden brown and set. Cool completely on a wire rack before cutting. **Yield:** 16 servings.

CELEBRATE THE SEASON with goodies like Fruity Pastel Cookies, Raspberry Ribbons and Gingerbread Cutouts (shown above, clockwise from top).

Raspberry Ribbons

(Pictured above)

I make these attractive cookies to serve at our guest lodge, and all the girls in the kitchen are addicted to them! —Patsy Wolfenden, Golden, British Columbia

    1 **cup butter (no substitutes), softened**
1/2 **cup sugar**
    1 **egg**
    1 **teaspoon vanilla extract**
2-1/4 **cups all-purpose flour**
1/2 **teaspoon baking powder**
1/4 **teaspoon salt**
1/2 **cup raspberry jam**
GLAZE:
    1 **cup confectioners' sugar**
    2 **tablespoons evaporated milk**
1/2 **teaspoon vanilla extract**

In a mixing bowl, cream butter and sugar. Beat in egg and vanilla. Combine the flour, baking powder and salt; gradually add to creamed mixture and mix well. Divide dough into four portions; shape each into a 10-in. x 2-1/2-in. log. Place 4 in. apart on greased or foil-lined baking sheets.

Make a 1/2-in. depression down center of each log. Bake at 350° for 10 minutes. Fill depressions with jam. Bake 10-15 minutes longer or until lightly browned. Cool for 2 minutes. Remove to a cutting board; cut into 3/4-in. slices. Place on wire racks.

In a small bowl, combine glaze ingredients until smooth. Drizzle over warm cookies. Cool completely. **Yield:** about 5 dozen.

— 🍽 🍽 🍽 —

Fruity Pastel Cookies

(Pictured above)

Lime Jell-O tints the dough and gives these wreaths a hint of fruity flavor. Try other flavors and shapes, too. —Conna Duff, Lexington, Virginia

3/4 **cup butter (no substitutes), softened**
1/2 **cup sugar**
    1 **package (3 ounces) lime gelatin *or* flavor of your choice**
    1 **egg**
1/2 **teaspoon vanilla extract**
1-3/4 **cups all-purpose flour**
1/2 **teaspoon baking powder**
Red and green colored sugar *and/or* sprinkles

In a mixing bowl, cream butter, sugar and gelatin powder. Beat in egg and vanilla. Combine flour and baking powder; gradually add to creamed mixture and mix well.

Using a cookie press fitted with the disk of your choice, press dough 2 in. apart onto ungreased baking sheets. Decorate as desired with colored sugar and/or sprinkles. Bake at 400° for 6-8 minutes or until set (do not brown). Remove to wire racks to cool. **Yield:** 6 dozen.

Gingerbread Cutouts

(Pictured at left)

Baking gingerbread cookies was a Christmas tradition when our three sons were at home. Now, our grand-daughter loves to help. —*Virginia Watson Kirksville, Missouri*

      1/2 cup butter (no substitutes), softened
      1/2 cup packed brown sugar
      1/2 cup molasses
        1 egg
        3 cups all-purpose flour
        1 teaspoon baking soda
        1 teaspoon ground ginger
      1/2 teaspoon salt
      1/4 teaspoon ground cinnamon
      1/8 teaspoon ground cloves
        1 to 2 tablespoons cold water

In a mixing bowl, cream the butter and brown sugar. Beat in molasses and egg. Combine the flour, baking soda, ginger, salt, cinnamon and cloves; add to the creamed mixture alternately with water. Mix well. Cover and refrigerate for 1 hour or until easy to handle.

On a well-floured surface, roll out dough to 1/4-in. thickness. Cut with a rocking horse cookie cutter or cutter of your choice dipped in flour. Place 2 in. apart on greased baking sheets. Bake at 350° for 9-11 minutes or until edges are firm. Remove to wire racks to cool. **Yield:** about 2 dozen.

Chocolate Coconut Neapolitans

These yummy striped cookies with a chocolaty twist are easy and fun to make, but they do need some time in the freezer. —*Lena Marie Brownell Rockland, Massachusetts*

        1 cup butter (no substitutes), softened
      1-1/2 cups sugar
        1 egg

        1 teaspoon vanilla extract
      2-1/2 cups all-purpose flour
      1-1/2 teaspoons baking powder
      1/2 teaspoon salt
        1 teaspoon almond extract
        4 drops red food coloring
      1/2 cup flaked coconut, finely chopped
      4-1/2 teaspoons chocolate syrup
      1/2 cup semisweet chocolate chips
      1-1/2 teaspoons shortening

Line a 9-in. x 5-in. x 3-in. loaf pan with waxed paper; set aside. In a mixing bowl, cream butter and sugar. Beat in egg and vanilla. Combine the flour, baking powder and salt; gradually add to creamed mixture and mix well.

Divide dough into thirds. Add almond extract and red food coloring to one portion; spread evenly into prepared pan. Add coconut to second portion; spread evenly over first layer. Add chocolate syrup to third portion; spread over second layer. Cover with foil; freeze for 4 hours or overnight.

Unwrap loaf and cut in half lengthwise. Cut each portion widthwise into 1/4-in. slices. Place 2 in. apart on ungreased baking sheets. Bake at 350° for 12-14 minutes or until edges are lightly browned. Remove to wire racks to cool.

In a microwave, melt chocolate chips and shortening; stir until blended and smooth. Dip one end of each cookie into chocolate. Place on wire racks until set. **Yield:** 5-1/2 dozen.

Coconut Cranberry Bars

I begged a neighbor for the recipe after tasting these yummy bars at a coffee she hosted. The red, white and pecan colors make them real eye-pleasers, too. —*Dolly McDonald, Edmonton, Alberta*

      1-1/2 cups graham cracker crumbs (about 24 squares)
      1/2 cup butter *or* margarine, melted
      1-1/2 cups vanilla *or* white chips
      1-1/2 cups dried cranberries
        1 can (14 ounces) sweetened condensed milk
        1 cup flaked coconut
        1 cup pecan halves

Combine cracker crumbs and butter; press into a greased 13-in. x 9-in. x 2-in. baking pan. In a bowl, combine the remaining ingredients; mix well. Gently spread over the crust. Bake at 350° for 25-28 minutes or until edges are golden brown. Cool on a wire rack. Cut into bars. **Yield:** 3 dozen.

Peppermint Pinwheels

(Pictured below)

Put a spin on your holidays with these rich-tasting bright swirls! —Marcia Hostetter, Canton, New York

   3/4 cup butter (no substitutes), softened
   3/4 cup sugar
     1 egg yolk
     1 teaspoon vanilla extract
     2 cups all-purpose flour
   1/2 teaspoon baking powder
   1/2 teaspoon salt
   1/2 teaspoon peppermint extract
   1/4 teaspoon red liquid food coloring

In a mixing bowl, cream butter and sugar. Beat in egg yolk and vanilla. Combine flour, baking powder and salt. Add to creamed mixture; mix well. Divide in half; add extract and food coloring to one portion.

Roll out each portion of dough between waxed paper into a 16-in. x 10-in. rectangle. Remove paper. Place red rectangle over plain rectangle; roll up tightly jelly-roll style, starting with a long side. Wrap in plastic wrap. Refrigerate overnight until firm.

Unwrap the dough and cut into 1/4-in. slices. Place 2 in. apart on lightly greased baking sheets. Bake at 350° for 12-14 minutes or until set. Cool for 2 minutes before removing to wire racks to cool completely. **Yield:** about 4 dozen.

— 🛒 🛒 🛒 —

Butter Cookie Snowmen

(Pictured on page 103)

I think it's great fun making these tasty cookies with my grandchildren. —Kathleen Taugher
East Troy, Wisconsin

     1 cup butter (no substitutes), softened
   1/2 cup sugar
     1 tablespoon milk
     1 teaspoon vanilla extract
 2-1/4 cups all-purpose flour
Red and yellow paste food coloring
Miniature chocolate chips

In a mixing bowl, cream butter and sugar. Add milk and vanilla; mix well. Gradually add flour. Tint 1/3 cup of dough with red food coloring. Tint 1/3 cup of dough with yellow food coloring; set aside.

For snowmen, shape white dough into 24 balls, 1-1/4 in. each; 24 balls, 1/2 in. each; and 24 balls, 1/8 in. each. For bodies, place large balls on two ungreased baking sheets; flatten to 3/8-in. thickness. Place 1/2-in. balls above bodies for heads; flatten.

Shape red dough into 24 balls, 1/8 in. each, and 24 triangles. Place triangles above heads for hats; attach 1/8-in. white balls for tassels. Place red balls on heads for noses. Divide yellow dough into 24 pieces. Shape into scarves; position on snowmen. Add chocolate chip eyes and buttons. Bake at 325° for 13-16 minutes until set. Cool 2 minutes before carefully removing to wire racks. **Yield:** 2 dozen.

— 🛒 🛒 🛒 —

Pumpkin Pecan Tassies

These delicious mini tarts are lovely for Christmas or to serve at a tea. —Pat Habiger, Spearville, Kansas

   1/2 cup butter (no substitutes), softened
     1 package (3 ounces) cream cheese, softened
     1 cup all-purpose flour
FILLING:
   3/4 cup packed brown sugar, *divided*
   1/4 cup canned pumpkin
     4 teaspoons plus 1 tablespoon butter, melted, *divided*
     1 egg yolk
     1 tablespoon half-and-half cream
     1 teaspoon vanilla extract
   1/4 teaspoon rum extract
   1/8 teaspoon *each* ground cinnamon and nutmeg
   1/2 cup chopped pecans

In a mixing bowl, cream butter and cream cheese. Beat in flour. Shape into 24 balls. Press onto bottom and up sides of greased miniature muffin cups. Bake at 325° for 8-10 minutes until edges are light brown.

Meanwhile, combine 1/2 cup brown sugar, pumpkin, 4 teaspoons butter, egg yolk, cream, extracts and spices. Spoon into warm cups. Combine the pecans and remaining brown sugar and butter; sprinkle over filling. Bake 23-27 minutes longer or until set and edges are golden brown. Cool for 10 minutes before removing from pans to wire racks. **Yield:** 2 dozen.

Evergreen Sandwich Cookies

(Pictured at right)

A vanilla filling makes these cookies a holiday favorite at our house. —Evelyn Moll, Tulsa, Oklahoma

  1 cup butter (no substitutes), softened
  2 cups all-purpose flour
  1/3 cup milk
  1/4 teaspoon salt
FILLING:
  1/4 cup shortening
  1/4 cup butter, softened
  2 cups confectioners' sugar
4-1/2 teaspoons milk
  1/2 teaspoon vanilla extract
Green paste food coloring
GLAZE:
1-1/3 cups confectioners' sugar
  4 teaspoons milk
Green paste food coloring
Green colored sugar

In a mixing bowl, combine the butter, flour, milk and salt; mix well. Cover and refrigerate for 1-1/2 hours or until easy to handle.

  Divide dough into thirds. On a floured surface, roll out each portion to 1/8-in. thickness. Cut with a 3-3/4-in. Christmas tree cookie cutter. Place on ungreased baking sheets. Pierce each with a fork several times. Bake at 375° for 8-11 minutes or until set. Remove to wire racks.

  For filling, in a mixing bowl, cream shortening, butter and confectioners' sugar. Add milk and vanilla. Tint with coloring. Spread a tablespoon each over half of cookies; top with remaining cookies.

  For glaze, combine confectioners' sugar and milk until smooth; set aside 1/4 cup. Stir food coloring into remaining glaze; spread a thin layer over cooled cookies. If desired, sprinkle tops of half of the cookies with colored sugar. Let stand until set. Pipe garland onto half of the cookies with reserved glaze. Let stand until set. **Yield:** about 2 dozen.

— 🍵 🍵 🍵 —

Apricot Pecan Bars

(Pictured on page 102)

A friend gave me this recipe years ago, and my grand-children and great-grandchildren really enjoy the moist sweet bars. —Verlene Hendricks, Roswell, New Mexico

  1 tube (8 ounces) refrigerated crescent rolls
1-1/2 cups chopped pecans, *divided*
  3/4 cup confectioners' sugar
  1/2 teaspoon ground cinnamon
  1/4 teaspoon ground nutmeg

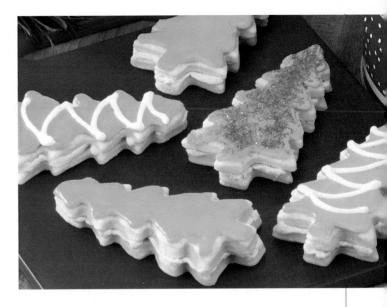

  1 jar (12 ounces) apricot preserves
  3/4 cup all-purpose flour
  1/2 cup packed brown sugar
  1/2 cup cold butter *or* margarine
  1 cup flaked coconut

Unroll crescent dough into a rectangle; press into a greased 13-in. x 9-in. x 2-in. baking pan. Sprinkle with 1 cup pecans, confectioners' sugar, cinnamon and nutmeg. Drop preserves over the top.

  In a bowl, combine the flour and brown sugar; cut in butter. Add the coconut and remaining pecans. Sprinkle over preserves. Bake at 375° for 25-30 minutes or until golden brown. Cool on a wire rack before cutting. **Yield:** about 1-1/2 dozen.

— 🍵 🍵 🍵 —

Cardamom Cookies

Cardamom, almond extract and walnuts enhance the flavor of these buttery cookies. —Mary Steiner
West Bend, Wisconsin

  2 cups butter (no substitutes), softened
2-1/2 cups confectioners' sugar, *divided*
1-1/2 teaspoons almond extract
3-3/4 cups all-purpose flour
  1 cup finely chopped walnuts
  1 teaspoon ground cardamom
  1/8 teaspoon salt

In a mixing bowl, cream butter and 1-1/2 cups confectioners' sugar until smooth. Beat in extract. Combine the flour, walnuts, cardamom and salt; gradually add to creamed mixture. Roll into 1-in. balls. Place 2 in. apart on ungreased baking sheets.

  Bake at 350° for 15-17 minutes or until edges are golden. Roll warm cookies in remaining confectioners' sugar. Cool on wire racks. **Yield:** 6 dozen.

Cherry Cheese Windmills

(Pictured above)

My pretty cookies look fancy, but they are really not much work. They're perfect for any occasion.
—Helen McGibbon, Downers Grove, Illinois

1/3 cup butter (no substitutes), softened
1/3 cup shortening
3/4 cup sugar
1 egg
1 tablespoon milk
1 teaspoon vanilla extract
2 cups all-purpose flour
1-1/2 teaspoons baking powder
1/4 teaspoon salt
FILLING:
1 package (3 ounces) cream cheese, softened
1/4 cup sugar
1/4 teaspoon almond extract
1/2 cup finely chopped maraschino cherries
1/4 cup sliced almonds, toasted and chopped

In a mixing bowl, cream butter, shortening and sugar. Beat in egg, milk and vanilla. Combine flour, baking powder and salt; gradually add to creamed mixture. Divide dough in half. Chill 3 hours or until easy to handle.

In a mixing bowl, beat cream cheese, sugar and extract. Fold in cherries. On a floured surface, roll each portion into a 10-in. square. With a sharp knife, cut into 2-1/2-in. squares. Place 2 in. apart on ungreased baking sheets. Make 1-in. cuts from each corner toward center of dough.

Drop teaspoonfuls of filling in the center of each square; sprinkle with almonds. Fold alternating points to the center to form a windmill; moisten points with water and pinch gently at center to seal. Bake at 350° for 8-10 minutes or until set. Cool on wire racks. **Yield:** about 2-1/2 dozen.

Watermelon Slice Cookies

These cute cookies are always popular at neighborhood events. —Sue Ann Benham, Valparaiso, Indiana

3/4 cup butter (no substitutes), softened
3/4 cup sugar
1 egg
1/2 teaspoon almond extract
2 cups all-purpose flour
1/4 teaspoon baking powder
1/8 teaspoon salt
Red and green gel food coloring
1/3 cup raisins
1 teaspoon sesame seeds

In a mixing bowl, cream butter and sugar. Beat in egg and extract. Combine flour, baking powder and salt; gradually add to creamed mixture. Set aside 1 cup dough. Tint remaining dough red; shape into a 3-1/2-in.-diameter log. Wrap in plastic wrap. Tint 1/3 cup reserved dough green; wrap in plastic wrap. Wrap remaining plain dough. Refrigerate 2 hours until firm.

On a lightly floured surface, roll plain dough into an 8-1/2-in. x 3-1/2-in. rectangle. Place red log on the end of a short side of the rectangle; roll up. Roll green dough into a 10-in. x 3-1/2-in. rectangle. Place red and white log on the end of a short side on green dough; roll up. Wrap; refrigerate overnight.

Unwrap and cut into 3/16-in. slices (just less than 1/4 in.). Place 2 in. apart on ungreased baking sheets. Cut raisins into small pieces. Lightly press raisin bits and sesame seeds into red dough to resemble watermelon seeds. Bake at 350° for 9-11 minutes until firm. Cut cookies in half. Remove to wire racks to cool. **Yield:** about 3 dozen.

—— 🥄 🥄 🥄 ——

Cream Cheese Brownies

You'll never eat plain brownies again after trying these!—Carol Gillespie, Chambersburg, Pennsylvania

1 package (19.8 ounces) brownie mix
1/2 cup vanilla *or* white chips
FILLING:
1 package (3 ounces) cream cheese, softened
2 tablespoons butter (no substitutes), softened
1/4 cup sugar
1 egg
1 tablespoon all-purpose flour
1/2 teaspoon orange extract
FROSTING:
2 tablespoons butter
1 ounce unsweetened chocolate
1 ounce semisweet chocolate
1 cup confectioners' sugar
2 to 3 tablespoons milk

Prepare brownies according to directions for cake-like brownies; fold in chips. Spread half of batter in a greased 13-in. x 9-in. x 2-in. baking pan. In a small mixing bowl, beat cream cheese, butter and sugar until smooth. Beat in egg, flour and orange extract.

Carefully spread cream cheese mixture over batter. Drop remaining batter by tablespoonfuls over cream cheese. Swirl through batter with a knife. Bake at 350° for 30-35 minutes or until a toothpick comes out almost clean. Cool on a wire rack.

In a microwave-safe bowl, melt the butter and chocolate. Cool slightly; stir in sugar and milk. Frost brownies. **Yield:** 16 brownies.

— 🍵 🍵 🍵 —

Cherry Streusel Bars

I came up with the recipe for these flavorful cherry bars myself. —Ellen Borst, Park Falls, Wisconsin

     4 **cups all-purpose flour,** *divided*
     2 **teaspoons sugar**
     1 **teaspoon salt**
  3/4 **cup butter-flavored shortening**
     1 **egg**
  1/4 **cup water**
1-1/2 **teaspoons cider vinegar**
     2 **cans (21 ounces** *each***) cherry pie filling**
     1 **tablespoon grated orange peel**
1-1/4 **cups packed brown sugar**
  1/2 **teaspoon ground cinnamon**
     1 **cup cold butter** *or* **margarine**

In a bowl, combine 2 cups flour, sugar and salt; cut in shortening until crumbly. Whisk egg, water and vinegar. Stir into flour mixture. On a lightly floured surface, roll dough into a 15-in. x 10-in. rectangle. Transfer to a greased 15-in. x 10-in. x 1-in. baking pan. Bake at 400° for 6-8 minutes until firm and dry.

Meanwhile, combine pie filling and orange peel; set aside. In a large bowl, combine brown sugar, cinnamon and remaining flour; cut in butter until crumbly. Spread cherry mixture over crust. Sprinkle with crumb mixture. Bake at 400° for 20-25 minutes or until golden brown. Cool on a wire rack for 20 minutes before cutting. **Yield:** about 2-1/2 dozen.

— 🍵 🍵 🍵 —

Peanut Butter Delights

(Pictured at right)

This recipe is one of my mom's. The cookies are rich and tasty. —Jennifer Moran, Elizabethtown, Kentucky

1/2 **cup shortening**
1/2 **cup butter** *or* **margarine, softened**
1/2 **cup creamy peanut butter**

1-1/2 **cups sugar,** *divided*
     1 **cup packed brown sugar**
     2 **eggs**
     3 **cups all-purpose flour**
  3/4 **teaspoon baking soda**
  1/2 **teaspoon salt**
FILLING:
  1/2 **cup creamy peanut butter**
     4 **ounces cream cheese, softened**
  1/4 **cup sugar**
     1 **egg yolk**
  1/2 **teaspoon vanilla extract**
2-1/2 **cups milk chocolate chips**
TOPPING:
     1 **tablespoon butter** *or* **margarine**
1-1/2 **cups confectioners' sugar**
     6 **tablespoons baking cocoa**
     3 **tablespoons water**
  1/4 **teaspoon vanilla extract**

In a large mixing bowl, cream shortening, butter, peanut butter, 1 cup sugar and brown sugar. Beat in eggs, one at a time. Combine flour, baking soda and salt; gradually add to creamed mixture. Roll into 1-1/2-in. balls; roll in remaining sugar. Place 2 in. apart on ungreased baking sheets. Make an indentation in the center of each ball.

In a small mixing bowl, beat peanut butter and cream cheese until smooth. Beat in sugar, egg yolk and vanilla. Spoon 3/4 teaspoon of filling into each indentation. Bake at 350° for 12-15 minutes or until firm to the touch. Remove to wire racks to cool.

Melt chocolate chips; stir until smooth. Dip bottoms of cookies in chocolate; shake off excess. Place chocolate side up on waxed paper-lined baking sheets. Refrigerate until set.

Melt butter in a saucepan. Whisk in confectioners' sugar and cocoa. Gradually add water, whisking until smooth. Stir in vanilla. Drizzle over tops of cookies. Chill until chocolate is set. Refrigerate in an airtight container. **Yield:** about 5 dozen.

Cakes & Pies

Serving a simply scrumptious dessert is as easy as pie— and cake—as these luscious treats deliciously prove! They're all crowd-pleasers.

SCRUMPTIOUS SLICES. Clockwise from upper left: Pear Custard Pie (p. 122), Christmas Cherry Pie (p. 115), Cupcake Easter Baskets (p. 124), Blackberry Nectarine Pie (p. 119) and Peach Pound Cake (p. 121).

Supreme Chocolate Cake

(Pictured above)

This dessert is so quick to make and looks stunning. My family loves it...and it's popular at church potlucks. Whenever this cake is in the fridge, a big "mouse" in our house eats the leftovers during the night!
—Helene Brule-Besner, Hamilton, Ontario

 3/4 cup butter *or* margarine, softened
 2 cups sugar
 4 eggs
 1-1/2 teaspoons vanilla extract
 3/4 cup baking cocoa
 3/4 cup boiling water
 1 cup buttermilk
 2-1/2 cups all-purpose flour
 1-1/2 teaspoons baking soda
 1/2 teaspoon baking powder
 1/2 teaspoon salt
FROSTING:
 1 carton (8 ounces) whipped cream cheese
 1-1/4 cups confectioners' sugar, *divided*
 2 teaspoons vanilla extract
 1-1/2 cups heavy whipping cream
Maraschino cherries and fresh mint, optional

In a mixing bowl, cream butter and sugar. Add eggs, one at a time, beating well after each addition. Beat in vanilla. In a bowl, whisk cocoa and water until smooth; stir in buttermilk. Sift together flour, baking soda, baking powder and salt; add to creamed mixture alternately with cocoa mixture. Beat until smooth.

Pour into three greased and floured 9-in. round baking pans. Bake at 350° for 25-30 minutes or until a toothpick inserted near the center comes out clean. Cool for 10 minutes before removing from pans to wire racks.

For frosting, in a mixing bowl, beat cream cheese until light. Add 1/2 cup confectioners' sugar; mix well. Add the vanilla, cream and remaining sugar; beat until frosting reaches desired consistency. Place one cooled cake layer on a serving plate; spread with a third of the frosting. Repeat layers twice. Garnish with maraschino cherries and mint if desired. Refrigerate leftovers. **Yield:** 12-14 servings.

— 🍴 🍴 🍴 —

Sour Cream Spice Cake

I perk up a meal with this old-fashioned layer cake. The dense cake is rich in spices, while the frosting is fluffy and sweet. —Edna Hoffman, Hebron, Indiana

 1/2 cup butter *or* margarine, softened
 1-1/2 cups packed brown sugar
 3 eggs, *separated*
 1 teaspoon vanilla extract
 1-3/4 cups cake flour
 1-1/2 teaspoons ground allspice
 1 teaspoon baking soda
 1 teaspoon ground cinnamon
 1 teaspoon ground cloves
 1/2 teaspoon salt
 1 cup (8 ounces) sour cream
FROSTING:
 1 cup packed brown sugar
 1/3 cup water
 2 egg whites
 1/4 teaspoon cream of tartar
 1-1/2 teaspoons vanilla extract

In a large mixing bowl, cream butter and brown sugar. Beat in the egg yolks and vanilla. Combine the dry ingredients; add to creamed mixture alternately with sour cream. In a small mixing bowl, beat egg whites until stiff; gently fold into batter.

Pour into two greased and floured 9-in. round baking pans. Bake at 350° for 25-30 minutes or until a toothpick inserted near the center comes out clean. Cool for 10 minutes before removing from pans to wire racks.

For frosting, in a heavy saucepan, bring brown sugar and water to a boil. Boil for 3-4 minutes or until a candy thermometer reads 242° (firm-ball stage). In a mixing bowl, beat egg whites and cream of tartar until foamy. Gradually add hot sugar mixture; beat on high for 7 minutes or until stiff peaks form.

Add vanilla; continue beating until frosting reaches desired consistency, about 2 minutes. Spread between layers and over top and sides of cake. Refrigerate leftovers. **Yield:** 12-16 servings.

— 🍽 🍽 🍽 —

Christmas Cherry Pie

(Pictured on page 113)

Vibrant color and a medley of fruit in its filling make this pretty pie a standout. This special dessert always brings compliments. The combination of cherries, pineapple, bananas and nuts appeals to most everyone.
—Mrs. Clifford Davis, Fort Smith, Arkansas

  1 **can (14-1/2 ounces) pitted tart cherries**
  1 **cup sugar**
1/4 **cup all-purpose flour**
  1 **can (8 ounces) crushed pineapple, undrained**
  1 **package (3 ounces) cherry gelatin**
10 **to 13 drops red food coloring, optional**
  3 **medium firm bananas, sliced**
1/2 **cup chopped pecans**
  1 **pastry shell (9 inches), baked**
Whipped topping

Drain cherries, reserving 2 tablespoons juice (discard remaining juice or save for another use). In a large saucepan, combine sugar and flour. Stir in the pineapple, cherries and reserved juice. Bring to a boil; cook and stir for 2 minutes or until thickened. Remove from the heat. Add gelatin powder; stir until dissolved. Stir in food coloring if desired. Cool until partially set.

Stir in bananas and pecans. Pour into the pie shell. Refrigerate for at least 3 hours before serving. Garnish with whipped topping. **Yield:** 6-8 servings.

— 🍽 🍽 🍽 —

Sweetheart Fudge Cake

(Pictured at right)

When asked to make dessert for a friend's engagement party, I came up with this cake. It's great for Valentine's Day. —Tiffany Taylor
St. Petersburg, Florida

  1 **package (18-1/4 ounces) chocolate fudge cake mix**
  1 **teaspoon vanilla extract**
1/4 **cup currant jelly, warmed**
3/4 **cup heavy whipping cream**

  3 **squares (1 ounce *each*) semisweet chocolate, chopped**
  1 **can (16 ounces) vanilla frosting**
  1 **carton (8 ounces) frozen whipped topping, thawed**
  2 **pints fresh raspberries**

Grease and flour two 9-in. heart-shaped or round baking pans. Prepare cake mix according to package directions; stir in vanilla. Pour into prepared pans. Bake at 350° for 25-30 minutes or until a toothpick inserted near the center comes out clean. Cool for 15 minutes before removing from pans to wire racks.

While cakes are still warm, poke several holes in cakes with a wooden skewer to within 1/4 in. of bottom. Brush jelly over top and sides of cakes. In a small saucepan, combine cream and chocolate; cook and stir over low heat until chocolate is melted. Brush over top and sides of cakes several times, allowing mixture to absorb between brushings. Cool completely.

In a mixing bowl, beat frosting until fluffy; fold in whipped topping. Place one cake on a serving plate; spread with frosting. Top with second cake; spread remaining frosting over top and sides. Garnish with raspberries. Refrigerate for 2 hours before cutting. **Yield:** 12-14 servings.

Sour Cream Rhubarb Pie

(Pictured below)

A hint of orange flavor and a nice blend of spices complement the tangy rhubarb in this pie. I like to serve it while it's still warm. —Doreen Martin
Kitimat, British Columbia

    1 cup sugar
    3 tablespoons cornstarch
    1/2 teaspoon ground cinnamon
    1/4 teaspoon ground nutmeg
    1 cup (8 ounces) sour cream
    1 egg
    3 cups chopped fresh *or* frozen rhubarb
    1 unbaked pastry shell (9 inches)
TOPPING:
    1/2 cup quick-cooking oats
    1/3 cup all-purpose flour
    1/3 cup packed brown sugar
    1/2 teaspoon grated orange *or* lemon peel
    1/3 cup cold butter *or* margarine

In a mixing bowl, combine the sugar, cornstarch, cinnamon and nutmeg. Beat in the sour cream and egg. Gently fold in the rhubarb. Pour into the pastry shell.

For topping, combine the oats, flour, brown sugar and orange peel. Cut in butter until crumbly. Sprinkle over the filling. Bake at 400° for 15 minutes. Reduce heat to 350°; bake 35-40 minutes longer or until topping is golden brown. Cool on a wire rack. Refrigerate leftovers. **Yield:** 6-8 servings.

Strawberry Hazelnut Torte

This beautiful dessert is a very big hit at parties. The tender meringues have a wonderful hazelnut flavor with layers of chocolate, whipped cream and berries.
—Phyllis Amboss, Pacific Palisades, California

    4 egg whites
    1 teaspoon white vinegar
    1 teaspoon vanilla extract, *divided*
Dash salt
1-1/4 cups sugar
    1/2 cup ground hazelnuts
    6 squares (1 ounce *each*) semisweet
        chocolate
    1 teaspoon shortening
1-1/2 cups heavy whipping cream
    1/3 cup confectioners' sugar
2-1/2 cups sliced fresh strawberries
Additional fresh strawberries, halved

Place egg whites in a large mixing bowl; let stand at room temperature for 30 minutes. Line a baking sheet with parchment paper. Trace two 8-in. circles 1/2 in. apart on the paper; set aside.

Add vinegar, 1/2 teaspoon vanilla and salt to egg whites; beat until soft peaks form. Add sugar, 1 tablespoon at a time, beating until stiff peaks form. Spread over paper circles. Sprinkle with hazelnuts; cut through meringues with a knife to swirl nuts.

Bake at 375° for 30-35 minutes or until the meringue and nuts are lightly browned. Cool on baking sheet. When completely cool, remove meringues from the paper; store meringues in an airtight container. In a microwave, melt chocolate and shortening until smooth; cool to room temperature.

To assemble, place one meringue, flat side down, on a serving plate; spread with half of the melted chocolate. In a mixing bowl, beat cream until it begins to thicken. Add confectioners' sugar and remaining vanilla; beat until stiff peaks form. Spread half over chocolate layer. Arrange sliced strawberries over whipped cream.

Spread flat side of the remaining meringue with melted chocolate. Place chocolate side down over the strawberries; spread with the remaining whipped cream. Refrigerate for up to 4 hours before serving. Garnish with halved strawberries. **Yield:** 10-12 servings.

———— 🦃 🦃 🦃 ————

Lemon Lover's Pound Cake

Everyone raves over this lovely, lemony cake—it sure doesn't last long. —Annettia Mounger
Kansas City, Missouri

1 cup butter (no substitutes), softened
3 cups sugar
6 eggs
5 tablespoons lemon juice
1 tablespoon grated lemon peel
1 teaspoon lemon extract
3 cups all-purpose flour
1/2 teaspoon baking soda
1/4 teaspoon salt
1-1/4 cups sour cream
ICING:
    1/4 cup sour cream
    2 tablespoons butter, softened
2-1/2 cups confectioners' sugar
    3 tablespoons lemon juice
    2 teaspoons grated lemon peel

In a large mixing bowl, cream butter and sugar until light and fluffy, about 5 minutes. Add eggs, one at a time, beating well after each addition. Stir in lemon juice, peel and extract. Combine the flour, baking soda and salt; add to the creamed mixture alternately with sour cream. Beat just until combined.

Pour into a greased and floured 10-in. fluted tube pan. Bake at 350° for 55-60 minutes or until a toothpick inserted near the center comes out clean. Cool for 10 minutes before removing from pan to a wire rack to cool completely.

For icing, in a small mixing bowl, beat the sour cream and butter until blended. Gradually add confectioners' sugar. Beat in lemon juice and peel. Drizzle over the cake. Store in the refrigerator. **Yield:** 12 servings.

Chocolate Strawberry Torte

(Pictured above)

I made this special dessert for my husband on Valentine's Day, and he really enjoyed it. It's pretty simple and tastes wonderful! —Suzanne Zick
Iron Station, North Carolina

1/2 cup plus 2 teaspoons butter (no substitutes), *divided*
    2 cups chocolate graham cracker crumbs (about 26 squares)
1/4 cup sugar
    1 carton (12 ounces) frozen whipped topping, thawed
    1 cup (8 ounces) sour cream
    1 package (3.9 ounces) instant chocolate pudding mix
    1 pint fresh strawberries, sliced
    1 square (1 ounce) semisweet chocolate

Melt 1/2 cup butter. In a bowl, combine the cracker crumbs, melted butter and sugar. Press onto the bottom and 1-1/2 in. up the sides of a greased 9-in. springform pan; refrigerate.

In a mixing bowl, beat the whipped topping, sour cream and pudding mix until blended. Spread half over crust. Arrange strawberries over the top. Spread with remaining filling. In a microwave, melt chocolate and remaining butter; stir until smooth. Cool to room temperature. Drizzle over filling. Refrigerate for at least 4 hours before serving. **Yield:** 10-12 servings.

Orange-Glazed Apple Pie

(Pictured above)

This is my favorite apple pie recipe. It's very easy to make and freezes well. —Katherine Moss
Gaffney, South Carolina

      3/4 cup sugar
        2 tablespoons all-purpose flour
      1/2 teaspoon ground cinnamon
      1/8 teaspoon salt
        6 cups sliced peeled tart apples (about 5 medium)
      1/3 cup raisins
Pastry for double-crust pie (9 inches)
        3 tablespoons butter *or* margarine
        2 tablespoons orange juice
GLAZE:
      1/2 cup confectioners' sugar
    4-1/2 teaspoons orange juice
      1/2 teaspoon grated orange peel

In a large bowl, combine the sugar, flour, cinnamon and salt. Add apples and raisins; toss to coat. Line a 9-in. pie plate with bottom pastry; trim to 1 in. beyond edge of plate. Spoon apple mixture into crust. Dot with butter; sprinkle with orange juice. Roll out remaining pastry to fit top of pie. Make cutouts in pastry with small cookie cutters if desired or cut slits in pastry. Place over filling; trim, seal and flute edges.

Bake at 400° for 40-45 minutes or until crust is golden brown and filling is bubbly. In a small bowl, whisk glaze ingredients until blended. Spread over warm pie. Cool on a wire rack. **Yield:** 6-8 servings.

---- 🍵 🍵 🍵 ----

Blueberry Upside-Down Cake

This cake is a family favorite when fresh blueberries are in season. We like it throughout the rest of the year, too. *It's also delicious served with vanilla ice cream.* —Charlotte Harrison, North Providence, Rhode Island

        6 tablespoons butter *or* margarine, softened, *divided*
      1/4 cup packed brown sugar
        2 cups fresh blueberries
      3/4 cup sugar
        1 egg
        1 teaspoon vanilla extract
    1-1/4 cups cake flour
    1-1/2 teaspoons baking powder
      1/2 cup milk
Whipped topping, optional

In a small saucepan, melt 2 tablespoons butter; stir in brown sugar. Spread into an ungreased 8-in. baking dish. Arrange blueberries in a single layer over brown sugar mixture; set aside. In a large mixing bowl, cream remaining butter; beat in sugar. Add egg and vanilla; mix well. Combine flour and baking powder; add to creamed mixture alternately with milk. Carefully pour over blueberries.

Bake at 350° for 40-45 minutes or until a toothpick inserted near the center of cake comes out clean. Immediately invert onto a serving platter. Cool. Serve with whipped topping if desired. **Yield:** 6-8 servings.

---- 🍵 🍵 🍵 ----

Orange Spice Cake

An orange marmalade glaze sweetens this moist, gingerbread-like cake. —Connie Simon
Reed City, Michigan

    1-2/3 cups all-purpose flour
      1/3 cup sugar
    1-1/2 teaspoons baking soda
        1 teaspoon ground ginger
        1 teaspoon ground cinnamon
      1/2 teaspoon ground cloves
      1/2 cup orange juice
      1/2 cup molasses
      1/3 cup vegetable oil
        1 egg
      1/2 cup orange marmalade
Whipped topping, optional

In a bowl, combine the flour, sugar, baking soda, ginger, cinnamon and cloves. Combine the orange juice, molasses, oil and egg; add to the dry ingredients and stir just until combined. Pour into a greased 9-in. square baking pan.

Bake at 350° for 16-20 minutes or until a toothpick inserted near the center comes out clean. Spoon marmalade over warm cake. Cool on a wire rack. Serve with whipped topping if desired. **Yield:** 9 servings.

Blackberry Nectarine Pie

(Pictured on page 112)

Blackberries are abundant here, so I've made this pretty double-fruit pie many times. —Linda Chinn
Enumclaw, Washington

✓ Uses less fat, sugar or salt. Includes Nutritional Analysis and Diabetic Exchanges.

- 1/4 cup cornstarch
- 1 can (12 ounces) frozen unsweetened apple juice concentrate, thawed
- 2 cups fresh blackberries, *divided*
- 5 medium nectarines, peeled and coarsely chopped
- 1 reduced-fat graham cracker crust (8 inches)

Reduced-fat whipped topping, optional

In a saucepan, combine cornstarch and concentrate until smooth. Bring to a boil. Add 1/2 cup blackberries; cook and stir 2 minutes or until thickened.

Toss the nectarines and remaining blackberries; place in the crust. Pour apple juice mixture over fruit (crust will be full). Cover and refrigerate for 8 hours or overnight. Garnish with whipped topping if desired. **Yield:** 8 servings.

Nutritional Analysis: One slice (calculated without whipped topping) equals 248 calories, 4 g fat (1 g saturated fat), 0 cholesterol, 106 mg sodium, 52 g carbohydrate, 3 g fiber, 2 g protein.

Low-Fat Pumpkin Pie

With its golden crust and creamy filling, this spicy pumpkin pie is so good, it's hard to believe it's low in fat. —Sharon Haugen, Fargo, North Dakota

✓ Uses less fat, sugar or salt. Includes Nutritional Analysis and Diabetic Exchanges.

- 1 can (15 ounces) solid-pack pumpkin
- 1 can (14 ounces) fat-free sweetened condensed milk
- 1/2 cup egg substitute
- 1/2 teaspoon salt
- 1/2 teaspoon ground cinnamon
- 1/2 teaspoon ground nutmeg
- 1/2 teaspoon ground ginger
- 1 unbaked pastry shell (9 inches)

In a large mixing bowl, combine the first seven ingredients; beat just until smooth. Pour into pastry shell. Bake at 425° for 15 minutes. Reduce heat to 350°; bake 25-30 minutes longer or until a knife inserted near the center comes out clean. Cool on a wire rack. Store in the refrigerator. **Yield:** 8 servings.

Nutritional Analysis: One piece equals 246 calories, 6 g fat (2 g saturated fat), 3 mg cholesterol, 334 mg sodium, 42 g carbohydrate, 3 g fiber, 8 g protein. **Diabetic Exchanges:** 2 starch, 1 fruit, 1/2 fat.

Chocolate Berry Angel Torte

(Pictured below)

This is an impressive way to dress up a purchased angel food cake! It has a chocolate filling between the layers and a lovely raspberry topping.
—Katherine Newman, Cedarburg, Wisconsin

- 3 tablespoons sugar, *divided*
- 1 tablespoon cornstarch
- 1 package (10 ounces) frozen raspberries, thawed
- 1/4 cup heavy whipping cream
- 1/4 cup packed brown sugar
- 2 squares (1 ounce *each*) unsweetened chocolate, melted
- 1 teaspoon rum extract *or* vanilla extract
- 1 carton (12 ounces) whipped topping, *divided*
- 1 prepared angel food cake (10 ounces)

In a saucepan, combine 1 tablespoon sugar, cornstarch and raspberries. Bring to a boil; cook and stir 2 minutes or until thickened. Cool. Strain and discard seeds; set aside. In a mixing bowl, beat cream, brown sugar and remaining sugar. Stir in chocolate and extract. Fold in 2 cups whipped topping.

Split angel food cake into three horizontal layers. Place bottom layer on a plate; spread with half of chocolate mixture. Repeat layers. Top with remaining cake. Spread remaining whipped topping over top and sides. Drizzle 1/4 cup raspberry sauce over top. Cover; refrigerate until serving. Serve with remaining raspberry sauce. **Yield:** 12 servings.

Coconut Cupcakes

(Pictured below)

I took these yummy treats to a picnic for our computer club one year, and they went like hotcakes! I should have made a double batch. With their creamy frosting and sprinkling of coconut, they appeal to kids and adults alike. —Judy Wilson, Sun City West, Arizona

1-1/2 cups butter *or* margarine, softened
2 cups sugar
5 eggs
1 to 1-1/2 teaspoons vanilla extract
1 to 1-1/2 teaspoons almond extract
3 cups all-purpose flour
1 teaspoon baking powder
1/2 teaspoon baking soda
1/2 teaspoon salt
1 cup buttermilk
1-1/4 cups flaked coconut
CREAM CHEESE FROSTING:
1 package (8 ounces) cream cheese, softened
3/4 cup butter *or* margarine, softened
1/2 teaspoon vanilla extract
1/2 teaspoon almond extract
2-3/4 cups confectioners' sugar
Additional flaked coconut, toasted

In a large mixing bowl, cream butter and sugar until light and fluffy. Add eggs, one at a time, beating well after each addition. Beat in extracts. Combine the flour, baking powder, baking soda and salt; add to creamed mixture alternately with buttermilk. Fold in coconut.

Fill paper-lined muffin cups two-thirds full. Bake at 350° for 18-20 minutes or until a toothpick comes out clean. Cool for 10 minutes before removing from pans to wire racks to cool completely.

For frosting, in a mixing bowl, beat cream cheese, butter and extracts until smooth. Gradually beat in confectioners' sugar. Frost the cupcakes; sprinkle with toasted coconut. **Yield:** 2-1/2 dozen.

Berry Tiramisu Cake

I love traditional tiramisu, but my husband was never crazy about the coffee flavor. So I got a little creative, leaving out the mocha and adding fresh berries.
—Diane Way, Harrisburg, Pennsylvania

4 cups assorted fresh berries
1 cup sugar
1 tablespoon lemon juice
2 teaspoons cornstarch
SPONGE CAKE:
1-1/2 cups all purpose flour
1 cup plus 2 tablespoons sugar, *divided*
2 teaspoons baking powder
1/2 teaspoon salt
4 eggs, *separated*
1/2 cup water
1/3 cup vegetable oil
CREAM FILLING:
1 package (8 ounces) cream cheese, softened
1/2 cup confectioners' sugar
2 cups heavy whipping cream, whipped

In a bowl, combine berries, sugar and lemon juice. Cover and refrigerate for 1 hour. Gently press berries; drain, reserving juice. Set berries aside. In a large saucepan, combine cornstarch and reserved juice until smooth. Bring to a boil; cook and stir for 1-2 minutes or until thickened. Cool completely.

In a large mixing bowl, combine the flour, 1 cup sugar, baking powder and salt. Whisk egg yolks, water and oil; add to dry ingredients, beating until smooth. In another mixing bowl, beat egg whites on medium speed until soft peaks form. Gradually add remaining sugar, beating on high until stiff peaks form; fold into batter. Spread into an ungreased 9-in. springform pan. Bake at 325° for 30-38 minutes or until cake springs back when lightly touched. Cool for 10 minutes; remove from pan and cool on a wire rack.

In a mixing bowl, beat cream cheese and confectioners' sugar until smooth. Fold in whipped cream. Split cake into three layers; place one layer on a serving plate. Spread with a third of the filling; top with a third of the berries and drizzle with 1/4 cup berry syrup. Repeat layers twice. Loosely cover; refrigerate for at least 2 hours before serving. **Yield:** 12 servings.

Peach Pound Cake

(Pictured on page 112)

Our state grows excellent peaches, and this is one recipe I'm quick to pull out when they are in season. It's a tender, moist cake that receives rave reviews.
—Betty Jean Gosnell, Inman, South Carolina

- 1 cup butter (no substitutes), softened
- 2 cups sugar
- 6 eggs
- 1 teaspoon almond extract
- 1 teaspoon vanilla extract
- 3 cups all-purpose flour
- 1/4 teaspoon baking soda
- 1/4 teaspoon salt
- 1/2 cup sour cream
- 2 cups diced fresh *or* frozen peaches

Confectioners' sugar

In a large mixing bowl, cream butter and sugar until light and fluffy. Add eggs, one at a time, beating well after each addition. Beat in extracts. Combine the flour, baking soda and salt; add to the batter alternately with sour cream. Fold in the peaches.

Pour into a greased and floured 10-in. fluted tube pan. Bake at 350° for 60-70 minutes or until a toothpick inserted near the center comes out clean. Cool for 15 minutes before removing from pan to a wire rack to cool completely. Dust with confectioners' sugar if desired. **Yield:** 12-16 servings.

Chocolate Macaroon Cake

(Pictured above right)

This cake is always popular with chocolate lovers, including my five children. I got the recipe from a dear friend more than 30 years ago. —Saburo Aburano
Ann Arbor, Michigan

- 1 egg white
- 3 tablespoons sugar
- 2 cups flaked coconut, finely chopped
- 1 tablespoon all-purpose flour

CAKE BATTER:

- 4 eggs, *separated*
- 1-3/4 cups sugar, *divided*
- 1/2 cup shortening
- 1/2 cup sour cream
- 2 teaspoons vanilla extract
- 1/2 cup brewed coffee
- 1/4 cup buttermilk
- 2 cups all-purpose flour
- 1/2 cup baking cocoa
- 1 teaspoon baking soda
- 1 teaspoon salt

FROSTING:

- 1 cup semisweet chocolate chips, melted and cooled
- 3 tablespoons butter (no substitutes), softened
- 2 cups confectioners' sugar
- 5 tablespoons milk

In a small mixing bowl, beat egg white on medium speed until soft peaks form. Gradually beat in sugar, 1 tablespoon at a time, on high until stiff glossy peaks form and sugar is dissolved. Fold in coconut and flour; set aside.

In a large mixing bowl, beat the egg whites on medium until soft peaks form. Gradually beat in 1/2 cup sugar, 1 tablespoon at a time, on high until stiff glossy peaks form and sugar is dissolved; set aside. In another mixing bowl, cream shortening and remaining sugar. Add the egg yolks, sour cream and vanilla; beat until creamy. Combine coffee and buttermilk. Combine the flour, cocoa, baking soda and salt; add to creamed mixture alternately with coffee mixture. Beat until combined. Fold in beaten egg whites.

Pour half of the batter into an ungreased 10-in. tube pan with removable bottom. Drop coconut filling by spoonfuls over batter. Top with remaining batter. Bake at 350° for 55-60 minutes or until a toothpick inserted near the center comes out clean. Immediately invert cake onto a wire rack; cool completely, about 1 hour. Run a knife around side of pan and remove.

In a mixing bowl, combine frosting ingredients. Beat until smooth and creamy. Spread over the top and sides of cake. **Yield:** 12-16 servings.

Hungarian Walnut Torte

(Pictured above)

This truly special cake with its creamy not-too-sweet filling is one I've made for many years. People say it is excellent. —Jeannette Jeremias, Kitchener, Ontario

6 eggs, *separated*
1 cup sugar
1 teaspoon vanilla extract
1 cup cake flour
1 teaspoon baking powder
5 tablespoons water
1/2 cup ground walnuts
FILLING:
1-1/4 cups milk
1 package (3.4 ounces) cook-and-serve chocolate pudding mix
1/2 cup butter *or* margarine, softened
1/2 cup shortening
1 cup confectioners' sugar
1 teaspoon vanilla extract
White and dark chocolate curls, optional

In a large mixing bowl, beat egg yolks and sugar for 10 minutes or until light lemon-colored. Beat in vanilla. Combine cake flour and baking powder; add to egg mixture alternately with water, beating well. Fold in walnuts.

In another mixing bowl, beat the egg whites until stiff peaks form; fold into batter. Pour into two greased and floured 9-in. round baking pans. Bake at 350° for 20-25 minutes or until a toothpick inserted near the center comes out clean. Cool for 10 minutes before removing from pans to wire racks to cool completely.

In a small saucepan, whisk the milk and pudding mix. Bring to a boil, stirring constantly. Remove from the heat. Pour into a bowl; press a piece of waxed paper or plastic wrap over pudding. Refrigerate for 30 minutes.

In a mixing bowl, cream the butter, shortening and confectioners' sugar until light and fluffy. Beat in vanilla and cooled pudding. Split each cake into two layers. Place one bottom layer on a serving plate; spread with about 3/4 cup filling. Repeat layers. Garnish with chocolate curls if desired. **Yield:** 12 servings.

Creamy Peach Pie

This pie always receives rave reviews and is especially good when peaches are in season.
—Mary Ann Bostic, Sinks Grove, West Virginia

Pastry for double-crust pie (9 inches)
3/4 cup plus 1 tablespoon sugar, *divided*
3 tablespoons cornstarch
1/2 teaspoon ground nutmeg
1/4 teaspoon ground ginger
1/4 teaspoon ground cinnamon
4 tablespoons heavy whipping cream, *divided*
1 tablespoon lemon juice
1/2 teaspoon almond extract
7 cups sliced peeled peaches (about 7 medium)

Line a 9-in. pie plate with bottom pastry; trim even with edge of plate. Set aside. In a bowl, combine 3/4 cup sugar, cornstarch, nutmeg, ginger and cinnamon; stir in 3 tablespoons cream, lemon juice and extract. Add the peaches; toss gently. Pour into the crust.

Roll out remaining pastry to fit top of pie; make decorative cutouts in pastry. Place top crust over filling; trim, seal and flute edges. Brush pastry and cutouts with remaining cream. Place cutouts on top of pie; sprinkle with remaining sugar.

Cover edges loosely with foil. Bake at 400° for 40 minutes. Remove foil; bake 8-12 minutes longer or until crust is golden brown and filling is bubbly. Cool on a wire rack. Refrigerate leftovers. **Yield:** 6-8 servings.

Pear Custard Pie

(Pictured on page 112)

When cooked, pears become incredibly sweet, soft and fragrant, and in this pie they are suspended in a rich creamy vanilla custard. —Marie Rizzio
Traverse City, Michigan

1 unbaked pastry shell (9 inches)
4-1/2 cups cubed peeled ripe pears (about 2-1/2 pounds)
1 cup sugar
1/4 cup all-purpose flour
1/4 teaspoon ground nutmeg
2 eggs
1 cup heavy whipping cream, *divided*
1/4 cup butter *or* margarine, melted
1 teaspoon grated lemon peel
1 teaspoon vanilla extract
1/4 teaspoon ground cinnamon

Line unpricked pastry shell with a double thickness of heavy-duty foil. Bake at 450° for 8 minutes. Remove foil; bake 3 minutes longer. Reduce heat to 350°. Place pears in shell. In a bowl, combine sugar, flour and nutmeg. Whisk in eggs, 1/4 cup cream, butter, lemon peel and vanilla. Pour over pears.

Cover edges loosely with foil. Bake for 50 minutes or until filling is just set (mixture will jiggle). Cool on a wire rack for 1 hour. Cover and refrigerate until serving. In a bowl, whip remaining cream with cinnamon. Serve with pie. **Yield:** 6-8 servings.

German Apple Cake

My mother made this cake for me and my brothers during our childhood. It's excellent any time of the year for potlucks or picnics. —Edie DeSpain, Logan, Utah

3 eggs
2 cups sugar
1 cup vegetable oil
1 teaspoon vanilla extract
2 cups all-purpose flour
2 teaspoons ground cinnamon
1 teaspoon baking soda
1/2 teaspoon salt
4 cups chopped peeled tart apples
3/4 cup chopped pecans
FROSTING:
1 package (8 ounces) cream cheese, softened
2 teaspoons butter *or* margarine, softened
2 cups confectioners' sugar

In a large mixing bowl, beat eggs, sugar, oil and vanilla. Combine flour, cinnamon, baking soda and salt; add to egg mixture and mix well. Fold in apples and nuts. Pour into a greased 13-in. x 9-in. x 2-in. baking dish. Bake at 350° for 55-60 minutes or until a toothpick comes out clean. Cool on a wire rack.

In a small mixing bowl, beat cream cheese and butter. Add confectioners' sugar, beating until smooth. Spread over cake. Refrigerate leftovers. **Yield:** 12-16 servings.

Orange Meringue Pie

(Pictured below)

This dessert is a citrus twist to a traditional favorite. Try this pie the next time you have company, and you're sure to be asked for the recipe. —Karyn Lee
West Columbia, South Carolina

3/4 cup sugar
1/4 cup cornstarch
1-1/2 cups orange juice
3 egg yolks, lightly beaten
1 tablespoon butter *or* margarine
MERINGUE:
3 egg whites
6 tablespoons sugar
1 pastry shell (9 inches), baked
Orange peel strips, optional

In a large saucepan, combine sugar and cornstarch. Gradually stir in orange juice until smooth. Bring to a boil; cook and stir for 2 minutes or until thickened. Reduce heat; cook and stir 2 minutes longer. Remove from the heat. Gradually stir 1/2 cup hot mixture into egg yolks; return all to the pan, stirring constantly. Bring to a gentle boil; cook and stir for 2 minutes. Stir in butter; keep warm.

In a small mixing bowl, beat the egg whites on medium speed until foamy. Gradually beat in sugar, 1 tablespoon at a time, on high just until stiff peaks form and sugar is dissolved. Pour hot filling into pastry shell. Spread meringue over filling, sealing edges to crust.

Bake at 375° for 15 minutes or until the meringue is golden brown. Cool on a wire rack for 1 hour. Refrigerate for at least 3 hours before serving. Garnish with orange peel if desired. Refrigerate leftovers. **Yield:** 6-8 servings.

Lemon Cherry Cake

(Pictured below)

The combination of sweet cherries and lemon peel gives the yellow cake a distinctive flavor.
—Janice Greenhalgh, Florence, Kentucky

1-1/2 cups coarsely chopped fresh *or* frozen pitted sweet cherries
3/4 cup butter *or* margarine, softened
1-3/4 cups sugar
3 eggs
2 teaspoons grated lemon peel
1-1/2 teaspoons vanilla extract
2-1/2 cups all-purpose flour
2-1/2 teaspoons baking powder
1/2 teaspoon salt
1-1/4 cups milk
TOPPING:
1 package (8 ounces) cream cheese, softened
2 tablespoons lemon juice
2 teaspoons grated lemon peel
3-1/2 to 4 cups confectioners' sugar

Pat cherries dry with paper towels; set aside. In a mixing bowl, cream butter and sugar. Add eggs, one at a time, beating well after each addition. Beat in lemon peel and vanilla. Combine the flour, baking powder and salt; add to creamed mixture alternately with milk.

Pour into a greased 13-in. x 9-in. x 2-in. baking pan. Sprinkle with cherries. Bake at 375° for 30-35 minutes or until a toothpick inserted near the center comes out clean. Cool on a wire rack.

In a mixing bowl, beat cream cheese, lemon juice and peel until smooth. Beat in enough confectioners' sugar until mixture achieves desired consistency. Cut cake; top each piece with a dollop of topping. **Yield:** 12-15 servings.

Strawberry Cream Cheese Pie

Cheesecake lovers will savor every bite of this light and pretty pie, even if they don't have to watch their diets.
—Kim Marie Van Rheenen, Mendota, Illinois

✓ Uses less fat, sugar or salt. Includes Nutritional Analysis and Diabetic Exchanges.

Pastry for a single-crust pie (9 inches)
1 package (8 ounces) reduced-fat cream cheese
1/2 cup egg substitute
3 tablespoons honey
1 teaspoon vanilla extract
3-1/2 cups sliced fresh strawberries
1 tablespoon cornstarch
1/2 cup cold water
1/2 cup reduced-sugar strawberry preserves
Nonfat whipped topping, optional

Roll out pastry to fit a 9-in. pie plate; transfer to plate. Trim pastry to 1/2 in. beyond edge of plate; flute edges. Prick bottom and sides of crust. Bake at 350° for 13-15 minutes or until lightly browned.

Meanwhile, in a mixing bowl, beat the cream cheese, egg substitute, honey and vanilla until smooth. Pour into crust. Bake 15-18 minutes longer or until center is almost set. Cool on a wire rack to room temperature.

Arrange strawberries over filling. In a saucepan, combine cornstarch and water until smooth. Stir in preserves. Bring to a boil; cook and stir for 2 minutes or until thickened. Spoon or brush over the strawberries. Refrigerate for 2 hours before cutting. Garnish with whipped topping if desired. Refrigerate leftovers. **Yield:** 8 servings.

Nutritional Analysis: One piece (calculated without whipped topping) equals 268 calories, 12 g fat (6 g saturated fat), 21 mg cholesterol, 119 mg sodium, 34 g carbohydrate, 2 g fiber, 5 g protein. **Diabetic Exchanges:** 2 fat, 1 starch, 1 fruit.

— 🍶 🍶 🍶 —

Cupcake Easter Baskets

(Pictured on page 113)

It's fun to dress up these cupcakes for Easter! As we raised four sons and a daughter, I prepared these springtime treats many times.
—Julie Johnston Shaunavon, Saskatchewan

1/2 cup butter *or* margarine, softened
1 cup sugar
1 egg
1 teaspoon grated orange peel
2 cups cake flour
3/4 teaspoon baking soda

1/2 teaspoon baking powder
1/4 teaspoon salt
2/3 cup buttermilk
FROSTING:
  3/4 cup butter *or* margarine, softened
    2 packages (3 ounces *each*) cream cheese,
      softened
    1 teaspoon vanilla extract
    3 cups confectioners' sugar
    1 teaspoon water
    4 drops green food coloring
1-1/2 cups flaked coconut
Red shoestring licorice
Jelly beans

In a large mixing bowl, cream butter and sugar. Beat in the egg and orange peel. Combine the flour, baking soda, baking powder and salt; add to creamed mixture alternately with buttermilk. Fill paper-lined muffin cups two-thirds full. Bake at 350° for 20-25 minutes or until a toothpick comes out clean. Cool for 10 minutes before removing from pans to wire racks to cool completely.

In a small mixing bowl, beat butter, cream cheese and vanilla until smooth. Gradually beat in confectioners' sugar; spread over cupcakes. Combine water and food coloring in a large re-sealable plastic bag; add coconut. Seal bag and shake to tint. Sprinkle over cupcakes.

Using a skewer, poke a hole in the top on opposite sides of each cupcake. Cut licorice into 6-in. strips for handle; insert each end into a hole. Decorate with jelly beans. **Yield:** 1-1/2 dozen.

— 🥤 🥤 🥤 —

Pistachio Bundt Cake

Pistachio pudding mix gives this moist cake a pretty tint of green. The cake slices beautifully and would make a fun dessert for St. Patrick's Day. —Becky Gant
South Bend, Indiana

  1 package (18-1/4 ounces) yellow cake mix
  3 packages (3.4 ounces *each*) instant
    pistachio pudding mix
  1 cup water
  1 cup vegetable oil
  4 eggs
GLAZE:
  1 cup confectioners' sugar
  1 tablespoon butter *or* margarine, softened
  2 to 3 tablespoons milk

In a mixing bowl, combine dry cake and pudding mixes, water, oil and eggs. Beat on low speed for 1 minute. Pour into a greased 9-in. fluted tube pan.

Bake at 350° for 60-70 minutes or until a toothpick inserted near the center comes out clean.

Cool for 10 minutes before removing from pan to a wire rack to cool completely. Combine the glaze ingredients; drizzle over cake. **Yield:** 10-12 servings.

— 🥤 🥤 🥤 —

Pineapple Meringue Pie

(Pictured above)

One of my dad's favorite pastimes was making this pie. You never left his house without a pie or two to take home with you. —Lyn Benedict, Dexter, New Mexico

  1 cup plus 6 tablespoons sugar, *divided*
  2 tablespoons cornstarch
1/8 teaspoon salt
  1 can (20 ounces) crushed pineapple,
    undrained
  3 eggs, *separated*
  1 tablespoon lemon juice
1/4 teaspoon cream of tartar
  1 pastry shell (9 inches), baked

In a saucepan, combine 1 cup sugar, cornstarch and salt. Stir in pineapple until blended. Bring to a boil; cook and stir 2 minutes or until thickened. Remove from heat. Gradually stir 1 cup hot filling into egg yolks; return all to pan, stirring constantly. Bring to a gentle boil; cook and stir 2 minutes. Remove from heat; stir in lemon juice. Keep warm.

For meringue, in a mixing bowl, beat egg whites and cream of tartar on medium speed until soft peaks form. Gradually beat in remaining sugar, 1 tablespoon at a time, on high until stiff peaks form. Pour hot filling into pastry shell. Spread meringue over hot filling, sealing edges to crust.

Bake at 350° for 15 minutes or until meringue is golden brown. Cool on a wire rack for 1 hour; refrigerate for at least 3 hours before cutting. Refrigerate leftovers. **Yield:** 6-8 servings.

Just Desserts

***There's no better way to finish off a fabulous meal than
with a luscious dessert like any of those featured here.***

HAPPY ENDINGS. Clockwise from upper left:
Chocolate Chip Cheesecake (p. 140), German Plum
Tart (p. 143), Peach Shortcake Towers (p. 132),
Chocolate Pecan Candies (p. 131) and Light
Cheesecake (p. 130).

Chocolate Velvet Dessert

(Pictured below and on front cover)

This creamy concoction is the result of several attempts to duplicate a dessert I enjoyed on vacation. It looks so beautiful on a buffet table that many folks are tempted to forgo the main course in favor of this chocolaty treat. —Molly Seidel, Edgewood, New Mexico

  1-1/2 **cups chocolate wafer crumbs**
     2 **tablespoons sugar**
    1/4 **cup butter (no substitutes), melted**
     2 **cups (12 ounces) semisweet chocolate
       chips**
     6 **egg yolks**
  1-3/4 **cups heavy whipping cream**
     1 **teaspoon vanilla extract**
CHOCOLATE BUTTERCREAM FROSTING:
    1/2 **cup butter, softened**
     3 **cups confectioners' sugar**
     3 **tablespoons baking cocoa**
     3 **to 4 tablespoons milk**

In a small bowl, combine wafer crumbs and sugar; stir in butter. Press onto the bottom and 1-1/2 in. up the sides of a greased 9-in. springform pan. Bake at 350° for 10 minutes. Cool on a wire rack.

In a microwave or heavy saucepan, melt chocolate chips; stir until smooth. Cool. In a mixing bowl, combine the egg yolks, whipping cream and vanilla; beat well. Gradually stir a third of the cream mixture into the melted chocolate until blended. Gradually stir in the remaining cream mixture. Pour into the crust.

Place pan on a baking sheet. Bake at 350° for 45-50 minutes or until center is almost set. Cool on a wire rack for 10 minutes. Carefully run a knife around edge of pan to loosen; cool 1 hour longer. Refrigerate overnight.

For frosting, in a mixing bowl, cream butter. Combine confectioners' sugar and cocoa; add to butter with enough milk to achieve frosting consistency. Pipe into center of dessert. Refrigerate leftovers. **Yield:** 12-16 servings.

— 🍸 🍸 🍸 —

Creamy Peppermint Patties

These smooth chocolate candies fill the bill for folks who like a little sweetness after a meal but don't want a full serving of rich dessert. —Donna Gonda
North Canton, Ohio

    1 **package (8 ounces) cream cheese,
     softened**
    1 **teaspoon peppermint extract**
    9 **cups confectioners' sugar**
  3/4 **cup milk chocolate chips**
  3/4 **cup semisweet chocolate chips**
    3 **tablespoons shortening**

In a large mixing bowl, beat the cream cheese and extract until smooth. Gradually add confectioners' sugar, beating well. Shape into 1-in. balls. Place on waxed paper-lined baking sheets. Flatten into patties. Cover and refrigerate for 1 hour or until chilled.

In a microwave, melt chips and shortening; stir until smooth. Cool slightly. Dip patties in melted chocolate; place on waxed paper until firm. Store in the refrigerator. **Yield:** about 4 dozen.

— 🍸 🍸 🍸 —

Chocolate-Covered Cherries

For these cute candies, maraschino cherries are dressed in a chocolate coating. Kids will have fun helping make the sweets, but they will have to wait a week or two for the filling to set before enjoying the fruits of their labors. —Janice Pehrson, Omaha, Nebraska

  60 **maraschino cherries with stems**
    2 **cups confectioners' sugar**
    3 **tablespoons butter (no substitutes),
     softened**
    3 **tablespoons light corn syrup**
  1/4 **teaspoon salt**
    2 **cups (12 ounces) semisweet chocolate
     chips**
    2 **tablespoons shortening**

Pat cherries dry with paper towels; set aside. In a small mixing bowl, combine the sugar, butter, corn syrup and salt; mix well. Knead until smooth. Cover and refrigerate for 1 hour.

Roll into 1/2-in. balls; flatten each into a 2-in. circle. Wrap each circle around a cherry and lightly roll in hands. Place cherries with stems up on waxed paper-lined baking sheets. Cover loosely and refrigerate for 1 hour.

In a microwave or heavy saucepan, melt chocolate chips and shortening; stir until smooth. Holding onto the stem, dip each cherry into chocolate; set on waxed paper. Refrigerate until hardened. Store in a covered container. Refrigerate for 1-2 weeks before serving. **Yield:** 5 dozen.

— ☕ ☕ ☕ —

Pear Tart

This pretty pastry looks like it came from a fancy bakery. My sister-in-law brought this fruity dessert to dinner one night, and we all went back for seconds. It is truly scrumptious.
—*Kathryn Rogers*
Suisun City, California

 Uses less fat, sugar or salt. Includes Nutritional Analysis and Diabetic Exchanges.

   3 tablespoons butter *or* stick margarine, softened
3/4 cup plus 1 tablespoon sugar, *divided*
3/4 cup all-purpose flour
1/3 cup finely chopped walnuts
   1 package (8 ounces) reduced-fat cream cheese
   1 egg
   1 teaspoon vanilla extract
   1 can (15 ounces) reduced-sugar sliced pears, drained and thinly sliced
   1 teaspoon ground cinnamon

In a small mixing bowl, beat butter and 1/2 cup of sugar for 2 minutes or until crumbly. Beat in flour and nuts. Press onto the bottom and up the sides of a 9-in. fluted tart pan with a removable bottom coated with nonstick cooking spray.

In another mixing bowl, beat cream cheese until smooth. Beat in 1/4 cup sugar, egg and vanilla; spread over the crust. Arrange pears over cream cheese mixture. Combine the cinnamon and remaining sugar; sprinkle over pears.

Bake at 425° for 10 minutes. Reduce heat to 350°; bake 15-20 minutes longer or until filling is set and a thermometer reads 160°. Cool for 1 hour on a wire rack. Refrigerate for at least 2 hours before serving. Remove sides of pan and slice. **Yield:** 12 servings.

Nutritional Analysis: One serving (1 slice) equals 192 calories, 9 g fat (4 g saturated fat), 36 mg cholesterol, 94 mg sodium, 25 g carbohydrate, 1 g fiber, 4 g protein. **Diabetic Exchanges:** 1 starch, 1 fruit, 1 fat.

English Toffee

(Pictured above)

Each Christmas I make several pounds of candy and cookies for friends, neighbors and business associates. This tasty toffee is covered in chocolate and sprinkled with nuts...and it won't stick to your teeth!
—*Don McVay, Wilsonville, Oregon*

   1 tablespoon plus 2 cups butter (no substitutes), softened, *divided*
   2 cups sugar
   1 tablespoon light corn syrup
1/4 teaspoon salt
   1 cup milk chocolate chips
   1 cup chopped pecans

Grease a 15-in. x 10-in. x 1-in. baking pan with 1 tablespoon butter; set aside. In a heavy 3-qt. saucepan, melt the remaining butter. Add sugar, corn syrup and salt; cook and stir over medium heat until a candy thermometer reads 295° (hard-crack stage). Quickly pour into prepared pan. Let stand at room temperature until cool, about 1 hour.

In a microwave, melt chocolate chips; spread over toffee. Sprinkle with pecans. Let stand for 1 hour. Break into bite-size pieces. Store in an airtight container at room temperature. **Yield:** about 2 pounds.

Editor's Note: We recommend that you test your candy thermometer before each use by bringing water to a boil; the thermometer should read 212°. Adjust your recipe temperature up or down based on your test.

Two-Tone Fudge

(Pictured above)

With its pretty butterscotch and chocolate layers, this creamy fudge looks fancy. It makes a great holiday gift. Both my husband and my dad love trying different kinds of fudge. They give this recipe a big thumbs-up!
—Jackie Hannahs, Cadillac, Michigan

1-1/2 teaspoons plus 1/2 cup butter (no substitutes), softened, *divided*
   2 cups packed brown sugar
   1 cup sugar
   1 cup evaporated milk
   1 jar (7 ounces) marshmallow creme
   1 teaspoon vanilla extract
1-1/2 cups semisweet chocolate chips
   1 cup chopped walnuts
 1/2 cup butterscotch chips

Line a 9-in. square pan with foil and grease the foil with 1-1/2 teaspoons butter; set aside. In a large heavy saucepan, combine the sugars, milk and remaining butter. Cook and stir over medium heat until sugar is dissolved. Bring to a rapid boil; boil for 5 minutes, stirring constantly. Reduce heat to low; stir in the marshmallow creme until melted and blended.

Remove from the heat; stir in vanilla. Pour 2-1/2 cups into a bowl; stir in the chocolate chips and walnuts until chips are melted. Pour into prepared pan. Add the butterscotch chips to the remaining marshmallow mixture; stir until chips are melted. Pour over the chocolate layer and gently spread to cover. Refrigerate overnight or until firm.

Using foil, remove fudge from pan; carefully peel off foil. Cut into 1-in. squares. Store in the refrigerator. **Yield:** 2-3/4 pounds.

Toffee Ice Cream Dessert

A lady at my church gave me the recipe for this yummy frozen treat. I make it for my husband's luncheons at work, and the dish comes home empty every time! A great dessert for a gathering any time of year, it can be prepared ahead and stored in the freezer.
—Sharon Pavlikowski, Virginia Beach, Virginia

   1 package (10 ounces) butter cookies, crushed (3 cups crumbs)
 1/2 cup butter *or* margarine, melted
   1 cup cold milk
   2 packages (3.4 ounces *each*) instant vanilla pudding mix
   1 quart vanilla ice cream, softened
   1 carton (8 ounces) frozen whipped topping, thawed
   2 Heath candy bars (1.4 ounces *each*), crushed

In a small bowl, combine cookie crumbs and butter. Press into a 13-in. x 9-in. x 2-in. dish; refrigerate. In a bowl, whisk milk and pudding mixes for 2 minutes. Fold in ice cream. Spread over crust. Top with whipped topping. Cover and refrigerate for at least 2 hours. Sprinkle with crushed candy bars before serving. **Yield:** 12-15 servings.

Light Cheesecake

(Pictured on page 126)

Our family loves cheesecake, but I wanted to serve something healthier, so I came up with this lighter version. I make it for holidays and everyday snacking.
—Diane Roth, Adams, Wisconsin

✓ Uses less fat, sugar or salt. Includes Nutritional Analysis and Diabetic Exchanges.

1-1/4 cups reduced-fat vanilla wafer crumbs (about 40 wafers)
   2 tablespoons butter *or* stick margarine, melted
   1 teaspoon plus 1-1/4 cups sugar, *divided*
   2 packages (8 ounces *each*) reduced-fat cream cheese
   1 package (8 ounces) fat-free cream cheese
   2 tablespoons cornstarch
   1 cup (8 ounces) reduced-fat sour cream
   1 teaspoon vanilla extract
   2 eggs
   2 egg whites
   1 cup sliced fresh strawberries

In a small bowl, combine wafer crumbs, butter and 1 teaspoon sugar. Press onto the bottom and 1/2 in. up the sides of a greased 9-in. springform pan. Bake at 350° for 8 minutes. Cool on a wire rack.

In a mixing bowl, beat reduced-fat and fat-free cream cheese until smooth. Combine cornstarch and remaining sugar; add to cream cheese mixture and beat well. Add sour cream and vanilla; beat just until blended. Add eggs and egg whites; beat on low speed just until combined. Pour into crust.

Place pan on a baking sheet. Bake at 325° for 60-65 minutes or until center is almost set. Cool on a wire rack for 10 minutes. Carefully run a knife around edge of pan to loosen; cool 1 hour longer. Refrigerate overnight. Remove sides of pan. Garnish with strawberries. Refrigerate leftovers. **Yield:** 12 servings.

Nutritional Analysis: One serving equals 311 calories, 13 g fat (7 g saturated fat), 74 mg cholesterol, 310 mg sodium, 39 g carbohydrate, trace fiber, 10 g protein. **Diabetic Exchanges:** 2 starch, 2 fat, 1 fruit.

Chocolate Pecan Candies

(Pictured on page 126)

When I give candy on Valentine's Day, I'm sure to include this homemade version of Turtles. This easy candy has brought many compliments. —Robert Watness Greenwood, Indiana

  1/2 **pound pecan halves**
   75 **caramels***
    3 **tablespoons milk**
    1 **pound dark chocolate candy coating, melted**

On waxed paper, place pecan halves in pairs 2 in. apart. In a heavy saucepan over medium-low heat, cook and stir the caramels and milk until melted. Pour about 2 teaspoons of caramel mixture over each pair of pecans. Let stand until set.

With buttered fingers, shape pecan clusters into balls. Dip in candy coating. Place on waxed paper-lined baking sheets. Refrigerate until set. Store in an airtight container. **Yield:** about 5 dozen.

*Editor's Note: This recipe was tested with Hershey caramels. A 14-ounce package contains about 65 caramels.

Coconut Cranberry Alaska

(Pictured at right)

This impressive treat is my favorite company dessert, and it's perfect for a holiday gathering! The recipe is easy to prepare in advance and makes such a beautiful presentation. I always receive raves when I serve it and predict that you will, too.   —Joan Hallford North Richland Hills, Texas

    1 **package (9 ounces) white *or* yellow cake mix**
    2 **envelopes unflavored gelatin**
  1/2 **cup sugar,** *divided*
1-1/2 **cups cranberry juice**
    1 **can (16 ounces) whole-berry cranberry sauce**
    3 **cups heavy whipping cream,** *divided*
  1/4 **cup chopped pecans**
1-1/2 **cups flaked coconut, toasted**

Prepare cake mix and bake in an 8- or 9-in. round baking pan according to package directions. Cool on a wire rack.

In a large bowl, combine gelatin and 1/4 cup sugar. Bring cranberry juice to a boil; stir into gelatin mixture until dissolved. Stir in cranberry sauce. Refrigerate until partially set.

Use nonstick cooking spray to grease a 2-qt. bowl with an 8- or 9-in.-diameter top. In a small mixing bowl, beat 1 cup of cream until soft peaks form. Fold whipped cream and pecans into gelatin mixture. Pour into prepared bowl. Refrigerate until set.

Place cake over gelatin mixture; trim if necessary. Invert dessert onto a serving plate. In a mixing bowl, beat remaining cream until it begins to thicken. Add remaining sugar; beat until stiff peaks form. Spread over gelatin mixture and cake. Sprinkle with coconut. **Yield:** 12-16 servings.

Valentine Napoleons

(Pictured below)

These pastries are quick to fix, thanks to convenient puff pastry! I fill the hearts with a pudding and cream mixture and strawberries. —Kathleen Taugher
East Troy, Wisconsin

> 1 package (17-1/4 ounces) frozen puff pastry, thawed
> 1 cup cold milk
> 1 package (3.4 ounces) instant vanilla pudding mix
> 1 cup heavy whipping cream
> 1/4 cup confectioners' sugar
> 1-1/4 cups sliced fresh strawberries
> Additional confectioners' sugar

On a lightly floured surface, roll out each pastry sheet to 1/8-in. thickness. Using a 3-1/2-in. heart-shaped cookie cutter, cut out 12 hearts. Place on ungreased baking sheets. Bake at 400° for 8-11 minutes or until golden brown. Remove to wire racks to cool.

In a bowl, whisk milk and pudding mix for 2 minutes. In a mixing bowl, beat cream until it begins to thicken. Beat in confectioners' sugar until soft peaks form. Fold into pudding.

Split puff pastry hearts in half. Place bottom halves on serving plates. Spoon 1/4 cup filling over each; top with strawberries and pastry tops. Sprinkle with confectioners' sugar. Serve immediately. **Yield:** 12 servings.

— 🍴 🍴 🍴 —

Macadamia Caramel Tart

I tried this recipe for an office potluck. When I returned from a break, I found a blue ribbon on my desk with a note from the boss, saying, "You get a blue ribbon for bringing us a 'slice of heaven'!" —Debbie Emerick
Castle Rock, Colorado

> 2-3/4 cups all-purpose flour
> 2-1/2 cups sugar, *divided*
> 1 cup cold butter (no substitutes), cut into chunks
> 2 eggs
> 1 cup heavy whipping cream
> 2-1/2 cups macadamia nuts, toasted
> 1 egg white, beaten

In a food processor, combine flour, 1/2 cup sugar and butter. Cover; pulse until blended. Add eggs; pulse until blended. On a lightly floured surface, gently knead dough 5 times until a ball forms.

Between two sheets of waxed paper, roll two-thirds of dough into a 13-in. circle; press onto the bottom and 2 in. up the sides of an ungreased 9-in. springform pan. Cover and chill. Roll remaining dough into a 9-in. circle; chill.

In a large heavy skillet, cook and stir the remaining sugar over medium heat until melted and dark brown, about 20 minutes. Slowly stir in cream until blended. Remove from the heat; stir in nuts. Cool for 15 minutes. Pour into prepared pan. Top with 9-in. pastry circle. Fold pastry from sides of pan over the top pastry; seal edges with a fork. Brush top with egg white.

Bake at 325° for 50-55 minutes or until golden brown. Cool on a wire rack for 20 minutes. Carefully run a knife around edge of pan to loosen. Remove sides of pan. Cool completely before cutting. **Yield:** 10-12 servings.

— 🍴 🍴 🍴 —

Peach Shortcake Towers

(Pictured on page 126)

These tender biscuits make wonderful peach or berry shortcakes that are always greeted with "oohs" and "aahs". They are very pretty when stacked pyramid-style. —Opal Sanders, Glouster, Ohio

> 3 cups all-purpose flour
> 1/4 cup finely chopped walnuts

2 tablespoons baking powder
1 teaspoon salt
1 cup plus 1 tablespoon heavy whipping cream, *divided*
1 egg
7 to 9 tablespoons sugar, *divided*
1 teaspoon vanilla extract
1 to 2 tablespoons cold water
4 cups sliced fresh peaches
Whipped topping

In a large bowl, combine the flour, walnuts, baking powder and salt. In a mixing bowl, beat 1 cup whipping cream, egg, 2 tablespoons sugar and vanilla until slightly thickened. Stir into dry ingredients until mixture forms a ball, adding cold water if necessary.

Turn dough onto a floured surface; knead 8-10 times. Roll out to 1/2-in. thickness. Cut into three 3-1/2-in. circles, three 2-3/4-in. circles and six 1-1/4-in. circles. Place on ungreased baking sheets. Brush the tops with remaining cream. Bake at 425° for 8-12 minutes or until golden brown.

In a bowl, combine the peaches and 5-7 tablespoons of sugar. Split the large and medium biscuits in half horizontally. Spoon a few peach slices on large biscuit halves; dollop with whipped topping. Top each with a medium biscuit half, remaining peaches and whipped topping and a small biscuit. **Yield:** 6 servings.

Cherry Cheese Blintzes

(Pictured above right)

These elegant blintzes can be served as an attractive dessert or a brunch entree. The bright cherry sauce gives them a delightful flavor. I sometimes substitute other fruits, such as raspberries, blueberries or peaches. —Jessica Vantrease, Anderson, Alaska

2/3 cup all-purpose flour
1/2 teaspoon salt
3 eggs
1-1/2 cups milk
2 tablespoons butter *or* margarine, melted
FILLING:
1 cup (8 ounces) small-curd cottage cheese
1 package (3 ounces) cream cheese, softened
1/4 cup sugar
1/2 teaspoon vanilla extract
CHERRY SAUCE:
1 pound fresh *or* frozen pitted sweet cherries
2/3 cup plus 1 tablespoon water, *divided*
1/4 cup sugar
1 tablespoon cornstarch

In a bowl, whisk the flour, salt, eggs, milk and butter. Cover and refrigerate for 2 hours. Heat a lightly greased 8-in. nonstick skillet; add 2 tablespoons batter. Lift and tilt pan to evenly coat bottom. Cook until top appears dry; turn and cook 15-20 seconds longer. Remove to a wire rack. Repeat with remaining batter. When cool, stack crepes with waxed paper or paper towels in between. Wrap in foil; refrigerate.

In a blender, process cottage cheese until smooth. Transfer to a mixing bowl; add cream cheese. Beat until smooth. Add sugar and vanilla; mix well. Spread about 1 rounded tablespoonful onto each crepe. Fold opposite sides of crepe over filling. Place seam side down in a greased 15-in. x 10-in. x 1-in. baking pan. Bake, uncovered, at 350° for 10 minutes or until heated through.

Meanwhile, in a saucepan, bring the cherries, 2/3 cup water and sugar to a boil over medium heat. Reduce heat; cover and simmer for 5 minutes or until cherries are tender. Combine cornstarch and remaining water until smooth; stir into cherry mixture. Bring to a boil; cook and stir for 2 minutes or until thickened. Serve over crepes. **Yield:** 9 servings.

In a bowl, combine the oats, flour, brown sugar and cinnamon. Cut in butter until the mixture resembles coarse crumbs. Spread in an ungreased 15-in. x 10-in. x 1-in. baking pan. Bake at 350° for 10-15 minutes or until golden brown. Cool on a wire rack.

Stir pie filling into cream mixture. Fill cylinder of ice cream freezer two-thirds full; freeze according to manufacturer's directions. Refrigerate remaining mixture until ready to freeze.

After removing from ice cream freezer, stir a portion of oat mixture into each batch. Transfer to a freezer container. Cover and freeze for at least 4 hours before serving. **Yield:** 2-1/2 quarts.

Cherry Crunch Ice Cream

(Pictured above)

I received this wonderful recipe many years ago from a friend. The creamy custard-style ice cream has a mild cherry flavor with a fun oat crunch. It takes some time to make, but it's worth the extra effort!
—Dorothy Koshinski, Decatur, Illinois

   6 eggs
   2 cups sugar
   2 cups milk
   1 package (3.4 ounces) instant vanilla
      pudding mix
   4 cups heavy whipping cream
   1 teaspoon vanilla extract
Dash salt
   1 cup old-fashioned oats
1/2 cup all-purpose flour
1/2 cup packed brown sugar
1/2 teaspoon ground cinnamon
1/3 cup cold butter *or* margarine
   1 can (21 ounces) cherry pie filling

In a large saucepan, whisk eggs, sugar and milk until combined. Cook and stir over low heat until mixture reaches 160° and coats the back of a metal spoon. Remove from the heat; cool. Beat in the pudding mix, cream, vanilla and salt. Cover and refrigerate for 8 hours or overnight.

Tart Cherry Meringue Dessert

I've made this cherry dessert for years to serve at baby showers, birthday parties and other special occasions. People really enjoy the tender crust, cherry filling and melt-in-your-mouth meringue. Every time I serve it, someone asks for the recipe.
—Kathryn Dawley, Gray, Maine

   2 cups all-purpose flour
   1 teaspoon salt
   1 cup shortening
   1 egg
FILLING:
   1 can (14-1/2 ounces) pitted tart cherries
   3 eggs, *separated*
1-1/2 cups sugar, *divided*
   3 tablespoons quick-cooking tapioca
   2 teaspoons lemon juice
   6 to 8 drops red food coloring, optional
   1 teaspoon vanilla extract
1/4 teaspoon cream of tartar
3/4 cup finely chopped almonds

In a bowl, combine the flour and salt. Cut in shortening until mixture resembles coarse crumbs. Add egg; mix well. Press onto the bottom and up the sides of a greased 11-in. x 7-in. x 2-in. baking dish. Bake at 375° for 20-22 minutes or until lightly browned.

Drain cherries, reserving the juice in a 1-cup measuring cup; set cherries aside. Add enough water to juice to measure 1 cup. In a saucepan, combine egg yolks, 3/4 cup sugar, tapioca and cherry juice mixture. Let stand for 5 minutes. Bring to a boil over medium heat, stirring constantly; cook and stir for 2 minutes or until thickened. Stir in the cherries, lemon juice and food coloring if desired. Pour into crust.

In a small mixing bowl, beat egg whites, vanilla and cream of tartar on medium speed until soft peaks form. Gradually add remaining sugar, beating on high until stiff peaks form. Fold in nuts. Spread evenly over hot filling, sealing edges to crust. Bake at 350° for 22-25 minutes or until meringue is golden brown. Cool on a wire rack for 1 hour; refrigerate for at least 3 hours before serving. Store in the refrigerator. **Yield:** 8-10 servings.

— 🍵 🍵 🍵 —

Apple Cranberry Cobbler

My family enjoys the sweetness of the apples as well as the tartness of the cranberries in this old-fashioned treat. It's a great dessert to make during the peak of apple season. —Regina Stock, Topeka, Kansas

>   5 cups sliced peeled tart apples
> 1-1/4 cups sugar
>   1 cup fresh *or* frozen cranberries
>   3 tablespoons quick-cooking tapioca
> 1/2 teaspoon ground cinnamon
>   1 cup water
>   2 tablespoons butter *or* margarine
> **TOPPING:**
> 3/4 cup all-purpose flour
>   2 tablespoons sugar
>   1 teaspoon baking powder
> 1/8 teaspoon salt
> 1/4 cup cold butter *or* margarine
> 1/4 cup milk

In a large saucepan, combine the apples, sugar, cranberries, tapioca, cinnamon and water. Let stand for 5 minutes, stirring occasionally. Cook and stir over medium heat until mixture comes to a full boil. Cook and stir 3 minutes longer. Pour into a greased 2-qt. baking dish. Dot with butter.

In a bowl, combine the flour, sugar, baking powder and salt. Cut in butter until crumbly. Stir in milk to form a soft dough. Drop dough by tablespoonfuls over hot apple mixture. Bake, uncovered, at 375° for 30-35 minutes or until topping is golden brown and a toothpick comes out clean. **Yield:** 8 servings.

— 🍵 🍵 🍵 —

Pistachio Cheesecake

(Pictured at right)

This appealing dessert, with its pretty pistachio filling, almond crust and chocolate drizzle, is creamy smooth. I created it one Christmas Eve and my family raved about it. I've never seen cheesecake disappear so quickly! —Karen Ankerson, Manistee, Michigan

>   2 cups all-purpose flour
> 1/2 cup ground almonds

> 1/2 cup cold butter *or* margarine
>   6 packages (8 ounces *each*) cream cheese, softened
>   1 can (14 ounces) sweetened condensed milk
>   2 packages (3.4 ounces *each*) instant pistachio pudding mix
>   5 eggs
> **Chocolate syrup**
> **Whipped cream and chopped pistachios, optional**

In a small bowl, combine the flour and almonds; cut in butter until crumbly. Press onto the bottom and 1-1/4 in. up the sides of a greased 10-in. springform pan. Bake at 400° for 10 minutes.

Meanwhile, in a large mixing bowl, beat cream cheese, milk and pudding mixes until smooth. Add eggs; beat on low speed just until combined. Pour over crust. Place pan on a baking sheet. Reduce heat to 350°. Bake for 55-60 minutes or until the center is almost set. Cool on a wire rack for 10 minutes. Carefully run a knife around edge of pan to loosen; cool 1 hour longer. Refrigerate overnight.

Remove sides of pan. Slice cheesecake; drizzle slices with chocolate syrup. Garnish with whipped cream and pistachios if desired. **Yield:** 12-14 servings.

HOP TO IT and make some fun homemade confections for Easter, like Jelly Bean Brittle, Marshmallow Easter Eggs and White Chocolate Easter Eggs (shown above, top to bottom).

Candy Any Bunny Can Make!

STIR UP a batch of these sweet treats, and the Easter bunny just might hire you to help fill Easter baskets!

— ▼ ▼ ▼ —

White Chocolate Easter Eggs

(Pictured at left)

My kids loved these homemade candies when they were growing up. The eggs are pretty and taste so sweet.
—*Diane Hixon, Niceville, Florida*

    1/2 cup butter (no substitutes)
      3 cups confectioners' sugar
    2/3 cup sweetened condensed milk
      1 teaspoon vanilla extract
      2 cups finely chopped pecans
      1 pound white candy coating, melted
Gel food coloring, optional

In a large saucepan, melt butter. Stir in confectioners' sugar, milk and vanilla until smooth. Stir in pecans. Transfer to a bowl. Cover; refrigerate for 2 hours or until easy to handle. Drop by level tablespoonfuls onto waxed paper-lined baking sheets. Form into egg shapes. Cover; refrigerate overnight.

Dip eggs into candy coating. Place on waxed paper until set. For a speckled look, dip a small crumpled ball of waxed paper into food coloring. First gently press waxed paper onto a paper plate to remove excess food coloring, then gently press color onto eggs. Repeat if needed. Blot eggs with a paper towel. **Yield:** about 4 dozen.

— ▼ ▼ ▼ —

Jelly Bean Brittle

(Pictured at left)

Here's a fun version of brittle that's perfect for Easter. The jelly beans add both color and flavor.
—*Kathy Kittell, Lenexa, Kansas*

      4 tablespoons butter (no substitutes), *divided*
2-1/2 cups miniature jelly beans
      3 cups sugar
      1 cup light corn syrup
    1/2 cup water
    1/2 teaspoon salt
      2 teaspoons baking soda

In a microwave-safe bowl, melt 1 tablespoon butter. Cube remaining butter and set aside. Line two 15-in. x 10-in. x 1-in. pans with foil; brush with melted butter. Arrange jelly beans evenly in pans.

In a saucepan, combine sugar, corn syrup and water. Bring to a boil over medium heat, stirring constantly, until a candy thermometer reads 240° (softball stage). Stir in cubed butter and salt. Cook and stir until mixture reaches 300° (hard-crack stage). Stir in baking soda (mixture will foam). Quickly pour over jelly beans. Spread with a buttered metal spatula. Cool; break into pieces. **Yield:** 2-1/2 pounds.

— ▼ ▼ ▼ —

Marshmallow Easter Eggs

(Pictured at left)

These eggs are a big hit with everyone who loves marshmallows. I've been making them for years.
—*Betty Claycomb, Alverton, Pennsylvania*

    25 cups all-purpose flour (about 8 pounds)
      1 large egg
      2 tablespoons unflavored gelatin
    1/2 cup cold water
      2 cups sugar
      1 cup light corn syrup, *divided*
    3/4 cup hot water
      2 teaspoons vanilla extract
      1 pound dark chocolate candy coating, melted
      2 ounces white candy coating, melted

Spread 7 cups flour in each of three 13-in. x 9-in. x 2-in. pans and 4 cups flour in a 9-in. square pan. Carefully wash the egg in a mild bleach solution (1 teaspoon chlorine bleach to 1 qt. warm water); dry. Press washed egg halfway into the flour to form an impression. Repeat 35 times; set aside.

In a small bowl, sprinkle the gelatin over cold water; set aside. In a large saucepan, combine the sugar, 1/2 cup corn syrup and hot water. Bring to a boil over medium heat, stirring constantly, until a candy thermometer reads 238° (soft-ball stage). Remove from the heat; stir in remaining corn syrup.

Pour into a large mixing bowl. Add reserved gelatin, 1 tablespoon at a time, beating on high speed until candy is thick and has cooled to lukewarm, about 10 minutes. Beat in vanilla. Spoon lukewarm gelatin mixture into egg depressions; dust with flour. Let stand for 3-4 hours or until set.

Brush excess flour off eggs. Dip each in chocolate candy coating. Place flat side down on waxed paper. Let stand until set. Pour white candy coating into a heavy-duty resealable plastic bag; cut a hole in one corner. Drizzle over eggs. **Yield:** 3 dozen.

Editor's Note: For safety reasons, we recommend that you discard the egg and all of the flour.

Raspberry Chocolate Puffs

(Pictured below)

This is my "show-off" dessert because it makes a spectacular presentation. Every time I serve it, my friends rave about this fancy and fun treat. Although it looks like you fussed, the recipe is actually quick and easy.
—Anneliese Deising, Plymouth, Michigan

- 1 cup vanilla *or* white chips
- 1 cup raspberry *or* milk chocolate chips
- 1 cup chopped pecans
- 1 package (17.3 ounces) frozen puff pastry, thawed
- 1 package (12 ounces) frozen unsweetened raspberries, thawed
- 1 cup confectioners' sugar

Fresh raspberries, additional vanilla and raspberry chips and confectioners' sugar, optional

In a bowl, combine the chips and pecans. On a lightly floured surface, roll each pastry sheet into a 12-in. square. Cut in half lengthwise and widthwise, making eight 6-in. squares. Spoon the chip mixture in the center of each square. Pull all corners together above the filling and pinch together below the tips of the corners, forming a pouch. Fold the corner tips down. Place on an ungreased baking sheet. Bake at 425° for 18-20 minutes or until golden brown. Remove to a wire rack to cool.

In a food processor or blender, puree raspberries and confectioners' sugar. Strain and discard seeds. Spoon raspberry sauce onto dessert plates; top with pastry pouches. If desired, garnish with raspberries and chips; dust with confectioners' sugar. **Yield:** 8 servings.

Rhubarb Shortbread Squares

I saw this recipe on the Internet and decided to try it since I had an abundance of rhubarb. It was a big hit!
—Marilyn Rodriguez, Fairbanks, Alaska

- 1 cup all-purpose flour
- 2 tablespoons sugar
- 1/4 teaspoon salt
- 1/2 cup cold butter *or* margarine

FILLING:
- 4 cups diced fresh *or* frozen rhubarb
- 1-1/4 cups sugar
- 1/4 cup water
- 1/8 teaspoon salt
- 2 envelopes unflavored gelatin
- 1/3 cup cold water
- 4 to 6 drops red food coloring, optional
- 1 cup heavy whipping cream, whipped

In a bowl, combine the flour, sugar and salt; cut in butter until crumbly. Press into a greased 8-in. square baking dish. Bake at 350° for 15-20 minutes or until edges are lightly browned. Cool on a wire rack.

In a saucepan, bring the rhubarb, sugar, water and salt to a boil. Reduce heat; simmer, uncovered, for 8-10 minutes or until rhubarb is tender, stirring occasionally. In a small bowl, sprinkle gelatin over cold water; let stand for 1 minute. Stir into rhubarb mixture. Cook and stir until gelatin is dissolved. Stir in food coloring if desired. Cover and refrigerate until cooled, about 2 hours.

Fold in whipped cream. Spread over crust. Cover and refrigerate for 3 hours or until set. Cut into squares. **Yield:** 9 servings.

Chocolate Fondue

This creamy, delectable dip is a chocolate lover's dream. —Jane Shapton, Tustin, California

- 1-1/2 cups sugar
- 1-1/4 cups water
- 1/4 cup light corn syrup
- 1 cup baking cocoa
- 1/2 cup heavy whipping cream
- 5 squares (1 ounce *each*) semisweet chocolate, chopped

Strawberries, banana chunks, apple slices *or* angel food cake cubes

In a small saucepan, bring the sugar, water and corn syrup to a boil. Reduce heat; simmer, uncovered, for 20 minutes, stirring frequently. In a bowl, combine the cocoa, cream and half of the syrup mixture until smooth; return all to the pan.

Bring to a boil, stirring constantly. Reduce heat; simmer, uncovered, for 5 minutes. Stir in chopped chocolate until melted. Serve warm with fruit or cake for dipping. Refrigerate leftovers. **Yield:** 2-1/2 cups.

🍷 🍷 🍷

Peachy Cream Dessert

(Pictured at right)

This is a pretty summer dessert that's "just peachy"! Cream cheese and fruit layers cover a nutty crust.
—*Deborah Ratliff, Leburn, Kentucky*

- 1 cup cold butter *or* margarine
- 2 cups self-rising flour*
- 1 cup chopped pecans
- 1 package (8 ounces) cream cheese, softened
- 2 cups confectioners' sugar
- 1 carton (8 ounces) frozen whipped topping, thawed
- 5 medium ripe peaches, peeled and thinly sliced
- 1 container (14 ounces) peach glaze

In a bowl, cut butter into the flour until crumbly; stir in the pecans. Press into a greased 13-in. x 9-in. x 2-in. baking dish. Bake at 350° for 25 minutes or until lightly browned. Cool on a wire rack.

In a small mixing bowl, beat cream cheese and confectioners' sugar until fluffy. Beat in whipped topping. Spread over crust. Arrange peaches over cream cheese layer. Carefully spread glaze over peaches. Cover and refrigerate until serving. **Yield:** 12-15 servings.

*Editor's Note: For *each* cup of self-rising flour, place 1-1/2 teaspoons baking powder and 1/2 teaspoon salt in a measuring cup. Add all-purpose flour to measure 1 cup.

🍷 🍷 🍷

Caramel Stripe Cheesecake

(Pictured above right)

I love to bake cheesecakes, and this recipe is one of the best I've tried.—*Brenda LaBrie, Clark, South Dakota*

- 2 cups vanilla wafer crumbs
- 1/3 cup butter *or* margarine, melted
- 3 packages (8 ounces *each*) cream cheese, softened
- 1 cup sugar
- 2 tablespoons all-purpose flour
- 3 eggs
- 2 tablespoons heavy whipping cream
- 1 teaspoon vanilla extract

CARAMEL TOPPING:
- 12 caramels*
- 2 tablespoons heavy whipping cream

CHOCOLATE TOPPING:
- 1/2 cup semisweet chocolate chips
- 2 teaspoons butter *or* margarine
- 4 teaspoons heavy whipping cream

Whipped cream and coarsely chopped pecans

In a small bowl, combine wafer crumbs and butter. Press onto the bottom and 1-1/2 in. up the sides of an ungreased 9-in. springform pan. Bake at 400° for 10 minutes. Cool on a wire rack. Reduce heat to 350°.

In a mixing bowl, beat cream cheese until smooth. Combine sugar and flour; add to cream cheese and mix well. Add eggs, beating just until combined. Stir in cream and vanilla. Pour into crust. Bake for 40-45 minutes or until center is almost set. Cool on a wire rack for 10 minutes. Carefully run a knife around edge of pan to loosen; cool 1 hour longer. Cover; refrigerate until completely cooled.

In a small saucepan over medium heat, cook and stir caramels and cream until melted and smooth. In another saucepan, cook and stir the chocolate chips, butter and cream until melted and smooth. Drizzle caramel and chocolate toppings over cheesecake. Refrigerate overnight. Remove sides of pan before serving. Garnish with whipped cream and pecans. Refrigerate leftovers. **Yield:** 12-14 servings.

*Editor's Note: This recipe was tested with Hershey caramels.

18-22 minutes or until golden brown. Remove to wire racks to cool. Serve with ice cream if desired. **Yield:** 2 dozen.

━━━━ 🍴 🍴 🍴 ━━━━

Chocolate Chip Cheesecake

(Pictured on page 126)

Cheesecakes are my specialty and my favorite dessert. Of the dozens of cheesecake recipes I've collected and created, this is one of the best! —Christina Till
South Haven, Michigan

- 2 cups vanilla wafer crumbs
- 1 cup flaked coconut, toasted
- 1/2 cup finely chopped walnuts
- 1/4 cup sugar
- 3 tablespoons baking cocoa
- 1/3 cup butter *or* margarine, melted

FILLING:
- 4 packages (8 ounces *each*) cream cheese, softened
- 1 cup sugar
- 4 teaspoons cornstarch
- 4 eggs
- 1/3 cup heavy whipping cream
- 3 teaspoons vanilla extract
- 1-1/2 cups miniature semisweet chocolate chips

TOPPING:
- 3 squares (1 ounce *each*) semisweet chocolate, melted
- 1 tablespoon butter (no substitutes), melted
- 1 cup confectioners' sugar
- 1/4 cup heavy whipping cream
- Toasted coconut, walnuts and maraschino cherries, optional

In a bowl, combine the first five ingredients; stir in butter. Press onto the bottom and 1 in. up the sides of a 10-in. springform pan. Refrigerate for 15 minutes.

In a mixing bowl, beat cream cheese until smooth. Combine sugar and cornstarch; beat into cream cheese. Add eggs; beat on low speed just until combined. Add the cream, vanilla and chocolate chips. Pour into prepared crust.

Place pan on a baking sheet. Bake at 350° for 60-65 minutes or until center is nearly set. Cool on a wire rack for 10 minutes. Carefully run a knife around edge of pan to loosen; cool 1 hour longer. (Cheesecake top may crack, but topping will cover.)

For topping, combine chocolate, butter and sugar in a mixing bowl. Slowly beat in cream until mixture achieves spreading consistency. Spread over cheesecake. Refrigerate overnight.

Remove sides of pan. Garnish the cheesecake with coconut, walnuts and cherries if desired. Refrigerate leftovers. **Yield:** 16-18 servings.

Mini Apple Turnovers

(Pictured above)

These cute little pastries are so yummy! I'm tempted to hoard them for myself when I make a batch, but I always end up sharing. —Merrill Powers
Spearville, Kansas

- 1 package (8 ounces) cream cheese, softened
- 3/4 cup butter *or* margarine, softened
- 1 egg, *separated*
- 3 tablespoons cold water, *divided*
- 2 cups all-purpose flour
- 7 cups thinly sliced peeled tart apples (about 6 medium)
- 3/4 cup sugar
- 1-1/2 teaspoons ground cinnamon
- Additional sugar, optional
- Vanilla ice cream, optional

In a mixing bowl, beat cream cheese and butter until smooth. Refrigerate the egg white. Beat egg yolk and 2 tablespoons water into cream cheese mixture. Gradually beat in flour until well blended. Shape pastry into a ball. Cover and refrigerate for 1 hour.

Meanwhile, in a large skillet, toss apples with sugar and cinnamon. Bring to a boil. Reduce heat; cover and simmer for 8-10 minutes or until apples are tender. Remove from the heat.

Turn the pastry onto a lightly floured surface. Roll to 1/8-in. thickness; cut into 4-in. circles. Top each circle with apple mixture. Brush edges of pastry with water; fold pastry over filling and seal edges well. In a small bowl, whisk egg white and remaining water; brush over pastry. Sprinkle with additional sugar if desired.

Place on greased baking sheets. Bake at 375° for

Blueberry Cheesecake Ice Cream

After sampling this flavor at an ice cream stand, I kept trying to duplicate it until it was just right. Everyone is impressed with its gourmet flavor.
—Melissa Symington, Neche, North Dakota

1/2 cup sugar
1 tablespoon cornstarch
1/2 cup water
1-1/4 cups fresh *or* frozen blueberries
1 tablespoon lemon juice
GRAHAM CRACKER MIXTURE:
2-1/4 cups graham cracker crumbs (about 36 squares)
2 tablespoons sugar
1/2 teaspoon ground cinnamon
1/2 cup butter *or* margarine, melted
ICE CREAM:
1-1/2 cups sugar
1 package (3.4 ounces) instant cheesecake *or* vanilla pudding mix
1 quart heavy whipping cream
2 cups milk
2 teaspoons vanilla extract

In a small saucepan, combine sugar and cornstarch. Gradually stir in water until smooth. Stir in blueberries and lemon juice. Bring to a boil. Reduce heat; simmer, uncovered, for 5 minutes or until slightly thickened, stirring occasionally. Cover and refrigerate until chilled.

In a bowl, combine cracker crumbs, sugar and cinnamon. Stir in butter. Pat into an ungreased 15-in. x 10-in. x 1-in. baking pan. Bake at 350° for 10-15 minutes or until lightly browned. Cool completely on a wire rack; crumble.

In a large bowl, whisk the ice cream ingredients. Fill ice cream freezer cylinder two-thirds full; freeze according to manufacturer's directions. Refrigerate remaining mixture until ready to freeze. Whisk before adding to ice cream freezer (mixture will have some lumps).

In a large container, layer the ice cream, graham cracker mixture and blueberry sauce three times; swirl. Freeze. **Yield:** 2 quarts.

Peach Frozen Yogurt

(Pictured at right)

When peaches are in season, we order them by the bushel and never have trouble using them up. This quick and creamy frozen treat has wonderful fresh fruit flavor. It's a big hit with everyone in my family.
—Stephanie Nohr, Cornell, Wisconsin

✓ Uses less fat, sugar or salt. Includes Nutritional Analysis and Diabetic Exchanges.

2 cups fresh *or* frozen unsweetened sliced peaches, thawed
1 envelope unflavored gelatin
1/4 cup cold water
1/4 cup sugar
2 cups (16 ounces) reduced-fat vanilla yogurt

Place the peaches in a blender or food processor; cover and process until pureed. Set aside. In a small saucepan, sprinkle gelatin over cold water; let stand for 1 minute. Stir in the sugar. Cook and stir over low heat until the gelatin and sugar are dissolved.

In a bowl, combine the yogurt, peach puree and gelatin mixture until blended. Pour into an ungreased 9-in. square dish. Cover and freeze for 3-4 hours or until partially set. Cut into pieces and place in a mixing bowl; beat on medium speed until smooth. Transfer to a freezer container. Cover and freeze until firm, about 2 hours. **Yield:** 6 servings.

Nutritional Analysis: One serving (1/2 cup) equals 179 calories, 1 g fat (1 g saturated fat), 4 mg cholesterol, 57 mg sodium, 39 g carbohydrate, 2 g fiber, 5 g protein. **Diabetic Exchanges:** 1-1/2 fruit, 1 fat-free milk.

Cranberry Mocha Cheesecake

(Pictured below)

I've made this delicious dessert for quite a few occasions, and it is always a hit. The cranberries make it a perfect finale to a holiday dinner. —Anissa Bednarski
Oronoco, Minnesota

    1 package (9 ounces) chocolate wafer
      cookies, crushed
1/3 cup butter *or* margarine, melted
FILLING:
    4 packages (8 ounces *each*) cream cheese,
      softened
1-1/3 cups sugar
    1 tablespoon all-purpose flour
    4 eggs
    2 tablespoons instant coffee granules
    1 tablespoon hot water
1/4 cup heavy whipping cream
1-1/2 teaspoons ground cinnamon
TOPPING:
    1 tablespoon cornstarch
    1 can (16 ounces) whole-berry cranberry
      sauce
3/4 cup heavy whipping cream
1/2 teaspoon vanilla extract
    2 tablespoons confectioners' sugar

Combine cookie crumbs and butter; press onto the bottom and about 2 in. up the sides of a greased 9-in. springform pan; set aside. In a mixing bowl, beat cream cheese until smooth. Combine sugar and flour; add to cream cheese and mix well. Add eggs; beat on low speed just until combined.

In a small bowl, dissolve coffee in water; add cream and cinnamon. Stir into the cream cheese mixture just until blended. Pour over crust. Place pan on a baking sheet. Bake at 350° for 50-55 minutes or until center is almost set. Cool on a wire rack for 10 minutes. Carefully run a knife around edge of pan to loosen; cool 1 hour longer.

In a large saucepan, bring cornstarch and cranberry sauce to a boil. Cook and stir for 2 minutes or until thickened. Cool. In a small mixing bowl, beat cream and vanilla until soft peaks form. Gradually add confectioners' sugar, beating until stiff peaks form. Spread over cheesecake. Refrigerate for 20 minutes or until set.

Carefully spread 1 cup of cranberry mixture to within 1 in. of edge; cover and refrigerate remaining cranberry mixture. Refrigerate cheesecake overnight; remove sides of pan. Serve with remaining cranberry mixture. **Yield:** 12-14 servings.

—— 🥄 🥄 🥄 ——

White Chocolate Cherry Parfaits

Layers of silky white chocolate mousse and sweet cherry sauce with a hint of orange alternate in this delectable dessert. —Rita Sherman, Coleville, California

1/2 cup sugar
    2 tablespoons cornstarch
1/2 cup water
    2 cups fresh *or* frozen pitted tart cherries
1/2 teaspoon orange extract
WHITE CHOCOLATE MOUSSE:
    3 tablespoons sugar
    1 teaspoon cornstarch
1/2 cup milk
    2 egg yolks, lightly beaten
    4 squares (1 ounce *each*) white baking
      chocolate, chopped
1/2 teaspoon vanilla extract
1-1/2 cups heavy whipping cream, whipped

In a small saucepan, combine sugar and cornstarch; stir in water until smooth. Add cherries. Bring to a boil over medium heat; cook and stir for 2 minutes or until thickened. Remove from the heat; stir in extract. Refrigerate until chilled.

In another saucepan, combine the sugar and cornstarch; stir in milk until smooth. Bring to a boil over medium heat. Reduce heat; cook and stir for 2 minutes. Remove from the heat. Stir a small amount of hot filling into egg yolks; return all to the pan, stirring constantly. Bring to a gentle boil; cook and stir for 2 minutes. Remove from the heat. Stir in chocolate and vanilla until chocolate is melted. Cool to room temperature. Fold in whipped cream.

Spoon 1/4 cup mousse into each parfait glass. Top with a rounded 1/4 cup of cherry mixture. Repeat layers. Refrigerate until chilled. **Yield:** 6 servings.

Country Apple Cobbler

This is my Aunt Goldie's recipe. She is without a doubt one of the family's best cooks. I like the touch of cheddar in the batter. —Mavis Diment, Marcus, Iowa

1-1/3 cups sugar, *divided*
1/4 cup water
2 tablespoons quick-cooking tapioca
1/4 teaspoon ground cinnamon
6 cups thinly sliced peeled tart apples (about 5 medium)
1 cup all-purpose flour
1 teaspoon baking powder
1/4 teaspoon salt
1/3 cup butter *or* margarine, melted
1/4 cup milk
1-1/2 cups (6 ounces) shredded cheddar cheese
1/2 cup chopped walnuts
Whipped topping, optional

In a large saucepan, combine 1 cup sugar, water, tapioca and cinnamon. Bring to a boil over medium heat, stirring occasionally. Remove from the heat; stir in the apples until coated. Pour into a greased 8-in. baking dish; set aside.

In a small bowl, combine the flour, baking powder, salt and remaining sugar. Stir in butter and milk just until moistened. Fold in cheese and walnuts. Sprinkle over apple mixture. Bake at 375° for 30-35 minutes or until filling is bubbly. Serve with whipped topping if desired. **Yield:** 6-8 servings.

German Plum Tart

(Pictured on page 126)

The buttery crust of this fruit-filled treat melts in your mouth. You can substitute sliced apples or peaches for the plums with great results. I've used this crust with blueberries, too. —Helga Schlape
Florham Park, New Jersey

1/2 cup butter *or* margarine, softened
4 tablespoons sugar, *divided*
1 egg yolk
3/4 to 1 cup all-purpose flour
2 pounds plums, quartered (about 4 cups)

In a mixing bowl, cream butter and 3 tablespoons sugar until fluffy. Beat in egg yolk. Gradually add flour, 1/4 cup at a time, until mixture forms a soft dough. Press onto the bottom and up the sides of a 10-in. pie plate.

Arrange plums, skin side up with edges overlapping, in crust; sprinkle with remaining sugar. Bake at 350° for 35-45 minutes or until crust is golden brown and fruit is tender. **Yield:** 6-8 servings.

Rhubarb Oat Dessert

(Pictured above)

I often make this old-fashioned favorite in spring when fresh rhubarb is plentiful. But it also works well with frozen rhubarb. It's pretty and pink...and has a nice crunch, thanks to the oatmeal crust and topping.
—Shirley Dreher, Clark, South Dakota

1-1/2 cups all-purpose flour
1-1/2 cups old-fashioned oats
1 cup packed brown sugar
1/2 cup chopped walnuts
1/4 teaspoon baking soda
1/4 teaspoon salt
1 cup cold butter *or* margarine
3 cups sliced fresh *or* frozen rhubarb
1-1/4 cups cold water, *divided*
1-1/2 cups sugar
3 tablespoons cornstarch
1 teaspoon vanilla extract
1/2 teaspoon red food coloring, optional
Ice cream, optional

In a large mixing bowl, combine the flour, oats, brown sugar, nuts, baking soda and salt. Cut in butter until crumbly. Press 3 cups into an ungreased 13-in. x 9-in. x 2-in. baking dish; set aside.

Soak rhubarb in 1 cup cold water for 3 minutes; drain. In a saucepan, combine sugar and cornstarch. Stir in remaining cold water until smooth. Add rhubarb, vanilla and food coloring if desired. Bring to a boil; cook and stir for 5 minutes or until thickened. Spoon over crust; sprinkle with remaining crumb mixture. Bake at 350° for 23-25 minutes or until golden brown. Serve with ice cream if desired. **Yield:** 12 servings.

Haunted House

(Pictured below)

One year I decided to try making a Halloween house out of sugar cookies. It was such fun!
—Joanne Woerlein, Etobicoke, Ontario

        3/4 cup butter *or* margarine, softened
        3/4 cup sugar
          2 eggs
          1 teaspoon vanilla extract
    2-3/4 cups all-purpose flour
          2 teaspoons baking powder
ICING AND ASSEMBLY:
    4-1/2 cups confectioners' sugar
          3 tablespoons meringue powder*
        1/2 teaspoon cream of tartar
          6 tablespoons warm water
          1 teaspoon vanilla extract
Blue, green, black and orange paste food coloring
Pastry tips-round #6 and #3
Additional confectioners' sugar
10 to 14 orange Spree candies

In a mixing bowl, cream butter and sugar. Beat in eggs, one at a time. Beat in vanilla. Combine flour and baking powder; gradually add to creamed mixture. Divide dough into thirds. Chill for 1-2 hours.

On a lightly floured surface, roll out one portion to 1/4-in. thickness. Position house side pattern on dough. With a sharp knife, cut one side piece. Reroll scraps; cut another side piece. Score and cut out window outlines; set window pieces aside. Transfer side pieces to an ungreased baking sheet.

Roll out second portion. Position house front pattern on dough. Cut out front; remove scraps. Cut out door and window pieces; set aside. Reroll scraps;

cut out house back. Cut out window piece; set aside.

Roll out remaining dough into two 5-1/2-in. x 4-in. rectangles for roof pieces. Transfer front, back and roof pieces to ungreased baking sheets. Bake at 400° for 10-12 minutes or until edges are lightly browned. Cool for 10 minutes before removing from pans to wire racks to cool completely.

Cut reserved window pieces in half for shutters. Place shutters and door on an ungreased baking sheet. Bake at 400° for 5-7 minutes or until edges are lightly browned. Cool for 10 minutes before removing to a wire rack to cool.

To make icing: In a mixing bowl, combine the first three ingredients. Add water and vanilla. Beat on low speed for 1 minute. Beat on high for 4-5 minutes or until stiff peaks form. Set aside 1 cup white icing. Tint remaining icing gray, using blue, green and black food coloring; set aside 1/2 cup. Thin remaining gray icing with 2 tablespoons water. Cover icing between uses.

To decorate: Place front, back, side and roof pieces on a work surface. Insert #6 tip into a pastry bag; fill with 1/2 cup gray icing. Outline windows, doors and edges of house and roof with icing; let dry. With thinned gray icing, fill in outlines.

To assemble: Transfer remaining thinned gray icing to a mixing bowl. Beat in 1-2 tablespoons confectioners' sugar until stiff peaks form. Pipe icing along sides of front and one side section. Position at right angles to each other on board. Press into place; prop with cans.

Pipe icing along inside edge for stability. Repeat with second side piece and back; let dry. Pipe icing along top edge of house. Position one roof piece; repeat. Pipe icing along top edge of roof pieces. Let dry.

To make decorations: Divide reserved white icing into thirds. Tint one portion black and one orange; leave the rest white. Using #3 tip and white icing, outline two large and three small ghosts on waxed paper; let dry. Thin remaining white icing with 1-2 teaspoons water. Fill in ghost outlines.

Use orange icing to make three pumpkins; use black for three bats. Let dry. Thicken remaining black with 1-2 teaspoons confectioners' sugar; pipe faces onto pumpkins and ghosts. Use a toothpick and thinned white icing to make bat eyes; let dry.

To remaining gray icing, add black coloring to make a darker gray. Using #6 tip and dark gray icing, pipe U-shaped designs on roof for shingles; let dry. Thin remaining icing if necessary with water; spread over shutters and doors. Let dry.

With remaining thickened black icing, pipe a tombstone onto door; write "RIP". Let dry. Attach door, shutters, ghosts, bats and pumpkins with icing. Attach Spree candies to roof. **Yield:** 1 house.

*Editor's Note: Meringue powder can be ordered from Wilton Industries, Inc.; 1-800/794-5866.

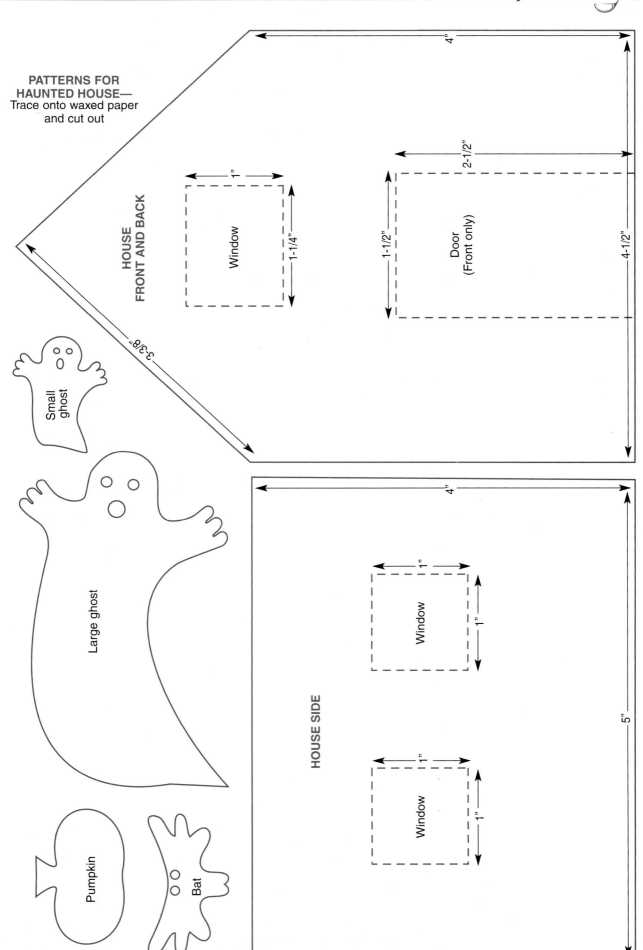

PATTERNS FOR
HAUNTED HOUSE—
Trace onto waxed paper
and cut out

HOUSE
FRONT AND BACK

4"

Window
1"
1-1/4"

2-1/2"
Door
(Front only)
1-1/2"
4-1/2"

3-3/8"

Small
ghost

Large ghost

Pumpkin

Bat

HOUSE SIDE

4"

Window
1"
1"

Window
1"
1"

5"

Potluck Pleasers

Cooking for a crowd doesn't have to be a challenge— not when you make any of these sizeable recipes.

— 🍴 🍴 🍴 —

GATHER THE GANG. Clockwise from upper left: Cherry Nut Bread (p. 150), Apple Lettuce Salad (p. 158), Peppered Rib Roast (p. 151), Crunchy Vegetable Bake (p. 162) and Chocolate Yule Log (p. 150).

TAKE-ALONG TREATS. Cranberry Biscuit Turkey Sandwiches, Tangy Party Punch, Citrus Spinach Salad and Strawberry Cream Dessert (shown above, clockwise from bottom left) make potlucks spectacular.

Citrus Spinach Salad

(Pictured above)

Grapefruit and orange segments add zest to this delightful salad that's tossed with a pleasant honey-lime dressing. It's perfect for a springtime luncheon or shower. —Pauline Taylor, Spokane, Washington

   3 tablespoons honey
   2 tablespoons lime juice
   1 teaspoon grated lime peel
1/8 to 1/4 teaspoon ground nutmeg
1/3 cup vegetable oil
 10 cups torn fresh spinach
   3 medium navel oranges, peeled and sectioned
   2 medium pink grapefruit, peeled and sectioned
   1 medium red onion, sliced and separated into rings

In a blender, combine the honey, lime juice, lime peel and nutmeg; cover and process until blended.

While processing, gradually add oil in a steady stream until dressing is thickened. In a large salad bowl, combine the spinach, oranges and grapefruit. Drizzle with dressing; toss to coat. Top with onion. Serve immediately. **Yield:** 12 servings.

———— 🏺 🏺 🏺 ————

Tangy Party Punch

(Pictured above)

As social chair one year during college, I tried to come up with a more interesting beverage than the usual cranberry juice and lemon-lime soda. This pastel punch was always a hit at receptions and parties.
—Jennifer Bangerter, Nixa, Missouri

1 can (46 ounces) pineapple juice, chilled
1 can (46 ounces) orange juice, chilled
1 can (12 ounces) frozen limeade concentrate, thawed
1 can (12 ounces) frozen lemonade concentrate, thawed

3 liters ginger ale, chilled
1 pint *each* orange, lemon and lime sherbet

In a large punch bowl, combine the first four in-gredients. Stir in ginger ale. Add scoops of sherbet. Serve immediately. **Yield:** 8 quarts.

— 🥄 🥄 🥄 —

Strawberry Cream Dessert

(Pictured at left)

This fluffy creation is a variation on two recipes—a de-licious four-layer dessert my mom used to make and a gelatin pie I came up with one day when I was short on ingredients. My family just loves it!
—*Rachel Lynn Rioux, Lisbon, Maine*

2-1/4 cups graham cracker crumbs (about 36 squares)
6 tablespoons sugar
10 tablespoons butter *or* margarine, melted
1 package (8 ounces) cream cheese, softened
1 cup confectioners' sugar
2 cartons (one 16 ounces, one 8 ounces) frozen whipped topping, thawed, *divided*
1 package (3 ounces) strawberry gelatin
1/2 cup boiling water
1 cup (8 ounces) strawberry yogurt
TOPPING:
2 tablespoons graham cracker crumbs
1-1/2 teaspoons sugar
1-1/2 teaspoons butter *or* margarine, melted

In a bowl, combine the cracker crumbs, sugar and butter. Press into an ungreased 13-in. x 9-in. x 2-in. dish. Refrigerate for 15 minutes. Meanwhile, in a mixing bowl, beat cream cheese and confection-ers' sugar until smooth. Whisk in 1 cup whipped topping. Spread over the prepared crust.

In a large bowl, dissolve gelatin in boiling water. Whisk in yogurt and 6 cups of whipped topping un-til blended. Pour over cream cheese layer. Refrig-erate for 1 hour. Spread remaining whipped top-ping over strawberry layer. Cover and refrigerate overnight. Just before serving, combine topping in-gredients; sprinkle over the whipped topping. **Yield:** 12-15 servings.

— 🥄 🥄 🥄 —

Cranberry Biscuit Turkey Sandwiches

(Pictured above left)

These flavorful buffet sandwiches are so fun and festive. Smoked turkey slices are layered inside tender biscuits flecked with dried cranberries and spread with a creamy cranberry butter. —*Barbara Nowakowski North Tonawanda, New York*

2 tablespoons cold butter (no substitutes)
4 cups biscuit/baking mix
1 cup milk
3/4 cup dried cranberries
CRANBERRY BUTTER:
1/2 cup butter, softened
1/4 cup honey
1/4 cup dried cranberries, chopped
1-1/2 pounds thinly sliced deli smoked turkey

In a large bowl, cut butter into biscuit mix until crumbly; stir in milk just until moistened. Fold in the cranberries. Turn onto a floured surface; knead 10-15 times. Roll out to 1/2-in. thickness; cut with a 2-1/2-in. biscuit cutter. Place on ungreased baking sheets. Bake at 400° for 14-16 minutes or until golden brown. Cool on a wire rack.

In a small mixing bowl, beat butter and honey until smooth; stir in cranberries. To assemble sandwiches, split biscuits. Spread with cranberry butter and top with turkey; replace biscuit tops. **Yield:** 20 sandwiches.

— 🥄 🥄 🥄 —

Two-Bread Dressing

At least 10 of us women made this old-fashioned dressing to feed over 1,500 people at our church's fall festival. Everyone thought it was wonderful. It's the best dressing I've ever made.
—*Patty Kierce, Weir, Texas*

2 cups water
2 large onions, chopped
1-1/2 cups chopped celery
1-1/2 cups minced fresh parsley
1 cup butter *or* margarine, cubed
1 teaspoon ground nutmeg
2 loaves (1-1/2 pounds *each*) bread, toasted and cubed
12 cups cubed corn bread, toasted
10 eggs, beaten
10 hard-cooked eggs, chopped
5 cups cubed cooked chicken
2 cans (14-1/2 ounces *each*) chicken broth

In a Dutch oven, combine the water, onions, cel-ery, parsley, butter and nutmeg. Bring to a boil; cook and stir until the vegetables are tender. Com-bine the bread, corn bread, eggs, chicken, broth and onion mixture. Divide among four greased 3-qt. baking dishes. Bake, uncovered, at 350° for 45-50 minutes or until a thermometer reads 160°. **Yield:** 36-40 servings.

Spinach Beef Macaroni Bake

(Pictured above)

This hearty casserole is great for a family reunion or church supper. I've also made half the recipe for smaller family gatherings.
—Lois Lauppe
Lahoma, Oklahoma

5-1/4 cups uncooked elbow macaroni
2-1/2 pounds ground beef
  2 large onions, chopped
  3 large carrots, shredded
  3 celery ribs, chopped
  2 cans (28 ounces *each*) Italian diced tomatoes, undrained
  4 teaspoons salt
  1 teaspoon garlic powder
  1 teaspoon pepper
1/2 teaspoon dried oregano
  2 packages (10 ounces *each*) frozen chopped spinach, thawed and squeezed dry
  1 cup grated Parmesan cheese

Cook macaroni according to package directions. Meanwhile, in a Dutch oven or large kettle, cook the beef, onions, carrots and celery over medium heat until meat is no longer pink; drain. Add the tomatoes, salt, garlic powder, pepper and oregano. Bring to a boil. Reduce heat; cover and simmer for 30 minutes or until vegetables are tender.
  Drain macaroni; add macaroni and spinach to beef mixture. Pour into two greased 3-qt. baking dishes. Sprinkle with Parmesan cheese. Bake, uncovered, at 350° for 25-30 minutes or until heated through. **Yield:** 2 casseroles (12 servings each).

Cherry Nut Bread

(Pictured on page 146)

Chopped pecans and maraschino cherries perk up this pound cake-like bread. The slices are rich and moist.
—Melissa Gentner, Tecumseh, Michigan

  2 cups butter *or* margarine, softened
  3 cups sugar
  5 eggs, *separated*
  1 teaspoon vanilla extract
  5 cups all-purpose flour
  1 teaspoon baking soda
1/2 teaspoon baking powder
1/2 teaspoon salt
  1 cup buttermilk
  2 jars (10 ounces *each*) maraschino cherries, drained and chopped
  1 cup chopped pecans

In a large mixing bowl, cream butter and sugar. Add egg yolks and vanilla; mix well. Combine the flour, baking soda, baking powder and salt; add to the creamed mixture alternately with buttermilk just until blended (batter will be thick). In a small mixing bowl, beat egg whites until stiff peaks form. Fold into batter. Fold in cherries and pecans.
  Transfer to four greased and floured 8-in. x 4-in. x 2-in. loaf pans. Bake at 350° for 50-55 minutes or until a toothpick inserted near the center comes out clean and loaves are golden brown. Cool for 10 minutes before removing from pans to wire racks. **Yield:** 4 loaves.

—— 🥄 🥄 🥄 ——

Chocolate Yule Log

(Pictured on page 146)

This eye-catching dessert is guaranteed to delight holiday dinner guests. Chocolate lovers will lick their lips over the cocoa cake, mocha filling and frosting.
—Jenny Hughson, Mitchell, Nebraska

  5 eggs, *separated*
  1 cup sugar, *divided*
1/2 cup cake flour
1/4 cup baking cocoa
1/4 teaspoon salt
1/2 teaspoon cream of tartar
MOCHA CREAM FILLING:
  1 cup heavy whipping cream
1/2 cup confectioners' sugar
1-1/2 teaspoons instant coffee granules
MOCHA BUTTERCREAM FROSTING:
1/3 cup butter *or* margarine, softened
1/3 cup baking cocoa
  2 cups confectioners' sugar

1-1/2 teaspoons vanilla extract
    1 tablespoon brewed coffee
    2 to 3 tablespoons milk

Line a 15-in. x 10-in. x 1-in. baking pan with parchment paper; grease the paper. Place egg whites in a small mixing bowl; let stand at room temperature for 30 minutes. In a large mixing bowl, beat egg yolks on high until light and fluffy. Gradually add 1/2 cup sugar, beating until thick and lemon-colored. Combine flour, cocoa and salt; gradually add to egg yolk mixture until blended.

Beat egg whites on medium until foamy. Add cream of tartar; beat until soft peaks form. Gradually add remaining sugar, beating on high until stiff peaks form. Stir a fourth into chocolate mixture. Fold in remaining egg whites until no streaks remain.

Spread batter evenly in prepared pan. Bake at 350° for 12-15 minutes or until cake springs back (do not overbake). Cool for 5 minutes; invert onto a linen towel dusted with confectioners' sugar. Peel off parchment paper. Roll up in the towel, starting with a short side. Cool on a wire rack. In a mixing bowl, beat cream until it begins to thicken. Add sugar and coffee granules. Beat until stiff peaks form; chill. Unroll cooled cake; spread filling to within 1/2 in. of edges. Roll up again. Place on serving platter; chill.

In a mixing bowl, beat frosting ingredients until smooth. Frost cake. Using a fork, make lines resembling tree bark. **Yield:** 12 servings.

— 🥄 🥄 🥄 —

Peppered Rib Roast

(Pictured on page 146)

The marinade tenderizes the meat, and the drippings make a savory sauce to accompany these beef slices.
—Mary Welch, Sturgeon Bay, Wisconsin

1/4 cup coarsely ground pepper
1/2 teaspoon ground cardamom
    1 boneless beef rib eye roast (5 to 6 pounds)
    1 cup soy sauce
3/4 cup red wine vinegar *or* cider vinegar
    1 tablespoon tomato paste
    1 teaspoon paprika
1/2 teaspoon garlic powder
1-1/2 teaspoons cornstarch
1/4 cup cold water

Combine the pepper and cardamom; rub over roast. In a gallon-size resealable plastic bag, combine the soy sauce, vinegar, tomato paste, paprika and garlic powder; add the roast. Seal bag and turn to coat; refrigerate overnight.

Drain and discard marinade. Place roast on a rack in a shallow roasting pan. Cover and bake at 350° for 2 to 2-3/4 hours or until meat reaches desired doneness (for rare, a meat thermometer should read 140°; medium, 160°; well-done, 170°). Let stand for 20 minutes before carving.

Meanwhile, for gravy, pour the pan drippings and loosened brown bits into a saucepan; skim fat. Combine cornstarch and cold water until smooth; gradually stir into the drippings. Bring to a boil; cook and stir for 2 minutes or until thickened. Serve with the roast. **Yield:** 16-18 servings.

— 🥄 🥄 🥄 —

Fake Steak

(Pictured below)

As hosts at a mission house, we cook for 30 to 60 people weekly. This ground beef entree is one we serve often.   *—Fran Wolfley, St. Mary, Jamaica*

    2 cups milk, *divided*
1-3/4 cups dry bread crumbs
    2 medium onions, finely chopped
    4 teaspoons salt
3/4 teaspoon pepper
    5 pounds ground beef
    2 cans (26 ounces *each*) condensed cream of mushroom soup, undiluted

In a bowl, combine 1-3/4 cups milk, bread crumbs, onions, salt and pepper. Crumble beef over mixture; mix well. Shape into 24 oval patties, about 4 in. x 2-1/2 in. Place in two greased 15-in. x 10-in. x 1-in. baking pans. Cover; refrigerate 8 hours or overnight. Bake, uncovered, at 350° for 15 minutes; drain. Combine soup and remaining milk; pour over patties.

Cover and bake 20-30 minutes longer or until a meat thermometer reads 160° (the patties will remain pink inside). **Yield:** 24 servings.

Italian Sausage and Peppers

(Pictured below right)

My sister was hosting a birthday party and asked me to bring sausage and peppers. I'd never made them before, so I altered a braised pepper recipe.
—*Jeanne Corsi, Arnold, Pennsylvania*

 Uses less fat, sugar or salt. Includes Nutritional Analysis and Diabetic Exchanges.

- 3 pounds Italian sausage links, cut into 3/4-inch slices
- 4 medium green peppers, cut into thin strips
- 1 medium onion, thinly sliced and quartered
- 1 tablespoon butter *or* stick margarine
- 1 tablespoon olive *or* canola oil
- 3 tablespoons chicken broth
- 6 plum tomatoes, coarsely chopped
- 1 tablespoon minced fresh parsley
- 1/2 teaspoon salt
- 1/4 teaspoon pepper
- 1/2 teaspoon lemon juice

In a Dutch oven, cook the sausage over medium heat until no longer pink; drain. Add the remaining ingredients. Cover and cook for 30 minutes or until vegetables are tender, stirring occasionally. Serve with a slotted spoon. **Yield:** 12 servings.
Nutritional Analysis: One serving (prepared with turkey Italian sausage) equals 230 calories, 13 g fat (4 g saturated fat), 63 mg cholesterol, 829 mg sodium, 8 g carbohydrate, 1 g fiber, 20 g protein.
Diabetic Exchanges: 2 lean meat, 2 fat, 1 vegetable.

Sweet Onion Corn Bake

(Pictured at right)

This tasty corn casserole gets plenty of flavor from sweet onions, cream-style corn and cheddar cheese plus a little zip from hot pepper sauce.
—*Jeanette Travis, Fort Worth, Texas*

- 2 large Vidalia *or* sweet onions, thinly sliced
- 1/2 cup butter *or* margarine
- 1 cup (8 ounces) sour cream
- 1/2 cup milk
- 1/2 teaspoon dill weed
- 1/4 teaspoon salt
- 2 cups (8 ounces) shredded cheddar cheese, *divided*
- 1 egg, lightly beaten
- 1 can (14-3/4 ounces) cream-style corn
- 1 package (8-1/2 ounces) corn bread/muffin mix
- 4 drops hot pepper sauce

In a large skillet, saute onions in butter until tender. In a small bowl, combine sour cream, milk, dill and salt until blended; stir in 1 cup cheese. Stir into onion mixture; remove from heat and set aside.

In a bowl, combine egg, corn, corn bread mix and hot pepper sauce. Pour into a greased 13-in. x 9-in. x 2-in. baking dish. Spoon onion mixture over top. Sprinkle with remaining cheese. Bake, uncovered, at 350° for 45-50 minutes or until top is set and lightly browned. Let stand for 10 minutes before cutting. **Yield:** 12-15 servings.

Tangy Salad Dressing

(Pictured at right)

This salad topper coats spinach or any greens so nicely...and it's easy to prepare. I like to use balsamic vinegar, which gives it a tart, refreshing flavor.
—*Alcy Thorne, Los Molinos, California*

- 1/2 cup balsamic vinegar *or* red wine vinegar
- 1/2 cup sugar
- 1/3 cup ketchup
- 1/4 cup finely chopped onion
- 1 tablespoon Worcestershire sauce
- 1 teaspoon salt
- 1 cup olive *or* vegetable oil
- Salad greens and croutons

In a blender or food processor, combine the vinegar, sugar, ketchup, onion, Worcestershire sauce and salt; cover and process until smooth. While processing, gradually add oil in a steady stream. Serve over salad greens and croutons. **Yield:** 2 cups.

Peanut Butter Chocolate Cake

(Pictured at right)

I'm a chocoholic and my kids love peanut butter, so a sweet slice of this cake is a real treat for all of us. A boxed mix cuts down on preparation time for busy moms like me. —*Fran Green, Linden, New Jersey*

- 1 package (18-1/4 ounces) devil's food cake mix
- 4 ounces cream cheese, softened
- 1/4 cup creamy peanut butter
- 2 tablespoons confectioners' sugar
- 1 cup whipped topping
- 1 cup heavy whipping cream
- 1 cup (6 ounces) semisweet chocolate chips

Prepare and bake cake mix according to package directions, using a 9-in. fluted tube pan. Cool for 10 minutes before removing from pan to a wire rack.

In a mixing bowl, beat cream cheese until smooth. Add peanut butter and confectioners' sugar; beat until blended. Fold in whipped topping. Split cake in half horizontally; place bottom layer on a serving plate. Spread with peanut butter mixture. Top with remaining cake. Refrigerate until chilled.

In a small heavy saucepan, bring cream to a boil. Reduce heat to low. Stir in chocolate chips; cook and stir until chocolate is melted. Refrigerate until spreadable. Frost top and sides of cake. Refrigerate until serving. **Yield:** 12-14 servings.

PLANT THE SEEDS for a spring potluck with Italian Sausage and Peppers, Sweet Onion Corn Bake, Peanut Butter Chocolate Cake and Tangy Salad Dressing with greens (shown below, clockwise from bottom).

Corn Bread Confetti Salad

(Pictured below)

This colorful and tasty salad is always well received at picnics and potlucks. Corn bread salads have long been popular in the South but may be new to people in other regions. No matter where you live, I think you'll like this one! —Jennifer Horst
Goose Creek, South Carolina

- 1 package (8-1/2 ounces) corn bread/muffin mix
- 2 cans (15-1/2 ounces *each*) whole kernel corn, drained
- 2 cans (15 ounces *each*) pinto beans, rinsed and drained
- 1 can (15 ounces) black beans, rinsed and drained
- 3 small tomatoes, chopped
- 1 medium green pepper, chopped
- 1 medium sweet red pepper, chopped
- 1/2 cup chopped green onions
- 10 bacon strips, cooked and crumbled
- 2 cups (8 ounces) shredded cheddar cheese

DRESSING:
- 1 cup (8 ounces) sour cream
- 1 cup mayonnaise
- 1 envelope ranch salad dressing mix

Prepare corn bread according to package directions. Cool completely; crumble. In a large bowl, combine the corn, beans, tomatoes, peppers, onions, bacon, cheese and crumbled corn bread. In a small bowl, combine the dressing ingredients until well blended. Just before serving, pour dressing over salad and toss. **Yield:** 20-22 servings.

Sweet 'n' Creamy Coleslaw

My grandmother taught me how to make the dressing for this coleslaw when I was very young. It's not too tart and not too sweet. Sometimes I make 8 gallon jars a week at the restaurant where I work! It gets lots of compliments. —Denise Elder, Hanover, Ontario

- 1/2 cup plus 2 tablespoons sugar
- 2-1/4 teaspoons all-purpose flour
- 2-1/4 teaspoons cornstarch
- 1 teaspoon ground mustard
- 1/2 teaspoon salt
- 1/2 teaspoon pepper
- 1/2 cup plus 2 tablespoons cider vinegar
- 1/2 cup water
- 1 egg, lightly beaten
- 1/2 cup milk
- 1/4 cup packed brown sugar
- 1/2 cup half-and-half cream
- 2 cups mayonnaise *or* salad dressing
- 3 medium heads cabbage (6 to 7 pounds), shredded
- 2 medium carrots, shredded
- 2 celery ribs, chopped
- 7 green onions, thinly sliced

In a large saucepan, combine the sugar, flour, cornstarch, mustard, salt and pepper. Gradually stir in vinegar and water. Add egg and milk. Cook and stir until mixture comes to a boil. Cook 2 minutes longer or until slightly thickened. Cool to room temperature, stirring several times.

In a large bowl, combine the brown sugar and cream. Stir in mayonnaise. Add cooked dressing; mix well. In several large bowls, combine the cabbage, carrots, celery and green onions. Add dressing and toss to coat. Serve immediately. **Yield:** 32 (3/4-cup) servings.

—— 🝙 🝙 🝙 ——

Fruited Turkey Salad

We served this delicious salad at a church luncheon along with a variety of homemade muffins and a dessert. The meal was a big hit, and many of the women attending asked for the salad recipe. If you prefer, use diced cooked chicken instead of turkey.
—Pat Swaney, Lima, Ohio

- 25 quarts cubed cooked turkey *or* chicken
- 20 cans (20 ounces *each*) pineapple chunks, drained
- 20 cans (15 ounces *each*) mandarin oranges, drained
- 20 cans (2-1/4 ounces *each*) sliced ripe olives, drained
- 5 bunches celery, thinly sliced

10 large green peppers, chopped
5 to 6 quarts mayonnaise *or* salad dressing
3 large onions, grated
1-1/2 cups prepared mustard
5 tablespoons salt
1 to 2 tablespoons lemon-pepper seasoning, optional
8 cans (5 ounces *each*) chow mein noodles

In several large bowls, combine the first six ingredients. In another large bowl, combine the mayonnaise, onions, mustard, salt and lemon-pepper if desired. Cover and refrigerate chicken mixture and dressing separately for at least 2 hours before tossing. Sprinkle with chow mein noodles. Serve immediately. **Yield:** 185 (1-cup) servings.

— 🍴 🍴 🍴 —

Danish Twists

(Pictured at right)

My twin sister and I love to bake together, and this was one of the first yeast breads we tried. Any day becomes a special occasion when these rich buttery twists are on the menu! But plan ahead...the dough needs to rise overnight.　　—Charys Rockey, Rochelle, Texas

2 packages (1/4 ounce *each*) active dry yeast
1-1/2 cups warm milk (110° to 115°)
4 cups all-purpose flour
1/2 cup sugar
2 teaspoons salt
1 cup cold butter (no substitutes)
4 egg yolks, beaten
2 egg whites, beaten
Seedless raspberry jam *or* apricot preserves
GLAZE:
1-1/2 cups confectioners' sugar
3/4 teaspoon vanilla extract
2 to 3 tablespoons milk

In a bowl, dissolve yeast in warm milk. In a large bowl, combine the flour, sugar and salt. Using a pastry blender, cut in butter until crumbly. Stir in yeast mixture and egg yolks. Cover and refrigerate overnight.

Punch dough down. Turn onto a lightly floured surface; divide into thirds. Roll each portion into a 9-in. x 7-in. rectangle. Cut into 7-in. x 1-in. strips. Pinch ends together, forming a circle; twist once to form a figure eight. Place 2 in. apart on greased baking sheets. Cover and let rise until doubled, about 20 minutes.

Brush with egg whites. Make an indentation in the center of each loop; fill with jam. Bake at 350° for 14-16 minutes or until golden brown. Remove from pans to wire racks. In a small bowl, combine glaze ingredients. Drizzle over warm rolls. **Yield:** 27 rolls.

— 🍴 🍴 🍴 —

Holiday Ribbon Gelatin

Layers of red and green make this festive salad a favorite during the Christmas season. Kids are sure to find it fun to eat, and adults will enjoy the combination of sweet-tart flavors.　　—Jenny Hughson, Mitchell, Nebraska

2 packages (3 ounces *each*) lime gelatin
5 cups boiling water, *divided*
4 cups cold water, *divided*
1 package (3 ounces) lemon gelatin
1/2 cup miniature marshmallows
1 package (8 ounces) cream cheese, softened
1 cup mayonnaise
1 can (8 ounces) crushed pineapple, undrained
2 packages (3 ounces *each*) cherry gelatin

In a bowl, dissolve lime gelatin in 2 cups boiling water. Add 2 cups cold water; stir. Pour into a 13-in. x 9-in. x 2-in. dish; refrigerate until set, about 1 hour.

In a bowl, dissolve lemon gelatin in 1 cup boiling water. Stir in marshmallows until melted. Cool for 20 minutes. In a small mixing bowl, beat cream cheese and mayonnaise until smooth. Gradually beat in lemon gelatin. Stir in pineapple. Carefully spoon over the lime layer. Chill until set.

Dissolve cherry gelatin in 2 cups boiling water. Add the remaining cold water; stir. Spoon over the lemon layer. Refrigerate overnight. Cut into squares. **Yield:** 12-15 servings.

FRIENDS AND FAMILY will warm up to this satisfying spread featuring tasty Bacon Onion Turnovers, Greens with Vinaigrette, Lemon Sheet Cake and Chicken and Ham Lasagna (shown above, clockwise from top).

Chicken and Ham Lasagna

(Pictured above)

This creamy version of lasagna goes over great at community get-togethers. My husband doesn't like broccoli, so I often substitute zucchini and yellow squash.
—Pamela Grady, Inman, South Carolina

3/4 **pound fresh mushrooms, sliced**
1 **large onion, chopped**
1 **large green pepper, chopped**
1/4 **cup butter *or* margarine**
1/2 **cup all-purpose flour**
1-2/3 **cups milk**
1 **can (14-1/2 ounces) chicken broth**
1 **package (16 ounces) frozen**
chopped broccoli, thawed and drained
2/3 **cup grated Parmesan cheese**
1/2 **teaspoon salt**
1/4 **to 1/2 teaspoon white pepper**
1/8 **teaspoon ground nutmeg**
12 **lasagna noodles, cooked and drained**
2 **cups cubed fully cooked ham**
2 **cups (8 ounces) shredded Swiss cheese**
2 **cups cubed cooked chicken**

In a large skillet, saute mushrooms, onion and green pepper in butter until tender. Stir in flour until blended. Gradually add milk and broth. Bring to a boil; cook and stir for 2 minutes or until thickened. Stir in broccoli, Parmesan, salt, pepper and nutmeg.

Spread 2 cups broccoli mixture in a greased 13-in. x 9-in. x 2-in. baking dish. Top with four noodles, overlapping if needed. Layer with 2 cups broccoli mixture, 1-1/2 cups of ham, 2/3 cup Swiss cheese, four noodles, 2 cups broccoli mixture, chicken, 2/3 cup Swiss cheese, four noodles and remaining broccoli mixture, Swiss cheese and ham. Cover; bake at 350° for 35-45 minutes until heated through. Let stand 15 minutes before cutting. **Yield:** 12 servings.

Greens with Vinaigrette

(Pictured at left)

_This slightly tangy oil and vinegar dressing comple-
ments a bowl of salad greens or a colorful vegetable toss
nicely._ —_Rosemarie Forcum, White Stone, Virginia_

- 1/4 **cup cider vinegar**
- 1/2 **to 1 teaspoon sugar**
- 1/4 **teaspoon salt**
- 1/8 **teaspoon seasoned salt**
- 1/8 **teaspoon pepper**
- 1/2 **cup vegetable oil**
- 4 **cups torn leaf lettuce**
- 4 **cups torn Bibb lettuce**
- 1/4 **cup thinly sliced onion**

In a small bowl, combine vinegar, sugar, salt, seasoned salt and pepper. Gradually whisk in oil. In a
large bowl, combine lettuces and onion. Serve with
dressing. **Yield:** 12 servings (about 1/2 cup dressing).

— 🥄 🥄 🥄 —

Bacon Onion Turnovers

(Pictured at left)

_Potluck-goers will enjoy these cute pastry packets. The
bacon-onion filling is tasty, and the turnover shell is
crispy on the outside, tender on the inside._
—_Cari Miller, Philadelphia, Pennsylvania_

- 3 **packages (1/4 ounce _each_) active dry yeast**
- 1/2 **cup warm water (110° to 115°)**
- 1 **cup warm milk (110° to 115°)**
- 1/2 **cup butter _or_ margarine, melted**
- 2 **teaspoons salt**
- 3-1/2 **to 4 cups all-purpose flour**
- 1/2 **pound sliced bacon, cooked and crumbled**
- 1 **large onion, diced**
- 1 **egg, lightly beaten**

In a large mixing bowl, dissolve yeast in warm
water. Add the milk, butter and salt; beat until
smooth. Stir in enough flour to form a soft dough.
Turn onto a floured surface; knead until smooth
and elastic, about 6-8 minutes. Place in a greased
bowl, turning once to grease top. Cover and let rise
in a warm place until doubled, about 30 minutes.
 Punch dough down. Turn onto a lightly floured
surface; divide into 30 pieces. Roll each into a 4-in.
circle. Combine bacon and onion; place about 2
teaspoons on one side of each circle. Fold dough
over filling; press edges with a fork to seal. Place 3
in. apart on greased baking sheets. Cover and let rise
in a warm place until doubled, about 20 minutes.
 Brush with egg. Bake at 425° for 10-15 minutes
or until golden brown. Remove to wire racks. Serve
warm. **Yield:** 2-1/2 dozen.

Lemon Sheet Cake

(Pictured at left)

_Lemon pie filling lends a splash of citrus flavor to con-
venient cake mix, and a rich cream cheese frosting
gives it sweetness. My family likes this cake cold, so I
cut it into squares and freeze before serving._
—_Alyce Dubisar, Coos Bay, Oregon_

- 1 **package (18-1/4 ounces) lemon cake mix**
- 4 **eggs**
- 1 **can (15-3/4 ounces) lemon pie filling**
- 1 **package (3 ounces) cream cheese,
softened**
- 1/2 **cup butter _or_ margarine, softened**
- 2 **cups confectioners' sugar**
- 1-1/2 **teaspoons vanilla extract**

In a large mixing bowl, beat the cake mix and eggs
until well blended. Fold in pie filling. Spread into a
greased 15-in. x 10-in. x 1-in. baking pan. Bake at
350° for 18-20 minutes or until a toothpick inserted
near the center comes out clean. Cool on a wire rack.
 In a small mixing bowl, beat cream cheese,
butter and confectioners' sugar until smooth. Stir in
vanilla. Spread over cake. Store in the refrigerator.
Yield: 30-35 servings.

— 🥄 🥄 🥄 —

Cheesy Noodle Casseroles

_This rich, cheesy side dish is such an excellent meal ex-
tender that I always keep it in mind whenever I feel
my menu needs a boost. It's a quick and easy casserole
to fix!_ —_Shirley McKee, Varna, Illinois_

- 2 **packages (1 pound _each_) wide egg noodles**
- 1/2 **cup butter _or_ margarine**
- 1/4 **cup all-purpose flour**
- 1 **teaspoon garlic salt**
- 1 **teaspoon onion salt**
- 5 **to 6 cups milk**
- 2 **pounds process cheese (Velveeta), cubed**

TOPPING:
- 1/2 **cup dry bread crumbs**
- 2 **tablespoons butter _or_ margarine, melted**

Cook noodles according to package directions;
drain. In a Dutch oven, melt butter. Stir in the flour,
garlic salt and onion salt until smooth. Gradually
stir in milk. Bring to a boil; cook and stir for 2
minutes or until thickened and bubbly. Add cheese;
stir until melted. Stir in noodles.
 Transfer to two greased shallow 2-qt. baking
dishes. Toss bread crumbs and butter; sprinkle over
casseroles. Bake, uncovered, at 350° for 25-30
minutes or until golden brown. **Yield:** 2 casseroles
(12 servings each).

Mom's Tamale Pie

(Pictured above)

My mom never used a recipe for her tamale pie, but I came up with this version that tastes very much like the one she used to make.
—_Waldine Guillott_
DeQuincy, Louisiana

- 2 pounds ground beef
- 1 large onion, chopped
- 1 large green pepper, chopped
- 1 can (15-1/4 ounces) whole kernel corn, undrained
- 1-1/2 cups chopped fresh tomatoes
- 5 tablespoons tomato paste
- 1 envelope chili seasoning
- 1-1/2 teaspoons sugar
- 1 teaspoon garlic powder
- 1 teaspoon dried basil
- 1 teaspoon dried oregano
- 6 cups cooked grits (prepared with butter and salt)
- 1-1/2 teaspoons chili powder, _divided_
- 1-1/2 cups (6 ounces) shredded cheddar cheese

In a large skillet, cook beef, onion and green pepper over medium heat until meat is no longer pink; drain. Add corn, tomatoes, tomato paste, chili seasoning, sugar, garlic powder, basil and oregano; mix well. Cook and stir until heated through; keep warm.
Spread half of the grits in a greased 3-qt. baking dish. Sprinkle with 1 teaspoon chili powder. Top with beef mixture and cheese. Pipe remaining grits around edge of dish; sprinkle with remaining chili powder. Bake, uncovered, at 325° for 20-25 minutes or until cheese is melted. Let stand for 5 minutes before serving. **Yield:** 12 servings.

Apple Lettuce Salad

(Pictured on page 146)

Apples and lettuce pair up in this colorful and crunchy salad that you can make ahead for a gathering.
—_Marlene Muckenhirn, Delano, Minnesota_

☑ Uses less fat, sugar or salt. Includes Nutritional Analysis and Diabetic Exchanges.

- 1/2 cup unsweetened apple juice
- 2 tablespoons lemon juice
- 2 tablespoons cider vinegar
- 2 tablespoons vegetable _or_ canola oil
- 4-1/2 teaspoons brown sugar
- 1 teaspoon Dijon mustard
- 1/4 teaspoon pepper
- 1/8 teaspoon salt
- 1/8 teaspoon ground cinnamon
- Dash ground nutmeg
- 1 medium red apple, chopped
- 1 medium green apple, chopped
- 6 cups torn green leaf lettuce
- 6 cups torn red leaf lettuce

In a large salad bowl, whisk the first 10 ingredients until blended. Add apples; toss to coat. Place lettuce over apple mixture (do not toss). Refrigerate; toss just before serving. **Yield:** 12 servings.
Nutritional Analysis: One serving (1 cup) equals 50 calories, 2 g fat (trace saturated fat), 0 cholesterol, 41 mg sodium, 7 g carbohydrate, 2 g fiber, 1 g protein. **Diabetic Exchanges:** 1/2 fruit, 1/2 fat.

Parmesan Zucchini Bread

This loaf has a rugged, textured look that adds to its old-fashioned appeal. The mild Parmesan flavor nicely complements the zucchini. —_Christine Wilson Sellersville, Pennsylvania_

☑ Uses less fat, sugar or salt. Includes Nutritional Analysis and Diabetic Exchanges.

- 3 cups all-purpose flour
- 3 tablespoons grated Parmesan cheese
- 1 teaspoon salt
- 1/2 teaspoon baking powder
- 1/2 teaspoon baking soda
- 2 eggs
- 1 cup buttermilk
- 1/3 cup sugar
- 1/3 cup butter _or_ stick margarine, melted
- 1 cup shredded peeled zucchini
- 1 tablespoon grated onion

In a bowl, combine the flour, Parmesan cheese, salt, baking powder and baking soda. In another bowl, beat the eggs, buttermilk, sugar and butter. Stir into dry ingredients just until moistened. Fold in zucchini and onion.

Pour into a greased and floured 9-in. x 5-in. x 3-in. loaf pan. Bake at 350° for 1 hour or until a toothpick comes out clean. Cool 10 minutes; remove from pan to wire rack. **Yield:** 1 loaf (16 slices).

Nutritional Analysis: One slice equals 144 calories, 5 g fat (3 g saturated fat), 38 mg cholesterol, 267 mg sodium, 23 g carbohydrate, 1 g fiber, 4 g protein. **Diabetic Exchange:** 1-1/2 starch.

——— 🥄 🥄 🥄 ———

Pumpkin Cheesecake Bars

The perfect dessert for an autumn celebration, these bars feature a gingery cookie crust and a spicy pumpkin filling. —_Marcie Matthews, Santa Rosa, California_

    2 cups crushed windmill cookies* (about 12 cookies)
  1/2 cup butter _or_ margarine, melted
    4 packages (8 ounces _each_) cream cheese, softened
1-1/4 cups sugar
    1 cup canned pumpkin
  1/4 cup heavy whipping cream
    3 tablespoons all-purpose flour
  1/2 teaspoon _each_ ground nutmeg, ginger, cinnamon and cloves
  1/4 teaspoon salt
  1/4 teaspoon vanilla extract
    4 eggs
    2 egg yolks
TOPPING:
  1/2 cup sugar
    1 cup pecan halves
    2 cups heavy whipping cream
  1/2 cup confectioners' sugar
  1/4 teaspoon vanilla extract

Combine cookie crumbs and butter; press into a greased 13-in. x 9-in. x 2-in. baking dish. Bake at 325° for 8-10 minutes until set. Cool on a wire rack.

In a large mixing bowl, beat cream cheese and sugar until smooth. Beat in the pumpkin, cream, flour, spices, salt and vanilla. Add the eggs and yolks; beat on low speed just until combined. Pour over prepared crust. Bake at 325° for 35-40 minutes or until center is almost set. Cool on a wire rack for 1 hour. Refrigerate for 3 hours or until chilled.

Sprinkle sugar into a large nonstick skillet. Without stirring, heat over medium-low until sugar is melted. Stir in pecans. Transfer to a piece of greased foil; cool. Break pecans into pieces.

In a small mixing bowl, beat cream until it begins to thicken. Add confectioners' sugar and vanilla; beat until stiff peaks form. Spread over chilled cheesecake. Sprinkle with sugared pecans. Cut into bars. Refrigerate leftovers. **Yield:** 2 to 2-1/2 dozen.

*Editor's Note: This recipe was tested with Archway windmill cookies.

——— 🥄 🥄 🥄 ———

Mushroom Veggie Chowder
(Pictured below)

This rich buttery broth is loaded with mushrooms, broccoli and corn. I made it for "Souper Sunday" at our church, and it sure didn't last long!
—_Edward Reis, Phoenix, Arizona_

    4 pounds fresh mushrooms, sliced
    4 large onions, chopped
1-1/2 cups butter _or_ margarine
1-1/2 cups all-purpose flour
    3 to 4 tablespoons salt
    2 to 2-1/2 teaspoons pepper
    3 quarts milk
    4 cartons (32 ounces _each_) chicken broth
    2 packages (24 ounces _each_) frozen broccoli cuts, thawed
    3 packages (8 ounces _each_) frozen corn, thawed
    8 cups (2 pounds) shredded cheddar cheese

In three or four soup kettles, saute the mushrooms and onions in butter until tender. Combine the flour, salt and pepper; stir into mushroom mixture until well blended. Gradually stir in milk. Cook and stir until mixture comes to a boil; cook 2 minutes longer or until thickened and bubbly.

Stir in the broth, broccoli and corn; heat through. Just before serving, stir in cheese until melted. **Yield:** 50 servings (12-1/2 quarts).

Three Potato Salad

(Pictured below right)

This pretty salad—made with white, red and sweet potatoes—tastes as good as it looks. The mild dill dressing enhances the tender spuds and onion, especially if you refrigerate it overnight. Even those who don't like sweet potatoes like this salad. —Nan Cairo Greenwood, Delaware

    3 medium russet potatoes, peeled and
      cubed
    3 medium unpeeled red potatoes, cubed
    1 large sweet potato, peeled and cubed
    1 medium onion, chopped
    1 cup mayonnaise
    2 tablespoons sugar
    1 tablespoon white vinegar
    1 teaspoon salt
  3/4 teaspoon dill weed
  1/2 teaspoon pepper

Place all of the potatoes in a Dutch oven; cover with water. Cover and bring to a boil. Reduce heat; cook for 20-30 minutes or until tender. Drain and cool. Place potatoes in a large bowl; add onion. In a small bowl, combine the remaining ingredients. Pour over potato mixture and toss gently to coat. Cover and refrigerate overnight. **Yield:** 15 servings.

———— ⚱ ⚱ ⚱ ————

Blueberry Pound Cake

(Pictured at right)

My husband and I have blueberry bushes in our backyard, so I developed this dessert using a basic pound cake recipe from my great-aunt. I pick and freeze the berries in 3-cup portions so I can make this yummy cake all year long. —Nancy Zimmerman Cape May Court House, New Jersey

    1 cup butter (no substitutes), softened
    3 cups sugar
1-1/2 teaspoons vanilla extract
  1/2 teaspoon lemon extract
    6 eggs
    3 cups all-purpose flour
  1/4 teaspoon baking soda
    1 cup (8 ounces) sour cream
    3 cups fresh *or* frozen blueberries*
Confectioners' sugar
BLUEBERRY SAUCE:
    1 cup sugar
  1/4 cup cornstarch
  1/2 cup cranberry juice concentrate
    6 cups fresh *or* frozen blueberries

In a large mixing bowl, cream butter and sugar. Beat in extracts. Add eggs, one at a time, beating well after each addition. Combine flour and baking soda; add to creamed mixture alternately with sour cream. Fold in blueberries.

Spoon into two greased and waxed paper-lined 9-in. x 5-in. x 3-in. loaf pans. Bake at 350° for 60-65 minutes or until a toothpick inserted near the center comes out clean. Cool for 10 minutes before removing from pans to wire racks. Sprinkle with confectioners' sugar.

In a saucepan, combine the sugar, cornstarch and cranberry juice concentrate until smooth. Add blueberries. Bring to a boil over medium heat; cook and stir for 2 minutes or until thickened. Serve warm or cold with the pound cake. **Yield:** 2 loaf cakes.

*Editor's Note: If using frozen blueberries, do not thaw before adding to the batter.

———— ⚱ ⚱ ⚱ ————

Zesty Sloppy Joes

(Pictured below right)

My mother-in-law created this recipe in the early 1950s. She prepared it many, many times before she was happy with the end result. Our family likes these satisfying sandwiches served with pickles and potato chips. —Sharon McKee, Denton, Texas

☑ Uses less fat, sugar or salt. Includes Nutritional Analysis and Diabetic Exchanges.

    2 pounds ground beef
    1 large green pepper, chopped
    2 cans (14-1/2 ounces *each*) diced
      tomatoes, undrained
    2 cans (8 ounces *each*) tomato sauce
    1 can (6 ounces) tomato paste
    2 tablespoons Worcestershire sauce
    1 tablespoon sugar
    2 teaspoons celery salt *or* celery seed
    2 teaspoons onion salt *or* onion powder
    1 teaspoon paprika
  1/4 to 1/2 teaspoon cayenne pepper
    3 bay leaves
16 hamburger buns, split

In a Dutch oven or large kettle, cook beef and green pepper over medium heat until meat is no longer pink; drain. Stir in the tomatoes, tomato sauce, tomato paste and seasonings. Bring to a boil. Reduce heat; cover and cook over low heat for 30 minutes.

Uncover; cook 30-40 minutes longer or until thickened. Discard bay leaves. Serve 1/2 cup of meat mixture on each bun. **Yield:** 16 servings.

Nutritional Analysis: One sloppy joe (prepared with lean ground beef, celery seed and onion powder) equals 249 calories, 6 g fat (2 g saturated fat), 28 mg cholesterol, 547 mg sodium, 31 g carbohydrate, 4 g fiber, 16 g protein. **Diabetic Exchanges:** 2 meat, 2 starch.

🍮 🍮 🍮

Grilled Corn on the Cob
(Pictured below)

Seasoned with cilantro, this easy-to-prepare corn on the cob is sure to be a standout at your Labor Day picnic. Wrapping the corn in foil locks in the flavors.
—Kara De la vega, Suisun City, California

  12 **medium ears sweet corn**
1/2 **cup butter *or* margarine, softened**
1/4 **cup sugar**
   1 **cup minced fresh cilantro *or* parsley**
Salt and pepper to taste

Soak corn in cold water for 1 hour. Drain and pat dry. In a small mixing bowl, beat the butter and sugar; spread over corn. On a shallow plate, combine the cilantro, salt and pepper. Roll corn in mixture until lightly coated. Wrap each ear in heavy-duty foil. Grill, covered, over medium heat for 25-30 minutes or until the corn is tender, turning occasionally. **Yield:** 12 servings.

🍮 🍮 🍮

Parmesan Salad Dressing

Served over your favorite salad greens, this rich and creamy dressing is a real treat. I first sampled it at an area restaurant, and the owners were kind enough to share the recipe.
—Lorraine LaVay Danz
New Holland, Pennsylvania

  5 **quarts buttermilk**
  4 **quarts mayonnaise**
64 **ounces sour cream**
  3 **pounds grated Parmesan cheese**
  1 **cup Worcestershire sauce**
  1 **cup minced chives**
  3 **tablespoons ground mustard**
  3 **tablespoons minced garlic**
  1 **tablespoon salt**
  1 **tablespoon pepper**

In a large bowl, combine all ingredients. Transfer to quart- or pint-size jars. Cover and refrigerate. **Yield:** 3 gallons.

A CROWD-PLEASING PICNIC is assured when Zesty Sloppy Joes, Grilled Corn on the Cob, Three Potato Salad and Blueberry Pound Cake (shown below, clockwise from bottom left) are served.

Hearty Beef Enchiladas

(Pictured below)

Since this recipe fills four 13-inch x 9-inch baking dishes, it's perfect for feeding a gang. I set out small bowls of shredded cheddar cheese, diced onions and diced tomatoes so folks can add their own garnishes.
—*Richard Clements, San Dimas, California*

   4 pounds ground beef
   4 medium onions, chopped
   4 cans (15-1/2 ounces *each*) chili beans, undrained
   4 cans (10 ounces *each*) enchilada sauce, *divided*
   1 jar (16 ounces) salsa, *divided*
Vegetable oil
  28 corn *or* flour tortillas (8 inches)
   4 cups (16 ounces) shredded cheddar cheese
   2 cans (2-1/4 ounces *each*) sliced ripe olives, drained

In a Dutch oven, cook beef and onions over medium heat until meat is no longer pink; drain. Stir in the beans, two cans of enchilada sauce and 1 cup salsa; set aside. In a skillet, heat 1/4 in. of oil. Dip each tortilla in hot oil for 3 seconds on each side or just until limp; drain on paper towels.

Top each tortilla with 2/3 cup beef mixture. Roll up and place seam side down in four 13-in. x 9-in. x 2-in. baking dishes. Drizzle with remaining enchilada sauce and salsa. Sprinkle with cheese and olives. Bake, uncovered, at 350° for 20-25 minutes or until bubbly. **Yield:** 28 servings.

Crunchy Vegetable Bake

(Pictured on page 146)

While traveling in Kentucky a few years ago, my husband and I enjoyed an excellent mixed vegetable dish at a restaurant...and the owners were kind enough to share the recipe. It makes four casseroles so it's great for a church supper.   —*Jean Voan, Shepherd, Texas*

   4 celery ribs, chopped
   2 large onions, chopped
 1/4 cup vegetable oil
   4 cans (10-3/4 ounces *each*) condensed cream of chicken soup, undiluted
4-1/2 cups (36 ounces) sour cream
   4 to 6 teaspoons salt
 1/2 to 1 teaspoon pepper
   8 packages (16 ounces *each*) frozen cut green beans, thawed
   8 packages (16 ounces *each*) frozen corn, thawed
   8 cans (8 ounces *each*) sliced water chestnuts, drained
   1 package (8 ounces) butter-flavored crackers, crushed
   1 cup sliced almonds
 1/2 cup butter *or* margarine, melted

In large skillets, saute celery and onions in oil until tender. Remove from the heat. Stir in the soup, sour cream, salt and pepper. Stir in the beans, corn and water chestnuts. Transfer to four greased 13-in. x 9-in. x 2-in. baking dishes.

In a bowl, combine cracker crumbs, almonds and butter. Sprinkle over bean mixture. Bake, uncovered, at 350° for 40-45 minutes or until the top is golden brown. **Yield:** 60-80 servings.

— 🍴 🍴 🍴 —

Au Gratin Party Potatoes

When putting on a party for their American Legion Post, my father and uncle prepared this yummy potato dish. I've used the recipe for smaller groups by making a half or quarter of it. It's simple to divide.
—*Crystal Kolady, Henrietta, New York*

  20 pounds potatoes, peeled, cubed and cooked
   4 cans (12 ounces *each*) evaporated milk
   3 packages (16 ounces *each*) process cheese (Velveeta), cubed
   1 cup butter *or* margarine, cubed
   2 tablespoons salt
   2 teaspoons pepper

In several large bowls, combine potatoes, milk, cheese, butter, salt and pepper. Transfer to four greased 13-in. x 9-in. x 2-in. baking dishes. Bake, uncovered, at 350° for 45-50 minutes or until bubbly. **Yield:** about 60 (3/4-cup) servings.

— 🥄 🥄 🥄 —

Chive Pinwheel Rolls

These light pleasant-tasting rolls complement almost any entree. With the chive filling swirled through the golden bread, they're attractive enough for special occasions. —Ann Niemela, Ely, Minnesota

    1 **package (1/4 ounce) active dry yeast**
1/4 **cup warm water (110° to 115°)**
    1 **cup milk**
1/3 **cup vegetable oil**
1/4 **cup mashed potatoes (prepared without milk and butter)**
    1 **egg**
    3 **tablespoons sugar**
1-1/2 **teaspoons salt**
3-1/2 **cups all-purpose flour**
CHIVE FILLING:
    1 **cup (8 ounces) sour cream**
    1 **cup minced fresh _or_ frozen chives**
    1 **egg yolk**
Butter _or_ margarine, melted

In a bowl, dissolve yeast in water. In a saucepan, heat milk, oil and potatoes to 110°-115°. Transfer to a mixing bowl; add yeast mixture, egg, sugar and salt. Add enough flour to make a soft dough. Turn onto a floured surface; knead until smooth and elastic, about 6-8 minutes. Place in a greased bowl; turn once to grease top. Cover and let rise in a warm place until doubled, about 1 hour.

Turn dough onto a floured surface. Roll into a 15-in. x 10-in. rectangle. In a bowl, combine sour cream, chives and egg yolk. Spread over dough to within 1/2 in. of edges. Roll up jelly-roll style, starting with a long side; pinch seam to seal. Cut into 1-in. slices. Place cut side down in a 13-in. x 9-in. x 2-in. baking pan. Cover and let rise until doubled, about 1 hour.

Bake at 350° for 30-35 minutes or until golden brown. Brush with butter. Cool on a wire rack. Refrigerate leftovers. **Yield:** 15 rolls.

— 🥄 🥄 🥄 —

Cinnamon-Swirl Raisin Bread

(Pictured above right)

Raisins give a delightful sweetness to this tender yeast bread, and cinnamon swirls beautifully through the slices. It makes terrific toast, too. —Ruth Crawford Tucson, Arizona

1-1/2 **cups warm milk (110° to 115°)**
    1 **cup mashed potatoes (prepared without milk and butter)**
1/2 **cup butter _or_ margarine, melted**
1/4 **cup sugar**
    2 **teaspoons salt**
    2 **packages (1/4 ounce _each_) active dry yeast**
1/2 **cup warm water (110° to 115°)**
6-1/2 **to 7 cups all-purpose flour**
1-1/2 **cups raisins**
FILLING:
1/2 **cup sugar**
    2 **teaspoons ground cinnamon**
    2 **tablespoons butter _or_ margarine, melted**

In a large bowl, combine the milk, potatoes, butter, sugar and salt. In a mixing bowl, dissolve yeast in warm water. Add potato mixture and 2 cups flour; beat until smooth. Fold in raisins. Stir in enough remaining flour to form a soft dough. Turn onto a lightly floured surface; knead until smooth and elastic, about 10 minutes. Place in a greased bowl, turning once to grease top. Cover and let rise in a warm place until doubled, about 1 hour.

Punch dough down. Turn onto lightly floured surface; divide in half. Roll each portion into a 16-in. x 8-in. rectangle. Combine sugar and cinnamon; sprinkle over rectangles to within 1/2 in. of edges. Roll up jelly-roll style, starting with a short side; pinch seam to seal and tuck ends under.

Place seam side down in two greased 9-in. x 5-in. x 3-in. loaf pans. Cover and let rise for 30 minutes or until doubled. Brush with butter. Bake at 350° for 40-45 minutes or until golden brown. Remove from pans to wire racks to cool. **Yield:** 2 loaves.

Cooking for One or Two

These small-quantity recipes that are big on taste will fill the bill when cooking for just yourself or the two of you.

—— 🏺 🏺 🏺 ——

BIG ON FLAVOR. Clockwise from upper left: Peach Smoothies (p. 179), Halibut with Shrimp Sauce (p. 171), Sausage Macaroni Bake (p. 172), Chili Bean Cheese Omelet (p. 166) and Apricot Mini Loaves (p. 179).

Smoked Sausage Scramble

I came up with this recipe one morning when we had smoked sausage left over from the day before—and my husband loved it. The combination of spicy sausage, spinach, eggs, potato and cheese makes a hearty morning meal or a satisfying light supper.
—Stephanie Leven, Warsaw, Missouri

   1 medium potato, cubed
   1 tablespoon chopped onion
   1 tablespoon vegetable oil
   1 cup torn fresh spinach
   1 cup cubed fully cooked smoked sausage
   4 eggs
   1 tablespoon water
   2 slices American cheese, diced

In a large skillet, cook the potato and onion in oil until potato is tender. Add spinach and sausage. In a bowl, whisk the eggs and water. Pour over sausage mixture. Cook over medium heat, stirring occasionally, until eggs are completely set. Top with cheese. Serve immediately. **Yield:** 2 servings.

Chili Bean Cheese Omelet

(Pictured on page 164)

In an effort to eat healthier, I've been playing around with some recipes, including this hearty omelet. The bountiful blend of tomatoes, kidney beans, cheese and onion makes it a satisfying centerpiece for breakfast, brunch or supper. —Cathee Bethel, Lebanon, Oregon

1/2 cup chopped fresh tomato
   1 green onion, chopped
1/4 cup canned kidney beans, coarsely chopped
   1 garlic clove, minced
1/8 teaspoon celery salt
1/8 teaspoon chili powder
1/8 teaspoon Worcestershire sauce
   2 teaspoons vegetable oil, *divided*
   2 eggs
1/4 teaspoon salt
1/4 cup shredded mozzarella cheese

In a skillet, saute the tomato, onion, beans, garlic, celery salt, chili powder and Worcestershire sauce in 1 teaspoon oil until liquid has evaporated; set aside and keep warm.

In a bowl, beat eggs and salt. Heat remaining oil in an 8-in. skillet over medium-low heat; add eggs. As eggs set, lift edges, letting uncooked portion flow underneath. When the eggs are nearly set, sprinkle vegetable mixture over one side. Fold omelet over filling. Sprinkle with cheese. Cover and let stand for 1-2 minutes or until cheese is melted. **Yield:** 1 serving.

Creamy Lime Chiller

(Pictured below right)

This frosty citrus refresher hits the spot. Neither too sweet nor too tart, this pretty pick-me-up will perk up any special occasion. —Maria Regakis
Somerville, Massachusetts

✓ Uses less fat, sugar or salt. Includes Nutritional Analysis and Diabetic Exchanges.

   1 cup milk
   1 cup lime sherbet
1/4 cup limeade concentrate

Place all ingredients in a blender; cover and process until smooth. Pour into chilled glasses and serve immediately. **Yield:** 2 servings.
   Nutritional Analysis: One 1-cup serving (prepared with fat-free milk) equals 215 calories, 2 g fat (1 g saturated fat), 7 mg cholesterol, 99 mg sodium, 47 g carbohydrate, trace fiber, 5 g protein. **Diabetic Exchanges:** 2 starch, 1 fruit.

Festive Chicken

(Pictured at right)

Moist golden chicken breasts are dressed up for the holidays in this special dish. Perched on a bed of sauteed spinach, the chicken is topped with a tangy cranberry, orange and pecan sauce. —Rebecca Baird
Salt Lake City, Utah

1/2 cup all-purpose flour
1/4 teaspoon salt
Dash pepper
   2 boneless skinless chicken breast halves
   2 teaspoons olive *or* vegetable oil
CRANBERRY ORANGE SAUCE:
   1 cup fresh *or* frozen cranberries
1/2 cup orange juice
   2 tablespoons brown sugar
   1 teaspoon grated orange peel
   2 tablespoons chopped pecans
   1 garlic clove, minced
   1 tablespoon butter *or* margarine
   2 cups fresh spinach

In a resealable plastic bag, combine the flour, salt and pepper. Flatten chicken to 3/8-in. thickness; place in the bag and shake to coat. In a skillet, cook chicken in oil for 3 minutes on each side or until juices run clear. Remove and keep warm.
   Add cranberries and orange juice to the skillet. Cover and cook over medium heat for 5 minutes or until the berries begin to pop. Add brown sugar and orange peel; cook 1 minute longer. Stir in pecans;

remove from the heat.

In another skillet, saute garlic in butter until tender. Add the spinach; saute for 1 minute or until spinach begins to wilt. Place spinach on serving plates; top with the chicken and cranberry sauce. **Yield:** 2 servings.

— ☕ ☕ ☕ —

Skillet Corn Bread

(Pictured below)

This skillet bread looks like a puffy pancake but has the easy-to-cut texture of conventional corn bread. It complements all sorts of main entrees from chicken to chili. —Kathy Teela, Tucson, Arizona

1/4 **cup all-purpose flour**
1/4 **cup cornmeal**
1/2 **teaspoon baking powder**
1/4 **teaspoon salt**
  1 **egg**
1/4 **cup milk**
  4 **teaspoons vegetable oil,** *divided*

In a bowl, combine the flour, cornmeal, baking powder and salt. In another bowl, beat the egg, milk and 3 teaspoons oil; stir into dry ingredients just until moistened. Heat remaining oil in a heavy 8-in. skillet over low heat. Pour batter into the hot skillet; cover and cook for 4-5 minutes. Turn and cook 4 minutes longer or until golden brown. **Yield:** 2 servings.

MERRY MENU for two features Festive Chicken, Skillet Corn Bread and Creamy Lime Chiller (shown above).

Chicken Cutlet

(Pictured below)

I love this combination of chicken and cheese. Parmesan cheese, garlic powder and onion powder flavor the golden cutlet, which is coated with seasoned bread crumbs. —Marie Hoyer, Lewistown, Montana

☑ Uses less fat, sugar or salt. Includes Nutritional Analysis and Diabetic Exchanges.

        1 teaspoon all-purpose flour
Dash *each* garlic powder, onion powder and
        pepper
        2 tablespoons grated Parmesan cheese
        2 tablespoons buttermilk
        3 tablespoons seasoned bread crumbs
        1 boneless skinless chicken breast half
            (4 ounces)
        2 teaspoons canola *or* vegetable oil

In a shallow bowl, combine the flour, garlic powder, onion powder and pepper. In another bowl, combine cheese and buttermilk. Place bread crumbs in a third shallow bowl.

Flatten chicken to 1/4-in. thickness. Coat chicken with flour mixture; dip in buttermilk, then coat with crumbs. In a skillet over medium heat, cook chicken in oil for 3-5 minutes on each side or until juices run clear. **Yield:** 1 serving.

Nutritional Analysis: One serving (prepared with 1% buttermilk) equals 357 calories, 15 g fat (3 g saturated fat), 75 mg cholesterol, 888 mg sodium, 20 g carbohydrate, 1 g fiber, 35 g protein. **Diabetic Exchanges:** 3 lean meat, 2 fat, 1 starch.

Fettuccine Primavera

(Pictured below)

This delicious dish is chock-full of crisp-tender vegetables that are delicately seasoned with garlic, cheese and chicken broth. You can serve it either as a colorful side dish or a light main course.
—Cassandra Corridon, Frederick, Maryland

        4 ounces uncooked fettuccine
        1/2 cup cauliflowerets
        1/2 cup fresh snow peas
        1/2 cup broccoli florets
        1/4 cup julienned carrot
        1 tablespoon vegetable oil
        1/2 cup julienned zucchini
        1/4 cup julienned sweet red pepper
        2 to 3 garlic cloves, minced
        1/3 cup chicken broth
        1/4 cup grated Romano cheese

Cook fettuccine according to package directions. Meanwhile, in skillet or wok, stir-fry cauliflower, peas, broccoli and carrot in oil for 2 minutes. Add zucchini, red pepper and garlic; stir-fry until vegetables are crisp-tender. Stir in broth. Reduce heat; cover and simmer for 2 minutes. Drain fettuccine; toss with vegetables. Sprinkle with cheese. **Yield:** 2 servings.

DINING ALONE? Treat yourself to a delicious Chicken Cutlet and Fettuccine Primavera (shown above).

Mini Egg Casserole

This savory casserole can be prepared the day before and popped into the oven in the morning.
—*Lynn Stephens, Hermann, Missouri*

    1 frozen hash brown patty, thawed
  3/4 cup frozen onion pepper stir-fry blend,
      thawed
  1/2 cup diced fully cooked ham
  1/3 cup sliced fresh mushrooms
  1/2 cup shredded Mexican cheese blend *or*
      cheddar cheese
    2 eggs
  1/4 cup heavy whipping cream
  1/4 teaspoon salt
  1/4 teaspoon pepper
  1/4 teaspoon ground mustard
    1 plum tomato, sliced

Place hash brown in a greased 3-cup baking dish. Arrange stir-fry blend around it. Sprinkle with ham, mushrooms and cheese. In a small bowl, whisk eggs, cream, salt, pepper and mustard; pour over cheese. Top with tomato. Bake, uncovered, at 350° for 45-50 minutes or until a knife inserted near center comes out clean. **Yield:** 1 serving.

—— 🍵 🍵 🍵 ——

Dilly Red Snapper

A light and creamy dill sauce lends lovely flavor to tender fish fillets in this recipe. —*Sharon Semph Salem, Oregon*

☑ Uses less fat, sugar or salt. Includes Nutritional Analysis and Diabetic Exchanges.

    1 medium lemon, thinly sliced
    2 green onions, sliced
    2 dill sprigs
    2 red snapper fillets (6 ounces *each*)
  1/8 teaspoon salt
Dash pepper
DILL SAUCE:
  1/3 cup mayonnaise
    1 garlic clove, minced
  1/2 teaspoon snipped fresh dill *or* 1/8
      teaspoon dill weed
  1/2 teaspoon lemon juice
  1/2 teaspoon minced green onion

Place the lemon slices, onions and dill sprigs in a foil-lined baking pan. Top with fish fillets; sprinkle with salt and pepper. Fold foil around fish and seal tightly. Bake at 400° for 20-25 minutes or until fish flakes easily with a fork.

In a small bowl, combine all of the sauce ingredients and serve over the fish. **Yield:** 2 servings.

Nutritional Analysis: One fillet with 2-1/2 tablespoons sauce (prepared with fat-free mayonnaise) equals 216 calories, 3 g fat (1 g saturated fat), 67 mg cholesterol, 580 mg sodium, 10 g carbohydrate, 2 g fiber, 35 g protein. **Diabetic Exchanges:** 5 very lean meat, 1/2 starch.

—— 🍵 🍵 🍵 ——

Spinach Salad Supreme

(Pictured above)

A tangy topping completes this fresh spinach salad, which is garnished with hard-cooked egg and crumbled bacon. —*Gail Sykora Menomonee Falls, Wisconsin*

  1/4 cup vegetable oil
    2 tablespoons red wine vinegar *or* cider
      vinegar
    1 teaspoon sugar
    1 teaspoon finely chopped onion
    1 teaspoon finely chopped green pepper
    1 teaspoon minced fresh parsley
    1 teaspoon ketchup
  1/4 teaspoon salt
  1/4 teaspoon ground mustard
  1/4 teaspoon paprika
    2 cups torn fresh spinach
    1 hard-cooked egg, sliced
    3 bacon strips, cooked and crumbled

In a jar with a tight-fitting lid, combine the first 10 ingredients; shake well. Divide spinach between two serving bowls or plates; top with egg and bacon. Drizzle with dressing. Serve immediately. **Yield:** 2 servings.

Pork Tenderloin with Gravy

(Pictured below)

I recently began experimenting with pork and came up with this easy dish, which has turned out to be a favorite. I like to vary it occasionally by using lemon-pepper or garlic-seasoned tenderloin for added flavor.
—Marilyn McGee, Tulsa, Oklahoma

1 envelope brown gravy mix
1/2 cup water
3 tablespoons soy sauce
2 tablespoons balsamic *or* red wine vinegar
1 garlic clove, minced
1 pork tenderloin (about 3/4 pound), cut into 1/2-inch slices
1/4 cup olive *or* vegetable oil

PERFECT FOR A PAIR. Win raves with this supper of Pork Tenderloin with Gravy, Ginger Veggie Stir-Fry and Berry Sponge Cakes (shown above).

1/2 pound fresh mushrooms, sliced
1 medium onion, sliced and separated into rings
Hot cooked rice

In a small bowl, combine the first five ingredients until blended; set aside. In a large skillet, brown pork in oil on all sides. Stir in the gravy mixture, mushrooms and onion. Bring to a boil. Reduce heat; cover and simmer for 10-15 minutes or until meat juices run clear and vegetables are tender. Serve over rice. **Yield:** 2 servings.

——— 🥄 🥄 🥄 ———

Ginger Veggie Stir-Fry

(Pictured at left)

Green beans blend nicely with the broccoli, carrots, red onion and sweet potato in this well-seasoned side dish. I created this colorful combination from the last remaining items in our refrigerator before a long vacation. —Jennifer Maslowski, New York, New York

1 teaspoon cornstarch
1/4 cup orange juice
2 tablespoons soy sauce
1 medium carrot, julienned
1 cup fresh broccoli florets
1 cup cut fresh green beans (2-inch pieces)
2 tablespoons olive _or_ vegetable oil
1 cup julienned peeled sweet potato
1 cup thinly sliced red onion
1 garlic clove, minced
1/2 teaspoon dried rosemary, crushed
1/4 teaspoon ground ginger
1/8 teaspoon crushed red pepper flakes, optional

In a small bowl, combine cornstarch, orange juice and soy sauce until smooth; set aside. In a large skillet or wok, stir-fry carrot, broccoli and beans in oil for 8 minutes. Add sweet potato and onion; stir-fry until vegetables are crisp-tender.

Stir the soy sauce mixture; add to the skillet with garlic, rosemary, ginger and pepper flakes if desired. Bring to a boil; cook and stir for 1 minute or until thickened. **Yield:** 2 servings.

——— 🥄 🥄 🥄 ———

Berry Sponge Cakes

(Pictured at left)

This fancy treat for two looks like you fussed, but it's easy to make with convenient prepared pudding and sponge cakes. My husband enjoys this dessert featuring seasonal fruit. —Bonnie Buckley, Kansas City, Missouri

1 individual prepared vanilla pudding cup*
(4 ounces)
1/2 teaspoon vanilla extract
2 individual sponge cakes
1/2 cup mixed fresh berries (blueberries, raspberries, blackberries, sliced strawberries)
2 tablespoons whipped topping
1 tablespoon sliced almonds, toasted

In a small bowl, combine pudding and vanilla until blended. Top each sponge cake with pudding and berries. Dollop with whipped topping; sprinkle with almonds. **Yield:** 2 servings.

*Editor's Note: This recipe was prepared with Jell-O pudding cups, which have six cups in each package.

——— 🥄 🥄 🥄 ———

Halibut with Shrimp Sauce

(Pictured on page 164)

I broil halibut with slices of onion and lemon, then serve the fish with a savory sauce of sour cream, seafood sauce, dill and baby shrimp. This is our favorite seafood recipe. —Wendy Bognar, Sparks, Nevada

2 halibut steaks (8 ounces _each_)
2 tablespoons butter _or_ margarine, melted
1 tablespoon lemon juice
1-1/4 teaspoons dill weed, _divided_
1 small lemon, sliced
1 small onion, sliced
2 garlic cloves, minced
1/2 cup sour cream
1/4 cup canned tiny shrimp
2 tablespoons seafood sauce

Place halibut on a broiler pan. Combine the butter, lemon juice and 1 teaspoon dill; drizzle over fish. Broil 3-4 in. from the heat for 8 minutes. Arrange lemon and onion slices over halibut. Sprinkle with garlic. Broil 2-4 minutes longer or until fish flakes easily with a fork.

In a small bowl, combine the sour cream, shrimp, seafood sauce and remaining dill. Serve with the fish. **Yield:** 2 servings.

🥄 Tip for Two

End up with leftover veggies after meals? Put them in a heavy-duty resealable plastic bag or freezer container and store in the freezer. When you have 3 to 4 cups, make soup!

Veggie Pork Kabobs

(Pictured above)

A refreshing orange glaze perks up these colorful kabobs. I serve this summery dish with baked potatoes and garlic bread. You could substitute some other vegetables if you like, but these are our favorites.
—Candy Gruman, Tucson, Arizona

    3/4 cup orange juice concentrate
    3/4 cup orange marmalade
      2 tablespoons teriyaki *or* soy sauce
      2 boneless pork loin chops (1-1/2 inches thick), cut into 1-inch pieces
      1 medium sweet red pepper, cut into 1-inch pieces
      1 medium green pepper, cut into 1-inch pieces
      1 medium sweet onion, cut into eighths

In a bowl, combine the orange juice concentrate, marmalade and teriyaki sauce. Pour 1-1/4 cups into a large resealable plastic bag; add the pork, peppers and onion. Seal bag and turn to coat; refrigerate for at least 1 hour. Cover and refrigerate remaining marinade.

Coat grill rack with nonstick cooking spray before starting the grill. Drain and discard marinade from pork and vegetables. Alternately thread onto metal or soaked wooden skewers. Grill kabobs, uncovered, over medium heat for 20-25 minutes or until meat juices run clear, turning often. Serve with the reserved marinade. **Yield:** 2 servings.

Sausage Macaroni Bake

(Pictured on page 164)

Everyone's bound to want seconds of this satisfying Italian-style bake. Oregano seasons the pork sausage, macaroni and tomato sauce mixture that's topped with a sprinkling of Parmesan cheese. It really hits the spot when you want a quick not-so-big meal.
—Kelli Bucy, Massena, Iowa

    1/2 cup uncooked elbow macaroni
    1/2 pound bulk pork sausage
    1/4 cup chopped green pepper
      2 tablespoons chopped onion
    1/4 teaspoon dried oregano
    1/8 teaspoon pepper
      1 can (8 ounces) tomato sauce
    1/2 cup water
      4 tablespoons grated Parmesan cheese, *divided*

Cook macaroni according to package directions; drain and set aside. In a small skillet, cook sausage over medium heat until no longer pink; drain if necessary. Add the green pepper, onion, oregano and pepper. Stir in tomato sauce and water. Bring to a boil. Reduce heat; simmer, uncovered, for 5 minutes.

Stir in macaroni and 2 tablespoons Parmesan cheese. Transfer to an ungreased 1-qt. baking dish. Sprinkle with the remaining Parmesan cheese. Bake, uncovered, at 350° for 20-25 minutes or until bubbly. **Yield:** 2 servings.

———— 🍴 🍴 🍴 ————

Stuffed Cornish Hens

(Pictured at right)

Cornish hens, basted with a delicious glaze of apricot preserves and cloves, make dinner for two something special. I use convenient packaged herb stuffing to complement the moist and tender meat. It's a delightful entree that's portioned just right. —Gusty Crum Dover, Ohio

      2 cups seasoned stuffing croutons
      5 tablespoons water
      2 tablespoons butter *or* margarine, melted
      2 Cornish game hens (20 ounces *each*)
GLAZE:
      1 envelope brown gravy mix
    1/2 cup water
    1/2 cup apricot preserves
Dash ground cloves

In a bowl, combine the croutons, water and butter. Loosely stuff into hens. Place breast side up on a rack in a shallow roasting pan; tie drumsticks together.

In a small saucepan, combine glaze ingredients. Bring to a boil. Spoon half over hens. Bake, uncovered, at 350° for 1-1/2 hours until a meat thermometer reads 180° for hens and 165° for stuffing, basting occasionally with remaining glaze. **Yield:** 2 servings.

— 🍺 🍺 🍺 —

Gingered Sweet Potatoes

(Pictured below)

Here's an easy and attractive way to spruce up sweet potatoes for Thanksgiving dinner. I coat the spud slices with a ginger, cinnamon and brown sugar sauce that's both sweet and spicy. —*Billie Moss*
El Sobrante, California

   2 tablespoons butter *or* margarine
   2 tablespoons olive *or* vegetable oil
1/3 cup packed brown sugar
   1 tablespoon honey
   1 teaspoon ground cinnamon
1/2 teaspoon salt
1/2 teaspoon ground ginger
1/4 teaspoon pepper
   1 medium sweet potato, peeled and cut into wedges

In a skillet, heat butter and oil over medium heat. Stir in the brown sugar, honey, cinnamon, salt, ginger and pepper. Add the sweet potato wedges; toss to coat. Cover and cook over low heat for 20-30 minutes or until potatoes are tender, stirring occasionally. **Yield:** 2 servings.

— 🍺 🍺 🍺 —

Green Bean Stir-Fry

(Pictured below)

Soy sauce and peanut butter flavor these crisp-tender green beans. They're a nice change from the usual green bean salads and casseroles. This dish always wows guests and brings plenty of recipe requests.
—*Robin Joss, Ashburn, Virginia*

   1 tablespoon soy sauce
   2 garlic cloves, minced
   1 teaspoon sesame seeds, toasted
   1 teaspoon brown sugar
   1 teaspoon peanut butter
3/4 pound fresh green beans, trimmed
4-1/2 teaspoons vegetable oil

In a bowl, combine the first five ingredients; set aside. In a large skillet, stir-fry green beans in oil until crisp-tender. Remove from the heat. Add the soy sauce mixture; stir to coat. **Yield:** 2 servings.

FORGO THE WHOLE TURKEY this Thanksgiving, and feast on Stuffed Cornish Hens, Gingered Sweet Potatoes and Green Bean Stir-Fry (shown above), which are sized right for two.

Grilled Triple-Decker Club

If you like ham and cheese, you'll savor this hearty sandwich. The meat and mozzarella delight is dipped in an egg batter before grilling. This is a delicious combination, but you can substitute other meats.
—Christine Nelson, Decatur, Arkansas

  3 slices whole wheat bread
  2 slices mozzarella cheese
  2 thin slices deli ham
  2 thin slices deli turkey
  2 tablespoons mayonnaise *or* salad dressing
  1 egg
  1 tablespoon milk
  1 tablespoon butter *or* margarine

Layer one slice of bread, one slice of cheese, ham, second slice of bread, turkey, mayonnaise, remaining cheese and remaining bread. In a small bowl, whisk egg and milk. Brush over the outsides of sandwich. In a skillet over medium heat, melt butter. Brown sandwich on both sides until cheese is melted. **Yield:** 1 serving.

———— 🍴 🍴 🍴 ————

Lemon Shrimp Ravioli Toss

Treat yourself to this attractive main dish for one that relies on shrimp and convenient cheese ravioli cooked in a light lemony sauce. Being an avid crafter and quilter, I'm usually running short on time, so I make this often. —Emma Magielda, Amsterdam, New York

1-1/2 cups refrigerated cheese ravioli
  2 tablespoons butter *or* margarine, melted
  1 tablespoon lemon juice
  3/4 teaspoon snipped fresh basil
  1/2 teaspoon grated lemon peel
1-1/3 cups cooked medium shrimp, peeled and deveined

Cook ravioli according to package directions; drain. In a microwave-safe 1-qt. dish, combine the butter, lemon juice, basil and lemon peel. Add shrimp and ravioli; toss to coat. Cover and microwave on high for 2-4 minutes or until heated through. **Yield:** 1 serving.
    Editor's Note: This recipe was tested in an 850-watt microwave.

———— 🍴 🍴 🍴 ————

Mini Turkey Loaf

(Pictured above right)

Onion, green pepper and apple juice flavor this moist ground turkey meat loaf. Drizzled with pan gravy, it makes a satisfying entree that's just right for two for an everyday or Sunday dinner. —Vikki Metz, Tavares, Florida

✓ Uses less fat, sugar or salt. Includes Nutritional Analysis and Diabetic Exchanges.

  1/4 cup chopped onion
  1/4 cup chopped green pepper
  1/4 cup chopped fresh mushrooms
    1 teaspoon olive *or* canola oil
    1 cup unsweetened apple juice, *divided*
  1/2 teaspoon garlic powder
  1/2 teaspoon onion powder
  1/4 teaspoon salt
  1/8 teaspoon pepper
  1/2 pound ground turkey
    2 tablespoons cornstarch
    3 tablespoons cold water
    1 teaspoon soy sauce

In a small skillet, saute onion, green pepper and mushrooms in oil until tender. Remove from heat; cool. In a large bowl, combine vegetables, 2 tablespoons apple juice, garlic powder, onion powder, salt and pepper. Crumble turkey over mixture; mix well.
    Shape into a loaf in an 11-in. x 7-in. x 2-in. baking dish coated with nonstick cooking spray. Bake at 350° for 40-45 minutes or until meat is no longer pink and a meat thermometer reads 165°.
    In a small saucepan, bring remaining apple juice to a boil. In a small bowl, combine the cornstarch, water and soy sauce until smooth. Gradually whisk into apple juice. Bring to a boil; cook and stir for 2 minutes or until thickened. Serve with turkey loaf. **Yield:** 2 servings.
    Nutritional Analysis: One serving (prepared with ground turkey breast and reduced-sodium soy sauce) equals 296 calories, 12 g fat (3 g saturated fat), 90 mg cholesterol, 507 mg sodium, 26 g carbohydrate, 1 g fiber, 21 g protein. **Diabetic Exchanges:** 2 lean meat, 1-1/2 starch, 1-1/2 fat.

———— 🍴 🍴 🍴 ————

Herbed New Potatoes

(Pictured above right)

I make these potatoes often for my husband and me. They're easy to prepare and have a nice dill flavor. We eagerly await farmers market season to get fresh new potatoes. —Vi Neiding, South Milwaukee, Wisconsin

  3/4 pound small red potatoes, quartered
    1 tablespoon butter *or* margarine, softened
    1 tablespoon sour cream
    2 teaspoons snipped fresh dill *or* 1/2 teaspoon dill weed
    2 teaspoons minced chives
  1/4 teaspoon salt
  1/8 teaspoon pepper
Dash lemon juice

PAIR UP with your favorite dining partner for a meal of Mini Turkey Loaf, Herbed New Poatoes and Chilled Strawberry Cream (shown above).

Remove a strip of peel from the middle of each potato. Place potatoes in a saucepan and cover with water. Bring to a boil over medium heat. Reduce heat; cover and simmer for 20 minutes or until tender. In small bowl, combine the remaining ingredients. Drain potatoes; add butter mixture and toss gently. **Yield:** 2 servings.

— 🌳 🌳 🌳 —

Chilled Strawberry Cream

(Pictured above)

Made with only three ingredients I usually have on hand, this cool and refreshing fruit-flavored dessert goes together in a jiffy. Yet everyone agrees it's pretty enough to serve for a special occasion if you double or triple the recipe.
— Ann Main
Moorefield, Ontario

- **2 cups frozen unsweetened whole strawberries**
- **1/4 cup confectioners' sugar**
- **1/2 cup heavy whipping cream**

Place the strawberries and sugar in a blender or food processor; cover and process until finely chopped. In a small mixing bowl, beat cream until stiff peaks form. Fold into berries. Pour into serving dishes. Refrigerate or freeze for 25 minutes. **Yield:** 2 servings.

Autumn Pear Dessert

(Pictured above)

After a filling meal, this elegant little dessert hits the spot...and it's a snap to fix! I serve a warm pear with a few simple ingredients. For a lighter dessert, substitute vanilla yogurt for the whipped topping.
—Patricia Olson, Germantown, Maryland

    1 medium firm pear
1/4 cup whipped topping
    3 tablespoons raisins
    2 tablespoons chopped pecans, toasted

Peel the top third of the pear; core from the bottom, leaving stem intact. Place on a microwave-safe plate; cover and cook on high for 2-3 minutes or until tender. Immediately transfer to a serving plate. Serve warm with whipped topping, raisins and pecans. **Yield:** 1 serving.
   Editor's Note: This recipe was tested in an 850-watt microwave.

Tarragon Salmon Steaks

I used this recipe often when I cooked for the "Meals on Wheels" program in our hometown. The salmon is mildly seasoned with lemon and tarragon.
—Helen Sandsbraaten, Naicam, Saskatchewan

    2 salmon steaks (about 1 inch thick)
    2 tablespoons butter *or* margarine, melted
    2 teaspoons lemon juice
    1 tablespoon minced fresh tarragon
    1 tablespoon minced fresh parsley
Salt and pepper to taste

Place the salmon steaks in an ungreased 13-in. x 9-in. x 2-in. baking dish. Drizzle with butter and lemon juice. Sprinkle with the tarragon, parsley, salt and pepper. Bake, uncovered, at 350° for 20-25 minutes or until fish flakes easily with a fork. **Yield:** 2 servings.

Fettuccine Alfredo

A creamy and comforting cheese sauce coats fettuccine noodles in fine fashion. This is wonderful as is, but sometimes I like to add sliced fresh mushrooms and black olives sauteed in butter and garlic.
—Jo Gray, Park City, Montana

    4 ounces uncooked fettuccine
    3 tablespoons butter *or* margarine
    1 cup heavy whipping cream
1/4 cup plus 2 tablespoons grated Parmesan cheese, *divided*
1/4 cup grated Romano cheese
    1 egg yolk, lightly beaten
1/8 teaspoon salt
Dash *each* pepper and ground nutmeg

Cook fettuccine according to package directions. Meanwhile, in a saucepan, melt butter over medium-low heat. Stir in the cream, 1/4 cup Parmesan cheese, Romano cheese, egg yolk, salt, pepper and nutmeg. Cook and stir over medium-low heat until a thermometer reads 160° (do not boil). Drain fettuccine; top with Alfredo sauce and remaining Parmesan cheese. **Yield:** 2 servings.

Lemony Chicken Noodle Soup

(Pictured at right)

This isn't Grandma's chicken soup, but it is comforting. The lemon juice adds a nice tang. —Bill Hilbrich
St. Cloud, Minnesota

    1 small onion, chopped
    2 tablespoons olive *or* vegetable oil
    1 tablespoon butter *or* margarine
1/4 pound boneless skinless chicken breast, cubed
    1 garlic clove, minced
    2 cans (14-1/2 ounces *each*) chicken broth
    1 medium carrot, cut into 1/4-inch slices
1/4 cup fresh *or* frozen peas
1/2 teaspoon dried basil
    2 cups uncooked medium egg noodles
    1 to 2 tablespoons lemon juice

In a small saucepan, saute onion in oil and butter until tender. Add chicken and garlic. Cook and stir until chicken is lightly browned. Stir in the broth, carrot, peas and basil. Bring to a boil.

Reduce heat; cover and simmer for 5 minutes. Add the noodles. Cover and simmer for 8-10 minutes or until noodles are tender. Stir in lemon juice. **Yield:** 2 servings.

— 🍲 🍲 🍲 —

Cheesy Texas Toast

(Pictured below)

My husband and I love garlic bread, but it's such a waste for just the two of us. So I came up with this cheesy recipe that calls for just a few slices of French bread instead of the whole loaf. You can make it in minutes, and it's yummy, too!
—*LaDonna Reed*
Ponca City, Oklahoma

> **2** tablespoons butter *or* margarine, softened
> **4** slices French bread (1 inch thick)
> **1/4 to 1/2** teaspoon garlic powder
> **1** cup (4 ounces) shredded mozzarella cheese
> **Chopped green onions *or* parsley, optional**

Spread butter over bread. Sprinkle with garlic powder and cheese. Place on an ungreased baking sheet. Bake at 400° for 5-7 minutes or until cheese is melted. Sprinkle with onions or parsley if desired. Serve warm. **Yield:** 2 servings.

YOU DON'T NEED to get out the big soup pot to make Lemony Chicken Noodle Soup, served with Cheesy Texas Toast (shown above). These recipes conveniently serve two.

Pork Chops with Cumin Rice

(Pictured below)

Cumin lends a real Southwestern flair to this satisfying main dish. The tender baked chops pick up extra flavor from the well-seasoned rice. Sometimes I use celery instead of green pepper and boneless skinless chicken breasts instead of the pork chops.
—*Loyse Keith, Enumclaw, Washington*

2 bone-in pork chops (3/4 inch thick)
1/4 teaspoon salt
1/4 teaspoon pepper
1 tablespoon vegetable oil
1 teaspoon chicken bouillon granules
1 cup hot water
1/2 cup uncooked long grain rice
2 tablespoons chopped onion
2 tablespoons chopped green pepper
2 teaspoons Worcestershire sauce
1/2 teaspoon ground cumin

Sprinkle pork chops with salt and pepper. In a small ovenproof skillet, brown chops in oil for 2-3 min-

DINING DUO. Set the table for two with Mini Sour Cream Biscuits, savory Pork Chops with Cumin Rice and Honey-Glazed Carrots (shown above).

utes on each side. Remove and keep warm. Dissolve bouillon in water; pour into skillet and stir to loosen the browned bits. Stir in the rice, onion, green pepper, Worcestershire sauce and cumin.

Place chops over rice. Cover and bake at 350° for 15-20 minutes or until meat juices run clear and rice is tender. Let stand for 5 minutes before serving. **Yield:** 2 servings.

— 🍵 🍵 🍵 —

Honey-Glazed Carrots

(Pictured at left)

It takes just four ingredients to prepare this sweet side dish. I like to serve the quick-to-fix recipe with fish, but it goes great with any entree. —*Molly Mason Denver, Colorado*

```
1-1/2 cups baby carrots
    3 tablespoons honey
    2 tablespoons brown sugar
    1 teaspoon lemon juice
```

Place 1 in. of water in a saucepan; add carrots. Bring to a boil. Reduce heat; cover and simmer for 8-10 minutes or until crisp-tender. Drain. In a small skillet, combine the honey, brown sugar and lemon juice. Cook and stir until bubbly. Add carrots and stir until well coated. **Yield:** 2 servings.

— 🍵 🍵 🍵 —

Mini Sour Cream Biscuits

(Pictured at left)

These buttery mini muffins are flaky, tender and a snap to make because you start with convenient biscuit mix. —*Sara Dukes, Bartow, Georgia*

```
  1 cup biscuit/baking mix
1/2 cup sour cream
1/4 cup butter or margarine, melted
```

In a bowl, combine all ingredients. Drop by rounded tablespoonfuls into greased miniature muffin pans. Bake at 425° for 15-18 minutes or until golden brown. **Yield:** 1 dozen.

— 🍵 🍵 🍵 —

Peach Smoothies

(Pictured on page 164)

Whip up this creamy concoction as a refreshing and nutritious snack or a quick chilled breakfast. Because you can use frozen fruit, you don't have to wait until fresh peaches are in season to enjoy this delicious drink. —*Martha Polasek, Markham, Texas*

✓ Uses less fat, sugar or salt. Includes Nutritional Analysis and Diabetic Exchanges.

```
1/2 cup peach or apricot nectar
1/2 cup sliced fresh or frozen peaches
1/4 cup vanilla yogurt
  2 ice cubes
```

In a blender, combine all ingredients. Cover and process until blended. Serve immediately in chilled glasses. **Yield:** 2 servings.
Nutritional Analysis: One serving (prepared with fat-free yogurt) equals 120 calories, trace fat (trace saturated fat), 1 mg cholesterol, 29 mg sodium, 29 g carbohydrate, 2 g fiber, 2 g protein. **Diabetic Exchange:** 2 fruit.

— 🍵 🍵 🍵 —

Apricot Mini Loaves

(Pictured on page 164)

These lightly spiced bread loaves are full of apricot-nut flavor with a honey and clove glaze. My young daughter, Miranda, helped me whip up these loaves with ingredients we had on hand, and they were surprisingly good. —*Kelly Koutahi, Moore, Oklahoma*

```
  1 egg, lightly beaten
  6 tablespoons milk
  5 tablespoons butter or margarine, melted
4-1/2 teaspoons honey
1/2 teaspoon vanilla extract
  1 cup pancake mix
1/4 cup finely chopped walnuts
1/4 cup finely chopped dried apricots
  2 tablespoons raisins
GLAZE:
1/2 cup confectioners' sugar
  1 teaspoon honey
1/8 teaspoon ground cloves
  2 to 3 teaspoons milk
```

In a bowl, combine the egg, milk, butter, honey and vanilla extract; stir in the pancake mix just until moistened. Fold in the walnuts, apricots and raisins. Pour into two greased 4-1/2-in. x 2-1/2-in. x 1-1/2-in. loaf pans.

Bake at 350° for 22-28 minutes or until a toothpick inserted near the center comes out clean. Cool for 5 minutes before removing from pans to wire racks.

In a small bowl, combine all of the glaze ingredients. Drizzle over the warm loaves. Cool completely. **Yield:** 2 loaves.

'My Mom's Best Meal'

Here, six daughters share their mom's best recipes for those special dinners that they remember the most.

            ▼ ▼ ▼

MADE BY MOM. Clockwise from upper left: Country-Style Supper (p. 198), From-Scratch Fare (p. 194), Traditional Turkey Dinner (p. 202) and French Christmas Feast (p. 182).

This mom gave her family a mouth-watering taste of Provence through an authentic French Christmas feast.

By Kerry Sullivan, Maitland, Florida

MY MOM, Nancy Larkin (above), is a true artist—both on canvas and in the kitchen. When she's not painting watercolors in her studio, she's busy creating in the kitchen.

So it was no surprise that when Mom returned from a 2-week watercolor workshop in Provence, France a year ago, she was all enthused about the meals she'd enjoyed there.

Our holidays are usually celebrated at her house...and the meals are always a real feast. Last Christmas, Mom wanted our family to experience the same country cuisine she'd relished in France. So she fashioned an unforgettable table feast with a French accent.

On Christmas Eve, the dining room table was aglow with candles, crystal and good china. Mom explained a little about each dish as she served it.

Her Raspberry Tossed Salad was a refreshing blend of mixed salad greens and sweet fresh raspberries, drizzled with a light vinaigrette dressing enhanced with raspberry juice.

Because some of us like our beef well-done and others prefer it medium-rare, Mom prepared not one Herbed Roast Beef, but two. She coated the roasts with a fragrant herb rub and covered them in onions before baking, then served the meat with horseradish sauce.

Roasted Root Vegetables showcased homey potatoes, turnips and carrots seasoned with garlic and rosemary. They were the perfect complement to the roast beef.

The finale was Orange Chantilly Cream, a recipe Mom found in a French cookbook. She scooped out the oranges and filled them with a fluffy orange-flavored whipped cream.

I'm thrilled to share Mom's French-inspired Yuletide menu and hope you'll enjoy this feast as much as our family did. *Joyeux Noel!*

PICTURED AT LEFT: Raspberry Tossed Salad, Herbed Roast Beef, Roasted Root Vegetables and Orange Chantilly Cream (recipes are on the next page).

Raspberry Tossed Salad

Red raspberries brighten this tossed green salad, making it the perfect ingredient for a festive Yuletide menu. Raspberry juice brings a special touch to the light oil and vinegar dressing.

✓ Uses less fat, sugar or salt. Includes Nutritional Analysis and Diabetic Exchanges.

- 9 cups torn mixed salad greens
- 3 cups fresh *or* frozen unsweetened raspberries
- 2 tablespoons olive *or* canola oil
- 2 tablespoons cider vinegar
- 4 teaspoons sugar
- 1/8 teaspoon salt

Dash pepper

In a large salad bowl, gently combine the salad greens and 2-3/4 cups raspberries. Mash the remaining berries; strain, reserving juice and discarding seeds. In a bowl, whisk the raspberry juice, oil, vinegar, sugar, salt and pepper. Drizzle over salad; gently toss to coat. **Yield:** 12 servings.

Nutritional Analysis: One serving (3/4 cup) equals 47 calories, 3 g fat (trace saturated fat), 0 cholesterol, 32 mg sodium, 6 g carbohydrate, 3 g fiber, 1 g protein. **Diabetic Exchanges:** 1 vegetable, 1/2 fat.

— 🍵 🍵 🍵 —

Herbed Roast Beef

A savory herb rub flavors this juicy roast that makes an impression every time my mom serves it for dinner.

The creamy horseradish sauce adds a little kick to the crispy-coated slices of beef. It's delicious served over the tender beef.

- 2 bone-in beef rib roasts (4 to 6 pounds *each*)
- 2 teaspoons fennel seed, crushed
- 2 teaspoons dried rosemary, crushed
- 2 teaspoons *each* dried basil, marjoram, savory and thyme
- 2 teaspoons rubbed sage
- 2 medium onions, sliced
- 6 fresh rosemary sprigs

HORSERADISH SAUCE:
- 1-1/2 cups (12 ounces) sour cream
- 1/4 cup prepared horseradish
- 2 tablespoons snipped chives
- 3 tablespoons lemon juice

Trim and tie roasts if desired. In a small bowl, combine the fennel seed, crushed rosemary, basil, marjoram, savory, thyme and sage; rub over roasts. Place with fat side up on a rack in a roasting pan. Top with onions and rosemary sprigs. Bake, uncovered, at 350° for 2-1/2 to 3-1/2 hours or until meat reaches desired doneness (for rare, a meat thermometer should read 140°; medium, 160°; well-done, 170°).

Discard onions and rosemary. Let roasts stand for 10-15 minutes before slicing. Meanwhile, in a small bowl, combine the sauce ingredients. Serve with beef. **Yield:** 10-12 servings.

— ♥ ♥ ♥ —

Roasted Root Vegetables

Pleasantly seasoned with rosemary and garlic, this appealing side dish showcases good-for-you turnips, carrots and potatoes. It's a nice homey addition to our family's holiday meal.

✓ Uses less fat, sugar or salt. Includes Nutritional Analysis and Diabetic Exchanges.

    5 medium red potatoes, cubed
    4 medium carrots, cut into 1/2-inch slices
    2 small turnips, peeled and cubed
    1 garlic clove, minced
    2 to 4 tablespoons olive *or* canola oil
    1 tablespoon minced fresh rosemary
      or 1 teaspoon dried rosemary, crushed
  1/2 teaspoon salt
  1/4 teaspoon pepper

Place the potatoes, carrots, turnips and garlic in a greased 13-in. x 9-in. x 2-in. baking dish. Drizzle with oil; sprinkle with rosemary, salt and pepper. Stir to coat. Bake, uncovered, at 350° for 35 minutes. Increase temperature to 450°; bake 10-15 minutes longer or until vegetables are tender. **Yield:** 10-12 servings.

Nutritional Analysis: One 3/4-cup serving (prepared with 2 tablespoons olive oil) equals 55

calories, 3 g fat (trace saturated fat), 0 cholesterol, 144 mg sodium, 7 g carbohydrate, 2 g fiber, 1 g protein. **Diabetic Exchanges:** 1 vegetable, 1/2 fat.

— ♥ ♥ ♥ —

Orange Chantilly Cream

Mom first tried this recipe from a French cookbook many years ago. She decorated the top of each light fluffy dessert cup with a slice of fresh orange from our trees! Everyone loved it.

   12 medium navel oranges
4-1/2 cups heavy whipping cream
    1 cup confectioners' sugar
2-1/4 teaspoons orange extract
  1/3 cup orange juice

Cut a thin slice off the top of each orange. With a grapefruit spoon, scoop out pulp. Invert oranges onto paper towels to drain. Remove and discard membranes from orange pulp; set pulp aside.

In a mixing bowl, beat the whipping cream until it begins to thicken. Add confectioners' sugar and extract; beat until stiff peaks form. Beat in the orange juice. Fold in reserved orange pulp. Spoon into orange shells. Cover and refrigerate until serving. **Yield:** 12 servings.

Her mom made holidays, birthdays and other occasions special with memorable meals seasoned with love.

By Susan Ormond, Jamestown, North Carolina

WHEN I THINK about my mom, the first things that come to mind are her fabulous meals and the joy it gave her to cook for others.

My mom, Mary Ann Emrick (above), loved to entertain and hosted many baby showers and dinner parties over the years. She made each event even more special with the loving care she put into the foods she prepared.

For our birthdays, my dad, two sisters and I got to pick any meal we wanted Mom to prepare. My favorite was Round Ham Loaf, Creamed Potatoes, Fluffy Lime Salad and Texas Sheet Cake.

Her Round Ham Loaf, a nice change from the usual meat loaf, was served with a pleasantly sweet raisin sauce. She garnished the loaf with pineapple and maraschino cherries, which made it pretty enough to serve for company.

Mom's Creamed Potatoes were comforting and chunky, while the tangy Fluffy Lime Salad was cool and refreshing.

There was no better way to end a birthday meal than with her chocolaty Texas Sheet Cake. Moist like a pudding cake, it was topped with a sweet cocoa icing.

My grandmother handed down the ham, potato and salad recipes to my mother. She learned to cook from Grandma, but my mom continued to refine her skills by gathering information and recipes from magazines, newspapers, television shows and friends. There were always scraps of paper and little notebooks around the house with recipes written on them.

Mom often served my favorite meal for Easter and other holidays, too. I have continued the tradition by making the dishes during the holidays for my husband, David, and our three children.

I'm glad that I've had this chance to pay tribute to my mom by sharing this special meal with you as well.

PICTURED AT LEFT: Round Ham Loaf, Creamed Potatoes, Fluffy Lime Salad and Texas Sheet Cake (recipes are on the next page).

Round Ham Loaf

Slices of pineapple and a maraschino cherry make my mom's homey ham loaf pretty enough for company. The accompanying vanilla and raisin sauce lends a distinctive flavor to the meat.

    1 egg
    3/4 cup milk
    1/4 cup crushed butter-flavored crackers
        (about 6 crackers)
      1 pound ground fully cooked ham
    1/2 pound ground pork
      1 can (8 ounces) sliced pineapple
RAISIN SAUCE:
    1/2 cup sugar
      1 tablespoon cornstarch
Pinch salt
      1 cup water
    1/3 cup golden raisins
      1 tablespoon butter *or* margarine
      1 teaspoon vanilla extract
      1 maraschino cherry, optional

In a large bowl, combine the egg, milk and cracker crumbs. Crumble ham and pork over mixture; mix well. Form into an 8-in. round loaf in an ungreased 9-in. pie plate. Drain pineapple, reserving juice. Cut pineapple slices in half if desired; place on top of loaf.

Bake, uncovered, at 325° for 45 minutes. Baste with reserved pineapple juice. Bake 45 minutes longer or until lightly browned and a meat thermometer reads 160°, basting occasionally with pan drippings.

For sauce, combine the sugar, cornstarch, salt and water in a saucepan; stir until smooth. Add the raisins. Bring to a boil; cook and stir for 2 minutes or until thickened. Remove from the heat; stir in butter and vanilla. Serve warm with ham loaf. Garnish with a cherry if desired. **Yield:** 6 servings.

Creamed Potatoes

These melt-in-your-mouth potatoes, baked in a mild creamy sauce, complement any meat entree, and they're a pleasant change from mashed or baked.

      6 medium potatoes (2 pounds), peeled and
        cut into 1/2-inch cubes
      3 tablespoons butter *or* margarine
    1/4 cup all-purpose flour
      1 teaspoon salt
    1/4 teaspoon pepper
      2 cups milk
Paprika and minced fresh parsley

Place potatoes in a saucepan and cover with water. Bring to a boil. Reduce heat; cover and cook for 15-20 minutes or until tender. Meanwhile, in another saucepan, melt butter. Stir in the flour, salt and pepper until smooth. Gradually add milk. Bring to a boil; cook and stir for 2 minutes or until thickened.

Drain potatoes and place in a serving bowl. Add cream sauce and toss gently. Sprinkle with paprika and parsley. **Yield:** 6 servings.

Fluffy Lime Salad

Crunchy walnuts, plump marshmallows and tangy pineapple dot this creamy lime salad. It's a refreshing side dish for a family meal or a yummy addition to a potluck dinner. It can be made in advance, giving you one less thing to do at dinnertime.

    1 can (8 ounces) crushed pineapple
    1 package (3 ounces) lime gelatin
    3 tablespoons water
    2 packages (3 ounces *each*) cream cheese, softened
    1 cup chopped walnuts
    1 cup miniature marshmallows
    1 cup heavy whipping cream, whipped

Drain pineapple, reserving juice; set the pineapple aside. In a saucepan, combine gelatin, water and reserved juice. Cook and stir over low heat until gelatin is dissolved. Refrigerate until syrupy, about 30 minutes.

In a small mixing bowl, beat cream cheese until fluffy. Stir in gelatin mixture, walnuts, marshmallows and reserved pineapple. Fold in the whipped cream. Transfer to a 1-qt. serving bowl. Cover and refrigerate for 2 hours or until set. **Yield:** 9 servings.

Texas Sheet Cake

This chocolaty delight was one of my favorites growing up. The cake is so moist and the icing so sweet that everyone who samples it wants a copy of the recipe. I'm always happy to share it.

    1 cup butter *or* margarine
    1 cup water
  1/4 cup baking cocoa
    2 cups all-purpose flour
    2 cups sugar
    1 teaspoon baking soda
  1/2 teaspoon salt
  1/2 cup sour cream
ICING:
  1/2 cup butter *or* margarine
  1/4 cup plus 2 tablespoons milk
    3 tablespoons baking cocoa
3-3/4 cups confectioners' sugar
    1 teaspoon vanilla extract

In a large saucepan, bring the butter, water and cocoa to a boil. Remove from the heat. Combine the flour, sugar, baking soda and salt; add to cocoa mixture. Stir in the sour cream until smooth. Pour into a greased 15-in. x 10-in. x 1-in. baking pan. Bake at 350° for 20-25 minutes or until a toothpick inserted near the center comes out clean.

In a saucepan, melt butter; add milk and cocoa. Bring to a boil. Remove from the heat. Whisk in confectioners' sugar and vanilla until smooth. Pour over warm cake. Cool completely on a wire rack. **Yield:** 15 servings.

This mom entertains often, treating family and friends to creative yet comforting meals from scratch.

By Mared Metzgar Beling, Eagle River, Alaska

A CLOSE FRIEND of my mother's once declared, "You don't meet Blanche, she meets you." And once Blanche Metzgar (above) meets you, you're likely to join the large circle of friends who relish dinner parties at my parents' home in Pennsylvania.

Mom absolutely loves to entertain, trying out new recipes on family and friends. She's always been just as creative cooking for my dad, sister and me. As kids, my sister and I were picky eaters, but Mom's mouth-watering meals exposed us to new dishes that helped us develop broader tastes.

My sister and I got to choose the entire menu for our summer birthday celebrations. My favorite meal still consists of Mom's Creamed Chicken in Patty Shells, Wild Rice Barley Salad, greens with Home-Style Salad Dressing and Zucchini Chip Snack Cake.

With its pretty presentation, Creamed Chicken in Patty Shells is the perfect entree for brunch or a special-occasion meal.

Mom's Wild Rice Barley Salad is a tangy accompaniment. I never thought I'd enjoy cold rice until I tasted this salad...now I serve it often. And people always request the recipe for Home-Style Salad Dressing with blue cheese to top a fresh tossed salad of mixed greens and vegetables.

Zucchini Chip Snack Cake is so moist, you don't even need a glass of milk to wash it down. When my dad harvests the overabundance of zucchini from his backyard garden, this scrumptious cake is the first thing everyone asks for.

Though my assignments as an Air Force nurse often take me far from my family, it's a comfort to have that little taste of home every time I make one of Mom's recipes. I hope you find them deliciously comforting as well.

— 🍽 🍽 🍽 —

PICTURED AT LEFT: Creamed Chicken in Patty Shells, Wild Rice Barley Salad, Home-Style Salad Dressing and Zucchini Chip Snack Cake (recipes are on the next page).

Bake pastry shells according to package directions. Meanwhile, in a large saucepan, saute the mushrooms, green pepper and broccoli in butter until tender; sprinkle with flour. Gradually stir in milk and reserved broth until blended. Bring to a boil; cook and stir for 2 minutes or until thickened. Add the pimientos, paprika, reserved chicken and remaining salt and pepper. Cook and stir until heated through. Spoon into pastry shells. **Yield:** 6 servings.

Wild Rice Barley Salad

I like this chilled salad because it's out of the ordinary. The rice is tossed with barley, green pepper, olives and cranberries, then coated with a tangy vinaigrette.

> 1 package (6 ounces) long grain and wild rice mix
> 1 cup cooked barley
> 1/2 cup chopped green pepper
> 1/2 cup sliced ripe olives
> 1/4 cup dried cranberries

DRESSING:

> 1/4 cup balsamic vinegar *or* red wine vinegar
> 2 tablespoons minced fresh basil
> 1 tablespoon chopped green onion
> 2 garlic cloves, minced
> 1/2 teaspoon pepper
> 1/3 cup olive *or* vegetable oil

Creamed Chicken in Patty Shells

My mom's tasty creamed chicken makes a wonderful main dish, and when you add extra vegetables, it becomes an entire meal. The recipe might look long, but it's well worth the effort.

> 1 broiler/fryer chicken (3 to 4 pounds), cut up
> 2 quarts water
> 1-1/2 teaspoons salt, *divided*
> 1-1/2 teaspoons pepper, *divided*
> 2 packages (10 ounces *each*) frozen puff pastry shells
> 1 cup sliced fresh mushrooms
> 1 medium green pepper, chopped
> 1/2 cup small fresh broccoli florets
> 5 tablespoons butter *or* margarine
> 6 tablespoons all-purpose flour
> 2 cups milk
> 1 jar (2 ounces) diced pimientos, drained
> 1/4 teaspoon paprika

In a large kettle, bring the chicken, water, 1 teaspoon salt and 1 teaspoon pepper to a boil. Reduce heat; cover and simmer for 1-1/2 to 2 hours or until chicken is tender.

Remove chicken from broth; cool. Remove meat from bones; cut into cubes and set aside. Discard skin and bones. Strain broth and skim fat; set aside 1 cup broth (refrigerate remaining broth for another use).

Cook the rice according to package directions. In a large serving bowl, combine the rice, barley, green pepper, olives and cranberries. In a blender, combine the vinegar, basil, green onion, garlic and pepper. While processing, gradually add the oil in a steady stream. Drizzle over salad and toss to coat. Cover; refrigerate until chilled. **Yield: 4-6 servings.**

— 🏳 🏳 🏳 —

Home-Style Salad Dressing

This pleasant-tasting salad dressing is delicious drizzled on a bed of greens with a sprinkling of crumbled blue cheese. Mom always gets requests for the recipe.

- 1 cup mayonnaise
- 1 small onion, cut into wedges
- 2 tablespoons sugar
- 2 tablespoons white vinegar
- 2 tablespoons ketchup
- 1 teaspoon salt
- 1/2 teaspoon celery seed
- 1/3 cup vegetable oil

Salad greens and vegetables of your choice
Crumbled blue cheese

Place the first seven ingredients in a blender; cover and process until smooth. While processing, gradually add oil in a steady stream. In a salad bowl, combine greens and vegetables; sprinkle with blue cheese. Serve with dressing. Refrigerate any leftover dressing. **Yield: 1-1/2 cups.**

Zucchini Chip Snack Cake

Here's a mouth-watering dessert that is so rich, it doesn't need frosting to top it off. The shredded zucchini makes it especially moist. With a scoop of vanilla ice cream, this cake makes an unbeatable finale for any occasion. My mom especially likes to serve it in summer, when the zucchini is fresh from my dad's garden.

- 1/2 cup butter *or* margarine, softened
- 1-3/4 cups sugar
- 1/2 cup vegetable oil
- 2 eggs
- 1 teaspoon vanilla extract
- 2-1/2 cups all-purpose flour
- 2 tablespoons baking cocoa
- 1 teaspoon baking soda
- 1/2 teaspoon baking powder
- 1/2 teaspoon ground cinnamon
- 1/2 teaspoon ground cloves
- 1/2 cup buttermilk
- 2 cups shredded peeled zucchini
- 2 cups (12 ounces) semisweet chocolate chips

In a large mixing bowl, cream butter and sugar. Beat in oil, eggs and vanilla. Combine dry ingredients; add to creamed mixture alternately with buttermilk. Stir in zucchini.

Pour into a greased 13-in. x 9-in. x 2-in. baking pan. Sprinkle with chocolate chips. Bake at 350° for 45-50 minutes or until a toothpick inserted near the center comes out clean. Cool on a wire rack. **Yield: 12-15 servings.**

Her mom prepares meals for family and friends from scratch...and she always makes it look easy!

By Nancy Holland, Morgan Hill, California

WHEN I was growing up, I loved to watch my mom cook. She made fixing a hearty mouth-watering meal from scratch appear so effortless.

My mom, LaVaun McMahon (above), made healthy, delicious dinners every night for my dad, younger brother, two older sisters and me. She served well-balanced meals, with something from every food group on the table.

Now when we visit my parents in Truckee, California, Mom asks what we'd like to eat...and that's a difficult decision! But no visit is complete without Cheeseburger Buns, Cauliflower Olive Salad, Dill Pickle Potato Salad and Custard Meringue Pie.

Mom came up with the Cheeseburger Buns recipe after my dad told her about the great meal they'd served in the school cafeteria (he's a teacher). So she made her yummy yeast rolls and stuffed them with meat and cheese.

Cauliflower Olive Salad, full of fresh veggies and tossed with a tangy dressing, is a recipe a neighbor shared with my mother.

Her Dill Pickle Potato Salad is legendary in our family. Mom flavors the salad with her homemade pickles, and because she doesn't care for sweet dressings, she coats it with a mixture of mayonnaise, mustard and dill pickle juice.

Mom's Aunt Emily used to make Custard Meringue Pie at Christmastime. It's so scrumptious that we enjoy it year-round.

My mom's ease and skill in the kitchen taught me the joys of cooking, too. I like trying new things, and I think that's because I don't feel intimidated by a new recipe. I just picture my mom whipping up something wonderful, and I dig in!

PICTURED AT LEFT: Cheeseburger Buns, Cauliflower Olive Salad, Dill Pickle Potato Salad and Custard Meringue Pie (recipes are on the next page).

Cheeseburger Buns

My mom stuffs soft homemade yeast rolls with ground beef, tomato sauce and cheese to make these tasty sandwiches. They're great leftovers, too.

✓ Uses less fat, sugar or salt. Includes Nutritional Analysis and Diabetic Exchanges.

- **2 packages (1/4 ounce *each*) active dry yeast**
- **1/2 cup warm water (110° to 115°)**
- **3/4 cup warm milk (110° to 115°)**
- **1/4 cup sugar**
- **1/4 cup shortening**
- **1 egg**
- **1 teaspoon salt**
- **3-1/2 to 4 cups all-purpose flour**
- **1-1/2 pounds ground beef**
- **1/4 cup chopped onion**
- **1 can (8 ounces) tomato sauce**
- **8 slices American cheese, quartered**

In a mixing bowl, dissolve yeast in warm water. Add milk, sugar, shortening, egg, salt and 2 cups flour; beat until smooth. Stir in enough remaining flour to form a soft dough. Turn onto a floured surface; knead until smooth and elastic, about 4-6 minutes. Place in a greased bowl, turning once to grease top. Cover and let rise in a warm place until doubled, about 30 minutes.

In a skillet, cook beef and onion until meat is no longer pink; drain. Stir in tomato sauce. Remove from the heat; set aside. Punch dough down; divide into 16 pieces. On a lightly floured surface, gently roll out and stretch each piece into a 5-in. circle. Top each circle with two pieces of cheese and about 3 tablespoons beef mixture. Bring dough over filling to center; pinch edges to seal.

Place seam side down on a greased baking sheet. Cover and let rise in a warm place until doubled, about 20 minutes. Bake at 400° for 8-12 minutes or until golden brown. Serve immediately. Re-

frigerate leftovers. **Yield:** 16 sandwiches.

Nutritional Analysis: One sandwich (prepared with fat-free milk, lean ground beef and reduced-fat cheese) equals 248 calories, 8 g fat (3 g saturated fat), 31 mg cholesterol, 374 mg sodium, 27 g carbohydrate, 1 g fiber, 15 g protein. **Diabetic Exchanges:** 2 lean meat, 2 starch.

— 🝙 🝙 🝙 —

Cauliflower Olive Salad

This colorful toss combines cauliflower and black and green olives with sweet peppers and red onion for a satisfying blend of flavors. The lemony vinaigrette coats the salad well and gives it a pleasing tartness.

- **5 to 6 cups cauliflowerets**
- **1 cup chopped green pepper**
- **1 cup stuffed olives, sliced**
- **1 can (4-1/2 ounces) chopped ripe olives, drained**
- **1/2 cup chopped sweet red pepper**
- **1/2 cup chopped red onion, optional**

DRESSING:
- **3 tablespoons lemon juice**
- **3 tablespoons cider vinegar**
- **1/2 teaspoon sugar**
- **1/4 teaspoon pepper**
- **1/2 cup vegetable oil**

In a large bowl, combine the cauliflower, green pepper, olives, red pepper and onion if desired. In a small bowl, whisk the lemon juice, vinegar, sugar and pepper; gradually whisk in oil. Pour over vegetables and stir to coat. Cover; refrigerate for at least 4 hours. Serve with a slotted spoon. **Yield:** 8 servings.

Dill Pickle Potato Salad

Dill pickles add pizzazz to this old-fashioned chilled salad. The creamy, well-dressed side dish makes a flavorful and attractive addition to a Fourth of July picnic or church supper.

> 3 pounds potatoes (about 8 medium)
> 6 hard-cooked eggs, chopped
> 3 celery ribs, chopped
> 6 green onions, chopped
> 2 medium dill pickles, finely chopped
> 1-1/2 cups mayonnaise
> 1/4 cup dill pickle juice
> 4-1/2 teaspoons prepared mustard
> 1 teaspoon celery seed
> 1 teaspoon salt
> 1/2 teaspoon pepper
> Leaf lettuce, optional

Place potatoes in a Dutch oven and cover with water. Bring to a boil. Reduce heat; cover and simmer for 20-30 minutes or until tender. Drain and cool.

Peel and cube potatoes; place in a large bowl. Add the eggs, celery, onions and pickles. In a small bowl, combine the mayonnaise, pickle juice, mustard, celery seed, salt and pepper. Pour over potato mixture; mix well. Cover and refrigerate for at least 4 hours. Serve in a lettuce-lined bowl if desired. **Yield:** 8-10 servings.

🍴 🍴 🍴

Custard Meringue Pie

Each bite of this light and fluffy pie will nearly melt in your mouth. The cracker-crumb crust holds a smooth vanilla filling topped with an airy meringue and a sprinkling of more crumbs.

> 1-1/4 cups crushed Holland Rusks *or* graham crackers
> 1/4 cup sugar
> 1/2 teaspoon ground cinnamon
> 6 tablespoons butter (no substitutes), melted
> **FILLING:**
> 2/3 cup sugar
> 1/4 cup cornstarch
> 1/2 teaspoon salt
> 3 cups milk
> 3 egg yolks, beaten
> 1 tablespoon butter, softened
> 1-1/2 teaspoons vanilla extract
> **MERINGUE:**
> 3 egg whites
> 1/4 teaspoon cream of tartar
> 1/8 teaspoon almond extract
> 6 tablespoons sugar

In a bowl, combine the first four ingredients; set aside 2 tablespoons. Press remaining crumb mixture onto the bottom and up the sides of an ungreased 9-in. pie plate. Bake at 350° for 10-12 minutes or until golden brown. Cool on a wire rack.

In a saucepan, combine the sugar, cornstarch and salt. Stir in milk until smooth. Bring to a boil; cook and stir for 1 minute. Remove from the heat. Stir in a small amount of hot filling into egg yolks; return all to pan, stirring constantly. Bring to a gentle boil; cook and stir for 2 minutes. Remove from the heat. Stir in butter and vanilla; keep warm.

In a small mixing bowl, beat the egg whites and cream of tartar on medium speed until foamy. Add extract; beat until soft peaks form. Beat in sugar, 1 tablespoon at a time, on high until stiff peaks form. Pour warm filling into crust. Spread meringue to edges, sealing to crust. Sprinkle with reserved crumbs. Bake at 350° for 15 minutes or until golden. Cool on a wire rack for 1 hour. Chill for 1-2 hours before serving. **Yield:** 6-8 servings.

Family and farm workers alike looked forward to dining on her mother's hearty country-style meals.

By Nancy Horsburgh, Everett, Ontario

FEEDING family and seasonal farmhands for more than 20 years meant that my mom, Jean Bailey (above), spent lots of time in her huge kitchen.

During the tobacco harvest, Mom would feed our family of five, in addition to 12 to 15 workers.

All of Mom's meals were wonderful, but during the harvest, they were the best! My favorite was Barbecued Spareribs, Yukon Mashed Potatoes, Carrot Broccoli Casserole, Fluffy Biscuits and Old-Fashioned Chocolate Pie.

The aroma of those spareribs baking in the oven had us drooling long before they were ready to eat!

The garlic-seasoned Yukon Mashed Potatoes were incredibly creamy. And Carrot Broccoli Casserole complemented the ribs and potatoes so nicely. This colorful side dish can be assembled ahead of time.

Fluffy Biscuits were the result of many years of practice. Mom didn't enjoy biscuit-making, so she gave that job to me. We both learned that the secret to good biscuits is to have cold ingredients and not over-mix.

My two brothers and I topped slices of Old-Fashioned Chocolate Pie with mounds of freshly whipped cream. It's hard to believe this yummy pie doesn't contain eggs or milk.

As I got older, I took over the harvest cooking and Mom planned the meals. I'm so thankful she gave me an early introduction to preparing nourishing foods. I've loved to cook ever since!

Every Sunday, I now prepare the big family meal. Our children, their spouses and our two grandsons live nearby. So do my brothers and their families…and Mom, of course.

I'm happy to share my mom's memorable meal with you and hope you enjoy it, too!

🍴 🍴 🍴

PICTURED AT LEFT: Barbecued Spareribs, Yukon Mashed Potatoes, Carrot Broccoli Casserole, Fluffy Biscuits and Old-Fashioned Chocolate Pie (recipes are on the next page).

uncovered, 1 hour longer or until the meat is tender, brushing frequently with remaining sauce. **Yield:** 6 servings.

— 🍶 🍶 🍶 —

Yukon Mashed Potatoes

(Pictured on page 199)

My mom liked to use Yukon Gold potatoes for this recipe instead of the usual white variety. These garlic-seasoned spuds are sensational served alongside spareribs.

> 8 to 9 medium Yukon Gold *or* russet
>   potatoes, peeled and quartered
> 1/2 cup half-and-half cream
> 2 tablespoons butter *or* margarine
> 1/2 to 1 teaspoon garlic salt
> 1/8 teaspoon pepper

Place potatoes in a Dutch oven and cover with water. Cover and bring to a boil; cook for 20-25 minutes or until very tender. Drain well. In a mixing bowl, mash the potatoes. Add the cream, butter, garlic salt and pepper; beat until light and fluffy. **Yield:** 6 servings.

— 🍶 🍶 🍶 —

Carrot Broccoli Casserole

This colorful side dish feels right at home with any entree. The veggies are coated in a buttery cheese sauce, then layered with cracker crumbs. Even kids who turn up their noses at broccoli will eat this up.

Barbecued Spareribs

You'll need extra dinner napkins when you serve these tender ribs because they're so finger-lickin' good. The thick and tangy sauce has bits of celery and onion as well as a cayenne pepper kick. The ribs are perfect for summer picnics.

> 6 pounds pork spareribs, cut into
>   serving-size pieces
> 2 tablespoons vegetable oil
> 1 medium onion, finely chopped
> 2 celery ribs, finely chopped
> 2 tablespoons butter *or* margarine
> 1 cup water
> 1 cup ketchup
> 3 tablespoons Worcestershire sauce
> 2 tablespoons brown sugar
> 2 tablespoons cider vinegar
> 1 tablespoon lemon juice
> 1 tablespoon Dijon mustard
> 1/8 teaspoon cayenne pepper

In a large skillet, brown ribs in batches in oil. Place ribs, bone side down, on a rack in a shallow roasting pan. Cover and bake at 350° for 1 hour. Meanwhile, in a skillet, saute onion and celery in butter until tender. Add the remaining ingredients. Bring to a boil. Reduce heat; simmer, uncovered, for 10-12 minutes or until slightly thickened.
   Drain ribs; brush with some of the sauce. Bake,

1 package (16 ounces) baby carrots
1-1/2 pounds fresh broccoli, chopped *or* 2 packages (10 ounces *each*) frozen chopped broccoli, thawed
8 ounces process cheese (Velveeta), cubed
3/4 cup butter *or* margarine, *divided*
1-3/4 cups crushed butter-flavored crackers (about 40 crackers)

Place 1 in. of water in a saucepan; add carrots. Bring to a boil. Reduce heat; cover and simmer for 5-8 minutes or until crisp-tender. Add broccoli; cover and simmer 6-8 minutes longer or until vegetables are crisp-tender. Drain and set aside. In a small saucepan, cook and stir the cheese and 1/4 cup butter until smooth. Stir in the broccoli and carrots until combined.

Melt the remaining butter; toss with cracker crumbs. Sprinkle a third of the mixture in a greased 2-1/2-qt. baking dish. Top with half of the vegetable mixture. Repeat layers. Sprinkle with the remaining crumb mixture. Bake, uncovered, at 350° for 35-40 minutes or until heated through. **Yield:** 6-8 servings.

— ☕ ☕ ☕ —

Fluffy Biscuits

If you're looking for a flaky basic biscuit, this recipe is the best. These golden-brown rolls bake up tall, light and tender. Their mild flavor tastes even better when the warm biscuits are spread with butter or jam.

2 cups all-purpose flour
4 teaspoons baking powder
3 teaspoons sugar
1/2 teaspoon salt
1/2 cup shortening
1 egg
2/3 cup milk

In a bowl, combine the flour, baking powder, sugar and salt. Cut in shortening until the mixture resembles coarse crumbs. In a small bowl, beat egg and milk; stir into dry ingredients just until moistened.

Turn onto a well-floured surface; knead 20 times. Roll to 3/4-in. thickness; cut with a 2-1/2-in. biscuit cutter. Place on a lightly greased baking sheet. Bake at 450° for 8-10 minutes or until golden brown. Serve warm. **Yield:** 1 dozen.

— ☕ ☕ ☕ —

Old-Fashioned Chocolate Pie

Rich and oh-so-chocolaty, this silky pie is a cinch to prepare. The mouth-watering filling and flaky crust are an unbeatable combination that's sure to make this pie one of your family's favorite desserts, too.

1 cup sugar
1/3 cup baking cocoa
1/4 cup all-purpose flour
Pinch salt
2-1/4 cups water
1 tablespoon butter *or* margarine
1 teaspoon vanilla extract
1 pastry shell (9 inches), baked
Whipped cream and chocolate sprinkles

In a large saucepan, combine the sugar, cocoa, flour and salt; gradually add water. Cook and stir over medium heat until mixture comes to a boil. Cook and stir for 1 minute or until thickened. Remove from the heat; stir in butter and vanilla. Pour into pastry shell. Refrigerate for 2-3 hours before slicing. Garnish with whipped cream and chocolate sprinkles. **Yield:** 6-8 servings.

Her mom's turkey dinner with all the trimmings is this 12-year-old's favorite holiday meal.

By Jacinta Ransom, South Haven, Michigan

AWESOME is the best way I know to describe the Thanksgiving dinner my mom, Marsha Ransom (above), prepares.

Dinner centers around Turkey with Grandma's Stuffing, which my grandma made when my mom was growing up. The yummy stuffing is flavored with poultry seasoning, and the gravy's great over mashed potatoes.

Gelatin Ring with Cream Cheese Balls is another recipe my mom enjoyed as a child. The cream cheese balls rolled in nuts make it fancy enough for a special occasion, but it's easy to make.

Aunt Mavis used to bring Special Layered Salad to our family feasts. Now my brothers and I help prepare it when we have Thanksgiving at our house.

I can hardly wait for dessert. Pumpkin Chip Cupcakes taste so good with all the nuts and chocolate chips inside, that I'd rather have them than pumpkin pie any day!

My mom, who's a *Taste of Home* field editor, cooks mostly from scratch. Mom learned to cook while growing up in Belle Vernon, Pennsylvania. Her mom taught her how to follow a recipe, but her grandmother taught her how to add a "pinch of this or a pinch of that". My mom has passed on her skills, too…to me and my three brothers.

I really love baking and cooking with my mom. She says I've been helping her since I was 3, when I'd climb up on a stool and tear lettuce for salads. She calls me her "right-hand girl". My brothers and I pitch in if we're expecting company or having a special meal…or whenever she needs extra help.

Someday I want to be as good a cook as my mom is. I hope you'll fix one of her recipes for one of your holiday meals.

PICTURED AT LEFT: Turkey with Grandma's Stuffing, Gelatin Ring with Cream Cheese Balls, Special Layered Salad and Pumpkin Chip Cupcakes (recipes are on the next page).

Turkey with Grandma's Stuffing

Everyone is ready to dig in when my mom sets this impressive Thanksgiving favorite on the dinner table. The moist turkey, seasoned bread stuffing and flavorful gravy remind her of holiday meals when she was growing up.

- 1 turkey (12 pounds) with giblets
- 4 celery ribs with leaves, chopped
- 1 small onion, finely chopped
- 4 tablespoons butter *or* margarine, *divided*
- 10 slices day-old white bread, cubed
- 10 slices day-old whole wheat bread, cubed
- 1/2 cup egg substitute
- 3/4 teaspoon poultry seasoning
- 1/2 teaspoon salt

Dash pepper
- 3 tablespoons cornstarch
- 1/4 cup cold water

Additional salt and pepper

Place giblets in a saucepan and cover with water; bring to a boil. Reduce heat; cover and simmer for 45-50 minutes or until tender. Remove giblets to a cutting board; dice. Set broth and giblets aside. In a skillet, saute celery and onion in 2 tablespoons butter until tender. In a bowl, combine bread cubes, celery mixture, giblets, egg substitute and seasonings. Stir in 1 cup giblet broth.

Just before roasting, loosely stuff turkey with 8 cups stuffing. Place remaining stuffing in a greased 2-cup baking dish; refrigerate. Skewer turkey openings; tie drumsticks together with kitchen string. Place breast side up on a rack in a roasting pan. Pour 1 cup giblet broth over turkey. Melt remaining butter; brush over turkey. Bake, uncovered, at 325° for 3-1/2 to 4 hours or until a meat thermometer reads 180° for turkey and 165° for stuffing, basting occasionally. (Cover loosely with foil if turkey browns too quickly.)

Bake additional stuffing, covered, for 25-30 minutes. Uncover; bake 10 minutes longer. Cover turkey and let stand for 20 minutes before carving. Pour pan drippings into a 2-cup measuring cup; skim fat. Add enough remaining giblet broth to measure 2 cups. In a saucepan, combine cornstarch and cold water until smooth. Stir in broth mixture. Bring to a boil; cook and stir for 2 minutes or until thickened. Season with salt and pepper. **Yield:** 8 servings (10 cups stuffing).

Gelatin Ring with Cream Cheese Balls

Here's a fun way to serve cranberry sauce that will please both kids and adults. The red gelatin and cranberry sauce ring is dressed up with cute cream cheese balls rolled in ground walnuts. It's cool, colorful and yummy, too!

- 2 packages (3 ounces *each*) raspberry gelatin
- 2 cups boiling water
- 2 cans (16 ounces *each*) whole-berry cranberry sauce
- 1 package (8 ounces) cream cheese
- 1 cup ground walnuts

In a bowl, dissolve gelatin in boiling water. Stir in cranberry sauce until well blended. Pour into a 6-cup ring mold coated with nonstick cooking spray; refrigerate overnight or until firm.

Roll cream cheese into 3/4-in. balls; coat with walnuts. Unmold gelatin onto a serving platter; place cream cheese balls in center of ring. **Yield:** 10-12 servings.

— ▼ ▼ ▼ —

Special Layered Salad

Tiny shrimp make my aunt's seven-layer salad something special. Layered with romaine, green pepper, onion, peas, cheese and crumbled bacon, this pretty salad never lasts long when my mom makes it.

1 pound romaine, torn
1 medium green pepper, chopped
1 medium onion, chopped
1 package (10 ounces) frozen peas
1-1/2 cups mayonnaise
2 cups (8 ounces) shredded cheddar cheese
1 can (4-1/4 ounces) tiny shrimp, rinsed and drained
4 bacon strips, cooked and crumbled
1 medium tomato, cut into wedges
3 hard-cooked eggs, cut into wedges
Paprika and minced fresh parsley

In a 3-qt. bowl or dish, layer the romaine, green pepper, onion, peas, mayonnaise and cheese. Cover and refrigerate for at least 2 hours or overnight. Just before serving, top with shrimp, bacon, tomato and eggs. Sprinkle with paprika and parsley. **Yield:** 8-10 servings.

Pumpkin Chip Cupcakes

I love these cupcakes that are loaded with chocolate chips and chopped walnuts. My mom makes them for dessert on special occasions or for a sweet autumn snack.

1 cup all-purpose flour
3/4 cup whole wheat flour
1 teaspoon baking powder
1 teaspoon baking soda
1/2 teaspoon salt
1/2 teaspoon ground cinnamon
1/4 teaspoon ground nutmeg
2 eggs, lightly beaten
1 cup canned pumpkin
1/2 cup vegetable oil
1/2 cup honey
1/3 cup water
1/2 cup chopped walnuts
1 cup miniature chocolate chips
FROSTING:
1 package (8 ounces) cream cheese, softened
1/4 cup butter *or* margarine, softened
1 teaspoon vanilla extract
2 cups confectioners' sugar

In a large bowl, combine the first seven ingredients. Combine the eggs, pumpkin, oil, honey and water; mix well. Stir into dry ingredients just until combined; fold in walnuts and chocolate chips. Fill greased or foil-lined muffin cups three-fourths full. Bake at 350° for 20-25 minutes or until a toothpick comes out clean. Cool for 10 minutes before removing from pans to wire racks to cool completely.

For frosting, in a small mixing bowl, beat the cream cheese, butter and vanilla until fluffy. Gradually beat in confectioners' sugar until smooth. Frost cooled cupcakes. **Yield:** 15 cupcakes.

Editors' Meals

Taste of Home is edited by 1,000 cooks across North America. Here, you'll "meet" some of those cooks who share a family-favorite meal.

———— 🍴 🍴 🍴 ————

FAMILY RECIPES. Clockwise from upper left: Special Spring Dinner (p. 216), Sizzling Warm-Weather Fare (p. 224), Supper Says "Summer" (p. 220) and Family-Favorite Foods.

Merry Morning Menu

This cook has time for merrymaking when she serves a Christmas brunch with convenient make-ahead dishes.

By Julie Sterchi, Harrisburg, Illinois

BRUNCH is a wonderful meal to enjoy on a special day like Christmas. I love to gather my family for Mushroom Sausage Strata, Fruit Medley, Warm Christmas Punch and Cinnamon Rolls.

My husband, Edd, is the minister for the Church of Christ here in Harrisburg, and we have three children—daughters Bethany and Brittany and son Ben.

Thanks to several recipes that can be made ahead, even the cook can relax and enjoy this appealing holiday brunch.

The hearty Mushroom Sausage Strata is a delightful do-ahead main dish. A friend brought this dish to serve to our Home Extension group one year, and I was so impressed with it. Made with whole wheat bread, sausage, mushrooms and two types of cheese, it's an appetizing combination.

Salad Was Mom's Creation

I remember my mom coming up with the colorful and tasty Fruit Medley salad one Christmas. Wanting something bright and refreshing for breakfast, Mom combined pineapple, sweet cherries, oranges, berries, grapes and more...and the whole family raved about it.

Some years later, I realized I had better write down the recipe so I could continue this popular tradition with my own family.

Warm Christmas Punch is another recipe you can mix up beforehand and simply heat in a slow cooker the morning of the brunch. Its rich color, inviting aroma and delightful flavor win over even those who aren't usually punch fans. I also serve this pretty beverage at a holiday open house we host each year, and it's always a hit.

Doing so much of the preparation the day before

frees up time for me to make Cinnamon Rolls the day of the brunch. They're such a treat, served fresh from the oven!

A dear friend brought these yummy rolls to a church fellowship meal several years ago. Edd was instantly hooked and encouraged her to bring them at every opportunity!

I love how easy it is to make these rolls. With the quick-rise yeast, they don't take as much time as traditional yeast rolls...and they are much less labor-intensive than others I've made.

Guests Drop in Often

Casual entertaining such as a brunch or open house blends well with my cooking style, which you could call "family friendly". I love whipping up a batch of cookies or a special pie or cake and having friends over on the spur of the moment.

We live just north of the high school football field, so most Friday nights when the Bulldogs (our school team) are in town, you'll find a group gathered around our kitchen counter after the game, drinking hot chocolate and eating a warm, sweet treat.

Our busy lifestyle—the kids play soccer, football, basketball and tennis—keeps me looking for everyday meals that go together quickly after I get home from work. Church activities also help fill our schedules to the brim.

All three children are showing an interest in cooking, and it's been fun to see their tastes expand as we've tried new foods. Their efforts make me think back to cooking projects during my years in 4-H. I especially loved baking.

Cooking on top of the stove, however, was a different story. But when I became engaged and realized I soon would be responsible for feeding a hungry man, I started taking mental notes when Mom cooked, especially Edd's favorites, such as cream gravy. I even asked her to measure ingredients that she usually just threw in until it "looked right".

It's a great honor to have been a field editor for *Taste of Home* since the magazine's inception. I laugh when people recognize my name from the masthead and exclaim, "Wow! You're famous!"

I hope you'll enjoy my brunch dishes and that they'll warm your holiday gatherings as they have ours.

PICTURED AT LEFT: Mushroom Sausage Strata, Fruit Medley, Warm Christmas Punch and Cinnamon Rolls (recipes are on the next page).

Mushroom Sausage Strata

This flavorful casserole is a hearty mainstay for our family's Christmas Day brunch menu. Being able to assemble the recipe ahead of time is a real plus!

    1 pound bulk pork sausage
  10 slices whole wheat bread, cubed
    1 can (4 ounces) mushroom stems and pieces, drained
1/2 cup shredded cheddar cheese
1/2 cup shredded Swiss cheese
    6 eggs, lightly beaten
    1 cup milk
    1 cup half-and-half cream
    1 teaspoon Worcestershire sauce
1/2 teaspoon pepper

In a skillet, cook sausage over medium heat until no longer pink; drain. Place bread cubes in a greased 13-in. x 9-in. x 2-in. baking dish. Sprinkle with the sausage, mushrooms and cheeses. In a bowl, combine the remaining ingredients; pour over the top. Cover and refrigerate overnight.

Remove from the refrigerator 30 minutes before baking. Bake, uncovered, at 350° for 35-45 minutes or until a knife inserted near the center comes out clean. **Yield:** 8-10 servings.

Fruit Medley

Whenever I take this eye-catching fruit salad to a party or gathering, people ask for the recipe. I like to use dark sweet cherries and blueberries to give this blend its distinctive flavor.

    1 can (20 ounces) pineapple chunks, undrained
    1 can (11 ounces) mandarin oranges, drained *or* 2 medium navel oranges, peeled and chopped
    1 large red apple, cubed
    1 cup sliced fresh strawberries
    1 cup halved seedless red grapes
    3 kiwifruit, peeled and sliced
    1 cup fresh *or* frozen blueberries
    1 cup fresh *or* canned pitted dark sweet cherries
    2 medium firm bananas, sliced

In a large bowl, combine the first six ingredients; cover and refrigerate overnight. Just before serving, fold in the blueberries, cherries and bananas; gently toss. **Yield:** 10 servings.

Warm Christmas Punch

Red-hot candies add rich color and spiciness to this festive punch, and the cranberry juice gives it a little tang. Our children always request it for our December 25th brunch.

    1 bottle (32 ounces) cranberry juice
    1 can (32 ounces) pineapple juice
1/3 cup red-hot candies
    1 cinnamon stick (3-1/2 inches)
Additional cinnamon sticks, optional

In a slow cooker, combine cranberry and pineapple juices, red-hots and cinnamon stick. Cook on low for 2-5 hours. Remove cinnamon stick before serving. Use additional cinnamon sticks as stirrers if desired. **Yield:** 2 quarts.

Cinnamon Rolls

I serve these yummy frosted rolls warm from the oven as a Christmas morning treat at our house. Even if you are not accustomed to working with yeast dough, you'll find this dough is easy to handle.

> **5 to 6 cups** all-purpose flour
> **1 package** (18-1/4 ounces) yellow cake mix
> **2 packages** (1/4 ounce *each*) quick-rise yeast
> **2-1/2 cups** warm water (120° to 130°)
> **1/4 cup** butter *or* margarine, melted
> **1/2 cup** sugar
> **1 teaspoon** ground cinnamon
> **FROSTING:**
> **6 tablespoons** butter *or* margarine, softened
> **3 cups** confectioners' sugar
> **1-1/2 teaspoons** vanilla extract
> **2 to 3 tablespoons** milk

In a mixing bowl, combine 4 cups flour, dry cake mix, yeast and warm water until smooth. Add enough remaining flour to form a soft dough. Turn onto a lightly floured surface; knead until smooth and elastic, about 5 minutes. Place in a greased bowl, turning once to grease top. Cover and let rise until doubled, about 45 minutes.

Punch dough down. Turn onto a lightly floured surface; divide in half. Roll each portion into a 14-in. x 10-in. rectangle. Brush with butter; sprinkle with sugar and cinnamon. Roll up jelly-roll style, starting with a long side. Cut each roll into 12 slices; place cut side down in two greased 13-in. x 9-in. x 2-in. baking pans. Cover and let rise until almost doubled, about 20 minutes.

Bake at 400° for 10-15 minutes or until golden brown. Cool for 20 minutes. For frosting, in a mixing bowl, cream butter, confectioners' sugar and vanilla. Add enough milk to achieve desired consistency. Frost warm rolls. **Yield:** 2 dozen.

Kneading Dough

To knead dough, turn it out onto a floured surface and shape into a ball. Fold the top of the dough toward you. With palms, push with a rolling motion. Turn dough a quarter turn; repeat motion until dough is smooth and elastic. Add flour to surface only as needed.

If you're kneading the dough on a pastry board, place a damp dishcloth underneath the board to prevent it from sliding.

Crowd-Pleasing Cuisine

Her homey menu is well-seasoned with tasty dishes and a generous helping of good fellowship.

By Erlene Cornelius, Spring City, Tennessee

I TRULY BELIEVE that good food and good fellowship hold family and friends together. During our almost 50 years of marriage, my husband, Loyal, and I have enjoyed entertaining both large and small groups of relatives and friends.

A delicious menu that always pleases those around our table includes Beef Brisket with Gravy, green salad with Blue Cheese Vinaigrette, Golden Carrot Coins, Pillow-Soft Rolls and Lemon Tart. Since most of the recipes can be made ahead, you can be at ease as you serve the meal and enjoy spending time with your friends and family.

The Beef Brisket becomes very tender as it bakes. It's my family's most-requested main dish.

Many years ago, our Sunday school class sponsored a progressive dinner, and we were asked to prepare brisket for 50. It was so good that I downsized the recipe. I usually fix the brisket and gravy 1 or 2 days ahead of time and reheat it in the oven or microwave the day of the dinner.

Dressing Brightens Greens

A tried-and-true recipe, Blue Cheese Vinaigrette is very tasty and goes well with any type of greens. The recipe was shared by one of the "helping moms" at a co-operative preschool where I was a teacher and director.

Later, I worked as a home economics teacher. I still use many of the quick and easy recipes created especially for our 45-minute classes. Loyal was a teacher and administrator for 30 years. Upon retirement, we moved from Ohio to our current home in Tennessee on Watts Bar Lake.

Golden Carrot Coins are colorful and easy to prepare.

Our oldest daughter, Kathy, said, "Mom, you've got to try this recipe from our church cookbook." It's such a simple method, but the carrots taste wonderful! Often, I include this popular side dish in our everyday menus.

Our two daughters, one son and their spouses have given us 10 grandchildren. The families are scattered throughout the United States, but when we do get together—what fun!

Can't Eat Just One

Pillow-Soft Rolls are light, fluffy and tender. Without realizing it, you can easily devour several. After the rolls cool, they can be wrapped in foil and reheated in the oven.

My first recollection of large meal preparation was helping my mother, grandmother and aunts take hours to fix supper for 12 to 15 neighborhood farmers who had spent the day threshing wheat or oats.

We made all the bread and even churned butter from cream skimmed off the milk. The threshers made it all disappear in about 15 minutes.

Lemon Tart is a delicious ending to any meal. For a fun variation, you can divide the creamy filling into individual tart shells.

I can't count how many times I have made this dessert at our cottage in Ontario, Canada. We spend time there in summer, when we swim, water-ski and boat. Loyal cuts and splits wood for the cottage stoves. I wish you could taste the biscuits I bake in our wood-burning cookstove! In winter, we go back to cross-country ski and snowmobile.

No matter where we are, I'm often working on one of my many quilt projects. And now that we have retired, we have time to volunteer. My most time-consuming job is working at "Our Daily Bread", a thrift shop. With the proceeds, we purchase food and pass it on to those in need.

Also, Loyal and I are volunteer tour guides at a unique electric power generating facility at Raccoon Mountain near Chattanooga.

It's a privilege to be one of *Taste of Home's* 1,000 editors, and it's a thrill whenever a friend, former home economics student, acquaintance or even a stranger contacts me to say they saw one of my recipes in print.

I hope you'll enjoy our family's favorite meal…and that it becomes as popular at your house as it is at ours.

PICTURED AT LEFT: Beef Brisket with Gravy, Blue Cheese Vinaigrette, Golden Carrot Coins, Pillow-Soft Rolls and Lemon Tart (recipes are on the next page).

Beef Brisket with Gravy

This tender roast has remained our very favorite family main dish over many years. Often, I make it ahead and reheat the beef in the gravy. It's delicious served with hot cooked noodles or mashed potatoes.

    1 fresh beef brisket* (about 2 pounds)
    2 tablespoons vegetable oil
    1 cup hot water
    1 envelope beefy onion soup mix
    2 tablespoons cornstarch
  1/2 cup cold water

In a Dutch oven, brown brisket in oil on both sides over medium-high heat; drain. Combine hot water and soup mix; pour over brisket. Cover and bake at 325° for 2 to 2-1/2 hours or until meat is tender.

Remove brisket to a serving platter. Let stand for 10-15 minutes. Combine cornstarch and cold water until smooth; gradually stir into pan juices. Bring to a boil; cook and stir for 2 minutes or until thickened. Thinly slice meat across the grain; serve with the gravy. **Yield:** 6-8 servings.

*Editor's Note: This is a fresh beef brisket, not corned beef.

Blue Cheese Vinaigrette

Even people who aren't big blue cheese fans have told me how much they enjoy this tangy dressing. It's refreshing and the flavors blend well.

    1 cup cider vinegar
  1/4 to 1/2 cup sugar
  1/2 to 1 cup crumbled blue cheese, *divided*
    1 small onion, chopped

    1 tablespoon Dijon mustard
    2 garlic cloves, minced
  1/2 teaspoon salt
    1 cup vegetable oil
Torn salad greens and vegetables of your choice

In a blender or food processor, combine the vinegar, sugar, 1/2 cup blue cheese, onion, mustard, garlic and salt. Cover and process until smooth. While processing, gradually add oil in a steady stream until dressing is thickened. Stir in the remaining blue cheese if desired. Serve over salad. Cover and refrigerate leftover dressing. **Yield:** 2-1/2 cups.

Golden Carrot Coins

(Pictured on page 212)

Once you try this simple yet scrumptious side dish, you'll never serve plain carrots again!

  1/4 cup butter *or* margarine
  3/4 cup chicken broth
    2 teaspoons sugar
    2 teaspoons salt
  1/8 teaspoon pepper
   14 medium carrots, cut into 1/4-inch slices
    3 tablespoons minced fresh parsley
    2 teaspoons lemon juice

In a large saucepan, melt butter. Stir in the broth, sugar, salt and pepper; bring to a boil. Add carrots. Return to a boil. Reduce heat; cover and simmer for 8-10 minutes or until carrots are crisp-tender. Stir in parsley and lemon juice. Serve with a slotted spoon. **Yield:** 6-8 servings.

Pillow-Soft Rolls

These rolls are always a treat, my children and grand-children tell me. Sour cream adds richness to the dough.

3-3/4 to 4-1/2 cups all-purpose flour
  1/2 cup sugar
    2 packages (1/4 ounce *each*) active dry yeast
1-1/4 teaspoons salt
    1 cup (8 ounces) sour cream
  1/2 cup water
    2 eggs
    1 tablespoon butter *or* margarine, melted

In a large mixing bowl, combine 1-1/4 cups flour, sugar, yeast and salt. In a saucepan, heat the sour cream and water to 120°-130°. Add to dry ingredients; beat until blended. Beat in eggs until smooth. Stir in enough remaining flour to form a soft dough. Turn onto a lightly floured surface; knead until smooth and elastic, about 6-8 minutes. Place in a greased bowl, turning once to grease top. Cover and refrigerate overnight.

Punch dough down. Turn onto a lightly floured surface; roll out to 1/2-in. thickness. Cut with a floured 2-1/2-in. biscuit cutter. Using the dull edge of a table knife, make an off-center crease in each roll. Fold along crease so the small half is on the top; press along folded edge.

Place in a greased 15-in. x 10-in. x 1-in. baking pan, allowing edges to touch. Cover and let rise in a warm place until doubled, about 25 minutes. Brush tops with butter. Bake at 375° for 12-15 minutes or until golden brown. **Yield:** 2 dozen.

Lemon Tart

Here's a luscious way to end a meal! Smooth and creamy, with a refreshing lemon taste, this tart gets rave reviews. Every time I serve it to someone new, it results in a request for the recipe.

    1 cup sugar
  1/4 cup cornstarch
    1 cup milk
    3 egg yolks, beaten
  1/4 cup butter *or* margarine
    1 tablespoon grated lemon peel
  1/3 cup lemon juice
    1 cup (8 ounces) sour cream
    1 pastry shell (9 inches), baked
Whipped topping

In a saucepan, combine the sugar and cornstarch. Gradually add milk until smooth. Cook and stir over medium-high heat until thickened. Reduce heat; cook and stir 2 minutes longer. Remove from the heat. Stir a small amount of hot liquid into egg yolks; return all to the pan. Bring to a gentle boil, stirring constantly. Cook 2 minutes longer (mixture will be very thick).

Remove from the heat; stir in the butter and lemon peel. Gently stir in the lemon juice. Cover and cool completely. Fold in sour cream. Pour into pastry shell. Refrigerate for at least 2 hours before cutting. Garnish with whipped topping. Refrigerate leftovers. **Yield:** 6-8 servings.

Special Spring Dinner

This cook's delectable springtime dinner is a delightful meal to share with family and friends for Easter.

By Vikki Rebholz, West Chester, Ohio

I LOVE having people over for dinner and making sure they enjoy themselves and the food.

For Easter and other special occasions, I can't go wrong with Applesauce Pork Loin, Roasted Asparagus, Sweet-Sour Spinach Salad, Sour Cream 'n' Chive Potatoes and Easter Bunny Carrot Cake. My husband, Andy, daughter, Bridget, and son, Brian, tell me I can make this meal anytime!

Applesauce Pork Loin is a recipe from a commercial cooking course I took before I was married. The meat was so flavorful that later, cooking for our family, I scaled down the size of the recipe. It has remained one of my favorite ways to prepare a pork loin and is perfect for company.

Some people are skeptical when I tell them I put applesauce, honey, mustard and rosemary on the roast. But after a taste, they concur that it's a great combination. This roast has evolved into one of my best springtime entrees since it goes so well with the rest of the menu.

Savor Spring "Greens"

Come springtime, fresh asparagus and spinach are abundant in Ohio. My daughter's friend Maria came to dinner one day when I served Roasted Asparagus and claimed she didn't like the vegetable. Bridget talked her into trying "just one piece" and by the end of the meal, Maria was asking if she could have the last spear on the serving dish.

Sweet-Sour Spinach Salad has been a favorite of mine since childhood. My mom made it a lot.

By the time I was 12 or so, I'd often help Mom with the cooking for our family of six. One day I decided to make the whole meal myself.

Mom worked third shift as a nurse in a newborn nursery and would have the meat out that she wanted to fix that evening for dinner. I thought, *I can cook that*! And I'd watched her fix other things often enough that I was able to come up with a whole meal. It was very well received.

Out of Milk

The Sour Cream 'n' Chive Potatoes came about by accident. I had no milk in the fridge, so I used sour cream instead, along with butter, salt and pepper.

I didn't tell anyone that I had made the switch—and they all loved the potatoes! The next time I mashed potatoes, I added chives in with the sour cream, knowing how good they are together on baked potatoes. Sometimes I also add shredded cheddar cheese if I have it on hand.

I've received a few recipe chain letters over the years, and the carrot cake recipe was one of them. I believe it's from a friend of my sister-in-law's who lives in Texas. It's a delicious dessert.

At Easter, I used a bunny-shaped pan to make it. After all, a carrot cake in a bunny pan seems perfect! I think people enjoy having a piece of the not-too-sweet cake as an alternative to Easter chocolates and marshmallow Peeps.

Day to day, I keep busy maintaining the household. Andy works swing shifts, often without days off for long periods of time. The kids' music lessons and Scouts, Bridget's horseback riding lessons and Brian's roller hockey keep me hopping.

Due to his schedule, Andy is often home during the daytime. We take advantage of that time and go out on "dates". We hike and fish, look for treasures in antique and thrift stores and go out to lunch.

I often come home and try to duplicate the entrees we've had at a restaurant. I like to experiment in the kitchen, read cookbooks and dabble in cake decorating.

When Andy's on second shift, I get the kids off to school and then begin preparing dinner so he can take a decent meal with him to microwave later at work.

As crazy as our schedule can be, we still find time to enjoy family meals and to invite others to share a special spring dinner with us. Perhaps our well-loved menu will inspire you to do the same!

PICTURED AT LEFT: Applesauce Pork Loin, Roasted Asparagus, Sweet-Sour Spinach Salad, Sour Cream 'n' Chive Potatoes and Easter Bunny Carrot Cake (recipes are on the next page).

1/4 teaspoon pepper
1/4 cup sesame seeds, toasted

Arrange asparagus in a single layer in two foil-lined 15-in. x 10-in. x 1-in. baking pans. Drizzle with oil. Sprinkle with salt and pepper. Bake, uncovered, at 400° for 12-15 minutes or until crisp-tender, turning once. Sprinkle with sesame seeds. **Yield:** 10-12 servings.

Sweet-Sour Spinach Salad

A tangy warm dressing pulls together all of the delicious elements in this great-tasting spring salad.

    1 cup sugar
    1 tablespoon all-purpose flour
  1/4 teaspoon ground mustard
Dash salt
  2/3 cup cold water
  1/3 cup white vinegar
    1 egg, lightly beaten
  18 cups fresh spinach, torn
    3 hard-cooked eggs, sliced
  1/2 pound sliced bacon, cooked and crumbled
    4 red onion slices, separated into rings

In a small saucepan, combine the sugar, flour, mustard and salt. Gradually stir in water and vinegar until smooth. Bring to a boil; cook and stir for 2 minutes or until thickened. Remove from the heat. Gradually stir a small amount of hot dressing into beaten egg; return all to the pan, stirring constantly. Bring to a gentle boil.

    Place spinach in a large salad bowl. Drizzle with warm dressing; toss to coat. Top with the hard-

Applesauce Pork Loin

I sampled this tasty pork roast in a commercial cooking course I took a number of years ago and saved the recipe. Later, I converted it to family-size and it's become a favorite.

    1 boneless pork loin roast (3 pounds)
  1/2 teaspoon salt
  1/4 teaspoon pepper
    2 tablespoons vegetable oil
    1 cup applesauce
    3 tablespoons Dijon mustard
    1 tablespoon honey
    3 fresh rosemary sprigs

Sprinkle roast with salt and pepper. In a large skillet, brown roast on all sides in oil. Place on a rack in a shallow roasting pan. Combine the applesauce, mustard and honey; spread over roast. Top with rosemary. Bake, uncovered, at 350° for 1-3/4 to 2-1/2 hours or until a meat thermometer reads 160°. Let stand for 10 minutes before slicing. **Yield:** 10-12 servings.

Roasted Asparagus

(Pictured on page 216)

Since asparagus is so abundant here come spring, I like to put it to great use with this recipe. We all look forward to this side dish each year.

    4 pounds fresh asparagus, trimmed
  1/4 cup olive *or* vegetable oil
  1/2 teaspoon salt

cooked eggs, bacon and onion. Serve immediately. **Yield:** 10-12 servings.

— 🎺 🎺 🎺 —

Sour Cream 'n' Chive Potatoes

These rich, creamy mashed potatoes are special enough for company, but my family won't wait for that. So I make them for everyday meals as well.

5-1/2 **pounds potatoes, peeled and cubed**
   3 **teaspoons salt,** *divided*
   1 **cup (8 ounces) sour cream**
1/2 **cup milk**
1/4 **cup butter** *or* **margarine, cubed**
1/4 **cup minced chives**
   1 **teaspoon pepper**

Place potatoes in a Dutch oven; cover with water. Add 1 teaspoon salt. Bring to a boil. Reduce heat; cover and cook for 20-25 minutes or until potatoes are very tender. Drain well. In a large mixing bowl, mash the potatoes, sour cream, milk and butter. Add the chives, pepper and remaining salt; mix well. **Yield:** 10-12 servings.

— 🎺 🎺 🎺 —

Easter Bunny Carrot Cake

At Easter, I hop to it and bake this delectable moist cake in a bunny-shaped pan.

   3 **eggs**
1-1/4 **cups sugar**
1/2 **cup vegetable oil**
1/3 **cup water**
   1 **teaspoon vanilla extract**
   2 **cups all-purpose flour**
   2 **teaspoons baking powder**

   1 **teaspoon ground cinnamon**
3/4 **teaspoon salt**
1/2 **teaspoon ground nutmeg**
1/4 **teaspoon ground cloves**
   2 **cups grated carrots**
   1 **can (16 ounces) cream cheese frosting**
Pink gel food coloring
Brown decorator icing
   1 **chocolate-covered peanut**
Red and green liquid food coloring
Flaked coconut

In a mixing bowl, combine the eggs, sugar, oil, water and vanilla; mix well. Combine the flour, baking powder, cinnamon, salt, nutmeg and cloves; beat into egg mixture. Stir in carrots. Pour into a greased and floured 2-qt. bunny-shaped pan. Bake at 350° for 25-30 minutes or until a toothpick comes out clean. Cool for 15 minutes before removing from pan to a wire rack.

Tint 1/3 cup frosting light pink and 1/3 cup frosting dark pink. Spread plain frosting over cake. With brown icing, outline bunny and form an ear, eyebrow, bow, nose, mouth and paws. Fill in ear and nose with light pink frosting and bow with dark pink. Add chocolate-covered peanut for the eye.

In a resealable plastic bag, combine 1/2 teaspoon water and a few drops of red food coloring; add 1/3 cup coconut. Seal bag and shake to coat. Sprinkle on tail. If desired, tint additional coconut green and sprinkle around bunny for grass. **Yield:** 10-12 servings.

Editor's Note: The Cottontail Bunny Pan can be ordered from Wilton Industries, Inc. Call 1-800/794-5866 or visit *www.wilton.com*. The carrot cake may also be baked in a greased 11-in. x 7-in. x 2-in. baking pan for 40-45 minutes.

Supper Says 'Summer'

Everyone loves eating their veggies when this cook dishes up her garden-fresh summertime meal!

By Catherine Dawe, Kent, Ohio

AS A NEW BRIDE living in Reno, Nevada 20-some years ago, I started collecting recipes for zucchini because our huge backyard vegetable garden produced giant zucchini every summer.

Zucchini Sausage Lasagna—the main course for my favorite meal—is handwritten in the little notebook I started back then. And we still enjoy it! I like to serve it with Dilly Romaine Salad, Cheddar Olive Loaf and Best-Ever Chocolate Cake.

Most people think that they won't like the taste of lasagna made with zucchini until they try it. These same people often ask for the recipe after they discover how good it is.

Our family eats a lot of salads, and I try to vary them so we don't get bored with the same old thing. My husband, Tom, and I have two sons and a daughter.

Dill Perks Up Dressing

I've found that homemade dressings, like the creamy dill blend for Dilly Romaine Salad, are really easy to concoct. Dill says summer to me. Often, I'll chop up dill pickles and add them to any salad for extra crunch and flavor.

Cheddar Olive Loaf adds a special touch to a meal. This delicious, moist bread smells wonderful while it's baking…and it's convenient, too, since you make it in a bread machine.

I love playing around with my bread machine. I've found that most of the time you can add extra ingredients to a basic bread recipe with good results. The most important thing to watch for is the dough consistency. It shouldn't be too stiff or too soft.

The recipe for old-fashioned, delectable Best-Ever Chocolate Cake was given to one of my friends by her grandmother. I was thrilled when she shared it with me.

The cake is rich and chocolaty without being too sweet. It's good all by itself, but I think the fluffy chocolate frosting (a family recipe from another friend) makes it even better. Like the cake, it's not overly sweet.

From-Scratch Background

Originally from Georgia, I've been cooking since I was a kid. My dad was a cotton farmer turned Merchant Marine, and he met my mom while on shore leave in Boston.

Dad taught me to bake. He baked a pie, or something else, almost every day. I could make a pie from scratch by the time I was 12.

Mom was a great cook but didn't use many recipes. Before she passed away a few years ago, I asked her to write down some of her recipes for me that were my favorites.

That notebook is one of my most cherished possessions, even though some of her measurements call for a "golf ball-size" amount of whatever ingredient. We never used prepackaged mixes.

Nowadays, I do use some convenience products and am the queen of speedy weeknight dinners. But I like to cook from scratch when I have the time, especially on the weekends.

I've been an in-home child-care provider for the past 23 years. I love working with babies and toddlers! I started watching children when my oldest son was a baby, thinking it would be a temporary thing. But I've pretty much made a career out of it.

My other son, who is a very good cook, often helps me out in the kitchen and occasionally makes a gourmet meal for the whole family. While in high school, he got a job as a dishwasher at a local country club and worked his way up to being a cook.

One of my community activities is the Kent Junior Mothers organization. We run a summer Safety School program for about 100 children who will be entering kindergarten…and sponsor a children's play area at Kent's Heritage Festival in July.

I love to entertain. In fact, I often serve the meal I shared with you here at small dinner parties. The menu is always a hit with our guests, as I'm sure it will be with you, too, if you decide to try my recipes.

PICTURED AT LEFT: Zucchini Sausage Lasagna, Dilly Romaine Salad, Cheddar Olive Loaf and Best-Ever Chocolate Cake (recipes are on the next page).

Zucchini Sausage Lasagna

This delicious zucchini and sausage casserole is a great way to sneak more vegetables into your family's diet. Even friends who didn't think they'd like lasagna made with zucchini have been won over by the taste!

- 1 pound bulk Italian sausage
- 1 large onion, chopped
- 2 garlic cloves, minced
- 2 cans (28 ounces *each*) crushed tomatoes
- 1 can (6 ounces) tomato paste
- 1/3 cup minced fresh parsley
- 2 teaspoons sugar
- 1 teaspoon dried basil
- 1 teaspoon dried oregano
- 1/4 teaspoon pepper
- 3 medium zucchini, sliced lengthwise
- 1 tablespoon butter *or* margarine
- 1 egg
- 15 ounces ricotta cheese
- 3/4 cup plus 2 tablespoons grated Parmesan cheese, *divided*
- 6 lasagna noodles, cooked and drained
- 3 cups (12 ounces) shredded mozzarella cheese, *divided*

In a large skillet, cook sausage, onion and garlic over medium heat until meat is no longer pink; drain. Add the tomatoes, tomato paste, parsley, sugar, basil, oregano and pepper. Cover and simmer for 30 minutes, stirring occasionally. In another large skillet, cook the zucchini in butter until tender. In a bowl, combine the egg, ricotta cheese and 3/4 cup Parmesan cheese; set aside.

Spread 1-1/2 cups meat sauce in an ungreased 13-in. x 9-in. x 2-in. baking dish. Layer with three noodles, half of the zucchini, half of the ricotta mixture, 2 cups of mozzarella cheese and 2 cups meat sauce. Layer with remaining noodles, zucchini and ricotta mixture. Top with 2 cups meat sauce.

Bake, uncovered, at 350° for 45-55 minutes or until bubbly. Sprinkle with remaining mozzarella and Parmesan. Bake 5 minutes longer or until cheese is melted. Let stand for 15 minutes before cutting. Serve with remaining meat sauce or save for another use. **Yield:** 12 servings.

Dilly Romaine Salad

I seldom use store-bought dressings anymore, now that I know how easy it is to mix up my own homemade versions.

- 8 cups torn romaine
- 1 medium cucumber, sliced
- 1 cup halved cherry tomatoes
- 1 small red onion, sliced and separated into rings

CREAMY DILL DRESSING:
- 1/2 cup evaporated milk
- 1/2 cup vegetable oil
- 3 tablespoons cider vinegar
- 2 teaspoons minced fresh dill
- 1/2 teaspoon onion salt
- 1/2 teaspoon dried minced onion
- 1/2 teaspoon salt
- 1/2 teaspoon ground mustard
- 1/8 teaspoon white pepper

In a large salad bowl, toss the romaine, cucumber, tomatoes and onion. In a jar with a tight-fitting lid, combine the dressing ingredients; cover and shake well. Serve with salad. Refrigerate any leftover dressing. **Yield:** 12 servings (1 cup salad dressing).

Cheddar Olive Loaf

Made in the bread machine, this moist loaf has nice texture and great flavor. The cheese also gives the bread an appealing light orange tint.

    1 cup water (70° to 80°)
  3/4 teaspoon salt
1-1/4 cups shredded sharp cheddar cheese
    3 cups bread flour
    4 teaspoons sugar
    2 teaspoons active dry yeast
  3/4 cup stuffed olives, well drained and sliced

In bread machine pan, place the first six ingredients in order suggested by manufacturer. Select basic bread setting. Choose crust, color and loaf size if available. Bake according to bread machine directions (check dough after 5 minutes of mixing; add 1 to 2 tablespoons of water or flour if needed).

Just before the final kneading (your machine may audibly signal this), add the olives. **Yield:** 1 loaf (1-1/2 pounds).

Editor's Note: If your bread machine has a time-delay feature, we recommend you do not use it for this recipe.

Best-Ever Chocolate Cake

You can't miss with this delightful old-fashioned dessert. The cake is moist and chocolaty, and its light, fluffy frosting stirs up in a jiffy. Use vanilla pudding instead of chocolate in the frosting if you wish.

  3 cups all-purpose flour
  2 cups sugar
  6 tablespoons baking cocoa
  2 teaspoons baking soda
  1 teaspoon salt
  2 cups water
2/3 cup vegetable oil
  2 teaspoons white vinegar
  2 teaspoons vanilla extract
FLUFFY CHOCOLATE FROSTING:
  1 cup cold milk
  1 package (3.9 ounces) instant chocolate pudding mix
  1 carton (8 ounces) frozen whipped topping, thawed

In a mixing bowl, combine the first five ingredients. Add the water, oil, vinegar and vanilla. Beat on low speed for 1 minute. Beat on medium for 1 minute. Pour into a greased 13-in. x 9-in. x 2-in. baking pan. Bake at 350° for 40-45 minutes or until a toothpick inserted near the center comes out clean. Cool on a wire rack.

For frosting, in a mixing bowl, beat the milk and pudding mix for 2 minutes. Beat in whipped topping. Spread over cake. Refrigerate leftovers. **Yield:** 12-15 servings.

Editor's Note: This cake does not contain eggs.

Sizzling Warm-Weather Fare

Come summer, this cook looks to her backyard grill to keep the kitchen cool. She fires up this savory chicken meal often.

By Jill Evely, Wilmore, Kentucky

ALTHOUGH I love to cook, I really don't like to be in the kitchen for very long in the summer. We use our gas grill a lot, with husband Bob usually flipping the burgers or sausage, and me getting the other things going for the meal.

The exception is Kentucky Grilled Chicken. Since this is one of my favorite foods, I often "man" the grill when it is on the menu. With it, I like to serve Picnic Bean Casserole, Deli-Style Pasta Salad and Blueberry Snack Cake.

A friend gave me the recipe for Kentucky Grilled Chicken several years ago, and it has been a standard at our house ever since. Crispy on the outside and tender on the inside, it is flavored with a tangy marinade and basting sauce that makes many folks declare it is the best chicken they have ever eaten.

We are Michigan natives and moved to this small town in Kentucky's Bluegrass region in 1992, after living in Florida for 8 years. Bob and I have been married 28 years and have five children.

Our two oldest sons were both married 2 years ago (I made the wedding cakes) and live nearby. A third son attends the University of Kentucky, while living in an apartment behind our house.

I home-school our daughter, a high school senior this fall, and our youngest son, who will begin his freshman year.

Tried-and-True Foods

Picnic Bean Casserole and Deli-Style Pasta Salad are two of my "staple" side dishes. The bean casserole has a great flavor and can be baked or cooked in a bean pot.

I usually put it in an electric bean pot because it looks so old-fashioned. And that way, I don't have to heat up my oven on a hot day. My mother gave me

this hearty recipe a number of years ago.

When I was growing up, Mom's rule was, "Do whatever you want in the kitchen, just be sure to clean up when you are done." My older sister, Gail, and I loved to bake and cook—from brownies and breads to shish kabobs.

I also helped my dad make beef jerky, stringing it and suspending it along the laundry room ceiling to dry. Our sons still use his jerky recipe, but they dry theirs in an electric smoker.

My sister went on to be a commercial foods teacher, while I had five children and put my culinary skills to good use at home.

Popular Dish to Pass

The Deli-Style Pasta Salad is a combination of two recipes that I tried and liked. Besides being attractive, it's easy to make and is a favorite at "pitch-in" dinners.

My Aunt Lalah, an excellent cook, gave me the recipe for Blueberry Snack Cake, which I've made literally hundreds of times since I was a newlywed.

The crisp sugar topping is inviting, and the delicious cake keeps people coming back for "just another sliver".

When I was a child, we picked blueberries every summer and froze nearly 100 pounds annually.

I do a bit of canning, and last year my daughters-in-law and I canned applesauce together. It was the first time they had ever canned, and they learned how wonderful it is when you hear those lids "pop" when the jars seal.

My first job as a teen was working as a kitchen girl in a German restaurant. There, I learned how to make many foods from scratch and in large quantities. I used to tell people I cooked in "vats".

That early training came in handy when my three oldest boys were all teenagers. Actually, I still cook large amounts, freezing or giving away the extras.

With the children and my in-laws living nearby, we often get together for family meals. We keep the extra table leaves close by, pull up stools and folding chairs and have a rather loud, fun time filled with laughter, stories and good-natured teasing. Good food is the foundation of those memorable gatherings.

As I plan meals and cook for family and friends, I am thankful for my childhood lessons in the kitchen, especially knowing that I can try anything—as long as I clean up!

PICTURED AT LEFT: Kentucky Grilled Chicken, Picnic Bean Casserole, Deli-Style Pasta Salad and Blueberry Snack Cake (recipes are on the next page).

Kentucky Grilled Chicken

This chicken is perfect for an outdoor summer meal, and my family thinks it's fantastic. It takes about an hour on the grill but is worth the wait. I use a new paintbrush to "mop" on the basting sauce.

✓ Uses less fat, sugar or salt. Includes Nutritional Analysis and Diabetic Exchanges.

   1 cup cider vinegar
1/2 cup vegetable *or* canola oil
   5 teaspoons Worcestershire sauce
   4 teaspoons hot pepper sauce
   2 teaspoons salt
 10 bone-in chicken breast halves (10 ounces *each*)

In a bowl, combine the first five ingredients; mix well. Pour 1 cup marinade into a large resealable plastic bag; add the chicken. Seal bag and turn to coat; refrigerate for at least 4 hours. Cover and refrigerate the remaining marinade for basting.

Coat grill rack with nonstick cooking spray before starting the grill. Drain and discard marinade from chicken. Grill bone side down, covered, over indirect medium heat for 20 minutes. Turn; grill 20-30 minutes longer or until juices run clear, basting occasionally with reserved marinade. **Yield:** 10 servings.

Nutritional Analysis: One serving (1 chicken breast half with skin removed) equals 252 calories, 8 g fat (1 g saturated fat), 105 mg cholesterol, 391 mg sodium, 1 g carbohydrate, trace fiber, 42 g protein. **Diabetic Exchanges:** 5 very lean meat, 1-1/2 fat.

Picnic Bean Casserole

Smoked bacon adds zest to this bean bake, a recipe I got from my mother. I must confess that lima beans have never been among my favorite foods. But I actually like them in this casserole, and their color brightens up the mixture.

   2 cans (15 ounces *each*) pork and beans
   1 can (16 ounces) kidney beans, rinsed and drained
   1 can (15 ounces) lima *or* butter beans, rinsed and drained
   1 medium onion, chopped
1/2 cup packed brown sugar
1/2 cup ketchup
   4 bacon strips, cooked and crumbled

In a large bowl, combine the beans, onion, brown sugar and ketchup. Transfer to a greased 2-1/2-qt. baking dish. Sprinkle with bacon. Cover and bake at 350° for 1 hour. Uncover; bake 30 minutes longer. **Yield:** 10 servings.

Deli-Style Pasta Salad

When I'm having weekend guests, I make this salad the day before they arrive. The flavors blend wonderfully when it is chilled overnight, and it keeps well for several days. It's also a great dish to take along to a picnic.

   1 package (16 ounces) tricolor spiral pasta
   2 medium plum tomatoes, seeded and julienned

1 teaspoon baking powder
1 cup milk
2 eggs, *separated*
2 cups fresh *or* frozen blueberries*

In a mixing bowl, combine flour and sugar. Cut in butter until crumbly. Set aside 3/4 cup for topping. Add the baking powder, milk and egg yolks to remaining mixture; mix well. Beat egg whites until soft peaks form; fold into batter.

Pour into a greased 13-in. x 9-in. x 2-in. baking dish. Sprinkle with blueberries and reserved crumb mixture. Bake at 350° for 30-35 minutes or until golden brown and a toothpick inserted near the center comes out clean. **Yield:** 15-18 servings.

*Editor's Note: If using frozen blueberries, do not thaw before adding to the batter.

Blueberries in Brief

Always choose blueberries that are plump, firm, uniform in size and a silver-frosted indigo blue color.

Refrigerate blueberries, tightly covered, for up to 10 days. Before using, discard shriveled or moldy berries and remove any stems.

Fresh blueberries won't bleed out their juice unless the skins are broken.

8 ounces sliced salami, julienned
8 ounces provolone cheese, julienned
1 small red onion, thinly sliced and separated into rings
1 jar (5-3/4 ounces) stuffed olives, drained and sliced
1 can (2-1/4 ounces) sliced ripe olives, drained
1/4 cup grated Parmesan cheese
1 bottle (8 ounces) Italian salad dressing

Cook pasta according to package directions; drain and rinse in cold water. In a large bowl, combine the pasta, tomatoes, salami, cheese, onion, olives and Parmesan cheese. Add dressing and toss to coat. Cover and refrigerate for several hours or overnight. **Yield:** 12 servings.

Blueberry Snack Cake

I love blueberries and have many recipes calling for them. One of my favorites is this quick dessert. I always freeze blueberries when they are in season so we can enjoy the summery flavor of this moist, tender cake all through the year.

2 cups all-purpose flour
1-1/2 cups sugar
1/2 cup cold butter *or* margarine

Family-Favorite Foods

When company's coming for Sunday dinner, this Pennsylvania Dutch cook relies on tried-and-true recipes from her past.

By Melody Mellinger, Myerstown, Pennsylvania

I ALWAYS ENJOY hosting guests for Sunday dinner...and the menu is sure to include some of the tasty Pennsylvania Dutch dishes I was raised on.

One of my favorite meals includes Sweet 'n' Sour Meatballs, Sunday Dinner Mashed Potatoes, Cheddar Broccoli Salad and Cherry Cream Cheese Dessert.

With two small children to care for, Brent and Lynette, it's a challenge to prepare a meal that is both delicious and attractive. So I use recipes that can be made ahead.

While this meal is special enough to serve Sunday dinner guests, it's also easy enough for a weeknight supper. All of the dishes seem to appeal to families.

Sweet 'n' Sour Meatballs were a family favorite when I was growing up, and they are now my husband John's favorite as well.

Gingersnap cookies are the "secret ingredient" in the tangy sauce for the meatballs. There's also plenty of it to pass around as gravy for the Sunday Dinner Mashed Potatoes.

I particularly like to serve these rich, creamy potatoes when I'm entertaining because they can be made the day before. Just store the dish in the refrigerator until you are ready to bake it.

To come up with my version of Cheddar Broccoli Salad, I combined several different recipes. Since chilling enhances the flavor, it is best made a day in advance. Guests often ask for a second helping...and John is always pleased to see it on the table. He never liked broccoli in salad until I came up with this recipe.

Herbs at Hand

We grow many of our own vegetables in a large garden, and I do a lot of canning and freezing. We've also

planted an herb garden. This 20- x 30-foot plot has lots of room for a variety of herbs. I'm really enjoying experimenting with them in my cooking.

Each summer when the area's Montmorency cherries are ripe, we go to the local orchard and pick them for my homemade pie filling.

Those cherries top my Cherry Cream Cheese Dessert, too. I carefully pit each one by hand, using a hairpin to lift out the stone. With this old-fashioned method, the cherries stay nice and round and look lovely.

This layered treat is quick and easy to prepare, and it looks delightful served in a glass dish. The tart cherries complement the sweet, creamy pudding and graham cracker base. My mom remembers making this pretty dessert when she was a young girl, and it still is popular with young and old alike.

Kids in the Kitchen

I started cooking at a young age, too. As soon as I could push a chair to the kitchen counter, I began helping Mom in the kitchen.

Over the years, I learned to make many of her specialties the same way she and Grandma have always made them, putting in a little of this and a little of that until it tastes just right.

Now Brent stands beside me, dumping premeasured ingredients into my mixing bowl. Helping Mommy cook is the highlight of his day!

As I mentioned earlier, growing up here in rural Pennsylvania has had a strong influence on my cooking. Pennsylvania Dutch food is basic, but so delicious. Although the recipes are simple and straightforward, the results are Mmmm...good!

I have quite a collection of recipes, including some from my former students. I taught at a local Amish and Mennonite school for several years. When I got married, my students made a cookbook for me with their favorite recipes. It is a special treasure, with each recipe handwritten by the student who shared it.

Besides cooking and baking, I enjoy gardening, sewing and doing counted cross-stitch. Music is another hobby. I play the piano, accordion and violin.

Being a *Taste of Home* field editor is an exciting part of my life. I consider it a privilege to share my best recipes with you and hope you like my Sunday dinner as much as we do. Enjoy!

PICTURED AT LEFT: Sweet 'n' Sour Meatballs, Sunday Dinner Mashed Potatoes, Cheddar Broccoli Salad and Cherry Cream Cheese Dessert (recipes are on the next page).

Wal-Mart Portrait Studio

Sweet 'n' Sour Meatballs

When we entertain friends for Sunday dinner, I frequently serve these tangy meatballs. Everyone loves the distinctive sauce, but they're often surprised to learn it is made with gingersnaps.

  3 eggs
  1 medium onion, chopped
1-1/2 cups dry bread crumbs
  1 teaspoon salt
  2 pounds ground beef
  2 tablespoons vegetable oil
SAUCE:
3-1/2 cups tomato juice
  1 cup packed brown sugar
 10 gingersnaps, finely crushed
1/4 cup white vinegar
  1 teaspoon onion salt

In a bowl, combine the eggs, onion, bread crumbs and salt. Crumble beef over mixture and mix well. Shape into 1-1/2-in. balls. In a large skillet, brown meatballs in batches in oil. Transfer to a greased 13-in. x 9-in. x 2-in. baking dish.

In a saucepan, combine the sauce ingredients. Bring to a boil over medium heat, stirring until cookie crumbs are dissolved. Pour over meatballs. Bake, uncovered, at 350° for 40-45 minutes or until meat is no longer pink. **Yield:** 8 servings.

Sunday Dinner Mashed Potatoes

Sour cream and cream cheese add delicious dairy flavors to these wonderful potatoes. They're special enough to serve guests and can be prepared in advance. Since I'm a busy mother of two young children, that's a convenience I appreciate.

  5 pounds potatoes, peeled and cubed
  1 cup (8 ounces) sour cream
  2 packages (3 ounces *each*) cream cheese, softened
  3 tablespoons butter *or* margarine, divided
  1 teaspoon salt
  1 teaspoon onion salt
1/4 teaspoon pepper

Place potatoes in a Dutch oven; cover with water. Cover and bring to a boil. Cook for 20-25 minutes or until very tender; drain well.

In a large mixing bowl, mash potatoes. Add sour cream, cream cheese, 2 tablespoons butter, salt, onion salt and pepper; beat until fluffy. Transfer to a greased 2-qt. baking dish. Dot with remaining butter. Bake, uncovered, at 350° for 20-25 minutes or until heated through. **Yield:** 8 servings.

Cheddar Broccoli Salad

I've received loads of compliments on this crunchy salad that is often on our Sunday dinner menu. It's also a great salad to take to a family picnic or a potluck. The flavors blend so nicely that we never tire of this good old standby recipe.

6 cups fresh broccoli florets
1-1/2 cups (6 ounces) shredded cheddar cheese
1/3 cup chopped onion
1-1/2 cups mayonnaise
3/4 cup sugar
3 tablespoons red wine vinegar *or* cider vinegar
12 bacon strips, cooked and crumbled

In a large bowl, combine the broccoli, cheese and onion. Combine the mayonnaise, sugar and vinegar; pour over broccoli mixture and toss to coat. Refrigerate for at least 4 hours. Just before serving, stir in bacon. **Yield:** 8 servings

———— 🍴 🍴 🍴 ————

Cherry Cream Cheese Dessert

Pretty layers of graham cracker crumbs, pudding and fruit topping make this dessert a standout! For a nice change, you can substitute blueberry pie filling or another fruit flavor for the cherry filling.

3/4 cup graham cracker crumbs (about 12 squares)
2 tablespoons sugar
2 tablespoons butter *or* margarine, melted
FILLING:
1 package (8 ounces) cream cheese, softened

1 can (14 ounces) sweetened condensed milk
1/3 cup lemon juice
1 teaspoon vanilla extract
1 can (21 ounces) cherry pie filling

In a bowl, combine cracker crumbs, sugar and butter. Divide among eight dessert dishes, about 4 rounded teaspoonfuls in each. In a small mixing bowl, beat cream cheese until smooth. Gradually add milk until blended. Beat in lemon juice and vanilla. Spoon 1/4 cup into each dish. Top with pie filling, about 1/4 cup in each. **Yield:** 8 servings.

Cheery Cherries

Canned pie cherries are usually not as red as nature intended due to their processing. Add a drop or two of red food coloring to a cherry pie or cobbler mixture to help bring back nature's blush.

There are two main groups of cherries—sweet and tart. The larger of the two are the firm, heart-shaped sweet cherries.

Meals in Minutes

Time is on your side with these speedy dinner solutions that can be on the table in 30 minutes or less.

——— 🍴 🍴 🍴 ———

FAST TO FIX. Clockwise from upper left: Yuletide Trimmings (p. 256), Soup's On...in Minutes! (p. 254), Speedy Summertime Fare Is Full of Sizzle (p. 242) and Homemade Meal for the Holidays Is Made in Minutes (p. 234).

Homemade Meal for the Holidays Is Made in Minutes

THE HOLIDAYS can be a hectic time, but putting a hot, homemade meal in front of your hungry family doesn't have to be.

The timely menu featured here is made up of favorite recipes from three cooks and combined by our Test Kitchen. You can have this festive dinner ready to serve in only 30 minutes!

Texas Lemon Shrimp, from Amy Parsons of League City, Texas, adds spice to any meal. "My family loves this simple yet elegant main dish," notes Amy.

Hot Spinach Apple Salad is just lightly coated in a sweet-tangy dressing so the spinach doesn't wilt and the apples retain their crunch. "We like this salad served with homemade bread," states Denise Albers from her home in Freeburg, Illinois.

"If you love chocolate, you'll find Chocolate Almond Tarts irresistible," assures Susan Martin of Chino Hills, California. "The rich filling blends chocolate, marshmallows and whipping cream for a treat that's hard to beat."

— 🥄 🥄 🥄 —

Texas Lemon Shrimp

✓ Uses less fat, sugar or salt. Includes Nutritional Analysis and Diabetic Exchanges.

    1 small onion, thinly sliced and separated
       into rings
1/2 cup chopped sweet red pepper
    2 tablespoons olive _or_ canola oil
1/3 cup water
    2 tablespoons lemon juice
    4 garlic cloves, minced
    1 to 3 teaspoons Cajun seasoning
    1 teaspoon grated lemon peel
1/4 teaspoon salt
    2 pounds uncooked medium shrimp, peeled
       and deveined
    1 tablespoon cornstarch
    2 tablespoons cold water
Hot cooked rice, optional

In a large skillet, saute onion and red pepper in oil until tender. Stir in the water, lemon juice, garlic, Cajun seasoning, lemon peel and salt. Add shrimp; cook and stir until shrimp turn pink.

Combine cornstarch and cold water until smooth; stir into shrimp mixture. Bring to a boil; cook and stir for 1 minute or until thickened. Serve over rice if desired. **Yield:** 8-10 servings.

Nutritional Analysis: One serving (1/2 cup shrimp mixture, calculated without rice) equals 164 calories, 5 g fat (1 g saturated fat), 172 mg cholesterol, 301 mg sodium, 4 g carbohydrate, trace fiber, 23 g protein. **Diabetic Exchanges:** 3 lean meat, 1/2 fat.

— 🥄 🥄 🥄 —

Hot Spinach Apple Salad

    6 bacon strips, diced
1/4 cup cider vinegar
    3 tablespoons brown sugar
    9 cups fresh baby spinach
    2 large red apples, thinly sliced
3/4 cup chopped red onion

In a skillet, cook bacon until crisp. Remove to paper towels. Drain, reserving 2 tablespoons drippings; add vinegar and brown sugar. Bring to a boil; cook and stir until sugar is dissolved. Cool slightly.

In a large salad bowl, combine spinach, apples, onion and bacon. Drizzle with warm dressing; toss to coat. Serve immediately. **Yield:** 8-10 servings.

— 🥄 🥄 🥄 —

Chocolate Almond Tarts

    2 milk chocolate candy bars with almonds
       (7 ounces _each_), chopped
    8 large marshmallows
1/4 cup milk
    1 cup heavy whipping cream, whipped
    8 individual graham cracker tart shells
Chocolate sprinkles, optional

In a microwave-safe bowl, combine the candy bars, marshmallows and milk. Microwave, uncovered, on high for 1 minute; stir. Heat 20-30 seconds longer or until the marshmallows are melted; stir until blended. Cover and chill for 7 minutes.

Fold in half of the whipping cream. Spoon into tart shells; top with the remaining whipped cream. Garnish with chocolate sprinkles if desired. Refrigerate until serving. **Yield:** 8 servings.

Editor's Note: This recipe was tested in an 850-watt microwave.

Speedy Supper Is Especially 'Souper' for Busy Days

AFTER A BUSY DAY at work, school or play, nothing will warm your family's spirit like this hot and hearty meal that can be put together in a hurry.

The complete-meal menu here is comprised of family favorites from three super cooks. It can go from start to "soup's on" in just 30 minutes!

"Vegetable Bean Soup is one of my favorite fast dishes on a cold winter day," shares Mary Ann Morgan from Cedartown, Georgia. "My husband and I like to eat this soup out of mugs in front of the fireplace."

Kids, in particular, will go for golden-brown Potato Chip Breadsticks with their crunchy coating. "I like to stand them up in a jar or stack them in a bread basket…either way, they don't last long," says Aneta Kish of LaCrosse, Wisconsin.

Instead of chips, brush the twists with olive oil and sprinkle with grated Parmesan cheese or your favorite herbs before baking.

Broiled Bananas a la Mode, from Charles Williams of Cincinnati, Ohio, can't be beat when you crave a delectable dessert. Dressed in a sweet apricot sauce with a sprinkling of toasted coconut, the warm bananas are extra yummy when you serve them with a scoop of ice cream on the side.

— 🍴 🍴 🍴 —

Vegetable Bean Soup

☑ Uses less fat, sugar or salt. Includes Nutritional Analysis and Diabetic Exchanges.

  3 cans (15-1/2 ounces *each*) great northern beans, rinsed and drained
  4 cups water
  2 cans (15-1/2 ounces *each*) hominy *or* 2 cans (15 ounces *each*) garbanzo beans, rinsed and drained
  1 package (16 ounces) frozen shoepeg corn
  1 can (15 ounces) crushed *or* diced tomatoes, undrained
  1 can (11-1/2 ounces) condensed bean and bacon soup, undiluted
  1 can (10 ounces) diced tomatoes and green chilies, undrained
  1 medium onion, chopped
  1 medium green pepper, chopped
  1 tablespoon dried cilantro flakes
  1 tablespoon dried parsley flakes
  1 teaspoon ground cumin
  2 bay leaves
  1 cup (4 ounces) shredded cheddar cheese

In a Dutch oven, combine the first 13 ingredients. Bring to a boil. Reduce heat; cover and simmer for 15 minutes. Discard bay leaves. Sprinkle with cheese. **Yield:** 12 servings (4 quarts).

Nutritional Analysis: One 1-1/3-cup serving (prepared with reduced-fat cheese) equals 328 calories, 4 g fat (2 g saturated fat), 8 mg cholesterol, 614 mg sodium, 56 g carbohydrate, 12 g fiber, 18 g protein.

— 🍴 🍴 🍴 —

Potato Chip Breadsticks

  1 tube (11 ounces) refrigerated breadsticks
  1 egg, lightly beaten
1/4 cup crushed sour cream and onion potato chips

Unroll dough; separate into 12 breadsticks. Twist each breadstick three times and place 1 in. apart on ungreased baking sheets. Carefully brush with egg; sprinkle with potato chips. Bake at 350° for 16-18 minutes or until golden brown. Serve warm. **Yield:** 1 dozen.

— 🍴 🍴 🍴 —

Broiled Bananas a la Mode

  2 jars (12 ounces *each*) apricot preserves
  1 cup orange juice
1/2 teaspoon rum extract *or* vanilla extract
 12 medium firm bananas, peeled
  1 cup flaked coconut
  1 quart peach, vanilla *or* strawberry ice cream

In a small saucepan, heat preserves over medium heat until warmed. Remove from the heat; stir in orange juice and extract. Halve bananas lengthwise; cut widthwise into thirds. Arrange cut side down in an ungreased 15-in. x 10-in. x 1-in. baking pan. Drizzle with apricot sauce; sprinkle with coconut. Broil 4 in. from the heat for 4-6 minutes or until coconut is lightly toasted. Serve with ice cream. **Yield:** 12 servings.

Have a Well-Rounded Meal Ready in Half an Hour

THINK preparing a balanced meal for your family means spending all day in the kitchen? Think again!

This menu made up of favorites from _Taste of Home_ readers can be on the table in 30 minutes!

Dijon mustard and grape juice combine in a flavorful sauce in this recipe for Cube Steak Diane, shared by Lauren Heyn of Oak Creek, Wisconsin.

Savory Rice Pilaf, from Grady Walker of Tulsa, Oklahoma, is a satisfying blend of flavors and textures, while Lena, Illinios cook Millie Vickery's Colorful Vegetable Medley brings together carrots, asparagus and water chestnuts.

Berries 'n' Cream Roll-Ups are easy to prepare and pretty, too, says Julianne Snell of Bellingham, Washington. "This recipe helped me win the top prize in a state cooking competition."

Cube Steak Diane

    4 beef cube steaks
1/4 cup butter _or_ margarine
1/2 cup white grape juice
    2 tablespoons Worcestershire sauce
    4 teaspoons Dijon mustard
Salt and pepper to taste

In a skillet, saute steaks in butter for 2 minutes on each side or until meat reaches desired doneness. Combine grape juice, Worcestershire and mustard; stir into cooking juices. Bring to a boil; cook for 1 minute. Remove steaks; keep warm. Cook sauce 1-2 minutes longer or until it reaches desired thickness. Season with salt and pepper. Serve over the cube steaks. **Yield:** 4 servings.

Savory Rice Pilaf

    2 cups uncooked instant rice
    2 celery ribs, chopped
    2 tablespoons butter _or_ margarine
1/4 cup chopped walnuts
    5 green onions, thinly sliced
    1 teaspoon salt
1/8 teaspoon _each_ pepper, curry powder and rubbed sage

Cook rice according to package directions. Meanwhile, in a skillet, saute celery in butter for 2 minutes.

Add walnuts, onions and seasonings; saute 2 minutes longer. Stir into rice. **Yield:** 4 servings.

Colorful Vegetable Medley

1/2 pound carrots, sliced
1/2 pound fresh asparagus, trimmed and cut into 1-inch pieces
    2 tablespoons butter _or_ margarine
    1 to 2 tablespoons cider vinegar
    1 to 2 tablespoons Worcestershire sauce
1/2 teaspoon dried thyme
1/2 teaspoon ground ginger
    1 can (8 ounces) sliced water chestnuts, drained
    1 tablespoon minced fresh parsley

Place 1 in. of water in a saucepan; add carrots. Bring to a boil. Reduce heat; cover and simmer for 4 minutes. Add asparagus; simmer 3-5 minutes longer or until vegetables are crisp-tender. Drain.

In a saucepan, melt butter over medium heat; stir in vinegar, Worcestershire, thyme and ginger. Add carrots, asparagus, water chestnuts and parsley. Cook and stir 1-2 minutes until heated. **Yield:** 4 servings.

Berries 'n' Cream Roll-Ups

    4 ounces cream cheese, softened
1/4 cup plus 6 tablespoons sugar, _divided_
    1 egg yolk
  10 slices firm white bread, crusts removed
1-1/2 teaspoons ground cinnamon
    3 tablespoons butter _or_ margarine, melted
1/2 cup sour cream
    1 cup sliced fresh strawberries

In a small mixing bowl, beat the cream cheese, 1/4 cup sugar and egg yolk until smooth. Spread 1 tablespoon over each slice of bread. Roll up jelly-roll style, starting with a long edge. In a shallow bowl, combine cinnamon and remaining sugar. Brush roll-ups with butter; coat with cinnamon-sugar.

Place seam side down in a greased 15-in. x 10-in. x 1-in. baking pan. Bake at 350° for 10-12 minutes or until lightly toasted. Serve with sour cream and strawberries. **Yield:** 10 servings.

Quick Cuisine Goes Well with Carefree Summer Days

FRESH AIR builds hearty appetites, so a filling and fast-to-fix meal is especially appropriate for the warm summer months.

The 30-minute menu here is made up of favorites from three great cooks and was combined by our Test Kitchen staff. It'll have you out of the kitchen and outdoors again in a flash.

Fresh mint and ground ginger flavor the fruity sauce served over Pear-Topped Ham Steak. "The sweetness of the pears contrasts nicely with the saltiness of the ham," notes Holly Ewan Nordheden of Champaign, Illinois.

"To streamline the quick recipe even more, I'll substitute a can of sliced pears with ginger flavoring and skip the ground ginger."

Lemon Mint Beans, from Dorothy Pritchett of Wills Point, Texas, taste so refreshing that they're a delightful addition to summer meals, but you'll want to enjoy them the rest of the year, too.

"If you need a no-fuss dessert that will please kids but is elegant enough for a grown-up gathering, try Banana Berry Tarts," suggests Barbara Nowakowski of North Tonawanda, New York. Marshmallows, banana and raspberries are stirred into the creamy treats for a fun dinner finale.

— ☕ ☕ ☕ —

Pear-Topped Ham Steak

1 can (15-1/4 ounces) sliced pears
1 fully cooked ham steak (about 1 pound and 1/2 inch thick)
1 tablespoon olive *or* vegetable oil
2 teaspoons cornstarch
1 teaspoon ground ginger
1 tablespoon cold water
1 to 3 teaspoons snipped fresh mint

Drain pears, reserving the juice; set the pears and juice aside. In a skillet, brown the ham steak on both sides in oil; remove and keep warm. Drain the skillet.

Combine cornstarch, ginger and water until smooth; stir in reserved pear juice. Add to the skillet. Bring to a boil. Reduce heat; simmer, uncovered, for 1-2 minutes or until thickened. Add ham and reserved pears; heat through. Sprinkle with mint. **Yield:** 4 servings.

Lemon Mint Beans

✓ Uses less fat, sugar or salt. Includes Nutritional Analysis and Diabetic Exchanges.

1 package (16 ounces) fresh *or* frozen cut green *or* wax beans
1 tablespoon lemon juice
1 tablespoon snipped fresh mint
1/4 teaspoon grated lemon peel
1/2 teaspoon salt

In a saucepan, cook beans in a small amount of water until tender; drain. Add remaining ingredients; toss to coat. **Yield:** 4 servings.

Nutritional Analysis: One serving (1 cup) equals 39 calories, trace fat (trace saturated fat), 0 cholesterol, 297 mg sodium, 9 g carbohydrate, 3 g fiber, 2 g protein. **Diabetic Exchange:** 2 vegetable.

— ☕ ☕ ☕ —

Banana Berry Tarts

4 ounces cream cheese, softened
2 tablespoons honey
1 package (10 ounces) frozen sweetened raspberries, thawed and undrained
1 cup miniature marshmallows
1 medium firm banana, chopped
1 cup whipped topping
1 package (6 count) individual graham cracker tart shells

In a small mixing bowl, beat the cream cheese and honey until smooth; whisk in raspberries until blended. Stir in marshmallows and banana. Fold in whipped topping. Spoon into tart shells. Refrigerate until serving. **Yield:** 6 servings.

🥄 Hamming It Up!

Ham steaks can be spruced up in no time. Rub both sides of a ham steak with a blend of 2 teaspoons Cajun seasoning and 1/2 teaspoon sugar. Fry or grill the steak until heated through.

Or cover a browned ham steak with thinly sliced apples, pour some maple syrup over the top and simmer until the fruit is cooked through.

Speedy Summertime Fare Is Full of Sizzle

IF YOU can't beat the summer heat…join it by whipping up this Mexican-style fare that is full of sizzling flavor.

The speedy supper is made up of tried-and-true recipes from three cooks that have been combined by our Test Kitchen home economists. You'll have this meal on the table in a mere 30 minutes, much to your family's delight.

Chicken Enchiladas put zip into this quick menu. The rolled tortillas are filled with a hearty mixture of Monterey Jack cheese, chicken and green chilies, then topped with a creamy sauce and shredded cheddar cheese.

"This dish is so easy to prepare," says Karen Bourne of Magrath, Alberta. "I sometimes substitute leftover turkey for the chicken."

"My colorful Guacamole Tossed Salad is a hit even with those who don't like avocados," says Lori Fischer of Chino Hills, California.

The fresh-tasting blend of avocados, tomatoes, red onion and greens gets added pizzazz from crumbled cooked bacon and a slightly spicy vinaigrette.

Peanut Butter Cashew Sundaes make a cool finale to any summer meal…and these tasty ice cream treats go together in a snap.

Betty Claycomb of Alverton, Pennsylvania simply mixes peanut butter and corn syrup, then drizzles the mixture over the ice cream and tops it all with crunchy cashews.

— 🍷 🍷 🍷 —

Chicken Enchiladas

2 tablespoons butter *or* margarine
1/4 cup all-purpose flour
2-1/2 cups chicken broth
1 teaspoon dried coriander
1 can (4 ounces) chopped green chilies, *divided*
2 cups cubed cooked chicken
1 cup (4 ounces) shredded Monterey Jack cheese
8 flour tortillas (7 to 8 inches)
1 cup (4 ounces) shredded cheddar cheese

For sauce, melt butter in a saucepan. Stir in flour until smooth. Gradually add broth. Bring to a boil; cook and stir for 2 minutes or until thickened.

Stir in coriander and half of the chilies. In a bowl, combine the chicken, Monterey Jack cheese and remaining chilies.

Spoon 1/3 cup chicken mixture onto each tortilla; roll up. Place seam side down in an ungreased 13-in. x 9-in. x 2-in. baking dish. Pour sauce over the enchiladas. Sprinkle with cheddar cheese. Bake, uncovered, at 375° for 15-18 minutes or until enchiladas are heated through and the cheese is melted. **Yield:** 4 servings.

— 🍷 🍷 🍷 —

Guacamole Tossed Salad

2 medium tomatoes, seeded and chopped
1/2 small red onion, sliced and separated into rings
6 bacon strips, cooked and crumbled
1/3 cup vegetable oil
2 tablespoons cider vinegar
1 teaspoon salt
1/4 teaspoon pepper
1/4 teaspoon hot pepper sauce
2 large ripe avocados, peeled and cubed
4 cups torn salad greens

In a bowl, combine the tomatoes, onion and bacon. In a small bowl, whisk the oil, vinegar, salt, pepper and hot pepper sauce. Pour over tomato mixture; toss gently. Add avocados. Place the greens in a large salad bowl; add avocado mixture and toss to coat. Serve immediately. **Yield:** 4 servings.

— 🍷 🍷 🍷 —

Peanut Butter Cashew Sundaes

1/3 cup light corn syrup
1/4 cup peanut butter
4 scoops vanilla ice cream
1/2 cup salted cashews

In a small bowl, combine the corn syrup and peanut butter until well blended. Serve sauce over ice cream; sprinkle with cashews. **Yield:** 4 servings.

Treat Your Family to a Fast Food Dinner Featuring Steak

DOES FALL find you on the go with kids' after-school activities and more? Well, drive by the drive-thru and head home to the kitchen instead.

Your family is sure to fall for the complete menu here that combines recipes from three super cooks …and it's ready to serve in just 30 minutes!

Mushroom Beef Tenderloin is quick to fix but seems special. A delightful mushroom sauce nicely complements the juicy beef. Blanche Stevens of Anderson, Indiana likes to serve it with toasted French bread.

"Lemony Brussels Sprouts is a fast and refreshing way to serve little cabbages," shares Joyce Guth of Mohnton, Pennsylvania. "The buttery lemon sauce really brings out the flavor of the sprouts. My youngest son loves them!"

"I always have the ingredients for Rapid Raspberry Torte on hand so I can make this dessert at a moment's notice," says Ruth Peterson of Jenison, Michigan. Whipped cream and lemon pudding are combined in the fluffy topping for this yummy pound cake that's layered with raspberry jam.

Mushroom Beef Tenderloin

- 3/4 pound fresh mushrooms, sliced
- 5 tablespoons butter *or* margarine, *divided*
- 2 teaspoons all-purpose flour
- 1 teaspoon salt
- 1/4 teaspoon pepper
- 1 cup heavy whipping cream
- 1 tablespoon minced fresh parsley
- 6 beef tenderloin steaks (1-1/2 inches thick)

In a large skillet, saute the mushrooms in 3 tablespoons butter for 6-8 minutes or until tender. Blend in the flour, salt and pepper. Gradually add the whipping cream. Bring to a gentle boil; cook and stir for 1-2 minutes or until thickened. Stir in parsley; keep warm.

In another large skillet, heat the remaining butter over medium-high heat. Cook steaks for 6-7 minutes on each side or until meat reaches desired doneness (for rare, a meat thermometer should read 140°; medium, 160°; well-done, 170°). Serve with the mushroom sauce. **Yield:** 6 servings.

Lemony Brussels Sprouts

- 1-1/2 pounds fresh brussels sprouts (about 2-1/2 cups), trimmed
- 1 teaspoon lemon juice
- 2 garlic cloves, minced
- 1/8 teaspoon salt
- 1/8 teaspoon pepper
- 1/3 cup butter *or* margarine

Cut an "X" in the core of each brussels sprout. Place in a saucepan; add 1 in. of water. Bring to a boil. Reduce heat; cover and simmer for 10-12 minutes or until crisp-tender. Drain. In a large skillet, saute the sprouts, lemon juice, garlic, salt and pepper in butter for 2-3 minutes or until flavors are blended. **Yield:** 6 servings.

Rapid Raspberry Torte

- 3/4 cup heavy whipping cream
- 1 tablespoon confectioners' sugar
- 2 cartons (3-1/2 ounces *each*) lemon pudding*
- 1 loaf (10-3/4 ounces) frozen pound cake, thawed
- 1/3 cup raspberry jam, divided

In a small mixing bowl, beat cream until soft peaks form. Add confectioners' sugar; beat until stiff peaks form. Place pudding in a bowl; fold in whipped cream.

Split cake into three horizontal layers. Spread half of the jam over the bottom layer; repeat layers. Top with third cake layer. Cut into slices; dollop with pudding mixture. **Yield:** 7-10 servings.

*Editor's Note: This recipe was tested with Hunt's Snack Pack lemon pudding.

Fast and Fruity Dessert

For an extra-easy dessert idea, puree 1-1/2 cups fresh fruit with 1 cup ricotta cheese. Cut a store-bought pound cake or sponge cake horizontally into three layers and spread the fruit mixture between the layers and on the top.

Fresh Catch Of The Day

LIKE MOST COOKS, you need food your family will fall for...hook, line and sinker! Our Test Kitchen staff had that in mind when they came up with this flavorful meal. With a creamy sauce and crunchy topping, Basil Walnut Fish Fillets will reel in rave reviews. While the fish bakes, simply toss together Carrot Saute and chill the Sunny Sherbet Cups.

☕ ☕ ☕

Basil Walnut Fish Fillets

Spreading fish fillets with a seasoned mayonnaise and sour cream mixture keeps the fish moist while baking. For the most flavor, use fresh basil.

1-1/2 **pounds fresh *or* frozen cod *or* haddock fillets**
3 **tablespoons mayonnaise**
2 **tablespoons sour cream**
2 **tablespoons grated Parmesan cheese**
1 **tablespoon minced fresh basil *or* 1 teaspoon dried basil**
1/4 **cup chopped walnuts**

Cut fish into serving-size pieces and place in a greased 13-in. x 9-in. x 2-in. baking dish. Combine the mayonnaise, sour cream, Parmesan cheese and basil; spread over fish. Sprinkle with walnuts. Bake, uncovered, at 425° for 10-15 minutes or until fish flakes easily with a fork. **Yield:** 4 servings.

☕ ☕ ☕

Carrot Saute

A simple side dish is all you need to accompany the fish. You can substitute zucchini or yellow squash for the carrots...just reduce the cooking time slightly.

3 **cups julienned carrots**
1 **tablespoon vegetable oil**
1/2 **cup sliced green onions**
1 **tablespoon lemon juice**
3/4 **teaspoon Italian seasoning**
1/2 **teaspoon garlic salt**
Dash pepper

In a skillet, saute carrots in oil for 3 minutes. Add onions; cook 4-5 minutes longer or until crisp-tender. Stir in lemon juice, Italian seasoning, garlic salt and pepper. **Yield:** 4 servings.

Sunny Sherbet Cups

The sky's the limit with this delicious dessert which is especially scrumptious in the warm summer months. Substitute raspberry, pineapple or orange sherbet for the lemon sherbet or replace the mandarin oranges with pineapple tidbits or fresh raspberries. Whipped cream and toasted nuts make tasty toppings.

1 **teaspoon cornstarch**
1/4 **cup orange *or* pineapple juice**
1/2 **teaspoon vanilla extract**

1 can (15 ounces) mandarin oranges, drained
3 to 4 cups lemon sherbet

In a small saucepan, combine the cornstarch and orange juice until smooth. Bring to a boil; cook and stir for 1-2 minutes or until thickened. Stir in the vanilla; cool for 5 minutes. Gently stir in the mandarin oranges. Scoop sherbet into individual dishes; top with the orange sauce. **Yield:** 4 servings.

Orange Tidbits

Did you know that all forms of orange juice—frozen concentrate, fresh squeezed or pasteurized—contain the same proportion of vitamin C? And orange juice retains up to 90% of its vitamin C for up to 1 week if stored in the refrigerator.

Mandarins are a relative to the orange. They peel more easily and have more pronounced sections.

Southwest Supper

YOUR FAMILY will run to the dinner table when this Mexican fare our Test Kitchen put together is on the menu. Chicken Tacos are a nice change of pace from the usual beef variety. A tasty tart dressing is the highlight of Tomato Avocado Salad. Keep the topping for Cinnamon Chocolate Sundaes on hand for anytime snacking.

Chicken Tacos

Even finicky eaters will love "Taco Night" because they can add toppings to suit their individual tastes. In this recipe, cubed chicken breasts are coated with taco seasoning and then stir-fried, so the zesty flavor really shines through.

> 1 envelope taco seasoning
> 1 pound boneless skinless chicken breasts, cut into 1/2-inch cubes
> 3 tablespoons butter *or* margarine, *divided*
> 1/3 cup chopped onion
> 1/3 cup chopped green pepper
> 8 taco shells, warmed
> Shredded lettuce and cheddar cheese
> Salsa, optional

Place taco seasoning in a large resealable plastic bag; add chicken, in batches, and shake to coat. In a large skillet, cook and stir chicken in 2 tablespoons butter for 4-5 minutes or until juices run clear. Remove chicken and keep warm.

In the same skillet, saute the onion and green pepper in remaining butter for 2-3 minutes or until crisp-tender. Combine the chicken, onion and green pepper; spoon into taco shells. Top with lettuce and cheese. Serve with salsa if desired. **Yield:** 4 servings.

Tomato Avocado Salad

Here's a cool alternative to guacamole. The slightly tart dressing showcases the garden-fresh flavors of ruby-red tomatoes and ripe avocados. It's a super salad to serve alongside any Mexican main entree.

> 2 tablespoons vegetable oil
> 2 tablespoons minced fresh cilantro *or* parsley
> 1 tablespoon lime juice
> 1/2 teaspoon garlic salt
> 1/2 teaspoon dried oregano
> 1/4 teaspoon ground cumin
> 2 medium tomatoes, cut into wedges
> 2 ripe avocados, peeled and sliced
> Lettuce leaves, optional

In a bowl, combine the oil, cilantro, lime juice, garlic salt, oregano and cumin. Arrange tomatoes and avocados on lettuce if desired. Drizzle with dressing. **Yield:** 4 servings.

Cinnamon Chocolate Sundaes

Kids will enjoy this tempting ice cream topping because it hardens on the ice cream as it stands.

1/2 cup butter *or* margarine
1/2 cup semisweet chocolate chips
1/3 cup packed brown sugar
1/4 cup corn syrup
1/4 cup half-and-half cream
1 teaspoon ground cinnamon
1 teaspoon vanilla extract

Vanilla ice cream
1 cup chopped walnuts

In a saucepan, combine the first five ingredients. Bring to a boil over medium-low heat, stirring constantly. Reduce heat; cook 5 minutes longer, stirring occasionally. Remove from the heat; stir in cinnamon and vanilla. Transfer to a heatproof measuring cup.

Cool for 10 minutes, stirring occasionally. Pour sauce over ice cream; top with walnuts. Refrigerate leftover sauce. Rewarm in a microwave before using.
Yield: 4 servings (about 1 cup sauce).

Old-World Appeal

WHEN cooler winds blow, this hearty fare from our Test Kitchen will keep you warm! Smoked Sausage Skillet has old-fashioned flavor that appeals to all. For a classic combination, try Apple Spinach Salad. Angel Toffee Dessert looks impressive but is easy to make.

—— 🍺 🍺 🍺 ——

Smoked Sausage Skillet

When the clock is ticking closer to dinnertime and you're nowhere near ready to call the clan to the dinner table, reach for this convenient recipe. Fully cooked sausage and quick-cooking cabbage make this meal-in-one a true time-saver.

> 1 pound fully cooked kielbasa *or* Polish sausage, sliced
> 3 cups shredded cabbage
> 1 celery rib, finely chopped
> 1 tablespoon vegetable oil
> 2 tablespoons Dijon mustard
> 1/2 teaspoon garlic salt
> 1/4 teaspoon rubbed sage
> 2 cups cooked noodles

In a large skillet, saute the sausage, cabbage and celery in oil for 5 minutes. Add the mustard, garlic salt and sage. Cook and stir over medium heat for 4-6 minutes or until vegetables are tender. Stir in noodles and heat through. **Yield:** 4 servings.

—— 🍺 🍺 🍺 ——

Apple Spinach Salad

This is an eye-catching addition to the table because the red apple contrasts nicely with the green spinach. The versatile dressing would taste great with any salad greens and toppings.

> 1/3 cup mayonnaise
> 4 teaspoons white vinegar
> 4 to 5 teaspoons sugar
> 1/4 teaspoon celery salt
> 1/8 to 1/4 teaspoon pepper
> 4 cups torn fresh spinach
> 1 small unpeeled red apple, sliced

In a small bowl, whisk together the mayonnaise, vinegar, sugar, celery salt and pepper. Let stand for

10 minutes; whisk until sugar is dissolved. In a salad bowl, combine the spinach and apple. Drizzle with salad dressing and gently toss to coat. **Yield:** 4 servings.

—— 🍺 🍺 🍺 ——

Angel Toffee Dessert

Although this dessert has a light and airy texture, the flavor is undeniably rich. Purchase a prepared angel food cake or, if time allows, bake one from scratch or

a boxed mix. Either way, it's a heavenly-tasting dessert you can even put together on a hectic weeknight. It's great for company as well.

2 **packages (3 ounces *each*) cream cheese, softened**
1/2 **cup confectioners' sugar**
2 **tablespoons milk**
1 **carton (8 ounces) frozen whipped topping, thawed**
5 **cups cubed angel food cake**
1/2 **cup chocolate syrup**

1/2 **cup English toffee bits *or* almond brickle chips, *divided***

In a mixing bowl, beat the cream cheese, sugar and milk until smooth. Fold in the whipped topping. Arrange angle food cake cubes in an ungreased 11-in. x 7-in. x 2-in. dish. Drizzle with chocolate syrup.

Set aside 1 tablespoon of toffee bits; sprinkle the remaining toffee bits over chocolate. Spread cream cheese mixture over top. Sprinkle with remaining toffee bits. Cover and chill until serving. Store leftovers in the refrigerator. **Yield:** 6-8 servings.

Hearty Fall Favorites

SURPRISE your family with a special dinner in the middle of the week. It's easy with this fast fare from our Test Kitchen. Cranberry Pork Chops capture the flavors of the season. Simple seasonings dress up Garlic Green Beans. And the aroma of Apricot Crisp baking is unbeatable.

— 🍴 🍴 🍴 —

Cranberry Pork Chops

Dried cranberries add a touch of sweetness—and autumn appeal—to this skillet supper.

> **4 bone-in pork loin chops (1/2 inch thick)**
> **2 tablespoons butter *or* margarine**
> **1 cup chicken broth, *divided***
> **1/2 teaspoon dried rosemary, crushed**
> **1/4 cup sliced green onions**
> **1/4 cup dried cranberries**
> **1/8 teaspoon pepper**
> **3 teaspoons cornstarch**
> **Hot cooked rice**

In a skillet, brown the pork chops in butter for 3 minutes on each side. Add 1/2 cup broth and rosemary. Reduce heat; cover and simmer for 5 minutes or until meat juices run clear. Remove chops to a serving dish and keep warm.

Add the onions, cranberries and pepper to skillet. Combine cornstarch and remaining broth until smooth; gradually add to skillet. Bring to a boil; cook and stir for 2 minutes or until thickened. Serve over pork and rice. **Yield:** 4 servings.

— 🍴 🍴 🍴 —

Garlic Green Beans

This savory side dish is a wonderful accompaniment to pork, beef and poultry.

> **1/2 cup water**
> **1/2 teaspoon chicken bouillon granules**
> **1 package (16 ounces) frozen green beans**
> **1 to 2 garlic cloves, minced**
> **1 tablespoon butter *or* margarine**
> **1/4 teaspoon seasoned salt**

In a saucepan, bring water and bouillon to a boil. Add the beans. Reduce heat; cover and simmer

for 10-12 minutes or until the beans are tender. In a large skillet, saute the garlic in butter for 1 minute. Drain the beans; add to the skillet. Sprinkle with seasoned salt and toss to coat. **Yield:** 4 servings.

— 🍴 🍴 🍴 —

Apricot Crisp

During the week, homemade fruit crisp is a treat you likely don't have time to prepare. But these individual-

serving crisps call for convenient canned fruit and bake for a mere 15 minutes. In place of the apricots, substitute another kind of fruit your family favors.

3 cans (15-1/4 ounces *each*) apricot halves, drained
2 tablespoons brown sugar
1/2 teaspoon ground ginger
TOPPING:
   1/4 cup all-purpose flour
   3 tablespoons brown sugar
   3 tablespoons quick-cooking oats
   2 tablespoons flaked coconut
1/4 cup cold butter *or* margarine

In a bowl, combine the apricots, brown sugar and ginger. Divide among four greased 8-oz. baking dishes. In another bowl, combine flour, brown sugar, oats and coconut. Cut in butter until mixture resembles coarse crumbs. Sprinkle over apricots. Bake at 400° for 15 minutes or until filling is bubbly and top is golden brown. **Yield:** 4 servings.

Editor's Note: Crisp may be baked in an 8-in. square baking dish for 23-25 minutes.

Soup's On... In Minutes!

NOTHING warms the body and soul like a steaming bowl of soup. But why rely on canned varieties when you can easily prepare your own like our Test Kitchen staff did? Teamed with Spicy Corn Bread Squares, Turkey Rice Soup is a satisfying meal for the whole family. Then satisfy a sweet tooth and whip up a batch of Crispy Chocolate Mounds.

— 🍲 🍲 🍲 —

Turkey Rice Soup

This tasty soup has a surprisingly short simmering time. You'll want to keep frozen mixed vegetables on hand to make this satisfying soup in a snap.

- 1/2 cup sliced fresh mushrooms
- 1/2 cup chopped onion
- 2 teaspoons vegetable oil
- 2 cans (14-1/2 ounces *each*) chicken broth
- 2 cups water
- 1/2 cup apple juice, optional
- 1 package (6 ounces) long grain and wild rice mix
- 2-1/2 cups cubed cooked turkey
- 2 cups frozen mixed vegetables

In a saucepan, saute mushrooms and onion in oil for 3 minutes. Stir in broth, water and apple juice if desired. Bring to a boil. Stir in rice mix. Reduce heat; cover and simmer for 20 minutes. Stir in turkey and vegetables; cook 5 minutes longer or until rice and vegetables are tender. **Yield:** 6 servings.

— 🍲 🍲 🍲 —

Spicy Corn Bread Squares

Corn bread captures the fabulous flavor of home-made bread without the hassle of rising and kneading the dough. Chili powder and red pepper flakes add zip to this hearty bread.

- 1 cup all-purpose flour
- 1 cup cornmeal
- 1/4 cup sugar
- 2 teaspoons baking powder
- 1/2 teaspoon baking soda

- 1/2 teaspoon salt
- 1/2 teaspoon chili powder
- 1 egg
- 1 cup buttermilk
- 2 tablespoons vegetable oil
- 1/2 teaspoon crushed red pepper flakes

In a large bowl, combine the first seven ingredients. In another bowl, beat the egg, buttermilk and oil; stir into dry ingredients just until moistened. Pour into a greased 9-in. square baking pan. Sprinkle with pepper flakes. Bake at 425° for 14-16 minutes

or until a toothpick inserted near the center comes out clean. Cool on a wire rack for 5 minutes. Cut into squares. Serve warm. **Yield:** 6 servings.

— 🛒 🛒 🛒 —

Crispy Chocolate Mounds

Make these bite-size treats while the Turkey Rice Soup is simmering and then chill. The recipe is so simple that the kids can help.

1 cup semisweet chocolate chips
1 cup peanut butter chips
1 cup crisp rice cereal
1/2 cup raisins
1/2 cup salted peanuts

In a microwave or heavy saucepan, melt chocolate and peanut butter chips; stir until smooth. Stir in the cereal, raisins and peanuts. Drop by table-spoonfuls onto waxed paper-lined baking sheets. Refrigerate for 15 minutes or until set. **Yield:** about 2 dozen.

Yuletide Trimmings

DURING the holiday hustle, present your family with this home-cooked meal our Test Kitchen put together in a hurry. The season's colors shine through in Artichoke Beef Steaks. To save time, use unpeeled potatoes in Creamy Mashed Potatoes. No one will think you're silly for gobbling up Cranberry Fool!

— 🝔 🝔 🝔 —

Artichoke Beef Steaks

Light green artichokes and vibrant pimientos make these colorful steaks perfect for the holiday season. If weather permits, grill the steaks outside and prepare the topping in a skillet as directed.

>   1 jar (6-1/2 ounces) marinated artichoke hearts
>   4 boneless beef rib eye steaks (3/4 inch thick and about 8 ounces *each*)
> 1/2 teaspoon salt
>   2 tablespoons butter *or* margarine
>   1 small onion, sliced and separated into rings
>   1 garlic clove, minced
>   1 jar (2 ounces) sliced pimientos, drained

Drain artichokes, reserving 1 tablespoon marinade. Cut artichokes in half and set aside. Sprinkle steaks with salt. In a large skillet, cook steaks in butter over medium-high heat for 4 minutes on each side or until the meat reaches desired doneness (for rare, a meat thermometer should read 140°; medium, 160°; well-done, 170°). Remove to a serving platter; keep warm.

In same skillet, saute the onion and garlic in reserved marinade for 3 minutes. Add the artichokes and pimientos; heat through. Serve over steaks. **Yield:** 4 servings.

— 🝔 🝔 🝔 —

Creamy Mashed Potatoes

These mashed potatoes are rich, thanks to the whipping cream. The pretty red potato skins peeking through the creamy mashed potatoes will draw comments.

>   6 medium unpeeled red potatoes (about 1-1/2 pounds), cut into 1-inch pieces*
> 1/3 to 1/2 cup heavy whipping

> cream, warmed
>   2 tablespoons butter *or* margarine
> 1/2 teaspoon salt
> 1/4 teaspoon pepper

Place potatoes in a saucepan; cover with water. Cover pan and bring to a boil. Reduce heat. Cook for 10-15 minutes or until tender; drain well. Add the cream, butter, salt and pepper; mash potatoes. **Yield:** 4 servings.

*Editor's Note: For a smoother consistency, peel potatoes before cooking.

Cranberry Fool

A "fool" is a dessert made by folding pureed fruit into whipped cream. In this delectable version, cranberry sauce is the featured fruit. If you're pressed for time, you can use 2 cups of thawed, frozen whipped topping instead of the whipping cream with just as delicious results.

**1 can (16 ounces) whole-berry cranberry
  sauce
1 teaspoon grated orange peel**

**1/4 teaspoon ground allspice
  1 cup heavy whipping cream, whipped
Additional grated orange peel, optional
Fresh mint, optional**

In a medium bowl, combine the cranberry sauce, orange peel and allspice and stir until well blended. Gently fold in the whipped cream. Spoon the cranberry mixture into individual dessert dishes. Refrigerate until serving. Before serving, garnish with orange peel and fresh mint if desired. **Yield:** 4 servings.

Meals on a Budget

Feed your family well without spending a lot on groceries with these frugal yet filling meals.

WON'T BREAK THE BANK. Clockwise from upper left: Grilled Meat Loaf, Beans with Parsley Sauce and Peanut Butter Pudding Pie (p. 266); Garlic Zucchini Frittata, Fresh Fruit Dip and Cinnamon Muffins (p. 264); Hash Brown Pork Bake, Braised Brussels Sprouts and Chocolate Mint Layer Cake (p. 260); Slow Cooker Beef Stew, Yellow Squash Muffins and Sweet Potato Custard Pie (p. 270).

Feed Your Family for $1.61 a Plate!

EVEN IF THE HOLIDAYS squeeze your household budget, you can still leave the table satisfied.

Three frugal cooks prove it with this delicious down-home dinner. Our Test Kitchen home economists estimate the total cost at just $1.61 per serving.

Hash Brown Pork Bake is a comforting family-style casserole Darlis Wilfer of Phelps, Wisconsin makes with convenient frozen hash browns.

Caraway, onion, bacon and chicken broth dress up Braised Brussels Sprouts, shared by Yvonne Anderson of New Philadelphia, Ohio.

With its rich chocolate icing and minty whipped cream filling, Chocolate Mint Layer Cake, from Jean Portwine of Recluse, Wyoming, makes a fitting finale to a special meal.

Hash Brown Pork Bake

- 2 cups (16 ounces) sour cream
- 1 can (10-3/4 ounces) condensed cream of chicken soup, undiluted
- 1 package (32 ounces) frozen cubed hash brown potatoes, thawed
- 2 cups cubed cooked pork
- 1 pound process cheese (Velveeta), cubed
- 1/4 cup chopped onion
- 2 cups crushed cornflakes
- 1/2 cup margarine, melted
- 1 cup (4 ounces) shredded mozzarella cheese
- 3 green pepper rings

In a bowl, combine sour cream and soup. Stir in hash browns, pork, process cheese and onion. Transfer to a greased 3-qt. baking dish. Toss cornflake crumbs and margarine; sprinkle over top. Bake, uncovered, at 350° for 50 minutes. Sprinkle with mozzarella. Bake 10 minutes longer or until bubbly. Garnish with green pepper. **Yield:** 8 servings.

Braised Brussels Sprouts

✓ Uses less fat, sugar or salt. Includes Nutritional Analysis and Diabetic Exchanges.

- 2 pounds fresh brussels sprouts
- 2 bacon strips, diced
- 1 medium onion, chopped
- 1 cup chicken broth
- 1 teaspoon caraway seeds
- 1/4 teaspoon salt
- 1/8 teaspoon pepper

Trim brussels sprouts; cut an "X" in the core of each. Place in a saucepan and cover with water; bring to a boil. Cook for 8-10 minutes or until crisp-tender. Meanwhile, in a large skillet, cook bacon until crisp; remove with a slotted spoon to paper towels.

Saute onion in the drippings until tender. Stir in the broth, caraway seeds, salt and pepper. Simmer, uncovered, until liquid has almost evaporated. Drain sprouts. Add sprouts and bacon to onion mixture; toss to combine. **Yield:** 8 servings.

Nutritional Analysis: One serving (1/2 cup) equals 68 calories, 1 g fat (trace saturated fat), 1 mg cholesterol, 205 mg sodium, 12 g carbohydrate, 5 g fiber, 5 g protein. **Diabetic Exchange:** 2 vegetable.

Chocolate Mint Layer Cake

1/2 cup butter, softened
1-3/4 cups sugar
3 eggs
4 squares (1 ounce *each*) unsweetened chocolate, melted and cooled
1 teaspoon vanilla extract
3/4 cup milk
1/2 cup water
1-3/4 cups all-purpose flour
3/4 teaspoon baking soda
1/2 teaspoon salt

FILLING:
1 cup heavy whipping cream
3 tablespoons confectioners' sugar
1/8 teaspoon peppermint extract
3 to 4 drops green food coloring, optional

ICING:
1 cup (6 ounces) semisweet chocolate chips
1/4 cup butter *or* margarine
1/3 cup evaporated milk
1 teaspoon vanilla extract
1-1/2 cups confecftioners' sugar

Line two greased 9-in. round baking pans with waxed paper. Grease and flour paper; set aside. In a mixing bowl, cream butter and sugar. Beat in eggs one at a time. Beat in chocolate and vanilla.

Combine milk and water. Combine the flour, baking soda and salt; add to creamed mixture alternately with milk mixture. Pour into prepared pans. Bake at 350° for 24-28 minutes or until a toothpick comes out clean. Cool for 10 minutes before removing from pans to wire racks.

For filling, in a mixing bowl, beat the cream until it begins to thicken. Add confectioners' sugar and extract; beat until stiff peaks form. Beat in food coloring if desired. Place one cake layer on a serving plate; spread with filling. Top with second cake.

For icing, in a microwave-safe mixing bowl, melt chips and butter; cool slightly. Beat in evaporated milk and vanilla. Gradually beat in confectioners' sugar. Frost and decorate cake. Chill 2 hours before slicing. **Yield:** 12 servings.

Feed Your Family for $1.56 a Plate!

YOU DON'T have to "shell out" a lot of money on grocery bills when feeding your family.

The recipes here are suggested by three budget-minded cooks and combined by our Test Kitchen into a delicious meal you can serve for just $1.56 per person.

Three-Cheese Shells make a hearty meatless entree. "It's easy to prepare ahead, then bake just in time for dinner," says June Barrus of Springville, Utah.

Bacon, brown sugar and cider vinegar season Beans 'n' Caramelized Onions. "I often serve this dish to guests, and it never fails to please," shares Jill Heatwole from Pittsville, Maryland.

With a tangy filling and a nutmeg-flavored crust, Lemon Cheese Squares hit the spot after a meal or as a snack. "My grandmother made these bars for me when I was growing up, and they were my favorite," recalls Emily Weedman of Milwaukie, Oregon.

— 🍮 🍮 🍮 —

Three-Cheese Shells

- 1 package (12 ounces) jumbo pasta shells
- 3 cups (24 ounces) ricotta cheese
- 3 cups (12 ounces) shredded mozzarella cheese
- 1/2 cup grated Parmesan cheese
- 1/2 cup chopped green pepper
- 1/2 cup chopped fresh mushrooms
- 2 tablespoons dried basil
- 2 eggs, lightly beaten
- 2 garlic cloves, minced
- 1/2 teaspoon seasoned salt
- 1/4 teaspoon pepper
- 2 jars (one 28 ounces, one 14 ounces) spaghetti sauce, *divided*

Cook pasta shells according to package directions. Drain and rinse in cold water. In a bowl, combine the next 10 ingredients. Divide the small jar of spaghetti sauce between two ungreased 13-in. x 9-in. x 2-in. baking dishes.

Fill shells with the cheese mixture and place in a single layer over sauce. Pour the remaining spaghetti sauce over shells. Cover and bake at 350° for 20 minutes. Uncover; bake 10 minutes longer or until heated through. **Yield:** 9 servings.

Beans 'n' Caramelized Onions

(Pictured on front cover)

- 4 bacon strips
- 2 large onions, cut lengthwise into 1/2-inch-thick wedges
- 2 pounds fresh green beans, trimmed
- 3 tablespoons cider vinegar
- 4-1/2 teaspoons brown sugar
- 1/4 teaspoon salt
- 1/4 teaspoon pepper

In a large skillet, cook bacon over medium heat until crisp. Remove to paper towels. Drain, reserving 2 tablespoons drippings. Crumble bacon and set aside. In the drippings, cook onions over medium-low heat until tender and golden brown, about 50 minutes.

Meanwhile, place the beans in a large saucepan and cover with water; bring to a boil. Cook, uncov-

ered, for 8-10 minutes or until crisp-tender. Drain. Stir the vinegar and brown sugar into onions; add beans. Cook, uncovered, over medium heat for 1 minute. Add bacon; toss gently. Season with salt and pepper. **Yield:** 9 servings.

─── 🍷 🍷 🍷 ───

Lemon Cheese Squares

1/3 cup stick margarine, softened
1/4 cup packed brown sugar
  1 cup all-purpose flour
1/4 teaspoon salt
1/4 teaspoon ground nutmeg
FILLING:
  1 cup (8 ounces) small-curd cottage cheese
  1 egg
  1 egg white

  3 tablespoons lemon juice
  1 cup sugar
  2 tablespoons all-purpose flour
  1 tablespoon grated lemon peel
1/4 teaspoon baking powder

In a mixing bowl, cream margarine and brown sugar. Combine flour, salt and nutmeg; add to creamed mixture. Press into a greased 8-in. square baking dish. Bake at 350° for 18-20 minutes until golden brown.

For filling, place cottage cheese, egg, egg white and lemon juice in a blender or food processor. Cover; process until smooth. Add the sugar, flour, lemon peel and baking powder. Cover; process until blended. Pour over crust. Bake at 350° for 30-34 minutes until edges are lightly browned. Cool on a wire rack 1 hour. Refrigerate until chilled. **Yield:** 9 servings.

Feed Your Family for $1.19 a Plate!

GROCERY BUDGET tight? Don't worry, you can still enjoy foods that satisfy and are full of flavor.

Three frugal cooks prove it with this mouth-watering meal that's perfect for Sunday brunch or a light supper. Our Test Kitchen home economists estimate the total cost at just $1.19 per setting.

"I love serving foods that both complement and contrast with each other, like my Garlic Zucchini Frittata," relates Michelle Krzmarzick of Redondo Beach, California. "This flavorful egg dish can be made in minutes and easily doubled. Sometimes I use leftover taco meat or chopped ham instead of bacon."

Elizabeth Hunter of Prosperity, South Carolina blends orange marmalade with sour cream and mayonnaise for her zesty Fresh Fruit Dip. It's a real refresher!

Cinnamon Muffins, with a dash of nutmeg in the batter, are seasoned to please. "My husband grew up enjoying these tender, yummy muffins that his mother made on special weekend mornings," says Katherine McVey from Raleigh, North Carolina.

Garlic Zucchini Frittata

- 1 tablespoon butter *or* margarine
- 1 tablespoon finely chopped onion
- 4 garlic cloves, minced
- 1 medium zucchini, shredded
- 6 eggs
- 1/4 teaspoon ground mustard
- 4 bacon strips, cooked and crumbled
- 1/4 teaspoon salt
- 1/8 teaspoon pepper
- 1/4 cup shredded Swiss cheese
- 1/4 cup sliced green onions

In a 10-in. ovenproof skillet, melt the butter over medium-high heat. Add the onion and garlic; saute for 1 minute. Add the zucchini and cook for 3 minutes or until tender. In a bowl, beat the eggs and mustard. Pour into skillet. Sprinkle with bacon, salt and pepper. As the eggs set, lift edges, letting uncooked portion flow underneath. Cook until eggs are nearly set, about 7 minutes. Meanwhile, preheat broiler.

Place the skillet under the broiler, 6 in. from the heat, for 30-60 seconds or until the eggs are completely set. Sprinkle with Swiss cheese and green onions. Broil 30 seconds longer or until the cheese is melted. Cut into wedges. **Yield:** 4 servings.

Fresh Fruit Dip

- 1/2 cup mayonnaise *or* salad dressing
- 1/2 cup sour cream
- 1/3 cup orange marmalade
- 1 tablespoon milk
- 1/2 pound green grapes
- 1/2 pound strawberries

In a small bowl, whisk the mayonnaise, sour cream, marmalade and milk. Refrigerate until serving. Serve with fruit. **Yield:** 1-1/3 cups.

— 🏺 🏺 🏺 —

Cinnamon Muffins

1/3 cup shortening
1/2 cup sugar
1 egg
1-1/2 cups all-purpose flour
1-1/2 teaspoons baking powder
1/2 teaspoon salt
1/4 teaspoon ground nutmeg
1/2 cup milk

TOPPING:
1/2 cup sugar
1-1/2 teaspoons ground cinnamon
3 tablespoons butter *or* margarine, melted

In a mixing bowl, cream shortening and sugar. Add egg; beat well. Combine the flour, baking powder, salt and nutmeg; add to creamed mixture alternately with milk and mix well. Fill greased muffin cups half full. Bake at 350° for 15-20 minutes or until a toothpick inserted near the center comes out clean.

In a shallow bowl, combine sugar and cinnamon. Dip muffin tops in butter, then in cinnamon-sugar. Serve warm. **Yield:** 1 dozen.

Feed Your Family for 99¢ a Plate!

FIRE UP the grill for this great-tasting meal that won't burn a hole in your pocketbook.

It combines three frugal yet flavorful recipes from fellow cost-conscious cooks. Our Test Kitchen staff estimates the total price at just 99¢ per serving!

Grilled Meat Loaf is the perfect summertime twist on a comforting family favorite. Catherine Carpenter of Barnesville, Ohio shapes the meat mixture into loaves and "bakes" them on the grill. Ketchup brushed over the meat lends a little sweetness to each slice.

You'll likely find the main ingredient for Beans with Parsley Sauce right in your garden. For a bit of extra color, try mixing wax beans with green beans. Veronica Teipel of Manchester, Missouri shares the recipe, saying, "The flavor is definitely worth the preparation time."

Peanut Butter Pudding Pie, from Valerie Sisson of Norton, Ohio, is pretty enough to serve company…if your family doesn't get to it first! No one will be able to resist a sweet piece of this creamy chocolate and peanut butter dessert.

Grilled Meat Loaf

1/2 cup ketchup
1/2 cup quick-cooking oats
1/4 cup chopped green pepper
  1 egg
  1 teaspoon dried parsley flakes
  1 teaspoon Worcestershire sauce
1/2 teaspoon garlic powder
1/2 teaspoon dried basil
1/4 teaspoon pepper
  2 pounds ground beef
Additional ketchup, optional

In a large bowl, combine the first nine ingredients. Crumble beef over mixture and mix well. Shape into two loaves. Place a sheet of heavy-duty foil in center of grill. Place meat loaves on foil (do not seal foil).

Grill, covered, over indirect medium heat for 50 minutes or until meat is no longer pink and a meat thermometer reads 160°. Brush tops with additional ketchup if desired. Let stand for 10 minutes before slicing. **Yield:** 2 loaves (4 servings each).

Beans with Parsley Sauce

  2 pounds fresh green beans, trimmed
  2 tablespoons butter *or* margarine
  2 tablespoons all-purpose flour
  1 teaspoon salt
1/8 teaspoon pepper
1-1/2 cups chicken broth
  2 egg yolks
1/2 cup milk
  1 cup minced fresh parsley

Place beans in a large saucepan and cover with water; bring to a boil. Cook, uncovered, for 8-10 minutes or until crisp tender. Meanwhile, in a large skillet, melt butter over medium heat. Stir in the flour, salt and pepper until smooth. Gradually

whisk in broth. Bring to a boil; cook and stir for 1-2 minutes or until thickened. Remove from the heat.

In a small bowl, combine egg yolks and milk. Stir a small amount of hot broth mixture into egg mixture. Return all to the pan, stirring constantly. Bring to a gentle boil; cook and stir for 2 minutes or until thickened. Stir in parsley. Drain beans; top with sauce. **Yield:** 8 servings.

— 🏮 🏮 🏮 —

Peanut Butter Pudding Pie

2 cups milk
1 package (3 ounces) cook-and-serve vanilla pudding mix
1 cup peanut butter chips
1 graham cracker crust (9 inches)
2-1/2 cups whipped topping
1/3 cup milk chocolate chips
1 teaspoon shortening

In a saucepan, whisk the milk and pudding mix. Cook and stir over medium heat until mixture comes to a boil.

Reduce heat; stir in the peanut butter chips until melted. Pour into the crust. Cover and refrigerate for 3-4 hours or until set.

Spread whipped topping over pie. In a microwave-safe bowl, melt chocolate chips and shortening. Cool for 5 minutes. Drizzle over topping. Refrigerate until serving. **Yield:** 8 servings.

Feed Your Family for $1.50 a Plate!

DISHING OUT hearty helpings of down-home foods doesn't mean you have to dish out hoards of money.

Our Test Kitchen home economists have combined the recipes here from three budget-minded cooks into a delicious and satisfying meal you can put on the table for just $1.50 per person.

Hay and Straw is not only quick and easy to prepare, it's pretty, too. This colorful pasta dish combines julienned ham, Parmesan cheese, peas and linguine. "The trick is to have all the ingredients ready at the same time, so you can toss it all together without having to reheat," says Priscilla Weaver of Hagerstown, Maryland.

Bits of crumbled bacon add texture to Creamy Bacon Salad Dressing from DeEtta Rasmussen of Fort Madison, Iowa. With a mayonnaise and vinegar base, this thick, slightly tangy blend coats tossed greens or spinach nicely.

"Chocolate Cream Dessert makes a cool and delicious treat on a warm summer day," says Pam Reddell of Linden, Wisconsin. "I bake a tender crust from a cake mix, then layer it with a cream cheese blend, chocolate pudding and whipped topping."

— 🛒 🛒 🛒 —

Hay and Straw

- 1 package (16 ounces) linguine
- 2 cups julienned fully cooked ham
- 1 tablespoon butter *or* margarine
- 3 cups frozen peas
- 1-1/2 cups shredded Parmesan cheese
- 1/3 cup heavy whipping cream

Cook linguine according to package directions. Meanwhile, in a large skillet, saute ham in butter for 3 minutes. Add peas; heat through. Drain linguine; toss with ham mixture, Parmesan cheese and cream. Serve immediately. **Yield:** 8 servings.

— 🛒 🛒 🛒 —

Creamy Bacon Salad Dressing

- 1/2 cup mayonnaise
- 2 tablespoons cider vinegar
- 2 tablespoons light corn syrup

- 1/8 teaspoon salt
- 4 bacon slices, cooked and crumbled
- 2 tablespoons finely chopped onion
- 6 cups torn mixed salad greens

In a small bowl, whisk mayonnaise, vinegar, corn syrup and salt until smooth. Stir in bacon and onion. Cover and refrigerate for at least 2 hours. Serve over salad greens. **Yield:** 8 servings (3/4 cup dressing).

— 🛒 🛒 🛒 —

Chocolate Cream Dessert

- 3/4 cup cold butter *or* margarine
- 1 package (18-1/4 ounces) chocolate cake mix
- 1 egg, lightly beaten

**1 package (8 ounces) cream cheese,
softened**
1 cup confectioners' sugar
4 cups whipped topping, *divided*
3 cups cold milk
**2 packages (3.9 ounces *each*) instant
chocolate pudding mix**
2 tablespoons chocolate curls

In a bowl, cut butter into the cake mix until crumbly. Add the egg and mix well. Press into a greased 13-in. x 9-in. x 2-in. baking dish. Bake at 350° for 15-18 minutes or until set. Cool completely on a wire rack.

In a small mixing bowl, beat cream cheese and confectioners' sugar until smooth. Fold in 1 cup of whipped topping. Carefully spread over the crust; refrigerate.

In a bowl, whisk the milk and pudding mix for 2 minutes; let stand until slightly thickened. Spread over the cream cheese layer. Top with the remaining whipped topping. Refrigerate for 2 hours before cutting. Garnish with chocolate curls. Refrigerate leftovers. **Yield:** 12 servings.

Coupon Clue

Having trouble keeping track of coupons when you're shopping? Write your grocery list on a business-size envelope and place corresponding coupons inside.

Feed Your Family for $1.35 a Plate!

YOU CAN BE FRUGAL and still prepare a satisfying, full-flavored fall dinner for your family. Three budget-conscious cooks prove it with these penny-pinching yet palate-pleasing recipes.

Our Test Kitchen home economists estimate the total cost for this meal is just $1.35 a serving!

When there's a chill in the air, nothing beats Slow Cooker Beef Stew from Earnestine Wilson of Waco, Texas. Seasoned with thyme and dry mustard, the hearty slow-cooked stew is chock-full of tender carrots, potatoes and beef.

Yellow Squash Muffins are so moist and golden, they're sure to become an instant family favorite. The muffins, shared by Doris Heath of Franklin, North Carolina, have a delicate squash flavor.

"I love to bake and experiment with ingredients," says Kathy Roberts of New Hebron, Mississippi. "Sometimes I get lucky and produce something that's new and tasty, like Sweet Potato Custard Pie."

— ☕ ☕ ☕ —

Slow Cooker Beef Stew

1-1/2 **pounds potatoes, peeled and cubed**
   6 **medium carrots, cut into 1-inch slices**
   1 **medium onion, coarsely chopped**
   3 **celery ribs, coarsely chopped**
   3 **tablespoons all-purpose flour**
1-1/2 **pounds beef stew meat, cut into 1-inch cubes**
   3 **tablespoons vegetable oil**
   1 **can (14-1/2 ounces) diced tomatoes, undrained**
   1 **cup beef broth**
   1 **teaspoon ground mustard**
1/2 **teaspoon salt**
1/2 **teaspoon pepper**
1/2 **teaspoon dried thyme**
1/2 **teaspoon browning sauce**

Layer the potatoes, carrots, onion and celery in a 5-qt. slow cooker. Place flour in a large resealable plastic bag. Add stew meat; seal and toss to coat evenly. In a large skillet, brown meat in oil in batches. Place over vegetables.

In a large bowl, combine tomatoes, broth, mustard, salt, pepper, thyme and browning sauce. Pour over beef. Cover; cook on high for 1-1/2 hours. Reduce heat to low; cook 7-8 hours longer or until meat and vegetables are tender. **Yield:** 8 servings.

— ☕ ☕ ☕ —

Yellow Squash Muffins

   1 **pound yellow summer squash, cut into 1-inch slices**
1/2 **cup butter *or* margarine, melted**
   1 **egg, lightly beaten**
1-1/2 **cups all-purpose flour**
1/2 **cup sugar**
2-1/2 **teaspoons baking powder**
1/2 **teaspoon salt**

Place 1 in. of water in a saucepan; add squash. Bring to a boil. Reduce heat; cover and simmer

for 5 minutes or until tender. Drain and mash; stir in the butter and egg. In a bowl, combine the flour, sugar, baking powder and salt. Stir in the squash mixture just until moistened.

Fill greased muffin cups three-fourths full. Bake at 375° for 20-25 minutes or until a toothpick comes out clean. Cool for 5 minutes before removing from pan to a wire rack. **Yield:** 1 dozen.

Sweet Potato Custard Pie

2 small sweet potatoes, peeled and chopped
3/4 cup marshmallow creme
1/2 cup butter *or* margarine, cubed
1 can (5 ounces) evaporated milk
3 eggs
1 teaspoon vanilla extract
1/4 teaspoon almond extract
3/4 cup sugar
1/4 cup packed brown sugar
1 tablespoon all-purpose flour
1/8 teaspoon ground cinnamon
1/8 teaspoon ground nutmeg
1 unbaked pastry shell (9 inches)
1/2 cup whipped topping

Place sweet potatoes in a large saucepan; cover with water. Bring to a boil. Reduce heat; cover and simmer for 10 minutes or until tender. Drain potatoes and place in a large mixing bowl; mash. Add marshmallow creme and butter; beat until smooth. Add milk, eggs and extracts; mix well.

Combine the sugars, flour, cinnamon and nutmeg; gradually beat into potato mixture until well blended. Pour into pastry shell. Bake at 350° for 45-50 minutes or until a knife comes out clean. Cool on a wire rack. Serve with whipped topping. Refrigerate leftovers. **Yield:** 8 servings.

Getting in the Theme of Things

Add a festive feel to any get-together with these theme-related menus featuring fabulous recipes and fun decorating ideas.

— 🥄 🥄 🥄 —

LIFE OF THE PARTY. Clockwise from upper left: Treat Guests to a Taste of the Tropics (p. 280), Valentine's Day Dinner Wins Hearts (p. 276), Christmas Meal with Country Appeal (p. 274) and A Birthday Feast Fit for "Jumbo" (p. 282).

Christmas Meal with Country Appeal

By Karen Darrell, Bethalto, Illinois

WHEN WE PLANNED a trip to Idaho to spend the holidays with my husband Robb's family, our daughter, Hailey, and I packed recipes and trims for a Country Christmas theme dinner to put on while we were there. Robb's mom always has a creative theme table and meal waiting for us when we visit, so I thought it would be fun to surprise her with one.

Idaho's woodsy landscape inspired my outdoorsy, old-fashioned country holiday decorations. And a traditional menu of Cornish Game Hens, Western Cubed Potatoes, Bacon-Onion Green Beans and Ice Cream Cake Dessert seemed to fit just right.

Everyone loved the seasonal table decorations and delicious meal. The Cornish Game Hens looked so festive and were something different from the usual ham or turkey. They're simple to make, and each

person gets an attractive individual serving.

Green chilies add a little zip to Western Cubed Potatoes but do not overpower this casserole's down-home appeal. It's a side dish the kids enjoyed as much as the adults did.

I threw together the recipe for Bacon-Onion Green Beans, wanting to give some color to the plate. I knew all the relatives liked green beans, so I added onion, bacon, toasted sesame seeds and a little vinegar for a nice tang.

The Ice Cream Cake Dessert was also a sweet success. It's a recipe you can have fun with by changing cake and ice cream flavors and using various sauces to suit your family's taste buds.

Set in the warmth of my in-laws' home with the family gathered, our Country Christmas dinner was an occasion to treasure. I hope you'll plan a similar celebration!

Cornish Game Hens

    6 **Cornish game hens (20 ounces** *each***)**
1/2 teaspoon salt
1/4 teaspoon pepper
1/4 cup butter *or* **margarine, melted**
1/4 cup orange juice
1/4 cup honey
SAUCE:
1/2 cup orange juice
    2 **tablespoons honey**
1/2 teaspoon cider vinegar
    1 **tablespoon cornstarch**
    1 **tablespoon cold water**

Place hens on a rack in a shallow baking pan. Tie legs with kitchen string if desired. Sprinkle with salt and pepper. Combine the butter, orange juice and honey; spoon over hens. Bake, uncovered, at 350° for 1 hour or until a meat thermometer reads 165° and juices run clear, basting every 15 minutes.

In a small saucepan, combine the orange juice, honey and vinegar. Combine cornstarch and water until smooth; stir into orange juice mixture. Bring to a boil; cook and stir for 1 minute or until thickened. Serve with hens. **Yield:** 6 servings.

— 🍵 🍵 🍵 —

Western Cubed Potatoes

1/2 cup butter *or* **margarine, melted**
    1 **can (4 ounces) chopped green chilies**
    2 **tablespoons finely chopped onion**
1/2 teaspoon salt
1/4 teaspoon garlic salt
1/4 teaspoon pepper
    6 **medium potatoes, cubed**
1/4 cup minced fresh parsley

In a large bowl, combine the first six ingredients. Add potatoes and toss to coat. Transfer to an ungreased 2-qt. baking dish. Cover and bake at 350° for 45 minutes. Uncover; bake 20-25 minutes longer or until the potatoes are tender. Sprinkle with parsley. **Yield:** 6 servings.

— 🍵 🍵 🍵 —

Bacon-Onion Green Beans

1-1/2 **pounds fresh green beans, trimmed**
    6 **bacon strips, diced**
    1 **medium onion, chopped**
    2 **tablespoons cider vinegar**
1/4 teaspoon salt
1/8 teaspoon pepper
    1 **tablespoon sesame seeds, toasted**

Place beans in a saucepan and cover with water; bring to a boil. Cook, uncovered, for 8-10 minutes or until crisp-tender. Meanwhile, in a skillet, cook bacon over medium heat until crisp. Remove to paper towels; drain, reserving 1 tablespoon drippings. Saute onion in the drippings until tender. Stir in vinegar, salt and pepper.

Drain beans; place in a large serving bowl. Stir in the onion mixture and bacon. Sprinkle with sesame seeds. **Yield:** 6-8 servings.

— 🍵 🍵 🍵 —

Ice Cream Cake Dessert

    1 **package (18-1/4 ounces) chocolate cake mix**
    1 **quart vanilla ice cream, softened**
    1 **cup sugar**
1/2 cup evaporated milk
1/2 cup light corn syrup
    3 **squares (1 ounce** *each***) unsweetened chocolate, chopped**
1/2 teaspoon vanilla extract
1/2 cup slivered almonds

Line a greased 15-in. x 10-in. x 1-in. baking pan with waxed paper. Grease the paper and set aside. Prepare the cake batter according to package directions; pour into the prepared pan. Bake at 350° for 23-28 minutes or until a toothpick inserted near the center comes out clean. Cool on a wire rack.

Invert cake and gently peel off waxed paper. Cut cake in half widthwise. Place one half on a serving platter. Spread with ice cream; top with remaining cake. Cover and freeze.

In a heavy saucepan, combine the sugar, milk and corn syrup. Bring to a boil over medium heat, stirring constantly. Cook and stir for 2 minutes. Remove from the heat; stir in chocolate until melted. Stir in vanilla.

Remove cake from freezer 15 minutes before serving. Serve sauce warm over cake. Sprinkle with almonds. **Yield:** 9 servings (1-3/4 cups sauce).

About Game Hens

Rock Cornish game hens (also called Cornish game hens) are miniature, 4- to 6-week-old chickens that weigh from 1-1/2 to 2-1/2 pounds. They're a hybrid of Cornish and White Rock chickens.

They look elegant and take less time to cook than a whole chicken. Typically, a game hen is just enough for one serving.

Valentine's Day Dinner Wins Hearts

By Barbara Birk, St. George, Utah

VALENTINE'S DAY has a special place in my heart since my husband, Gordon, and I were engaged on this romantic holiday 42 years ago.

It's a wonderful day for us to reminisce, and we often invite friends or neighbors to join us for a Valentine's Day dinner. It's fun for me because I love to prepare delicious, attractive foods.

People really like my Cupid's Chicken 'n' Stuffing. This main dish looks attractive and is easy to fix. The chicken stays moist, and the savory stuffing that bakes right with it is the perfect accompaniment.

Early in the day, I prepare the stuffing and place it in the baking dish. Later, all I need to do is brown the chicken, assemble the few other ingredients and it's ready to pop into the oven.

Tangy Bacon Salad Dressing is always a hit. I serve it over assorted salad greens or sometimes fresh spinach,

adding different kinds of berries, radishes or tomatoes for color. This thick and flavorful dressing is slightly sweet with a light tang.

I go overboard on sweets for my valentine parties. If you have time, it's nice to write guests' names on the Shortbread Hearts with white icing. These flaky cookies melt in your mouth. Dipped in chocolate, they look festive.

I don't think you can overdo chocolate for this holiday. Candy sprinkles dress up my tried-and-true Favorite Frosted Brownies for the occasion. Everyone always agrees that they are so yummy!

Last year I ended up sending desserts home with guests. Not a one refused! They always comment that Valentine's Day is a fun time to receive a dinner invitation and are so enthusiastic about the good food and decorations.

I enjoy planning the evening and hope you might want to try out my recipes and theme on your own family and friends. I predict that the party will win their hearts, too!

— 🥄 🥄 🥄 —

Cupid's Chicken 'n' Stuffing

✓ Uses less fat, sugar or salt. Includes Nutritional Analysis and Diabetic Exchanges.

    1 package (6 ounces) seasoned stuffing mix
    8 boneless skinless chicken breast halves (4 ounces *each*)
    1 tablespoon canola *or* vegetable oil
1/4 teaspoon salt
1/4 teaspoon pepper
    4 Swiss cheese slices (2 ounces), halved
    2 tablespoons butter *or* stick margarine, melted
    1 can (10-3/4 ounces) condensed cream of chicken soup, undiluted
1/4 cup water

Prepare stuffing mix according to package directions. Transfer to a greased 13-in. x 9-in. x 2-in. baking dish. In a large skillet, brown chicken in oil. Sprinkle with salt and pepper; place over stuffing. Top with cheese. Drizzle with butter.

Combine soup and water; spoon over stuffing. Cover and bake at 350° for 40 minutes. Uncover; bake 10-15 minutes longer or until chicken juices run clear. **Yield:** 8 servings.

Nutritional Analysis: One chicken breast with 1/3 cup stuffing (prepared with reduced-fat cheese and reduced-fat reduced-sodium cream of chicken soup) equals 268 calories, 6 g fat (3 g saturated fat), 79 mg cholesterol, 869 mg sodium, 18 g carbohydrate, 1 g fiber, 32 g protein. **Diabetic Exchanges:** 4 lean meat, 1 starch.

— 🥄 🥄 🥄 —

Tangy Bacon Salad Dressing

3/4 cup sugar
1/3 cup white vinegar
1/3 cup ketchup
    1 teaspoon Worcestershire sauce
1/2 cup vegetable oil
    8 bacon strips, cooked and crumbled
    1 small onion, finely chopped
Torn salad greens, shredded red cabbage and sliced cucumbers *or* vegetables of your choice

In a small bowl, whisk the sugar, vinegar, ketchup and Worcestershire sauce. Gradually whisk in the oil in a steady stream. Stir in the bacon and onion. Serve with tossed salad. **Yield:** about 2 cups.

Shortbread Hearts

    2 cups all-purpose flour
1/2 cup sugar
Dash salt
    1 cup cold butter (no substitutes)
    1 tablespoon cold water
    1 teaspoon almond extract
1/2 pound dark chocolate candy coating, melted

In a large bowl, combine the flour, sugar and salt; cut in butter until mixture resembles coarse crumbs. Stir in water and extract until mixture forms a ball. On a lightly floured surface, roll out dough to 1/4-in. thickness. Cut with a 2-1/2-in. cookie cutter dipped in flour. Place 1 in. apart on ungreased baking sheets. Cover and refrigerate for 30 minutes.

Bake at 325° for 13-16 minutes or until edges are lightly browned. Cool for 2 minutes before removing to wire racks to cool completely. Dip one side of cookies in candy coating; place on waxed paper until set. **Yield:** about 2 dozen.

— 🥄 🥄 🥄 —

Favorite Frosted Brownies

    1 cup butter *or* margarine, softened
    2 cups sugar
    4 eggs
    2 teaspoons vanilla extract
1-3/4 cups all-purpose flour
    6 tablespoons baking cocoa
    1 teaspoon baking powder
1/4 teaspoon salt
FROSTING:
1/2 cup butter *or* margarine, softened
1/4 cup evaporated milk
    1 teaspoon vanilla extract
    2 tablespoons baking cocoa
    3 cups confectioners' sugar
Decorating sprinkles, optional

In a large mixing bowl, cream butter and sugar. Add eggs, one at a time, beating well after each addition. Beat in vanilla. Combine the flour, cocoa, baking powder and salt; gradually add to creamed mixture and mix well.

Spread into a greased 13-in. x 9-in. x 2-in. baking pan. Bake at 350° for 25-30 minutes or until a toothpick inserted near the center comes out clean. Cool on a wire rack.

For frosting, in a mixing bowl, beat the butter, milk and vanilla; add cocoa. Gradually beat in confectioners' sugar until smooth. Spread over cooled brownies. Decorate with sprinkles if desired. **Yield:** 12-15 servings.

Tax Day Party Really Pays Off!

By Betty Jean Jordan, Monticello, Georgia

WHEN APRIL 15 is not too far away, maybe a Tax Day Party will give you some lighthearted fun to look forward to! I had a good time planning the theme party my husband and I gave one spring, and our guests really got a kick out of it.

We began the evening with CPA Snack, a yummy mixture of seasoned nuts. People picked up on the certified public accountant abbreviation right away. But the title has a double meaning—the initials also stand for the main ingredients, cashews, pecans and almonds.

Who doesn't feel poor after they've paid their taxes? That's why Shrimp Po'boys, a sandwich with Louisiana flair, starred on my party menu. I coated peeled shrimp with a special light batter, fried them and served them on crusty French rolls with lettuce,

tomato and a tasty homemade tartar sauce.

Sprinkling the shrimp with a little cayenne pepper after deep-frying gives them some zip. Use as much as pleases your palate.

We made a playful attempt to recoup some of our tax payments with Greenback Salad. My quick-and-easy vinaigrette dressing adds a pleasant tang to any mixture of salad greens and ingredients.

For dessert, we had Pay Dirt Cake. With layers of crushed chocolate sandwich cookies and creamy filling, it certainly is "rich". I decorated the top with a few wrapped chocolate coins.

We all enjoyed an evening of good food, a little commiserating and a lot of laughs. I'm happy to share my party idea. It's a good way to gear up for another year of working for yourself and your uncle—Uncle Sam, that is! I hope you won't find the recipes too taxing.

CPA Snack

1/2 cup butter *or* margarine, melted
4-1/2 teaspoons Worcestershire sauce
3/4 teaspoon hot pepper sauce
1-1/2 teaspoons salt
1/2 teaspoon pepper
2-1/4 cups pecan halves
2 cups whole cashews
1-1/2 cups whole almonds

In a large bowl, combine the butter, Worcestershire sauce, hot pepper sauce, salt and pepper. Stir in the pecans, cashews and almonds until coated. Transfer mixture to a 15-in. x 10-in. x 1-in. baking pan.

Bake nuts at 300° for 30 minutes, stirring them every 10 minutes. Spread out on waxed paper to cool completely. Store nuts in an airtight container in the refrigerator for up to 2 weeks. **Yield:** 6 cups.

— 🍳 🍳 🍳 —

Shrimp Po'boys

1/2 cup mayonnaise
1/2 cup finely chopped onion
1/2 cup chopped dill pickles
1-1/3 cups all-purpose flour
1 teaspoon salt
4 eggs, *separated*
1-1/3 cups milk
2 tablespoons vegetable oil
8 French sandwich rolls, split
Additional oil for deep-fat frying
2 pounds uncooked large shrimp, peeled and deveined
Cayenne pepper to taste
4 cups shredded lettuce
16 tomato slices

In a small bowl, combine the mayonnaise, onion and pickles; set aside. For batter, combine flour and salt in a mixing bowl. Add the egg yolks, milk and oil; beat until smooth. In a small mixing bowl, beat egg whites until stiff peaks form; fold into batter.

Wrap the sandwich rolls in foil. Bake at 350° for about 10 minutes or until warmed. Meanwhile, in a large skillet or deep-fat fryer, heat 1/2 in. of oil to 375°. Dip the shrimp in the batter; fry shrimp for 2-3 minutes on each side or until golden brown. Drain on paper towels; sprinkle with cayenne pepper.

Spread mayonnaise mixture over rolls; top with lettuce, tomato slices and shrimp. Serve immediately. **Yield:** 8 servings.

Greenback Salad

4 teaspoons Dijon mustard
1/4 cup red wine vinegar *or* cider vinegar
1/2 teaspoon salt
1/2 teaspoon pepper
1/2 cup vegetable oil
1/2 cup finely chopped onion
1/2 cup minced fresh parsley
8 cups torn salad greens

In a small bowl, whisk the mustard, vinegar, salt and pepper. Slowly add oil while whisking. Stir in onion and parsley. Place the greens in a large salad bowl; drizzle with dressing and toss to coat. **Yield:** 8 servings (1 cup dressing).

— 🍳 🍳 🍳 —

Pay Dirt Cake

28 cream-filled chocolate sandwich cookies
1 package (8 ounces) cream cheese, softened
1/4 cup butter *or* margarine, softened
1 cup confectioners' sugar
3-1/3 cups cold milk
2 packages (3.4 ounces *each*) instant French vanilla pudding mix
1 carton (8 ounces) frozen whipped topping, thawed
Foil-wrapped chocolate coins, optional

Line a 2-1/2-qt. clean new pail or container with plastic wrap or use a serving bowl; set aside. In a food processor or blender, process the cookies until finely crushed. Set aside 2 tablespoons of crumbs for topping.

In a large mixing bowl, beat cream cheese, butter and sugar. In a bowl, whisk the milk and pudding mix for 2 minutes. Add to cream cheese mixture; mix well. Fold in whipped topping.

Place half of the cookie crumbs in prepared container or bowl; top with half of the pudding mixture. Repeat layers. Sprinkle with reserved crumbs. Refrigerate until serving. Top with foil coins if desired. Refrigerate any leftovers. **Yield:** 8-10 servings.

🥄 *Table Toppers*

For a frugal but fun table setting, use tax forms and tax tables as place mats. A "money tree" centerpiece can be the focal point. Just decorate a small artificial tree with play money.

Treat Guests to a Taste of the Tropics

By Carol Wakley, North East, Pennsylvania

TWO of my closest friends and I, along with our mothers, get together for a "new recipe" dinner each year. When it was my turn to host, I chose a Hawaiian Luau theme.

As guests arrived, we sipped on refreshing Sunny Slush I stirred up…and then watched my friend Lori Needham assemble a clever Luau Centerpiece.

We couldn't bear to dig into the centerpiece early in the party, so we started with Polynesian Meatballs brought by Maxine Ryder. Linda Cravener shared her Tropical Tossed Salad.

The party erupted when Mom brought in her Volcano Cake! She baked the layers in three different-sized pans.

Our tropical evening was a great success—one we'd like to share so you, too, can catch the aloha spirit!

— 🍹 🍹 🍹 —

Sunny Slush

    6 cups pineapple juice
    4 pints lemon sherbet
   24 ice cubes
    1 teaspoon rum extract

In a blender, combine pineapple juice, sherbet, ice and extract in batches; cover and process until smooth. Pour into chilled glasses. **Yield:** 3 quarts.

Luau Centerpiece

    4 packages (3 ounces *each*) berry blue gelatin
    3 cups boiling water
    3 cups cold water
    2 medium unpeeled potatoes
    4 medium carrots
    4 medium green peppers
Strawberries, grapes, and chunks of honeydew, cantaloupe, star fruit and pineapple
    1 whole pineapple

In a large bowl, dissolve gelatin in boiling water. Stir in cold water. Pour into an 8-cup ring mold coated with nonstick cooking spray. Refrigerate for 2 hours or until set.

Cut each potato in half lengthwise for base of palm trees. Make a hole in the uncut side of potato halves that's large enough to hold a carrot; set aside. For tree trunks, use a sharp knife to make a thin petal-shaped cut on one side of each carrot toward the bottom, leaving slice attached. Rotate carrot a quarter turn and make another cut. Repeat one or two more times around carrot. Make another series of cuts about 1-1/2 in. above first set. Make a third series of cuts about 1-1/2 in. above second set. Insert carrots into potatoes.

For palm leaves, cut tops off green peppers and remove seeds (discard tops). Make deep V-shape cuts around bottom edge of pepper. Place a pepper on top of each carrot; secure with toothpicks.

Thread fruit onto wooden skewers; insert into whole pineapple. Unmold gelatin ring and place on a 19-in. x 12-in. platter. Place whole pineapple in center of gelatin, and palm trees and any additional chunks of fruit around gelatin. **Yield:** 1 centerpiece.

— 🍵 🍵 🍵 —

Polynesian Meatballs

    1 can (5 ounces) evaporated milk
1/3 cup chopped onion
2/3 cup crushed saltines
    1 teaspoon seasoned salt
1-1/2 pounds lean ground beef
SAUCE:
    1 can (20 ounces) pineapple tidbits
    2 tablespoons cornstarch
1/2 cup cider vinegar
    2 tablespoons soy sauce
    2 tablespoons lemon juice
1/2 cup packed brown sugar

In a bowl, combine the milk, onion, saltines and seasoned salt. Crumble beef over mixture and mix well. With wet hands, shape into 1-in. balls. In a large skillet over medium heat, brown meatballs in small batches, turning often. Remove with a slotted spoon and keep warm. Drain skillet.

Drain pineapple, reserving juice; set pineapple aside. Add enough water to juice to measure 1 cup. In a bowl, combine the cornstarch, pineapple juice mixture, vinegar, soy sauce, lemon juice and brown sugar until smooth. Add to skillet. Bring to a boil; cook and stir for 2 minutes or until thickened. Add meatballs. Reduce heat; cover and simmer for 15 minutes. Add the pineapple; heat through. **Yield:** about 6 dozen.

— 🍵 🍵 🍵 —

Tropical Tossed Salad

    6 tablespoons sugar, *divided*
1/2 cup slivered almonds
1/4 cup vegetable oil
    2 tablespoons cider vinegar
    1 tablespoon minced fresh parsley
1/2 teaspoon salt
Dash *each* pepper and hot pepper sauce
    6 cups torn iceberg lettuce
    5 cups torn romaine
    1 can (11 ounces) mandarin oranges, drained
1/2 cup chopped red onion

In a heavy saucepan over medium-low heat, cook and stir 4 tablespoons of sugar until melted and golden brown. Stir in the almonds until well coated. Remove to waxed paper to cool.

In a bowl, whisk oil, vinegar, parsley, salt, pepper, hot pepper sauce and remaining sugar. In a large bowl, combine lettuces, oranges and onion. Break apart caramelized almonds; add to salad. Drizzle with dressing; toss to coat. **Yield:** 12 servings.

— 🍵 🍵 🍵 —

Volcano Cake

    1 package (18-1/4 ounces) yellow cake mix
    2 cans (8 ounces *each*) crushed pineapple, drained
    1 cup chopped walnuts
FROSTING:
    1 package (8 ounces) cream cheese, softened
1/2 cup butter *or* margarine, softened
    4 cups confectioners' sugar
    3 to 4 tablespoons milk
    2 teaspoons vanilla extract
1/2 cup baking cocoa
Orange and red food coloring

Prepare cake batter according to package directions. Stir in pineapple and walnuts. Pour 2 cups into a greased 9-in. round baking pan and 2 cups into a greased 8-in. round baking pan. Pour remaining batter into a greased 1-1/2-qt. ovenproof bowl.

Bake the layer cakes at 350° for 18-22 minutes or until a toothpick inserted comes out clean. Bake the bowl cake for 35-40 minutes or until a toothpick comes out clean. Cool for 10 minutes before removing from pans to wire racks to cool completely.

In a mixing bowl, beat cream cheese and butter. Add confectioners' sugar alternately with milk. Beat in vanilla. Set aside 3/4 cup frosting. Add cocoa to remaining frosting; beat until smooth. Place 9-in. layer on a serving plate; frost with chocolate frosting. Top with 8-in. layer and bowl cake, frosting between layers. Spread the remaining chocolate frosting over top and sides of cake.

Divide the reserved white frosting in half; tint half orange and half red. Drop by spoonfuls over top and down sides of cake. **Yield:** 12-14 servings.

A Birthday Feast Fit for 'Jumbo'

By Kristen Proulx, Canton, New York

THE IDEA for a theme for my son Joshua's fourth birthday party came to me in a big way when I thought of the beloved elephant "blankie" he used to take everywhere.

Joshua and I made elephant-shaped invitations with a foldout trunk that read, "Let out a roar…Joshua is turning four!" Behind the ear flap were details of the party.

The menu was fit for an elephant. It featured Peanut Butter Dip, Peanutty Chicken Wings, Peanut Cookies and an Elephant Cake.

Both the children and adults really enjoyed the Peanut Butter Dip, which includes mini chocolate chips. It's so easy to whip up.

A pleasant, mild blend of peanut and curry flavors the sauce for Peanutty Chicken Wings. I doubled the recipe, and was I glad I did! The tasty wings were gobbled right up.

To shape the Peanut Cookies, just flatten each dough log with a fork, then pinch in the center before baking.

The Elephant Cake was a huge hit. One look tells you that this giant pachyderm is friendly and sweet. It was fun to make—and I'm no cake decorator.

The children had a terrific time playing "pin the tail on the elephant" and tossing peanuts into a large elephant's mouth.

If you choose to re-create this elephant theme for your child or grandchild, you can bet it will be a memorable party no one will soon forget!

Peanut Butter Dip

1/2 cup vanilla yogurt
1/2 cup peanut butter
1/4 teaspoon ground cinnamon
1/4 cup miniature semisweet chocolate chips
Apple wedges and miniature pretzels

In a small bowl, combine the yogurt, peanut butter and cinnamon. Stir in chocolate chips. Serve with apples and pretzels. **Yield:** 1 cup.

———— 🐘 🐘 🐘 ————

Peanutty Chicken Wings

1/2 cup creamy peanut butter
1/3 cup honey
1/4 cup soy sauce
  3 tablespoons vegetable oil
  1 garlic clove, minced
  1 teaspoon curry powder
2-1/2 pounds chicken wings

In a large mixing bowl, combine the peanut butter, honey, soy sauce, oil, garlic and curry powder until blended. Cut chicken wings into three sections; discard wing tips. Add wings to peanut butter mixture; stir to coat. Cover and refrigerate for 2 hours.

Transfer to an ungreased 13-in. x 9-in. x 2-in. baking dish. Bake, uncovered, at 375° for 35-45 minutes or until chicken juices run clear. **Yield:** 6-8 servings.

Peanut Cookies

1 cup butter *or* margarine, softened
1 cup creamy peanut butter*
1 cup sugar
1 cup packed brown sugar
2 eggs
1 teaspoon vanilla extract
2-1/2 cups all-purpose flour
1 teaspoon baking powder
1 teaspoon baking soda
Additional sugar

In a large mixing bowl, cream butter, peanut butter and sugars. Add eggs, one at a time, beating well after each addition. Beat in vanilla. Combine the flour, baking powder and baking soda; gradually add to creamed mixture. Refrigerate for 1 hour.

Roll dough into 1-in. balls; roll in sugar. Shape into logs. Place 2 in. apart on ungreased baking sheets. Flatten with a fork. Pinch center to form peanut shape. Bake at 375° for 7-10 minutes or until golden brown. Cool for 2 minutes before removing to wire racks. **Yield:** about 5-1/2 dozen.

Editor's Note: Reduced-fat or generic brands of peanut butter are not recommended for this recipe.

Elephant Cake

1 package (18-1/4 ounces) yellow cake mix
1 package (18-1/4 ounces) devil's food cake mix
1-1/2 cups shortening
1-1/2 cups butter *or* margarine, softened
12 cups confectioners' sugar
1 tablespoon vanilla extract
4 to 7 tablespoons milk
Black and blue paste food coloring

Line two 9-in. round baking pans and one 13-in. x 9-in. x 2-in. baking pan with waxed paper; grease the paper. Prepare both cake batters and bake according to package directions, using the 9-in. pans for the yellow cake and the 13-in. x 9-in. pan for the chocolate cake. Cool for 10 minutes; remove from pans to wire racks to cool completely. Level cake tops if necessary.

Referring to Fig. 1 (above right) and using a serrated knife, cut out a trunk and two feet from one yellow cake. Referring to Fig. 3, cut out an ear and tail from second yellow cake. (Discard leftover cake pieces or save for another use.)

Center chocolate cake on a 28-in. x 16-in. covered board. Referring to Fig. 2, position trunk along left bottom edge of cake and tail on right side. Place feet at bottom corners of cake. Place ear 2 in. from left side of cake.

For frosting, in a large mixing bowl, cream shortening and butter until fluffy. Gradually add the confectioners' sugar, beating well. Add vanilla and enough milk to achieve a spreading consistency. Tint 1/4 cup of frosting black; set aside. Set aside 1/2 cup white frosting. Tint remaining frosting blue-gray, using small amounts of black and blue food coloring. Spread 2 cups of the blue-gray frosting over top and sides of cake.

Trace a 1-1/2-in. x 1-1/4-in. oval for the eye. Cut a small hole in the corner of a pastry or plastic bag; insert round tip #4. Fill bag with black frosting. Outline eye and fill in pupil; pipe eyelashes and mouth. Using star tip #25 and reserved white frosting, pipe stars to fill in eye and add nostril and toes.

With blue-gray frosting and star tip #16, pipe stars over top and sides of elephant. **Yield:** 24-30 servings.

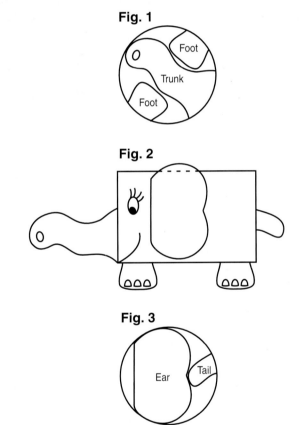

Autumn Menu Celebrates the Season-ing!

By Laurel Leslie, Sonora, California

DREAMING UP a theme is part of the fun when it's my husband Bob's and my turn to host our gourmet dinner group.

I picked "For Everything There Is a Seasoning" for a theme one October. I was thinking about fall and about the way herbs and spices enhance the flavor of food when Ecclesiastes 3:1 came to mind: "To everything there is a season…".

Herbed Cheese Spread, definitely lives up to its name. Flavored with six different herbs, it is one of the best cream cheese spreads I've had.

Everyone liked the beautiful golden color and creamy consistency of Ginger Squash Soup. A touch of ginger really sparks the mild flavor of butternut squash.

The Rosemary Plum Pork Roast is delicious…and slices of it make such a pretty presentation.

With the roast, we had herbed mashed potatoes and Green Beans with Basil. These crisp-tender beans are accented with garlic, rosemary, basil, onions and celery.

Apple Spice Bundt Cake is perfect for the season. Not too sweet and not too heavy, the moist bundt cake has a mild fruit flavor and a pleasant spice level.

Our party was a big success. I hope you spice up your next gathering with some of these same recipes!

— 🛒 🛒 🛒 —

Herbed Cheese Spread

  1 package (8 ounces) cream cheese, softened
1/4 cup butter *or* margarine, softened
  1 tablespoon minced fresh parsley
  2 teaspoons minced chives
  2 teaspoons minced fresh chervil *or* 1/2 teaspoon dried chervil
  1 to 2 garlic cloves, minced
3/4 teaspoon minced fresh tarragon *or* 1/4 teaspoon dried tarragon
1/4 teaspoon lemon-pepper seasoning
Assorted crackers

In a mixing bowl, beat cream cheese and butter until smooth. Add the parsley, chives, chervil, garlic, tarragon and lemon-pepper; mix well. Transfer to a serving dish. Cover and refrigerate for 4-24 hours. Remove from the refrigerator 15 minutes before serving. Serve with crackers. **Yield:** 1-1/2 cups.

Ginger Squash Soup

✓ Uses less fat, sugar or salt. Includes Nutritional Analysis and Diabetic Exchanges.

3 cups chicken broth
2 packages (10 ounces *each*) frozen cooked winter squash, thawed
1 cup unsweetened applesauce
3 tablespoons sugar
1 teaspoon ground ginger
1/2 teaspoon salt
1/2 cup heavy whipping cream

In a large saucepan, simmer broth and squash. Add the applesauce, sugar, ginger and salt. Bring to a boil. Reduce heat to low; stir in cream. Cook for 30 minutes or until soup reaches desired consistency, stirring occasionally. **Yield:** 6 servings.
Nutritional Analysis: One 1-cup serving (prepared with reduced-sodium broth) equals 163 calories, 8 g fat (5 g saturated fat), 29 mg cholesterol, 260 mg sodium, 22 g carbohydrate, 3 g fiber, 3 g protein. **Diabetic Exchanges:** 1 starch, 1 vegetable, 1 fat.

— ▼ ▼ ▼ —

Rosemary Plum Pork Roast

16 pitted dried plums
1 cup boiling water
2 bunches fresh rosemary, *divided*
1 center-cut boneless pork loin roast (about 2 pounds)
1/2 teaspoon salt, *divided*
1/2 teaspoon coarse ground pepper, *divided*

Place plums in a bowl; add boiling water. Let stand for 15 minutes; drain well. Mince enough rosemary to measure 1 tablespoon; stir into plums. Cut a slit along top of roast 2 in. deep, leaving 1 in. at each end uncut. Sprinkle inside of cut with 1/4 teaspoon salt and pepper. Fill with plum mixture. Cover top with overlapping rosemary sprigs.

Tie roast at 1-in. intervals with kitchen string. Sprinkle with the remaining salt and pepper. Place several rosemary sprigs in a shallow roasting pan. Top with roast. Bake, uncovered, at 350° for 1 to 1-1/4 hours or until a meat thermometer reads 160°. Let stand for 10 minutes before slicing. **Yield:** 6 servings.

— ▼ ▼ ▼ —

Green Beans with Basil

1 pound fresh green beans
1/4 cup water
2 to 3 tablespoons butter *or* margarine
1/2 cup chopped onion
1/4 cup chopped celery
1 garlic clove, minced
1-1/2 teaspoons minced fresh rosemary *or* 1/2 teaspoon dried rosemary, crushed
1-1/2 teaspoons minced fresh basil *or* 1/2 teaspoon dried basil

Place beans and water in a saucepan. Bring to a boil; cook, uncovered, for 7 minutes or until crisp-tender. Drain; add the remaining ingredients. Cover and cook for 4 minutes or until vegetables are tender. **Yield:** 6 servings.

— ▼ ▼ ▼ —

Apple Spice Bundt Cake

1/3 cup butter *or* margarine, softened
1/3 cup shortening
3/4 cup sugar
2/3 cup packed brown sugar
1 teaspoon grated lemon peel
2 eggs
1-1/4 teaspoons vanilla extract
2-1/4 cups all-purpose flour
2 teaspoons ground cinnamon
1 teaspoon baking soda
1 teaspoon ground allspice
1 teaspoon ground nutmeg
1/4 teaspoon salt
1 cup unsweetened applesauce
2/3 cup finely chopped peeled tart apple
3/4 cup chopped pecans, toasted
BROWN SUGAR GLAZE:
3 tablespoons butter *or* margarine
3 tablespoons brown sugar
3 tablespoons heavy whipping cream
3/4 cup confectioners' sugar
1/2 teaspoon vanilla extract
2 tablespoons chopped pecans, toasted

In a large mixing bowl, cream butter, shortening, sugars and lemon peel until fluffy. Add eggs, one at a time, beating well after each addition. Beat in vanilla. Combine flour, cinnamon, baking soda, allspice, nutmeg and salt; add to creamed mixture alternately with applesauce. Stir in apple and pecans.

Pour into a greased and floured 9- or 10-in. fluted tube pan. Bake at 350° for 55-60 minutes or until a toothpick inserted near the center comes out clean. Cool for 10 minutes before removing from pan to a wire rack to cool completely.

For glaze, in a heavy saucepan, melt butter and brown sugar over low heat. Stir in cream. Cook and stir until mixture comes to a boil; boil for 1 minute. Remove from the heat; whisk in sugar and vanilla until smooth, about 1 minute. Pour over cake; immediately sprinkle with pecans. **Yield:** 12 servings.

Substitutions & Equivalents

Equivalent Measures

3 teaspoons	= 1 tablespoon	16 tablespoons	= 1 cup
4 tablespoons	= 1/4 cup	2 cups	= 1 pint
5-1/3 tablespoons	= 1/3 cup	4 cups	= 1 quart
8 tablespoons	= 1/2 cup	4 quarts	= 1 gallon

Food Equivalents

Grains

Macaroni	1 cup (3-1/2 ounces) uncooked	=	2-1/2 cups cooked
Noodles, Medium	3 cups (4 ounces) uncooked	=	4 cups cooked
Popcorn	1/3 to 1/2 cup unpopped	=	8 cups popped
Rice, Long Grain	1 cup uncooked	=	3 cups cooked
Rice, Quick-Cooking	1 cup uncooked	=	2 cups cooked
Spaghetti	8 ounces uncooked	=	4 cups cooked

Crumbs

Bread	1 slice	=	3/4 cup soft crumbs, 1/4 cup fine dry crumbs
Graham Crackers	7 squares	=	1/2 cup finely crushed
Buttery Round Crackers	12 crackers	=	1/2 cup finely crushed
Saltine Crackers	14 crackers	=	1/2 cup finely crushed

Fruits

Bananas	1 medium	=	1/3 cup mashed
Lemons	1 medium	=	3 tablespoons juice, 2 teaspoons grated peel
Limes	1 medium	=	2 tablespoons juice, 1-1/2 teaspoons grated peel
Oranges	1 medium	=	1/4 to 1/3 cup juice, 4 teaspoons grated peel

Vegetables

Cabbage	1 head	=	5 cups shredded	Green Pepper	1 large	=	1 cup chopped
Carrots	1 pound	=	3 cups shredded	Mushrooms	1/2 pound	=	3 cups sliced
Celery	1 rib	=	1/2 cup chopped	Onions	1 medium	=	1/2 cup chopped
Corn	1 ear fresh	=	2/3 cup kernels	Potatoes	3 medium	=	2 cups cubed

Nuts

Almonds	1 pound	=	3 cups chopped	Pecan Halves	1 pound	=	4-1/2 cups chopped
Ground Nuts	3-3/4 ounces	=	1 cup	Walnuts	1 pound	=	3-3/4 cups chopped

Easy Substitutions

When you need...		Use...
Baking Powder	1 teaspoon	1/2 teaspoon cream of tartar + 1/4 teaspoon baking soda
Buttermilk	1 cup	1 tablespoon lemon juice *or* vinegar + enough milk to measure 1 cup (let stand 5 minutes before using)
Cornstarch	1 tablespoon	2 tablespoons all-purpose flour
Honey	1 cup	1-1/4 cups sugar + 1/4 cup water
Half-and-Half Cream	1 cup	1 tablespoon melted butter + enough whole milk to measure 1 cup
Onion	1 small, chopped (1/3 cup)	1 teaspoon onion powder *or* 1 tablespoon dried minced onion
Tomato Juice	1 cup	1/2 cup tomato sauce + 1/2 cup water
Tomato Sauce	2 cups	3/4 cup tomato paste + 1 cup water
Unsweetened Chocolate	1 square (1 ounce)	3 tablespoons baking cocoa + 1 tablespoon shortening *or* oil
Whole Milk	1 cup	1/2 cup evaporated milk + 1/2 cup water

Cooking Terms

HERE'S a quick reference for some of the cooking terms used in *Taste of Home* recipes:

Baste—To moisten food with melted butter, pan drippings, marinades or other liquid to add more flavor and juiciness.

Beat—A rapid movement to combine ingredients using a fork, spoon, wire whisk or electric mixer.

Blend—To combine ingredients until *just* mixed.

Boil—To heat liquids until bubbles form that cannot be "stirred down". In the case of water, the temperature will reach 212°.

Bone—To remove all meat from the bone before cooking.

Cream—To beat ingredients together to a smooth consistency, usually in the case of butter and sugar for baking.

Dash—A small amount of seasoning, less than 1/8 teaspoon. If using a shaker, a dash would comprise a quick flip of the container.

Dredge—To coat foods with flour or other dry ingredients. Most often done with pot roasts and stew meat before browning.

Fold—To incorporate several ingredients by careful and gentle turning with a spatula. Used generally with beaten egg whites or whipped cream when mixing into the rest of the ingredients to keep the batter light.

Julienne—To cut foods into long thin strips much like matchsticks. Used most often for salads and stir-fry dishes.

Mince—To cut into very fine pieces. Used often for garlic or fresh herbs.

Parboil—To cook partially, usually used in the case of chicken, sausages and vegetables.

Partially set—Describes the consistency of gelatin after it has been chilled for a small amount of time. Mixture should resemble the consistency of egg whites.

Puree—To process foods to a smooth mixture. Can be prepared in an electric blender, food processor, food mill or sieve.

Saute—To fry quickly in a small amount of fat, stirring almost constantly. Most often done with onions, mushrooms and other chopped vegetables.

Score—To cut slits partway through the outer surface of foods. Often used with ham or flank steak.

Stir-Fry—To cook meats and/or vegetables with a constant stirring motion in a small amount of oil in a wok or skillet over high heat.

Guide to Cooking with Popular Herbs

HERB	APPETIZERS SALADS	BREADS/EGGS SAUCES/CHEESE	VEGETABLES PASTA	MEAT POULTRY	FISH SHELLFISH
BASIL	Green, Potato & Tomato Salads, Salad Dressings, Stewed Fruit	Breads, Fondue & Egg Dishes, Dips, Marinades, Sauces	Mushrooms, Tomatoes, Squash, Pasta, Bland Vegetables	Broiled, Roast Meat & Poultry Pies, Stews, Stuffing	Baked, Broiled & Poached Fish, Shellfish
BAY LEAF	Seafood Cocktail, Seafood Salad, Tomato Aspic, Stewed Fruit	Egg Dishes, Gravies, Marinades, Sauces	Dried Bean Dishes, Beets, Carrots, Onions, Potatoes, Rice, Squash	Corned Beef, Tongue Meat & Poultry Stews	Poached Fish, Shellfish, Fish Stews
CHIVES	Mixed Vegetable, Green, Potato & Tomato Salads, Salad Dressings	Egg & Cheese Dishes, Cream Cheese, Cottage Cheese, Gravies, Sauces	Hot Vegetables, Potatoes	Broiled Poultry, Poultry & Meat Pies, Stews, Casseroles	Baked Fish, Fish Casseroles, Fish Stews, Shellfish
DILL	Seafood Cocktail, Green, Potato & Tomato Salads, Salad Dressings	Breads, Egg & Cheese Dishes, Cream Cheese, Fish & Meat Sauces	Beans, Beets, Cabbage, Carrots, Cauliflower, Peas, Squash, Tomatoes	Beef, Veal Roasts, Lamb, Steaks, Chops, Stews, Roast & Creamed Poultry	Baked, Broiled, Poached & Stuffed Fish, Shellfish
GARLIC	All Salads, Salad Dressings	Fondue, Poultry Sauces, Fish & Meat Marinades	Beans, Eggplant, Potatoes, Rice, Tomatoes	Roast Meats, Meat & Poultry Pies, Hamburgers, Casseroles, Stews	Broiled Fish, Shellfish, Fish Stews, Casseroles
MARJORAM	Seafood Cocktail, Green, Poultry & Seafood Salads	Breads, Cheese Spreads, Egg & Cheese Dishes, Gravies, Sauces	Carrots, Eggplant, Peas, Onions, Potatoes, Dried Bean Dishes, Spinach	Roast Meats & Poultry, Meat & Poultry Pies, Stews & Casseroles	Baked, Broiled & Stuffed Fish, Shellfish
MUSTARD	Fresh Green Salads, Prepared Meat, Macaroni & Potato Salads, Salad Dressings	Biscuits, Egg & Cheese Dishes, Sauces	Baked Beans, Cabbage, Eggplant, Squash, Dried Beans, Mushrooms, Pasta	Chops, Steaks, Ham, Pork, Poultry, Cold Meats	Shellfish
OREGANO	Green, Poultry & Seafood Salads	Breads, Egg & Cheese Dishes, Meat, Poultry & Vegetable Sauces	Artichokes, Cabbage, Eggplant, Squash, Dried Beans, Mushrooms, Pasta	Broiled, Roast Meats, Meat & Poultry Pies, Stews, Casseroles	Baked, Broiled & Poached Fish, Shellfish
PARSLEY	Green, Potato, Seafood & Vegetable Salads	Biscuits, Breads, Egg & Cheese Dishes, Gravies, Sauces	Asparagus, Beets, Eggplant, Squash, Dried Beans, Mushrooms, Pasta	Meat Loaf, Meat & Poultry Pies, Stews & Casseroles, Stuffing	Fish Stews, Stuffed Fish
ROSEMARY	Fruit Cocktail, Fruit & Green Salads	Biscuits, Egg Dishes, Herb Butter, Cream Cheese, Marinades, Sauces	Beans, Broccoli, Peas, Cauliflower, Mushrooms, Baked Potatoes, Parsnips	Roast Meat, Poultry & Meat Pies, Stews & Casseroles, Stuffing	Stuffed Fish, Shellfish
SAGE		Breads, Fondue, Egg & Cheese Dishes, Spreads, Gravies, Sauces	Beans, Beets, Onions, Peas, Spinach, Squash, Tomatoes	Roast Meat, Poultry, Meat Loaf, Stews, Stuffing	Baked, Poached & Stuffed Fish
TARRAGON	Seafood Cocktail, Avocado Salads, Salad Dressings	Cheese Spreads, Marinades, Sauces, Egg Dishes	Asparagus, Beans, Beets, Carrots, Mushrooms, Peas, Squash, Spinach	Steaks, Poultry, Roast Meats, Casseroles & Stews	Baked, Broiled & Poached Fish, Shellfish
THYME	Seafood Cocktail, Green, Poultry, Seafood & Vegetable Salads	Biscuits, Breads, Egg & Cheese Dishes, Sauces, Spreads	Beets, Carrots, Mushrooms, Onions, Peas, Eggplant, Spinach, Potatoes	Roast Meat, Poultry & Meat Loaf, Meat & Poultry Pies, Stews & Casseroles	Baked, Broiled & Stuffed Fish, Shellfish, Fish Stews

General Recipe Index

This handy index lists every recipe by food category, major ingredient and/or cooking method, so you can easily locate recipes to suit your needs.

✓ Recipe includes Nutritional Analysis and Diabetic Exchanges

✓ *Recipe includes Nutritional Analysis and Diabetic Exchanges*

✓ *Recipe includes Nutritional Analysis and Diabetic Exchanges*

✓ Recipe includes Nutritional Analysis and Diabetic Exchanges

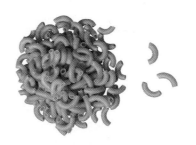
✓ Recipe includes Nutritional Analysis and Diabetic Exchanges

✓ Recipe includes Nutritional Analysis and Diabetic Exchanges

✓ *Recipe includes Nutritional Analysis and Diabetic Exchanges*

✓ *Recipe includes Nutritional Analysis and Diabetic Exchanges*

Alphabetical Recipe Index

This handy index lists every recipe in alphabetical order
so you can easily find your favorite recipes.

✓ Recipe includes Nutritional Analysis and Diabetic Exchanges

✓ Recipe includes Nutritional Analysis and Diabetic Exchanges

✓ Recipe includes Nutritional Analysis and Diabetic Exchanges